Effective
Social Work
Practice

◆▸◀◆▸◀◆▸◀◆▸◀◆▸◀◆▸◀◆▸◀◆▸◀◆▸◀◆▸◀◆▸◀◆▸◀◆

Advanced Techniques for
Behavioral Intervention with Individuals,
Families, and Institutional Staff

Elsie M. Pinkston
John L. Levitt
Glenn R. Green
Nick L. Linsk
Tina L. Rzepnicki

Effective Social Work Practice

Jossey-Bass Publishers

San Francisco • Washington • London • 1982

EFFECTIVE SOCIAL WORK PRACTICE
Advanced Techniques for Behavioral Intervention with Individuals,
Families, and Institutional Staff
by Elsie M. Pinkston, John L. Levitt, Glenn R. Green,
Nick L. Linsk, and Tina L. Rzepnicki

Copyright © 1982 by: Jossey-Bass Inc., Publishers
433 California Street
San Francisco, California 94104
&
Jossey-Bass Limited
28 Banner Street
London EC1Y 8QE

Library of Congress Cataloging in Publication Data
Main entry under title:

Effective social work practice.

Bibliography: p. 457
Includes indexes.
1. Social service—Addresses, essays, lectures.
I. Pinkston, Elsie M.
HV40.E388   1982   361.3   82-48057
ISBN 0-87589-534-4

Manufactured in the United States of America

The paper in this book meets the guidelines for
permanence and durability of the Committee on
Production Guidelines for Book Longevity of the
Council on Library Resources.

JACKET DESIGN BY WILLI BAUM

FIRST EDITION

Code 8220

The Jossey-Bass
Social and Behavioral Science Series

To our colleague
Evelyn Harris Ginsburg, A.C.S.W., C.S.W.

Preface

◆◆◆◆◆◆◆◆◆◆◆◆◆◆◆◆◆◆◆◆◆◆◆◆◆◆◆◆◆◆◆◆◆

The focal point of this book is the application of scientific methodology to developing and evaluating social work interventions to solve human problems. This methodology has been built around objective tools for evaluating the client's interactions with the environment and the interventions that alter those interactions; it also emphasizes ongoing evaluations of client progress and the outcomes of interventions.

Although behavioral research literature has extensively reported progress in all these areas, there is less information on how these advances are used in social work. Our aim in writing this book is to show how this empirically based methodology can be incorporated into social work practice. To achieve this end, we organized the material sequentially and defined the elements to be included from the perspective of the social work practitioner. The book is directed to all professionals whose primary interests are providing effective help to clients and contributing to the knowledge base of social work.

Chapter One defines an applied science approach to social work using a behavioral model of intervention. The rationale for this methodology is presented in terms of its functions to improve interventions with clients and add to the knowledge base of social work. The model is discussed according to its appropriateness to include empirical evidence, accountability, educational value, and ease of implementation. The ways both practitioners and clients can learn and benefit from the evaluation process are detailed.

Chapter Two presents the theoretical view of human behavior and the behavior principles from which our practice model is derived. To show the ways the principles can be used to develop intervention techniques, specific techniques that have been developed and evaluated are discussed.

The practice methodology of the behavior analysis model of social work is the topic of Chapter Three. Methods for assessing client problems and resources, including information on interviews with the client, designing and accomplishing interventions, and planning maintenance and generalization of effects, are described in detail.

Chapter Four presents the methods for applying scientific procedures to the research and evaluation of social work practice. It explains methods for use with experimental research, clinical evaluation, and structured practice as well as basic procedures for defining and recording behavior change in single-case research designs.

Chapter Five is an overview of methods for analyzing who should be trained—clients, significant others, and institutional staff (as well as what training procedures should be used) —and how to examine potential consequences. The analysis and selection of educational components of practice is divided into the following segments: selecting the change agent, analyzing the agent's relevant characteristics and response requirements, selecting the change setting by analyzing potential contingencies in that setting, and selecting specific training techniques.

Chapter Six details how to use behavior analysis when intervention occurs directly between social workers and clients experiencing a behavioral problem or deficiency. Specifically emphasized are self-control and self-management procedures. The worker acts as a behavioral educator, engineer, and consultant to teach clients to analyze their own behavior or the behaviors of others in their environment and to develop interventions appropriate to both. Alternatively, the worker may serve as behavior change agent and directly observe and have an impact on the client environment. The chapter elaborates self-analysis and intervention methods and procedures for identifying and selecting appropriate intervention settings, including ways to modify environmental and social consequences to effect and maintain behavior change. The end-of-chapter practice illustrations focus on research-based practice using this approach, including examples of clinical work with children.

Chapter Seven focuses on the behavior analysis model of social work practice applied to families. The social worker's roles in training and teaching family members as behavior change agents are detailed. Whether the identified clients are children, the aged, or spouses, the model of achieving change in family interactions is described in five steps: selecting family members as change agents, selecting the setting for that change, defining the change agents' response requirements and contingencies, presenting the treatment techniques available, and evaluating how effectively these techniques produce the desired change. The practice illustrations cover clinical applications to families with coercive interaction patterns, single-parent–child interaction problems, and families with adult retardates.

Chapter Eight describes indirect practice procedures within institutional settings, such as psychiatric hospitals and schools. Social worker functions include behavior consultation, staff education, program design, and ongoing monitoring of programs. Behavior change agents may include teachers, care-givers, nursing staff, or other workers. Methods for identifying possible change agents, teaching them behavior analysis, and identifying the relevant resources and contingencies necessary to ensure program adherence are discussed. The uses of administrative supports to develop, implement, and maintain institution-based behavior analysis programs and suggestions for behavior analysis of agency systems and procedures are important parts of this chapter. The specific techniques emphasize simplicity, continuity within staff, minimizing competing demands on change agents, environmental design, and group contingencies. Practice evaluations with children and adults, including the elderly, provide excellent examples of how the model is used. These practice illustrations describe token systems, time-out and response-cost procedures, stimulus control, and positive reinforcement procedures.

Chapter Nine discusses the extension of intervention effects through planned behavior procedures designed to achieve maintenance and generality. These procedures are less well developed than some other aspects of the model, but recent research and development suggest that consideration of generality and long-term effectiveness should be a built-in part of intervention in social work practice. Generality and maintenance are first defined, and then methods for programming appropriate to assessment, intervention, and follow-up are introduced. The practice illustrations describe examples of such research and show how such research can be evaluated.

Chapter Ten summarizes the behavioral model of social work and provides suggestions for workers who are integrating behavioral social work into practice and into the clinical structure of agencies.

Our model evolved from seven years of training social work practitioner-researchers to conduct direct social work practice with individuals, families, and institutional staffs. The coauthors are all graduates of these practice-research classes, confirming that practitioner-researchers can contribute to knowledge building in social work practice. The practice illustrations are examples of research conducted by second-year social work students from these classes. Students are taught how to assess, intervene, quantify, and evaluate. If methods for quantifying a problem are not developed, it is the worker's responsibility to attempt one by applying such questions as, "How do I know that?"; "Under what circumstances can I expect this intervention to be effective?"; and "Was the evaluation appropriate to the goals and questions involved in the intervention?" The students learn various ways to integrate behavioral theories and procedures into diverse intervention settings and are instructed in research design and data-recording techniques. The critical evaluation of publications is used to supplement fieldwork and classroom experience.

It is our pleasure to acknowledge the contributions of Arthur Schwartz, who was responsible for conceptualizing a behavioral sequence. He organized and participated in the first two years of its development and taught courses relevant to its success. Donald Baer was the strongest influence on the direction of this book through his original conceptualization of applied behavior analysis and his continued advice and consultation.

We also appreciate the administrative contributions of Harold Richmond and John Schuerman, who found the money for us to get started. Special appreciation is tendered to Lynn Vogel and Margaret Rosenheim for their support during the writing of this book. We are grateful to Jeanne Marsh, Eleanor Tolson, John Schuerman, and William Reid for reading and commenting on drafts.

Finally, we would like to thank our families for providing stimulating and reinforcing consequences for our work. Our productivity was enhanced by their prodding to have some fun in addition to work.

Chicago, Illinois
August 1982

Elsie M. Pinkston
John L. Levitt
Glenn R. Green
Nick L. Linsk
Tina L. Rzepnicki

Contents

Preface   ix

The Authors   xix

1. Scientific Methods of Social Work Practice   1

2. Principles of Behavior Change   16

3. Developing and Implementing Intervention
   Strategies   33

4. Evaluating the Effectiveness of Intervention   61

5. Selecting and Training Behavior Change Agents   92

6. Intervention with Individuals   105

   Practice Illustration 6.1. Social-Skills Training
   for a Depressed Woman   139
      Marcia M. McCabe, Charlotte M. Mallon-Wenzel,
      William J. Reid, Elsie M. Pinkston

   Practice Illustration 6.2. Negotiation:
   Modification of Communication Processes   158
      Charlotte Mallon-Wenzel, Marcia M. McCabe,
      William J. Reid, Elsie M. Pinkston

   Practice Illustration 6.3. Increasing Prosocial
   Behavior of a First-Grade Boy   171
      Carol A. Moses, Elsie M. Pinkston

7. Intervention with Families   183

   Practice Illustration 7.1. Home-Based
   Behavioral Social Work with the Elderly   220
      Nick L. Linsk, Elsie M. Pinkston,
      Glenn R. Green

   Practice Illustration 7.2. Treating Stuttering
   by Using Parental Attention and a Structured
   Program for Fluency   233
      Tina L. Rzepnicki, Matsujiro Shibano,
      Elsie M. Pinkston, Wendell H. Cox

   Practice Illustration 7.3. Intervention for
   Coercive Family Interactions   247
      Elsie M. Pinkston, Richard A. Polster,
      Benjamin S. Friedman, Mary Ann Lynch

   Practice Illustration 7.4. Group Training
   Parents to Negotiate Behavior Change with
   Their Mentally Retarded Adult Children   261
      Ronald Molick, Brian T. Love,
      Paul D. Henderson, Elsie M. Pinkston

8.   Intervention in Institutional Settings   272

     Practice Illustration 8.1. A Response-Cost
     Token Economy: Effectiveness and Side
     Effects   307
       Glenn R. Green, Elsie M. Pinkston

     Practice Illustration 8.2. An Analysis of
     Time-Out and Response-Cost Procedures in
     a Special Education Class   320
       *Richard Dougherty, Benjamin S. Friedman,
       Elsie M. Pinkston*

     Practice Illustration 8.3. Applying Behavior
     Analysis to Social Group Work with the
     Elderly   342
       Nick L. Linsk, Elsie M. Pinkston

     Practice Illustration 8.4. Differential
     Reinforcement of a Low Rate of Behavior
     in an Applied Setting   353
       Lorelle K. Banzett

     Practice Illustration 8.5. Using Behavioral
     Analysis to Develop Adaptive Social Behavior
     in a Depressed Adolescent Girl   364
       Ronald Molick, Elsie M. Pinkston

9.   Extending Intervention Effects: Procedures for
     Maintaining Positive Change   376

     Practice Illustration 9.1. Programming for
     the Establishment, Maintenance, and
     Generality of a Self-Initiated Greeting
     Response Using a Token Economy   402
       Sheila A. Lullo, Elsie M. Pinkston

     Practice Illustration 9.2. A Training-Maintenance
     Program for Reestablishing Appropriate Utensil
     Use Among the Impaired Elderly   412
       Donald K. Blackman, Elsie M. Pinkston

Practice Illustration 9.3. A Single-Parent
Intervention to Increase Parenting Skills
over Time   422
   Matsujiro Shibano, Wendell H. Cox,
   Tina L. Rzepnicki, Elsie M. Pinkston

Practice Illustration 9.4. A Creativity
Enhancement Program for Preschool Children
in an Inner City Child-Parent Center   435
   Theodore W. Lane, Miriam Z. Lane,
   Benjamin S. Friedman, Elizabeth M. Goetz,
   Elsie M. Pinkston

Summary: Using Behavioral Methods Effectively   452

References   457

Name Index   485

Subject Index   493

The Authors

Elsie M. Pinkston is associate professor, School of Social Service Administration, University of Chicago. She was awarded the B.A. degree (1969) in child development and psychology, the M.A. degree (1971) in child development, and the Ph.D. degree (1974) in developmental and child psychology—all from the University of Kansas. From 1973 to 1977 at the University of Chicago, she chaired the Applied Behavior Analysis Sequence in direct practice methods. She has published articles in the *Journal of Applied Behavior Analysis, Social Work,* the *Social Service Review, Social Work Research and Abstracts,* and the *Gerontologist.* As the principal investigator of several behavioral family treatment grants involving family members as behavioral change agents or therapists, she has developed a family treatment model for families of persons with special problems. Pinkston's current research is on the development of home-based treatment for the impaired elderly. She has been awarded a grant from the National Institute on Aging in support of her efforts, which include development of assessment tools for research with the elderly.

John L. Levitt is a social worker in the Medical Ecology Unit of Lutheran General Hospital in Park Ridge, Illinois. He was awarded the M.A. degree (1978) in social work and the Ph.D. degree (1981) in social service administration—both from the University of Chicago. As an Edith Abbott Fellow, he supervised the field experience of master's degree students at the School of Social Service Administration. His publications are in the area of evaluation methods development in social work. Currently, he is interested in psychosomatic and somatophysic disorders, especially anorexia nervosa, and is conducting research on the psychosocial aspects of the problem.

Glenn R. Green is director of Behavior Management at Chicago Services for Work and Rehabilitation. He was awarded the B.A. degree (1974) in psychology and educational psychology from the University of Michigan and the M.A. degree (1979) and the Ph.D. degree (1982) in social service administration—both from the University of Chicago. He was co-investigator on the Elderly Support Project at the University of Chicago with Pinkston and Linsk, examining methods of intervention with the elderly. His other research interests include behavioral programming for impaired populations and family interventions.

Nick L. Linsk is director of the Elderly Support Project, a home-based intervention program for older families at the University of Chicago. He is also a researcher for the Illinois Citizens for Better Care, Chicago. He was awarded the B.A. degree (1972) in social welfare from the University of Minnesota and the M.A. degree (1974) and the Ph.D. degree (1982) in social service administration—both from the University of Chicago. He has nine years of experience in direct practice with the elderly, and his research and practice interests include behavioral family intervention, behavioral group work with the elderly, long-term care policy and community advocacy, and empirically based practice education.

Tina L. Rzepnicki is project director of the West Virginia Intake Decision Project in Child Welfare Service, University of Illinois at Chicago Circle. She was awarded the B.A. degree (1973) in sociology from DePauw University and the M.A. degree (1978) and the Ph.D. degree (1982) in social service administration—both from the University of Chicago. She was project coordinator for the Parent Education Program and the Child Welfare Curriculum Development grant at the School of Social Service Administration, University of Chicago. Rzepnicki has provided field instruction for graduate students and conducted permanency planning training for child welfare staff in several states. Her practical and research interests lie in the development of empirically based models of intervention for use with individuals and families.

Pinkston and her colleagues have worked together on several research projects and publications. Levitt, Green, Linsk, and Rzepnicki were students in Pinkston's social treatment sequence during their second year at the School of Social Service Administration. Their ongoing collaborative relationship is a part of the model of reinforcement distribution discussed in this book.

Effective
Social Work
Practice

◆▬◆▬◆◆▬◆◆▬◆◆▬◆◆▬◆◆▬◆◆▬◆◆▬◆◆▬◆◆▬◆

Advanced Techniques for
Behavioral Intervention with Individuals,
Families, and Institutional Staff

1

◆-◆◆-◆◆-◆◆-◆◆-◆◆-◆◆-◆◆-◆◆-◆◆-◆◆-◆◆-◆◆-◆◆-◆

Scientific Methods
of Social Work Practice

*Why do social workers need to learn a scientific methodology
for conducting direct practice?* Most importantly, scientific
methodology enables social workers to determine that clients
are receiving the most effective assistance possible. Behavioral
scientists determine how people function within a laboratory or
within the context of the social environment, whereas social
workers encourage people to function at their maximum potential by helping their clients obtain training, personal support,
and material services. Because the goals of behavioral scientists
differ from those of social workers, social workers cannot depend on these scientists to conduct the research for and the
evaluation of the improvement of social work methods. Thus
social workers must arm themselves with a scientific practice-
research methodology that will advance their field systematically and scientifically.

Behavior analysis is such a methodology. It includes effective interventions, built-in methods for evaluation, and ongoing development of sophisticated practice knowledge. This
book describes how to use this approach and details its effec-

1

tiveness and the ease with which such an empirically based practice methodology can be implemented. Based upon rapidly developing technologies and procedures that have been experimentally evaluated, extensive methodology, used to test operant principles, is available for practitioners to evaluate the effectiveness of their interventions with clients and to help develop future programs and interventions. Certainly, the methodology requires further development before its application to social work problems fits perfectly, but evaluated practice is now possible along many dimensions (Thomas, 1978). What are needed are both social workers with the skills to employ scientific practice and make appropriate modifications and agencies that will support the workers' efforts. This book is directed toward making these two goals possible.

In their original definition of an analytical behavioral orientation, Baer, Wolf, and Risley (1968) suggested that behavioral applications should include a "self-examining, self-evaluating, and discovery-oriented research procedure for studying behavior" (p. 91). They delineated many important elements recently recognized as relevant to empirical models of social work (Briar, 1973; Fischer and Gochros, 1975; Jayaratne and Levy, 1979; Thomas, 1975), including precise definitions, reliable measurement, demonstration of effectiveness, and experimental control.

An important dimension when applying behavior analysis to social work practice is its well-developed methodology for examining and demonstrating the effectiveness of intervention procedures. Journals that discuss various types of intervention research based on this model—such as *Behavior Modification, Journal of Applied Behavior Analysis, Behavior Therapy,* and *Education and Training of Children*—are excellent sources of documented intervention research and practice methodology for a wide variety of human problems. Behavior analysis has been used as a major theoretical and practice base for individual achievement problems, a wide range of psychological problems, skill deficits, marital and family problems, educational programs, and community intervention. This literature is a rich resource for those applying scientific principles to the direct practice of social work and contains well-defined and -evaluated techniques for treating socially relevant problems. The solution to the problems of applying behavioral procedure and single-case methodology is incomplete (Thomas, 1978), but the rich arsenal of effective intervention methods is a useful beginning.

Defining Scientific Behavioral Practice

This model of social work practice is the direct application of principles of behavior (Skinner, 1953) and scientific methodology to the *solution* of rather than the study of human problems. Skinner stated in *Science and Human Behavior*: "An adequate science of human behavior should make a greater contribution to therapy than to diagnosis" (p. 368). An important part of behavior is viewed as a collection of learned responses accumulated through interaction with the environment. Behaviors can be altered, then, by altering the environment. This view is compatible with the tradition of social work, in which the worker's efforts are directed toward increasing the resources within the environment to enable individuals to achieve "common human needs" (Towle, 1965). This concept is extended a step further to help individuals develop skills to increase their personal effectiveness. Effectiveness is defined as the achieving of desires and needs while engaging in activities that lead to positive consequences and avoid negative consequences. Behaviors directed toward gaining positive consequences are usually associated with feelings of satisfaction, whereas behaviors that avoid negative consequences are more often accompanied by anger, frustration, and feelings of deprivation and anxiety.

This book provides no insight into the nature-nurture conflict; it addresses the abundant evidence which proves that positively altering the environment can improve human behavior. Because the helping professions are not always as helpful as they desire (Fischer, 1978; Mullen and Dumpson, 1972), a strong evaluation component is included to aid workers in their scientific self-evaluation. The words "science" and "evaluation" may arouse anxiety in those students and practitioners whose humanistic views and talents for working with clients have led them in other directions. It is valuable for such people to consider the following quotation from the justification of the first single-case dissertation at the School of Social Service Administration at the University of Chicago:

> Historically, social workers have responded to conditions of misery and injustice by arming themselves with whatever tools or weapons that were available, whether scientific, political, or interpersonal. They have not tended to look upon human adversity and say that nothing can be done because it is not "our kind of problem." Instead, social workers have focused on a wide range of human problems and moved to develop ways to help individuals gain the basic necessities for life and human dignity by improving their interactions with their environments. When individuals were not capable of fulfilling these common human needs and maintaining satisfactory levels of social functioning, social workers have found it necessary to develop a multiplicity of responsive methods for the solution of these needs. The development of innovative methods has been especially relevant as new problems arose and old problems have been reevaluated. Obviously the mere fact that social workers have not dealt with a problem has rarely thwarted or deterred their fundamental commitment to the total bio-social welfare of individuals in need (Howe, 1975, pp. 2-3).

Notable, then, in this approach is the lack of separation between intervention and the evaluation of effects, which is particularly important when modifying or altering the course of intervention. In addition, the approach is a basis for clients and workers as well as funding agents, policy makers, and social agents for deciding whether a specific technique is helpful. Furthermore, the method contributes to an understanding of the interaction process between people and their environments. We assume that the answers to how to proceed in remediation and intervention of social problems are most likely to be found within the analysis of this interaction.

The scientific methods of social work practice vary from other methods of practice in their integration of treatment and evaluation components. Therefore, characteristics of the behavior analysis model include *commitment to scientific method* and *treatment of behavioral and environmental variables*; it should also be *analytical, technological, conceptually systematic,* and *educational* and should demonstrate *effectiveness, generality,* and *social relevance.* This conceptual framework was developed by Baer, Wolf, and Risley (1968) to define the scientific methodology for applied behavioral research. This framework is expanded in this book to develop a practice methodology that incorporates scientific procedures into social work practice.

Commitment to Scientific Method. Scientific methods help develop intervention and evaluation methods more effective than those previously used in social work practice. Through scientific demonstration, social work can be brought from systematic practice to science. By doing this, we intend not to replace the worker-client relationship aspect of practice but to explore the causality of behavior change among relationships, techniques, and functional analyses. Practice within this model includes both applying carefully defined principles and procedures toward improving specifically defined behaviors or environmental variables and validating the effects of these principles and procedures through scientific demonstration. This practice is accomplished by exercising scientific control over specific variables, carefully analyzing results from an empirical and clinical perspective, and replicating effects. The careful delineation of relevant problems, environmental effects, and social components has a long history in social work, beginning in 1922 with Mary Richmond, who first described scientific social work in *Social Diagnosis* (1965). Although refined examination of controlling variables occurs less often in actual practice than it does in laboratories and various demonstration projects, it is nevertheless a laudable goal and improves the quality of interventions by building a firmer, more well-defined field of practice. In those cases where scientific demonstration is accomplished, the worker will experience the satisfaction of knowledge building and increased professionalism.

Commitment to scientific method is reinforced by teaching practitioners to use effective empirically evaluated practice methods, to evaluate their own practice using scientific methods, to experimentally control untested intervention procedures, and to share their results with others (Briar, 1977). Workers who have participated in this discovery-oriented approach during their education are more likely to engage in research activities and to continue to use research articles to inform their practice than those who have not. From her study surveying social-treatment graduates of the University of Chicago, Teigiser (1980) found that students who graduated from sequences in which scientific methods were emphasized reported more involvement in and use of research in their practice. A larger proportion of these students also felt that their second-year methods classes were quite valuable. Therefore, for social work to have a commitment to scientific method in the future, workers must receive integrated research and clinical training.

Treatment of Behavioral and Environmental Variables. The concept of behavior change is well within the tradition of social casework. Helen Harris Perlman, in her classic work *Social Casework: A Problem-Solving Process* (1957), stated that behavior change is a legitimate goal of social casework and that systematic attempts to understand the process are certainly desirable (pp. 3-39). Defining the effectiveness of intervention on positive behavioral outcome should meet with little resistance in a field of practice devoted to helping people obtain more life satisfaction. Within the behavior analysis model, we are more interested in what the clients are actually able to do about their problems than in how clients talk about their problems. Implicit in any change in interpersonal relationship is some change in behavior. For example, it is one thing for a father to understand the anger that "drives" him to abuse his child but quite another for him to engage in positive, nurturing parental behaviors.

Using behavior as a medium for assessing change has clear advantages. Behavior is accessible to treatment, and by focusing on behavior, the worker is able to help clients analyze the problems currently causing havoc in their lives. Clearly, it is desirable both to change destructive behavior patterns as soon as possible and to guide clients in understanding the role of those patterns in their difficulties. The very direct application of intervention procedures to behavior bypasses the almost impossible task of helping clients improve their situations without altering the contingencies within their environments. Reports of cognitive changes are not adequate evidence of interventive effectiveness.

Predictable methods of behavior change are essential for establishing effective intervention. Defining human interaction problems as to behavior change allows the worker to build a public data base for evaluating treatment; that is, it provides visible information beyond the worker's inference regarding the client's private mental events.

Analytical Component. Behavior analysis in social work practice reduces the costly errors of subjective inference by determining environmental relationships to behavior change. Adequate analysis requires convincing demonstrations that specified interventions are responsible for behavior change. This demonstration may be explored through replication and control procedures. In behavior analysis methods, the worker establishes certain control variables by functional analysis. Environmental variables are analyzed by their function; then, if variables tend to increase or decrease rates of behavior, they are considered directly related to the behavior. This relationship is often referred to as *experimental control.* Conducting this kind of functional analysis enables the worker to make more informed decisions when devising and evaluating an intervention strategy. A question frequently debated among social workers is how much control is necessary to infer causal relationships between intervention procedures and targeted behaviors.

It is helpful to practitioners-researchers to think of functional analysis as simply the use of research tools to build a believable case as to whether a causal relationship does or does not exist. What is acceptable depends somewhat on the sophistication and experience of the workers or those they intend to convince. The ability of practitioners-researchers to experimentally control behavior heightens their ability to analyze the behavior's functions. The behavior analysis methodology may enlarge the audience that will find results of clinical research worthwhile

to include other helping professionals and researchers who demand scientific proof.

Intra- and intersubject replication designs, usually referred
to as reversal and multiple-baseline designs, are the vehicles for
the analysis of each intervention plan and the methods for the
analysis of separate components. These designs are used extensively in the behavior analysis research on social work practice
(for example, Fischer, 1978; Gambrill, 1977). Briefly, these
single-case designs involve recording for five to ten days, baseline measures of carefully specified and defined target behaviors, accompanied by measures of predicted consequence events.
Before deciding on a treatment plan, the worker inspects the
data and analyzes functional events (those events that may be
controlling the behavior and are most frequently associated
with the behavior under study). The reversal design involves repeated applications of the treatment procedure alternated with
a baseline condition. When this approach is accompanied by
repeated behavior changes, evidence for experimental control
is established. As is noted in more detail in later chapters, in
the multiple-baseline design, behavioral baseline measures may
be recorded across one of several dimensions (behaviors, subjects, and settings). For example, for a multiple baseline across
behaviors, the baseline is recorded concurrently across three to
five behaviors. Then the treatment is applied serially to each
behavior at different times. The replication of results with each
behavior is evidence that the intervention has a direct relationship to the behavior change. These designs are highly developed;
further explication of their varied uses is discussed in Chapter
Four.

Technological Component. Technology is the means for
accomplishing specific goals and the basis of all applied science.
Scientific social work practice includes specific techniques that
are transmittable between workers. A technological approach
requires careful, clear, and objective descriptions of procedures.
Descriptions must include sufficient information so that an in-
telligent worker can read and follow them. These descriptions
facilitate both clinical applications and the experimental study
of intervention and provide the alternative behaviors workers

may engage in under a variety of circumstances. Such careful
attention to definition increases the probability that practitioner-
researchers and their colleagues will be able to replicate positive
results with future clients. This likelihood is germane to the development of a unified practice model composed of empirically
tested procedures.

Technology is particularly important when treatment
procedures do not rest on a solid foundation of empirical findings (and this is often the case). For instance, the development
of such advances as task-centered casework (Reid and Epstein,
1972) was possible because of careful technological development of practice methods. Each step of the method was so carefully defined that the trip from systematic practice to empirically validated procedures was short. Therefore, it is important
to define target problems, intervention techniques, and evaluation procedures with extreme care. Technology is thus the key
for turning practice wisdom or experience into clearly defined
practice principles and systematic practice into a discipline.

Conceptually Systematic Component. To be conceptually
systematic, knowledge building must integrate technology,
analysis, and previous research when the worker is developing,
publishing, and using intervention evaluations. Systematic practice research leads to the development of empirically evaluated
practice principles, and the approach then includes a tested
knowledge base rather than a mere collection of techniques.
These components provide a unified framework against which
to measure the reasonableness of future nonempirically based
intervention plans, giving the practitioner the opportunity to
contribute to the knowledge and building of social work practice principles.

Conceptually systematic practice develops treatment
knowledge through scrupulous documentation, evaluation, and
discussion of failures and successes relative to earlier assertions
and empirical findings. Particularly interesting are discussions of
both the failure and success of interventions. What can be
learned from the experience? How does a specific piece of research fit into a total practice method? Do the research results
support previous findings? If not, what should be examined

next? Analysis of failure is as important as analysis of success, and carefully analyzed failure may yield more important implications.

The scientific demonstration of effective procedures for practice interventions is primary. However, eliminating ineffective procedures clears the attic and saves suffering, time, and money. For instance, one "secret of the attic" of behavioral parent training is the issue of discontinuance. Few published articles and even fewer papers even mention this widespread problem, yet it is of major importance (as it is with most family therapies) and deserves study. Mention discontinuance among parent trainers and one finds an instant audience willing to exchange war stories! Unfortunately, there are few systematic studies (Friedman, 1979).

Thus, careful analysis of all research findings relative to past research is necessary to formulate future intervention questions and build both a theory of practice and a useful base of knowledge.

Educational Component. Behavior analysis is an educational approach to the solution of human problems and involves three levels: (1) Clients learn new ways to alter and analyze their interaction with their environment; (2) workers add to their knowledge of how to help clients function more effectively by developing more useful practice methods; and (3) social work practice is informed by the resulting research and evaluation. Part of the approach, then, is an arsenal of teaching techniques. Through the educational process, both the worker and the client learn to analyze behavior in functional terms (see Chapter Five for educational procedures).

Systematic research supports the hypothesis that generality (extension) of behavior change to other behaviors and settings is enhanced by teaching clients how to functionally examine the relationship between their own behavior and environmental variables. Therefore, an established goal of social work practice is education of the worker and the client (Perlman, 1957).

The educational responsibility of the social worker extends to colleagues through the publication of experimentally

examined clinical techniques. Because of the need for accountability and demonstration and the rarity of researchers with
clinical experience, this additional role falls to the practitioner-
researcher. Knowledge building has always been an important
part of the function of a social work discipline and adds a note
of professionalism and prestige to the worker's career. Therefore, an important goal of this book is to provide the worker
with good practice-research methods and to allow the practitioner involvement in the advancement of the field.

Effectiveness. Because the primary requirement for a social work practice model is effectiveness, intervention procedures must generate enough behavior change to be socially important to the client or to society. If behavior changes do not
cause important changes in the clients' lives, the interventions
are not successful. Even when the clients are diagnosed correctly and the behaviors are defined precisely, improved behavior is
the fundamental requirement for effective treatment.

Although theories describing human behavior, or more
precisely the interaction between people and their environments, may be interesting and thought to contribute to "understanding" the process of therapy, the criterion for effective
intervention remains meaningful behavior change. This includes
the opportunity for behavior change by the clients or persons
within their support system or environment. This is as true with
the delivery of services as with difficulties in interpersonal relationships.

How much behavior needs to be changed can be answered
most readily by the client and the people who interact with the
client. When setting goals, it may be possible for the worker to
determine how much behavior change is needed by referring to
the client's or change agent's experience with that particular behavior. It is unreasonable to assume that all defined behaviors of
all participants will need to change. For instance, parents who
are dissatisfied with their relationship with their child could be
using primarily coercive means to obtain compliance. In such a
case, the parents might be taught more positive means for dealing with their child while the child's compliant behavior (which
was not really the problem) remains stable.

Generality. Good practice methods should produce some degree of generality. In social work, generality means that practice procedures can be implemented by a variety of workers and can affect the client's behavior change across time, in several environments, and/or with a number of people. The advantage of developing methods for extending intervention effects across time and to a wide variety of problems and behaviors will be obvious to the clinician. This does not mean that clients always maintain the same level of behavior achieved during treatment but that they will maintain satisfactory levels of functioning in their search for life satisfaction once their relationship with the worker ends.

Because it cannot be assumed that future environmental factors will support newly learned behavior patterns, intervention should include a plan for extending treatment effects. A worker who regards generality as something that needs to be carefully programmed and evaluated is more likely to find generality of behavior change than one who regards extension of treatment effects as a given. Because extension of intervention is so important, Chapter Nine includes a detailed discussion of generality.

Social Relevance. Behavioral targets for change are selected because they have current social importance to the client, recipients of the client's behavior, or social agents. Although it is relevant to study why people behave the way they do, the primary role of social work practitioners is to effect improvement in the client's behavioral functioning. For instance, it is more interesting for practitioners to help the elderly client reestablish appropriate self-help skills than it is to describe, however accurately, the aging process. The social relevance criterion stresses the applied, rather than the basic or developmental, aspects of research.

Successful behavior development is certainly not guaranteed if the client chooses the target behavior, but it is indeed futile to attempt to get the client to engage in self-modification procedures to achieve behaviors the client considers unimportant. Not only should the practitioner and the client choose relevant behavior, but for the intervention to be successful, there needs to be enough positive change to enhance the quality of the client's life. For self-help skills, the desired goal for elderly persons might be the ability to maintain reasonable functioning within their own homes. For many targeted behaviors, subtle changes often are not adequate to be considered important or relevant to the individual's total functioning, although in some cases small changes may beget other changes and reinforce a chain of positive events.

When developing programs for specific populations, it is reasonable to spend some time determining the behaviors that clients and societal agents consider important. Dangel and Polster (1981) reported the results of a parent discussion group that not only identified socially relevant problems for parent training but provided feedback regarding procedures and training materials. Although this is not the only criterion for selecting behaviors for change, a survey of the relevant population is usually informative. In cases where societal agents determine acceptable behaviors, such as in a home for delinquent children, it may be necessary to validate the proposed responses more formally (Kazdin, 1977; Minkin and others, 1976).

Rationale for Using an Applied Behavior Analysis Model

Empirical evidence and accountability are strongly emphasized in the current social work literature (Briar, 1977; Fischer, 1978; Gambrill, 1977; Jayaratne and Levy, 1979). Generally, social workers are advised to use treatment procedures that have been empirically validated, although it is not always clear what constitutes empirical validation. This seems an excellent, self-evident idea; why not use what is so obviously effective? Social workers, however, deal with numerous practical and psychological problems, and in many instances the worker cannot find an empirically tested procedure proved effective with a specific problem or client population. Therefore, it is productive to concentrate on a practice methodology that includes methods for designing and evaluating intervention procedures; producing evidence; and providing an accountability system for the client, social worker, and society.

As public and private funding sources become more judicious in their granting of funds, they are demanding more accountability. The sources want clients to experience demonstrable changes, and they expect agencies to document these changes. Therefore, social workers and other service providers are being asked hard questions about the effectiveness of their services and being encouraged to budget evaluation plans. Workers who are trained to ask questions regarding procedures, effectiveness, and maintenance have definite advantages over those who cannot provide scientific evidence of changes.

Behavior analysis is an educational approach to treating human problems by direct practice methods. The clients' learning may affect more permanent behavior changes. These behavior changes will also depend on adequate resources within the environment to support positive client change. Although more evidence is necessary before this assumption is scientifically demonstrated, initial findings are encouraging. As stated earlier, the educational component is also built into the method via the analytical component. Both the worker and the client benefit from the learning experience of defining and measuring behavioral operations as to their interaction with the environment. Behavior analysis is also a good model for educating practitioners-researchers because it integrates practice and research methods.

The methodology of behavior analysis is relatively simple to teach to a beginning social worker because it so carefully specifies what the worker does. The information needed to implement intervention is directly available through observation and structured interviews. The worker learns to ask the client questions directly relevant to the problem definition and then shapes the design of interventions. Development of intervention occurs within two or three interviews and is enhanced by between-session data recording and analysis. The worker learns to use readily available information, that is, information the worker can see or elicit from the client.

It is frequently possible to develop workable (if not always perfect) single-subject evaluation designs. These designs are essential for interventions that have not been adequately evaluated and are desirable for more well-evaluated interventions. The model also offers the opportunity to make treatment decisions based on data and gives the clients the opportunity to obtain immediate feedback on their own and others' behavior change.

Historically, the social work profession has always been committed to the development of an applied science of social work (Perlman, 1957; Reid and Epstein, 1977; Richmond, 1965; Towle, 1954). This development has moved from recorded practice wisdom to systematically defined practice to empirically tested procedures and evaluation of outcomes. This book offers a method for combining scientific and practice procedures.

◆◆◆◆ ◆◆ ◆ ◆◆ ◆ ◆◆ ◆ ◆◆ ◆ ◆◆ ◆ ◆◆ ◆ ◆◆ ◆ ◆◆ ◆ ◆◆ ◆ ◆◆ ◆ ◆◆ ◆◆◆

Principles of Behavior Change

The theoretical basis for the behavior analysis model of social work is primarily behavioral principles applied to the solution of human problems. This model focuses on the clients and their interactions with the environment. Understanding the underlying theory gives workers a view of their clients and their problems that leads to specific kinds of interventions directed toward altering these interactions. It also provides a means for analyzing the interactions as applied to current events in the clients' lives.

When behavioral theories are applied to behaviors, applications focus on new behavior patterns that need to be learned, functional analysis of behavioral interactions with the environment, continuous assessment of interventions effects, and empirical validation of intervention procedures (Redd, Porterfield, and Anderson, 1979). Therefore, most behavioral interventions are directed toward increasing behaviors that enhance individual functioning and decreasing or eliminating behaviors that lead to unhappiness and dissatisfaction. Clients are taught new ways to gain desired outcomes, usually to achieve desired reinforcers.

During this process, the worker analyzes clients' behavioral interactions with their environment and how the environment controls their behavior. This functional analysis is enhanced by continuous assessment of the interaction, which involves examining clients' records of behaviors and the consequences of those behaviors. Interventions are either drawn from the empirical literature or evaluated by using experimental techniques (see Chapter Four for evaluation procedures).

Human behavior is influenced by genetic endowment, physical states, historical events, and recent environmental events. The behavior analysis model is particularly suited for social work because the worker can gather information about current environmental events in clients' lives and strive to implement any necessary change, whereas the worker cannot alter the other influential variables. Obviously, then, a conceptual view should include a perspective that leads to environmental interventions. Environmental interventions, for our purposes, include working with clients in ways to help them use themselves and their environments more effectively. Most interventions in this model are directed toward developing delivery systems and strategies to give clients additional reinforcement. However, this is not an easy task, and it is useful for the worker to learn behavioral theories both to design interventions and to analyze the clients' behaviors and the consequences of these behaviors.

Behavioral Principles

A basic assumption of behavioral theory is that human behaviors are lawful phenomena and therefore can be studied and altered scientifically. The roots of this assumption are in the works of Pavlov (1927, 1928), Watson and Rayner (1920), Thorndike (1898), and Skinner (1935, 1938, 1953). These scientists' research provided only the beginning of scientific proof, but their work led directly to human applications of Thorndike's *law of effect*: Essentially, behavior is affected by its consequences. Bijou and Baer (1961, 1965, 1967) expanded behavior theory to a theory of child development and began an area of applications research called *applied behavior analysis* (Baer, Wolf, and Risley, 1968).

The behavioral principles of human behavior determined by environmental events are called *respondent* and *operant*. Most experimental evidence in applied behavior analysis is based on operant events (see *Journal of Applied Behavior Analysis*, 1968 to present), so this chapter discusses mainly operant procedures for behavior change.

Operant Behaviors. Operant behaviors operate on their environment to produce specific results. The future predictability of a behavior is established by its current consequences or its function. Consequences are defined by their effect on behavior. There are essentially two ways operant behaviors are altered by their consequences in the environment: Something is removed from the environment, or something is added. The procedures for affecting this alteration are reinforcement, punishment, and extinction. The functional properties of a consequence determine the future probability of a response.

Positive Reinforcement. Reinforcement is either positive or negative. *Positive reinforcement* is the occurrence of a desirable consequence (stimulus) following a behavior which increases the future probability of that behavior. The stimulus is called a positive reinforcer. In Practice Illustration 8.5, Molick and Pinkston demonstrated that teacher attention plus tokens were positive reinforcers for increasing the social behaviors of a depressed adolescent girl. As in most interventions, this procedure was directed to arrange the delivery of positive reinforcers following desired client behaviors to increase the client's potential for achieving successful interactions with individuals in the environment.

Negative Reinforcement. Negative reinforcement is the removal of an unwanted consequence following a behavior which increases the future probability of that behavior. That is, the client escapes negative consequences by engaging in specific behaviors. Clients who spend inordinate time behaving in ways to avoid real or imagined negative consequences are likely to experience anxiety and dissatisfaction. However, it is important for clients to have behavior for escaping negative consequences. This principle explains why mothers may be shaped by their children toward yelling at them to stop engaging in behaviors the mothers find unacceptable. For a few moments, at least, a mother escapes those behaviors, and therefore she may develop a pattern of yelling at the children when she wants them to stop making so much noise or fighting with each other. Note that negative reinforcement increases her yelling behavior—all reinforcers increase behavior.

Punishment. Punishment is the addition of a consequence following a behavior which decreases the future probability of that behavior. Critical comments following an irrelevant statement may decrease the future probability of irrelevant contributions. Unfortunately, other behaviors occurring in conjunction with irrelevant statements may also be decreased such as participation, and the person administering the punishment and the setting in which the punishment is administered may acquire aversive characteristics for the client. For instance, an individual working in an office and who receives critical comments as a consequence of an irrelevant statement may keep quiet but may also respond with a critical remark and leave the office or quit because all aspects of the environment are associated with the punishment. Although punishment may be necessary to break up long-term dysfunctional behavior patterns, it is never used by itself in a clinical situation. Punishment procedures are more useful to the worker as a way of understanding why clients behave as they do. In groups where discipline is an important factor, the person(s) in charge—parent, teacher, institutional staff—may resort to criticism, physical punishment, and withdrawal of privileges as the "easiest" way to gain behavioral control of individuals. Punishment, however, does not give clients the opportunity to learn what they need to know to function in a desirable way: what they should be doing. If the worker can analyze punishing consequences, it is easier to design programs that are based on positive reinforcement and the escape of punishment. When trying to change extreme behaviors, the most effective use of punishment is to reinforce desired behaviors while punishing negative ones.

Extinction. With extinction, previously administered reinforcers are discontinued following a behavior, to decrease the future probability of that behavior. This principle is usually involved in any procedure which removes attention from undesirable behaviors that have been receiving a considerable amount of attention. The purpose is to stop reinforcing behaviors that are not wanted. In many cases, naturally occurring extinction may be one reason that clients seek help in the first place. Almost any major loss, such as the loss of a job or spouse, leads to a loss of reinforcement and extinction. Like punishment, extinction may result in emotional behaviors by clients. When extinction is used as an intervention method, it should be combined with reinforcement of desired behaviors. Reinforcers then can be discontinued following undesired behaviors while they are administered for desired behaviors. When using this procedure, the total amount of reinforcement should not be decreased abruptly and usually not at all. (Extinction is more fully discussed in the following section.)

Behavioral Interventions

Functional and Contingency Analysis. Before using specific techniques, the worker conducts an extensive functional analysis of the client's interaction with the environment. A functional analysis is an examination of environmental events that appear to be causally related. The worker analyzes the current situation and determines who is doing what to whom and with what effect. The functional analysis is one of the most important tools the worker brings to the client-worker relationship. As an alternative to diagnosis, functional analysis looks at the client's complex situation rather than identifying the client according to categories (Redd, Porterfield, and Anderson, 1979). The analytical dimensions of the functional analysis were defined by Kanfer and Saslow (pp. 426-427, 1969):

1. Since the individual operates in a complex system, psychological variables are not the only ones considered in the assessment; biological, economic, and social factors are also included.
2. Since it is probable that many of the individual's behaviors are operant (maintained by the consequent stimuli provided

by the social environment), the client's behaviors can be organized in terms of the consequences they produce.

3. Since individual behavioral repertoires are limited by individual biological, social, and intellectual attributes and by the norms of peer groups, knowledge of the client's history, capacities, and group norms is necessary.

4. Assessment is always individualized.

5. Assessment does not necessarily lead to psychological intervention. If the controlling factors are economic, for example, the recommended intervention would be economic.

This analytical approach to intervention is useful to the worker as both an interpretative and intervention assessment. It is a major part of the information the worker transmits to the client, serving as a conceptual framework for the client and worker.

The foundation for the functional analysis is the contingency analysis, which specifies the relationship between a behavioral performance and its outcome (Ferster, Culbertson, and Boren, 1975). O'Leary and Wilson (1975) defined contingency as "the extent to which the occurrence of one event is dependent upon the occurrence of another event" (p. 481). The concept "contingency" refers to the probabilistic relationship between at least two events: an individual's behavior and the ensuing consequences of that behavior and the environment. For instance, if a parent yells at a child every time tantrums occur, the unwritten contract is that the tantrums will be followed by parent attention. The worker's task is to discover the implied contracts or established relationships that exist. These established relationships are frequently referred to as *schedules of reinforcement* and fall into two general categories: ratio and interval. A *ratio schedule* is the specific number of responses that occur before reinforcement is presented. For example, if every time a child throws a tantrum a parent provides attention, the probabilistic relationship between behavior and reinforcement is one to one (1:1). Reinforcement following each instance of behavior is referred to as a continuous reinforcement schedule (CRF) or fixed ratio of one (FR 1) schedule. The schedule is "fixed," but it could be any number. Usually, reinforcement schedules in naturalistic environments do not follow a fixed number of behaviors; they tend to vary around an average or mean number of responses, which is a variable ratio schedule. For example, the parent does not follow each occurrence of a child's noncompliant behavior with attention; the parent attends following varying instances of behavior. The total child behavior divided by the numbers of occurrences of parent attention is the variable ratio of reinforcement.

The *interval schedule* represents reinforcement that follows a specified fixed or variable period of time. Two examples of an interval schedule are reinforcing a child for studying following a specified length of time or paying adults higher amounts for certain work after a specified length of time, that is, overtime. Variable interval schedules occur when reinforcers are available following a variable length of time.

Reinforcement-Based Procedures. Reinforcement procedures are designed to increase behaviors that help the clients obtain what they need from the environment. The procedures include shaping, differential reinforcement, token and point systems, increased opportunity for reinforcement, and cueing and reinforcement.

A reinforcer is a behavior, material, or event that follows a specific behavior and increases the future likelihood of that behavior. Primary reinforcers, such as food and sex, have a universal tendency to increase future behavior, particularly among deprived persons. Social reinforcers, including attention and praise, have such powerful effects on increasing behaviors that they are a general focus in social work. These phenomena occur whether the worker deliberately or inadvertently reinforces clients' behaviors.

The arrangement of a reinforcer after a behavior to increase the future occurrence of that behavior is a reinforcement procedure. A frequent reinforcement technique is *shaping,* which is applying reinforcers following incremental changes in behavior to develop a desirable behavior. Use of shaping may result in substantially complex behavior patterns. The worker, a change agent, or a client may all learn to apply shaping techniques to foster specific behaviors. When clients lack sufficient skills to attain their goals, it may be necessary to develop these skills through small steps. A person who is working to regain the use of bodily functions following an illness may first be praised for attempting to do exercises and, as improvement occurs, the standard for receiving praise may be raised. This is not totally unlike sports training, in which the coach may praise a player for a good try. Shaping is programmed into the intervention through the planning of small steps to be reinforced or approximations of the small steps. Increments are a way of setting up the program so that shaping is likely to occur.

The most frequently suggested reinforcement technique is *differential attention,* which includes the reinforcement of desirable behavior and the extinction or ignoring of undesirable behavior. This technique is effective with clients who are suffering from extreme social deprivation and who find attention very reinforcing. Although this procedure has gained use, it is not always effective. It is sometimes difficult for individuals and families with long histories of inappropriate interaction to change that pattern with this simple procedure (Herbert and others, 1973). When a worker is attempting to modify long-standing behaviors, it is better to use this technique in conjunction with other procedures that involve more powerful reinforcer systems than social attention. For example, differential reinforcement may include material reinforcers or be combined with mild punishment procedures; these techniques are often components of reinforcement systems. (See the "Punishment-Based Procedure" section for a discussion of differential attention as an extinction method.)

When more structure is required to change a long-standing interaction problem, *token* and *point systems* can be added to differential reinforcement for a powerful behavior change intervention (Kazdin, 1977). These techniques are particularly useful in schools, institutions, and families. Tokens or points are presented following a desired behavior; these tokens or points are exchanged later for material or social reinforcers. The presentation of tokens is an easily discriminated occasion for rewarding an individual for desirable behavior, a bridge to reinforcers not easily available at a specific moment, and has been demonstrated as more powerful than differential attention (Phillips and others, 1971; Kazdin, 1977). The difficulties with token and point systems are that they require considerable skill to administer and behaviors may be lost if tokens are discontinued too quickly; some clients may also find them cumbersome. Generally, token systems should not be used between people of equal status, and they may create an imbalance in the power structure between two people, such as a married couple.

Token economies are one of the most powerful tools that behavioralists have developed to date and have proved effective in a wide range of settings, with different therapists, clients, and behavioral difficulties (see Kazdin, 1977 for an excellent review of successful token economies). An effective token economy has four components: the token, the target behavior that is to be increased or decreased, backup reinforcers, and specific contingencies (Kazdin, 1977). The specific contingencies define whether the token takes on reinforcing or punishing value. For example, when the token is delivered contingent upon the occurrence of a specific behavior and reinforcing backup stimuli are made available, the token assumes reinforcing value and increases the likelihood that the behavior will occur in the future. When the token is removed contingent upon the occurrence of a behavior, the token assumes punishing value and decreases the likelihood that the behavior will occur in the future.

Successful settings for token economies have included a residential treatment center for predelinquents (Phillips, 1968; Phillips and others, 1971), the classroom (Kaufman and O'Leary, 1972; Iwata and Bailey, 1974), a psychiatric hospital (Ayllon and Azrin, 1968; Winkler, 1970), and the home, on the part of parents (Patterson and others, 1975). A token economy may be programmed three different ways: based on response cost (which is a punishment-based procedure), based on reinforcement, or based on a mixture of cost and reinforcement. During the early development of the token economy, most programs were based on reinforcement, partly because of Azrin and Holz's article (1966) that discussed punishment with animals and negative side effects. They hypothesized that similar examples of negative side effects would occur in humans: undesired emotional outbursts or states, flight, increased aggression, and attempts at escape. As the token economy's methodology matured, clinicians learned how to program for and control negative side effects when they occurred. Doty, McInnis, and Paul (1974) successfully programmed for the aversive side effect of clients not paying off their fines. They were able to successfully reduce the number of fines accumulated by proportionally reducing the number of accumulated fines by the number of "fineless" days.

In another study, Kaufman and O'Leary (1972) found that a classroom token economy based on response cost was as effective as one based on reinforcement. Kaufman and O'Leary compared two classrooms, one with a token economy based on response cost alone and the other based on reinforcement alone. In the cost-response classroom, "free" tokens were removed contingent on disruptive behavior. In the reinforcement classroom, appropriate behaviors were contingently reinforced by the addition of tokens. In both classes, backup reinforcers were available contingent upon the number of tokens remaining or earned at the end of each session. Unique to this study is that the authors observed for side effects but found none in either classroom. However, they did state that ". . . more powerful reinforcers might have generated side effects in the cost class" (p. 308).

Iwata and Bailey (1974) also studied side effects in a classroom token economy based on response cost alone and reinforcement alone. The results demonstrated that both programs equally controlled disruptive behaviors. The results did not indicate any side effects exhibited by the children in their classroom. The teachers were slightly more approving when the reinforcement program was used. Data indicated unprogrammed positive side effects in both classes, namely, increased academic output and accuracy in completing problems. The authors followed Kaufman and O'Leary's concept of increased potency of the response cost leading to increased aversive side effects. After reviewing four studies, they concluded that removing previously earned tokens is more punishing than removing free tokens contingent upon undesired behavior. Iwata and Bailey concluded that the removal of earned tokens may lead to more aversive side effects because the tokens are more potent.

Reinforcers may be available for desirable behaviors in an environment, but clients must learn how to get them. The worker teaches and helps clients arrange the *opportunity for reinforcement*. This may be a very simple technique, such as saying "good morning" to a teacher (Lullo and Pinkston, Practice Illustration 9.1), or very complex, such as determining what behaviors are reinforced in one's job and under what circumstances. In other instances, it involves the worker engineering a change in the client's environment. As examples, providing a daycare situation so that an elderly person can engage in social behavior facilitates possible social consequences. Or the worker teaches the client techniques for achieving needed services by using public programs. Increasing reinforcers may be gained by teaching the client to ask a friend for what is needed: something so simple as saying "I need a hug." Environmental arrangements are made to increase the probability that specific prosocial behavior occurs. Arranging juice and coffee in the sitting room of a nursing home increases the probability that the residents will talk to each other (Blackman, Howe, and Pinkston, 1976); instructing a group leader to ask more questions increases group participation (Linsk and Pinkston, Practice Illustration 8.3). These techniques contain a strong element of stimulus control; that is, they provide cues for behavior which eventually leads to reinforcement.

Clients unable to discriminate when to use a behavior may benefit from a combination of *cueing and reinforcement*. In the cueing procedure, an antecedent event before a behavior helps individuals discriminate the behaviors necessary to acquire positive consequences. This occurs naturally in most environments. For example, the presence of a teacher may be a cue for a student to say "help" and receive desired attention. A more obvious cue may be needed; for example, the client may learn to greet a teacher at specific times. The cue or reminder is given to increase the probability of the occurrence of a desired behavior; reinforcement is given to ensure the future probability of that behavior. With most adults and children, cues can be eventually faded out. With mentally impaired persons, the cues may need to remain as an ongoing part of their environment to maintain the desired behavior. It is helpful to use cues to remind persons within the environment to reinforce the client. A parent who has difficulty discriminating when to praise a child's behaviors is given a chart with specific times to check if the behavior has occurred.

Contingency Contracting. The contingency contract (Homme and others, 1969) is the agreement regarding the circumstances under which specific techniques will be used in relation to specific behaviors. It is the mutual agreement between two or more persons as to the consequences of specific behaviors. These consequences are usually positive, although response cost and time-out can be included with reinforcement. (Time-out is discussed in the "Punishment-Based Procedures" section.) The rules for setting up a contract may vary according to the circumstances, but the seven-step sequence is usually: (1) The involved persons sit down together; (2) one or two behaviors are selected and defined in observable terms; (3) all important aspects of the behavior are determined, such as how often it could be done, when it should be done, and where it should be done; (4) a reward that will be given for performing the behavior is agreed on; (5) it is decided who will determine whether the behavior was completed according to the definition; (6) all the above information is written into a contract; (7) participants sign the contract. The contract is a versatile instrument and can be used in numerous ways: between the worker and the client, parents and children, married partners, teachers and children, and so on. It has even been suggested as a way of more clearly defining requirements of parents and foster parents by public agencies (Stein and Gambrill, 1976). In addition to the contract, it is useful to include a reward menu, with a variety of reinforcers listed with the behavioral requirement or number of points for each item.

An important skill that can be learned in the contracting process is *negotiation*. Essentially, negotiation is the ability to state what one wants and what one will do to get it—more simply, asking for what one needs. Because authority figures will not always be pleased to have those over whom they have power exhibit this skill, when teaching clients to negotiate, it is relevant to teach them by using ways currently acceptable within their environment. For instance, it may be better for a child to say "I'll mow the lawn and in return I'd like to go to the movies Saturday" instead of "What will you give me to mow the lawn?" Specific times should be set for altering and renegotiating the terms of the contract, and usually the contracts should be reviewed weekly to determine the participants' satisfaction or dissatisfaction with the terms and effectiveness of the contract.

Extinction-Based Procedures. As defined earlier, extinction, part of most behavioral interventions, is the withholding of reinforcers following an undesirable behavior that has previously been reinforced, to decrease the future probability of that behavior. With human beings, *extinction is never used alone; it is always used in combination with some reinforcement system.* Extinction used alone will very likely elicit overt emotional behavior or withdrawal. It is important that desirable behaviors be defined and reinforced at the same time so that the client can discriminate what to do to obtain reinforcers. A characteristic of extinction techniques is the extinction curve, which indicates the increase in undesirable behavior that occurs before the client is able to discriminate the new contingency system. The curve denotes the circumstances that maintain behaviors. The increase is generally followed by a sudden decrease in undesirable behavior and, if an adequate reinforcement technique is being used, an increase in desirable behavior.

The simplest extinction technique is *differential attention*: Undesirable behavior is ignored, desirable behavior is reinforced. Other extinction techniques are *ignore-protect-reinforce* and *ignore-redirect-reinforce.* It is important that the worker understand how the extinction curve may occur and that the change agent implementing the program be alerted to the possibility of an increase in inappropriate behavior before improvement occurs. Otherwise, the worker will hear a phrase such as "I tried your procedure but he just got worse," and the change agent may discontinue the intervention procedure.

Although acting-out behavior is frequently maintained by social attention, a few procedures have been developed to incorporate extinction to alter dangerous aggressive behavior. With the *ignore-protect-reinforce* procedure, the aggressive behavior is ignored, the victim is protected, and the target person is reinforced for prosocial behavior (Pinkston and others, 1973). Although this procedure is a hopeful alternative to punishment, it should be evaluated carefully when used because of the lack of research findings demonstrating its generality to other situations and populations.

The *ignore-redirect-reinforce* procedure is useful with clients who have a high rate of inappropriate behavior and practically a nonexistent rate of appropriate behavior, as is the case with many behavior-problem children and institutional residents. It is also useful in normal adult interactions when it is necessary to ignore criticism, state a specific need, and thank the individual for fulfilling that need. Or a worker might ignore a child's inappropriate behavior, suggest appropriate behavior, and reinforce those appropriate behaviors with praise and tokens (Moses and Pinkston, Practice Illustration 6.3).

Punishment-Based Procedures. Punishment procedures are used to decrease the future probability of undesirable behavior. These procedures include techniques for presenting an aversive event following an undesirable behavior, to lead to a decreased probability of that behavior, or removing a reinforcing event following a behavior, to lead to a decrease in the probability of that behavior. Punishment is used when a dysfunctional behavior prevents the implementation of reinforcement procedures to decrease behavior deficits. Clinically, punishment procedures are used in conjunction with reinforcement of other specifically defined behaviors. *No punishment procedures should be used alone*; again, as with extinction, the predicted result will be withdrawal or emotional behavior by the client. The four most frequently evaluated punishment techniques are *presentation of an aversive event, response cost, time-out,* and *overcorrection.*

An *aversive event* includes such common punishments as criticism, slapping, spanking, and yelling. In many ways, this technique is the least tolerable to workers. Frequently, however, the worker develops the intervention plan to minimize aversive methods of interaction between family members to improve relationships (Pinkston and others, Practice Illustration 7.3). Extreme cases of self-destruction and aggression have been altered by presenting such aversive events as shock, spanks, and yells, which have produced sharp decreases in highly undesirable behavior (Lovaas and Bucher, 1974). Even though it is often effective, the use of these aversive techniques should be subject to a review committee and not be the decision of any individual worker.

Response-cost techniques involve removing a reinforcing event to decrease the future probability of a behavior. In naturalistic situations, these techniques often take the form of fines or loss of privileges. This technique works well in conjunction with token and point systems, whereby tokens or points are lost. It is unlikely to apply to other settings or behaviors that are not being treated or to apply beyond the termination of its use. That is, when used alone, response cost merely suppresses negative behavior rather than develops new behavioral repertoires. As with all other punishment procedures, response cost should be combined with strong reinforcement systems.

Response-cost token economies are effective, and there are two ways to program to control aversive side effects. In the first option, the clinician can wait and see what side effects develop and then program for the side effects within the token economy. The second option is to reduce the probability of aversive side effects by using free tokens. Further exploring the use of free tokens, Hall and others (1972) reduced whining, complaining, and crying by removing free tokens contingent upon the occurrence of those behaviors. The unique aspect of the treatment is that no backup reinforcers were made available.

Researchers have systematically explored the effectiveness of response cost within the token economy and the nature of any side effects. Buchard and Barrera (1972) compared the effectiveness of time-out and response cost on a retarded population. They found that in all subjects but one, a higher magnitude of the punishment led to a greater suppression of behavior. The authors found that time-out and response costs are equally effective in reducing behavior, but they felt that response cost has two primary advantages over time-out: The client is not removed from the environment, so the client may engage in reinforcing behavior after the response-cost procedure has been implemented; and response cost is more realistic. Buchard and Barrera noted the disadvantage that fining and using response-cost procedures may actually reinforce the client.

Time-out, a form of aversive event, is the brief removal of a person from a reinforcing situation following an occurrence of undesirable behavior, with the expectation that the time-out will decrease the future occurrence of that behavior. This technique combines elements of extinction, response cost, and presentation of an aversive stimulus. Time-out periods range from three to ten minutes, and the procedure has been tested most frequently with aggressive, acting-out children, although it is sometimes used with others (Bostow and Bailey, 1969; Wolf, Risley, and Mees, 1964; Clark and others, 1973). With this technique, the precise conditions under which it is to be used should be defined in observable terms.

Overcorrection is a technique for decreasing the probability of undesirable behavior and increasing the probability of desirable behavior. Following an instance of undesirable behavior, a practice period of appropriate behavior occurs repetitiously for a specified time (Foxx and Azrin, 1972, 1973). Generally, this technique was researched in institutional settings with research or institutional staff. In practice, however, many children require a physical rehearsal of the appropriate behavior, and families and staff dislike putting the child through these procedures, decreasing the possibility that the intervention will be used. This form of punishment is an alternate to other, sometimes less available procedures, such as time-out or the presentation of an aversive stimulus.

Modeling Procedures. In direct intervention, modeling procedures are used to teach both new skills and new ways to combine old skills. Modeling techniques are designed to elicit specific behaviors to provide the opportunity to reinforce behavior or to model the reinforcement of a specific behavior. Modeling is combined with rehearsal, feedback, and/or reinforcement. The effects of modeling alone are not likely to last long without some form of additional reinforcement. To avoid this difficulty, modeling usually occurs in the following combinations: modeling and rehearsal; modeling, rehearsal, and feedback; and modeling and reinforcement (Bandura, 1969; Nay, 1979).

The *modeling and rehearsal* technique gives the client the opportunity to first observe another person exhibiting the desired behavior and then enables the client to practice the desired behavior before trying it outside the interview. This procedure can be used with individuals, families, or groups. Modeling can be enhanced further by the addition of *feedback* following the client's rehearsal. Whenever possible, feedback should stress the positive aspects of the client's performance. If additional improvement is required, the behavior should be modeled for the client, again, with particular stress on the area needing improvement; *avoid negative feedback*. Although modeling, rehearsal, and feedback are excellent techniques for teaching behavior, they do not enhance the likelihood that the behavior will be maintained over time. Reinforcement should be included as part of the training technique and faded out gradually once the behavior has been established. The behavior being taught may be reinforced by the consequences occurring naturally in the environment, but the worker should plan this, not expect it to occur spontaneously (see Chapter Five for a detailed description of how to use these techniques).

3

◆◆◆◆◆◆◆◆◆◆◆◆◆◆◆◆◆◆◆◆◆◆◆◆◆◆◆◆◆◆◆◆◆

Developing and Implementing Intervention Strategies

A practice model is a set of practice procedures designed to assess problems, develop interventions, evaluate progress, and maintain intervention effects, to increase the likelihood of producing desirable solutions to clients' problems. It is also a description of the operation, and alternative operations, involved when working with clients, their significant others, institutions, and the community. The behavior analysis model includes scientific methods for gathering evidence that helps the worker select and evaluate the specific intervention which most likely will produce favorable outcomes. Science is a way of accumulating evidence to establish the correctness or incorrectness of an assumption (a hypothesis). In practice situations, the worker is required to make many on the spot assumptions while assessing and designing an intervention strategy. Systematic data gathering should enhance the worker's ability to produce correct assumptions. And applying rules of evidence is even more important when making decisions that affect people's lives than when testing abstract principles.

Before embarking on an intervention, the worker requires information which indicates that there is at least some hope the intervention is directed toward factors associated with the occurrence of the problem and that the problem as stated by the client and others actually exists. Objective scientific and systematic methods are logical ways of organizing and evaluating practice procedures for effective intervention outcomes. This chapter shows how these methods can be incorporated with behavioral principles for a behavior analysis practice model. We begin with a description of the behavioral interview, which is the basis of the workers' interactions with clients and other relevant persons. The intervention process is divided into four phases: assessment, intervention, maintenance, and follow-up. Steps for implementing each phase are discussed, along with important questions the worker should ask before proceeding to the next step.

Interviews

In the behavior analysis model of social work practice, each interview is directed toward specific goals that fulfill certain functions. The interview is the setting for the development of planned interventions to be carried out in the clients' environments. The interview is the occasion for defining problems in behavioral terms, assessing resources, setting goals, planning intervention, evaluating progress, and planning the extension of intervention effects. Interviews should be nonpunishing events in which clients need not fear negative consequences (Skinner, 1953; Kanfer and Goldstein, 1975; Wilson and Evans, 1977). Within this context, the worker gives clients or the clients' group opportunities to experience increased access to reinforcement and to learn new behaviors that extend a pattern of behavior change outside the interview.

It is not known which components of interviews are most important or even what all the components are likely to be. Worker behaviors, empathy, warmth, and genuineness are frequently offered as basic conditions for successful intervention (Fischer, 1978; Traux and Carkhuff, 1967). However, conclusive evidence regarding the actual impact of these variables upon client behavior change is not yet available. Carefully defined problems and systematic intervention procedures may be more important, or there may be great individual difference among clients as to the importance of specific variables. A client in need of material services may not need the same kind of relationship with the worker as a client who has received considerable negative feedback from the environment and who depends upon the worker to show understanding in the form of accepting and positive statements regarding the client's personal worth.

Characteristics. The four basic features for behaviorally oriented interviews are: (1) Provides a nonpunishing setting in which clients can analyze their problems and discuss possible solutions, (2) provides access to increased reinforcement, (3) allows avoidance of punishment, and (4) provides the opportunity for mutual shaping to occur between the worker and the clients. Although these features have not been empirically validated, existing evidence of positive outcomes suggests that the features can serve as basic guidelines for the behavior analysis model of practice. The point is that the interview context is conceived in behavioral terms, as a setting in which learning can occur, and is carefully managed regarding consequences following clients' behavior.

Workers provide a nonpunishing environment to obtain adequate information from clients to determine the nature of the clients' problem, the circumstances under which it occurs, and the clients' reasons for seeking help. The interview's context facilitates discussion between the worker and the client about personal problems that may not present a positive view of the client. Although it is not always possible to predict which worker behaviors will elicit fear and anxiety, the worker should not behave in any way (verbal or nonverbal) that reflects negative feelings or moral judgments (a possible punishing consequence) about the client's behavior. Negative feedback from the worker may decrease the self-revealing statements necessary for obtaining a clear view of the problems and the client's motivation for solving them.

Instead, the interview should increase the likelihood of positive feedback and access to reinforcement to the client from both the worker and others. This is relatively easy to accomplish because most clients come to the interview in a state of social deprivation. They may not have satisfactory personal relationships, may not receive adequate compensation for their work, or may not feel life satisfaction. As a result, most likely the worker will be able to provide a situation that the client will view as helpful and reinforcing because it is so unlike the "real world," in which much of the client's behavior is directed toward avoiding punishing consequences. For instance, many clients live in fear of rejection if they make an error, live in a state of deprivation, or lack skills.

Avoidance of punishment and increased reinforcement in the interview may stimulate a helping relationship that will enhance the worker's ability to help clients solve problems. The interview represents one place where clients can come with confidence that they will not receive excessive negative feedback or criticism. This security often provides relief from outside pressures even before a specific intervention is designed to remediate identified problems.

The interaction within interviews is characterized by mutual shaping processes in which both worker and client behaviors are subject to change. The clients' behaviors play a major part in determining the worker's behavior and formulating the decisions made in the interview. The more aware the worker is of the mutuality of the interview and the importance of specific events involved in this process, the more likely the client and worker will be able to formulate a mutually satisfactory intervention plan.

In behaviorally oriented interventions, a major task is to focus clients on the *functional aspects of their behavior,* which are those aspects that result in changes in reinforcement and punishment as consequences of specific behaviors within the surrounding environment. These interactions with the environment affect both the clients' behavior and feelings and those of others. Initially, most clients will not see the problem as a need for behavior change. Instead, clients may view themselves as incompetent, or even slightly crazy, rather than as persons requiring behavioral change. The worker's first task is to help clients reconceptualize the problems in behavioral terms that facilitate intervention. It is then possible to show clients how the "dysfunctional" behavior has led to negative outcomes in previous problem situations. Clients may have received positive reinforcers by engaging in behavior that also led to negative consequences, which leaves the clients in the position of bank robbers who have stolen much money but cannot spend it because they are in jail!

The worker must also be able to elicit adequate information from the client through thoughtful questions. This information provides data used to assess problems and design interventions likely to help the client avoid negative experiences or obtain more life satisfaction. For example, in early interviews the worker ascertains the client's view of a positive outcome (Goldiamond, 1974; Schwartz and Goldiamond, 1975); the client's views following the intervention should then be different. This provides the worker with better ideas of what changes need to occur.

It is useful for the worker to develop a relationship that provides positive social consequences for the client. Most often this can take the form of verbal praise and attention, by articulating the client's strengths most likely to be helpful in solving problems or by focusing on the client's attempts to do something about the problems. Positive statements about the client's efforts to obtain assistance direct the client's attention toward strengths and support motivation, increasing the likelihood of desirable change. When clients have limited skills, such as an autistic child or a mentally impaired adult, it may be necessary to pair the worker with a material object like food to strengthen social reinforcement. In any event, helping potential is maximized by the worker's ability to focus on the positive aspects of the client and the client's behavior and by ensuring that the interview is an occasion for receiving social reinforcement.

It is also useful for the worker to spend some time clarifying the client's role in the interview. Clients provide initial information, continuous feedback to the worker, and help focus the worker on important and relevant events. Making clients aware of the importance of their participation in the intervention and their contributions by providing information for the solution of the problem is another way to reinforce the client.

The Behavior Analysis Model

Phase 1—Assessment. Initial assessment interviews are designed to gather information about the client and the client's environment. This information involves specifying desirable outcomes of the intervention, evaluating available resources, defining target behaviors, selecting the evaluation techniques, orienting the client or significant other(s) to observation and data collection of baseline information, and supervising the collection of baseline data (the data recorded before intervention).

Step 1: initial assessment. Initial assessment is the foundation of successful intervention. The worker spends much of the early sessions gathering information about the client and the client's reason for seeking help. In this respect, the model is not essentially different from other models of social work practice (Fischer, 1978; Hollis, 1970, 1974; Perlman, 1957; Pincus and Minahan, 1973; Reid and Epstein, 1972). The five important questions are: (1) What problems are the most troublesome to the client? (2) Why has the client sought help at this time? (3) Whose behavior needs to be changed? (4) What behaviors need to be changed? (5) Who will act as the behavior change agent? These questions help the worker focus clients on the environmental aspects of what is happening to them and what is currently being done about the problems.

The client is usually an excellent source for determining the problems most relevant for intervention. Questions regarding the reasons for coming for help should lead to the discovery of the most important problems from the client's viewpoint. Even if clients are not totally voluntary, such as adjudicated delinquents, it is still important to explore their opinion of this issue. More detailed exploration is necessary if the client's complaint is very general. "If we are successful, what do you think will change?" is a good way to expand the problem exploration. Furthermore, the worker might ask a client, "How would you like to behave differently or have others around you behave differently?"

It is also important to determine *why the client has come for help at this time*. If others have insisted that the client seek help (for example, courts, schools, or relatives), it is informative to note the client's agreement or disagreements with the referral. This is very important when selecting behaviors to be changed and the person to be the change agent because the change agent is the person who will provide the restructuring of the environment. Sometimes the change agent is the client, and it will be impossible to implement the intervention if the client disagrees with the goals of the intervention.

As the interview progresses, the worker must seek some indication of *whose behavior needs to be changed*. The referred client may or may not be the person whose behavior needs to be altered. For instance, if a child is not doing well in school, the teacher's behavior may be the primary focus of intervention, whereas the child's performance is secondary. On the other hand, if the teacher is unwilling to cooperate with the worker, it may be necessary to teach the child how to cope with a bad situation or to focus on parent and principal behaviors to get the child transferred to a more favorable environment.

As discussed in Practice Illustration 7.2, the worker took the child out of his classroom to teach him cooperative play skills. Although the teacher complained about the child's lack of social skill, she refused to act as the change agent. After observations confirmed that the child lacked positive social behaviors, the worker taught the child how to play by bringing other students to play with him and providing positive consequences for his appropriate behaviors. The child was able to take his increased social skills out of the session and onto the playground.

After the worker determines whose behavior needs to be changed, it is important to determine *what behaviors need to be changed*. It may be very simple to determine behaviors because the client is able to provide such a clear picture of what is happening that specific behaviors can be defined on the spot. However, to the other extreme, direct observation of the client interacting with significant others or institutional staff may be necessary to determine which behaviors need changing. With mentally competent clients, agreement with the behaviors selected is crucial for analyzing and intervening in complex problems. With the mentally incompetent individual, agreement is sought when possible; otherwise, staff, family, and caretakers are consulted.

Chapters Six to Eight are organized around the decision as to *who will act as the behavior change agent.* The behavior change agent is the person who manages the intervention program. The primary change agents are usually the client (Chapter Six), family members (Chapter Seven), or institutional staff (Chapter Eight). Selection of the change agent is fully discussed in Chapter Five and depends on who controls the social and material contingencies in a specific situation. Quite often both the change agent and the client (when they are not the same person) need to alter their behavior to achieve desired outcomes. Family members who inadvertently have been reinforcing an aggressive child's behavior through their attention are an example of when both the change agent (parents) and the client (child) need to alter their behavior before a successful intervention to improve child behavior can be affected. The primary requirements for the change agent include adequate time, social skills, and motivation to engage in the intervention.

Step 2: specifying desirable outcomes. Desirable outcomes (as discussed in step 1) indicate *what will be different following the intervention* or what will change if the intervention is successful. Developing goals this way maximizes the client's positive behaviors, enhances the client's participation, and helps the worker shape the client's goals toward behaviorally specific obtainable ends. A client who initially specifies "feeling happy" as an outcome may redefine the goal as "participating in social events" or "having fewer fights with spouse," thus targeting specific problem areas on which behavior change efforts can be focused. In pursuing this issue further, the worker may ask *how will the client behave and how will others behave toward the client.* As the worker and the client examine some possible outcomes, the solutions to problems emerge as more clearly defined behaviors. For instance, what specific personal skills will the client have? What behavioral evidence of new supportive relationships will there be? A woman client may complain that no one likes her at work and report as evidence that she is never invited to lunch and that the men swear in her presence. The behaviors she might desire are to be asked to lunch and for the men to talk respectfully in her presence. The worker may decide to include client assertiveness as one possible alternative for client target behaviors.

Step 3: evaluating available resources. The worker evaluates the client's personal skills that will be necessary for achieving the desired outcomes. Throughout the practice illustrations it can be seen that clients often exhibit low rates of necessary skills to achieve their goals; the intervention's goals become the improvement or increase of these skills. Examples include negotiation skills (Practice Illustration 6.2) and parental praise following positive child behavior (Practice Illustration 9.3). Assessment of the client and/or the change agent's physical and intellectual abilities is essential before designing an intervention. Clients' ability to read, understand, and follow directions, notice changes in their own or others' behaviors, or to come to interviews as scheduled are all important resources to include in planning interventions. One often ignored variable is whether the client and/or change agent have time to engage in an intensive change effort. This is particularly important when working with single mothers who hold two jobs to achieve financial stability.

The worker will also want to determine *what supportive relationships the client can rely on for help in solving the current problem.* These relationships range from a good friend, a supportive employer, or a family member who may be willing to help the worker and client with the intervention. For instance, the ability of elderly clients with various impairments to stay at home outside an institutional environment is sometimes dependent upon the health of a significant other, such as a spouse. Supportive relationships (outside the interview) increase the spouse's possibility of obtaining additional reinforcement to compensate for the increased effort usually necessary for the family to affect behavior change. Enlisting these relationships not only increases the possibility of reinforcement for the client but decreases the likelihood that supportive persons will sabotage the intervention by punishing or neglecting the client's efforts.

An assessment of *what current behaviors are in the client's repertoire* helps the worker guide the client toward more realistic goals. It is desirable to find out the behaviors (for example, work skills, family interaction patterns, and recreational abilities) that the client has performed successfully because they are also resources which can be used in the intervention plan. With this information the worker designs the intervention around the client's past as well as the present strengths.

Finally, it is important to note *what community resources are available* to enhance the intervention and to increase the individual's quality of life. Community resources include such diverse events as church sponsored activities, in-home medical and physical care, or financial aid. They include all the social, financial, and physical resources available to the client and in this model are regarded as a way of increasing the total amount of available reinforcers in the client's life. Some of these resources are critical for extending and maintaining intervention effects by providing the client with new support networks. At the end of the structured intervention, it may be these networks that provide the resources for continued client improvement. For instance, a good daycare facility may enable a mother to stay off public aid and continue working.

Step 4: defining target behaviors. By this stage of the assessment, the worker should have a fairly complete picture of the client's problems and the resources available for solving those problems. With this information in mind, the worker helps the client define likely target behaviors for intervention. Although clients frequently present their problems in negative terms, it is the worker's responsibility to help them define possible targets for intervention positively as well as negatively. Behavioral excesses are sometimes more easily defined because they are more easily identified. Instead of saying that a client is depressed, the worker may decide to define rate of prosocial behavior and then immediate behavioral consequences of those behaviors. What should the client and the behavior change agent be *doing*? Frequently clients can state exactly what the appropriate behaviors should be, and they can sometimes tell the worker what the consequences necessary to maintain those behaviors should be. An adequate intervention is more valuable if it is directed toward building positive behavior rather than toward "stamping out" negative behavior. The client is focused on what to do rather than what not to do, which is accomplished by defining targets regarding behavioral deficits and excesses.

Behavioral deficits include positive behavior that does occur but at a rate too low to be helpful in the management of the client's life. Occasionally the necessary behaviors for coping do not exist in the client's repertoire, so the components of those behaviors need to be defined as the immediate target, while the complete set of behaviors is retained as long-term goals. For example, parents with coercive behavior patterns often do not have a repertoire of positive statements to make to their children. It is necessary to define specific positive remarks before asking parents to reinforce their children's positive behaviors (Pinkston and others, Practice Illustration 7.3). For effective intervention to occur, it is necessary to *define with the client the observable components of the target behaviors.*

After behaviors have been defined, it is also important to determine *the specific circumstances under which the target behavior(s) occur or should occur.* The occurrence of negative behavior is usually accompanied by specific consequences that are discovered during the interview or later when baseline data is examined. Time, place, others present, and others' behavior are important as to their relation to target behaviors. It is also important to ascertain the temporal relationship of those events to the target behaviors: whether they occur before or after the target behaviors and in what time frame (Skinner, 1938; 1957). Our research and that of others indicates that social consequences following behavior have powerful effects on future client behaviors (Pinkston and Herbert-Jackson, 1975; Pinkston and others, 1973). Therefore, the social consequences of the client's behavior are examined and must be defined, which is accomplished through discussion with the client, requiring the client to record a behavioral diary, asking significant others to keep records on client behavior, or by direct observation of client behavior.

The environmental events occurring most frequently in conjunction with the target behaviors should be noted carefully. In some cases, the physical events in the environment are important when planning an intervention to increase positive behavior (Blackman, Howe, and Pinkston, 1976; Goldiamond, 1965; Polster and Pinkston, 1979). When increasing these behaviors—such as appropriate social behavior, sexual activity, or studying at home—the client often finds specific arrangement of the physical environment an asset to intervention procedures. Studies have found that simple environmental changes, such as including juice in a social area, using a light as a cue for lovemaking, and a desk, lamp, and chair arrangement, are beneficial. It is of interest to the worker to explore these environmental arrangements before recording extensive data. A good question to ask is whether the physical environment supports the desired behavior.

As the worker focuses the client on specific target behaviors, it is essential that the target behaviors are described so the worker and the client both agree that they have occurred. When doing this, the observable aspects of the behavior, including what the behavior looks like and what the worker would see if watching the client or others perform the behaviors, are described. Then the worker and the client formulate a more formal definition of behavior, which is included in a behavioral code. This behavioral code provides instructions for using the behavioral definitions as a basis for recording observations (see Chapter Four). The data from these observations are used to make decisions about interventions.

Because the intervention is behaviorally specific, it is necessary to explore in *what time period does or should the target behavior occur at the highest rate.* This information clarifies the *antecedents* and *consequences* of the target behavior. In some cases, recording data for an entire day is not possible, or even relevant. It is better to select a specific period of one or two hours when the problem usually occurs and ask the client to record information during this time rather than to record every instance throughout the day. This includes, for example, children who have high rates of inappropriate behavior after returning home from school (Shibano and others, Practice Illustration 9.3) or adults who experience extremely low activity levels and subjective states of loneliness and depression at particular times of day (McCabe and others, Practice Illustration 6.1). Of course, if behaviors occur sporadically or at a low rate throughout the day, it is desirable to record each event. These recordings are the basis for most behavioral interventions. (For a discussion of observation, see Chapter Four.)

Step 5: selecting measurement techniques. A major achievement during the assessment phase is developing a methodology to measure relevant qualities of the targeted client behaviors. These qualities may include the frequency, duration, specific timing of behaviors of interest, and client attitudes. When designing measurement techniques, the worker and client seek ways to achieve *repeated measures* that will be *sensitive to changes over time.* Such measurements are used to verify a client's verbal reports about stress or behavior problems. In addition, specific measurement provides additional information often not noticed or inaccurately reported by the client. Green and Wright (1979) reported that teachers did not accurately reconstruct data on child behavior.

Direct observation is the most reliable method of measuring client behavior (Baer, Wolf, and Risley, 1968). Direct observation consists of direct *access* of observers (worker, client, or others) to view and *record* data on relevant behaviors. Access may be achieved by physical presence in the same environment (of the worker or outside observers), use of audio- or videotapes, or recordings made by supportive persons already in the client's environment who have been involved in intervention efforts. Often relatives, teachers, or others usually present when behavior occurs can be trained as effective observers. Of course, observation by a more objective observer is desirable, but such people are not usually available to the practitioner.

The first question considered after target behaviors have been selected is *"Are direct observational techniques possible?"* To decide the feasibility of direct observation, the worker evaluates the stability of the client's environment. In institutions, the activity schedule is predictable, but persons in their own homes might have a less stable or predictable environment. Initiating observation may be easier in schools, hospitals, activity programs, or other institutions because staff observers may be available. In the home, the *willingness of various family members to be observed must be evaluated* by asking for their consent, evaluating their skill, and determining their availability. Although it may be easier initially to observe within institutions, home observations can usually be negotiated via agreements about specific times for observation. Generally, outlining the potential benefits of observation for effective intervention facilitates this negotiation.

Indirect measurement techniques are available as supplementary data. These include questionnaires, pencil-paper tests, and scales. Often these techniques can be administered repeatedly, to determine changes over time. These methods can be used in combination with more direct data collection or may be helpful when administrative limitations or recording failure impede more direct approaches. Specific data-collection procedures are discussed fully in Chapter Four.

Step 6: orienting client or significant other(s) to data recording. Very few individuals like to record data; even people with successful outcomes report that they disliked recording data (Cox, 1982; Friedman, 1979; and Levitt and others, 1980). Therefore the practitioner should provide the rationale for the data recording before training the client or change agents to use the recording procedure. Also, social praise should be provided for recording as part of the intervention. The behavioral codes should be kept simple and the recording time as convenient as possible. Levitt (1981) showed data recording as an important part of intervention; the time spent orienting the observers pays off during the intervention because it increases the effectiveness the change agents implement during the intervention procedures and during assessment.

The worker verifies whether the client has the basic skills for recording the data. The first necessary skill is the recorder's ability to discriminate if the target behavior occurs. For instance, some research indicates that mothers poorly discriminate the occurrence of negative behavior in their children, even when such behaviors are part of their complaints about the child (Herbert and Baer, 1973; Jones, Reid, and Patterson, 1975), whereas other studies report higher reliabilities from mothers who have been trained in observation procedures (Pinkston, Friedman, and Polster, 1981). The second skill is the recorder's ability to record the occurrence or nonoccurrence of the behavior, which is verified by asking the recorder to describe and demonstrate the procedures. A client-recorder may appear resistant and not record the data, but in fact, the recorder may not understand the worker's expectations. To enable the client to demonstrate an understanding of the instructions, the worker may wish to model the recording procedure, have the client practice the data recording during the session, and conduct out-of-session reliability observations. These steps give the worker an opportunity to correct and model needed additional behaviors for the client.

If the client cannot record data accurately, it may be necessary to ask the client's family, institutional staff, or others who are present when the problems occur to be the primary data recorders. For instance, Dougherty, Friedman, and Pinkston (Practice Illustration 8.2) asked teachers to record students' behaviors and then recorded reliability sessions with the teachers. Essentially the same training procedures are followed for nonclients; thus it is the worker's responsibility to assess these issues and *teach the client or a significant other data-recording techniques.* This entails several forms of training: instructions, modeling, practice, and feedback. (See Chapter Five for detailed educational procedures.)

Step 7: baseline data. The client or other observer should have time to accumulate at least five or six days of targeted behavior. As discussed further in Chapter Four, a minimum of three data points is required for baseline periods. The baseline period is generally as limited as possible, ranging from a few days to two or three weeks, depending on the type and frequency of the behavior. To be considered a valid baseline, the data should be stable and reliable.

Are the data reliable and valid is an important question that should be answered to make good intervention decisions. *Valid* data are representative measures of the behaviors the worker and the client intended to measure. *Reliability* assesses the accuracy of the measurement techniques. For an elegant intervention evaluation, independently recorded data are essential. Access or time constraints may require the worker to use less formal sources of reliability, including family members and indirect data in the form of checklists and questionnaires (Hersen and Barlow, 1976). The *stability* of the data or verification of preintervention trends are necessary for later comparisons after intervention to determine if desired changes have occurred. Stable behaviors occur at comparable rates under similar conditions, as opposed to trends showing increasing or decreasing rates of behavior.

Baseline data also may be used to examine the actual importance of the behavior targeted for change. Observing levels of behavior can help the client and significant others determine *if the behaviors are really problematic* and if the relevant behaviors or events are being measured. Occasionally a very low frequency of targeted behaviors indicates that the behaviors are either trivial or occur so infrequently that they are not a problem for current intervention. If this happens, the worker reinstitutes assessment procedures and redefines the problem if one is still thought to exist.

To plan interventions, the baseline data are *graphed* for display and feedback to the client. Graphs give the client the chance to inspect the data during and after intervention to determine how well the program is working. Data recording is an intervention, but it is rarely strong enough to cause permanent behavior change because it does not sufficiently alter the consequences of the behaviors being recorded. A mother's negative statements to her child may decrease briefly in reaction to recording, but the child's reaction will probably maintain the negative statements. However, graphs often serve as part of intervention to reinforce clients' behavior change.

Phase 2—Designing Interventions, Training, and Evaluation. Design, training, and evaluation interviews are the heart of the development of effective intervention procedures. In these interviews, the data are reviewed (via preliminary functional analysis), with feedback from the client. The worker supervises the design and implementation of the intervention, which includes training the client to use procedures and providing supportive and evaluative feedback on progress. These interviews are also used to evaluate and revise the intervention.

Step 1: functional analysis of data. During the analysis of baseline data, the worker, and sometimes the client, discriminates *relationships between the client's target behavior and aspects of the environment.* It is important to assess possible functional or causal relationships by analyzing *the client's behavior and its temporal relationship to the behavior of others in the environment.* Probably the client's future rates of behaviors will be controlled by events following the occurrences of past and future behaviors, as well as current events. Because behavior can be increased after it has occurred, we are discussing here future rates of behavior. For example, in the Molick and Pinkston study (Practice Illustration 8.5), a preliminary functional analysis revealed that, for practical purposes, no environmental reinforcers for appropriate behavior, such as praise or attention, were available to the client. Therefore, the behavioral targets for change were the teachers' positive statements plus the administration of points following prosocial behaviors. It looked as if the young woman had shaped the teachers not to respond or initiate to her, although her schizophrenic label may have been a cue for them to underestimate her abilities.

The practitioner, especially for long-standing behaviors, also analyzes events that most frequently precede the target behaviors or lack of behaviors. In institutional environments, there may be very few preceding events that stimulate or elicit prosocial behaviors. The goal therefore may be to increase cues for engaging in social behaviors. These can be simple and inexpensive cues, such as worker questions to elicit participation in group activities that can then be praised or acknowledged (Linsk and Pinkston, Practice Illustration 8.3). If such cues are not there, they should be programmed at once.

Inspecting the data also gives the client and the practitioner the opportunity to *discuss alterations needed to change the relevant behaviors.* This is true whether the client is involved in changing the level of social interactions with friends and family or trying to obtain a service from a public welfare worker. For instance, if housing is required, client and worker must decide which client behaviors are necessary to gain certain behaviors from the public welfare worker. The next question is *"whose behaviors need to be changed?"* There may be nothing wrong with the client's behaviors, but it is usually necessary to make some changes to influence others to change their behaviors. The selection of behaviors and the people requiring change are thus usually paired. In Practice Illustration 8.3, note that both the worker's and the client's behaviors were targeted for change.

Specific aspects of the environment that need to be altered are decided by examining the baseline data. These aspects may include the behaviors of others who are present when desired or undesired behaviors occur; the physical arrangement of the environment, which may reinforce or punish specific behaviors; the presence of resources necessary to engage in the behavior, such as books needed to engage in study behavior; or competing demands that affect behavioral patterns. As described in Chapter Five, the worker then determines which aspects of the environment are most available for change, in which settings, and with what effects. This analysis determines the most probable events that are maintaining the client's positive or negative behaviors.

Step 2: determining intervention strategy. To increase the client's positive functioning, the *intervention most likely to enhance positive behaviors* is given priority. Both general procedures and specific techniques are selected. Procedures are general strategies based upon specific behavioral principles. Procedures include time-out, positive reinforcement, response cost, shaping, and differential attention. Techniques include specific means for change agents to carry out a procedure through intervention steps. Each intervention consists of specific techniques based on behavioral procedures.

A fundamental part of the behavior analysis model is remediating behavioral deficits by increasing available reinforcers following desired behaviors rather than eradicating behavioral excesses. The worker helps clients develop behaviors that enhance their pleasurable life functioning. This priority is critical when clients exhibit low rates of appropriate prosocial behavior. Mary (Practice Illustration 8.5) had little prosocial behavior, so intervention techniques were systematically developed to initiate those behaviors one by one and to increase available reinforcers in her school and dormitory. This approach is preferrable to punishing undesired behavior.

However, sometimes it is necessary to decrease dangerous or inappropriate behaviors so the client can experience improvement, such as when bizarre behaviors work as distancing mechanisms between the clients and others. That is, the client's behavior is aversive to others to the extent they ignore or avoid the client. Such odd behaviors include arm flapping, tantrums, repetitious verbal behaviors, or attacks on others. These behaviors are viewed as obstacles to positive adaptive behavior instead of as symptoms of a psychological process. Inappropriate behavior is selected as the first intervention target when it impedes learning with the client or with the persons with whom the client interacts. Desirable behaviors are always reinforced concurrently with punishment of undesirable behaviors, to provide behaviors that gain reinforcers or the opportunity for reinforcing the client's behavioral repertoire. When considering intervention strategies, ask *what the client should be doing instead of the dangerous or inappropriate behavior.* For instance, in the Dougherty, Friedman, and Pinkston study (Practice Illustration 8.2), it was necessary to control violent and aggressive student behaviors for the students to study. The research examined response cost as a less aversive technique to administer than time-out, one that more efficiently used the token economy to control aggression.

The intervention strategy is therefore determined by the client's interaction with the environment during the assessment of the baseline. The general strategy is to design interventions that will increase behaviors to desirable rates and decrease excessive rates of undesirable behaviors. Chapter Two presented a variety of procedures and techniques for altering behaviors. Additional methods of change can be found in the works of Fischer (1978), Gambrill (1977), Leitenberg (1976), and Redd, Porterfield, and Anderson (1979), all excellent texts organized around types of problems and specific populations.

When selecting the strategy of change for a specific behavior or set of behaviors, it is useful to ask *what is maintaining the behavior now or what is controlling the behavior now.* This analysis points the way to potential solutions of the problem, which is the reason for all the careful analysis during assessment. If, as in the McCabe and others (Practice Illustration 6.1) and Mallon-Wenzel and others (Practice Illustration 6.2) studies, the clients have low skill levels and depressed and angry behaviors have emerged to gain social attention, some skills training may be in order. Or if, as in Banzett's study (Practice Illustration 8.4), inappropriate behaviors are receiving high rates of a childcare worker's attention, then a technique for reducing that attention should be devised. In the Green and Pinkston study (Practice Illustration 8.1), an environmental cue (in this case a token pad worn by the child) can be added to increase the probability that the response-cost procedures will be carried out by staff; teachers removed a token when the child engaged in such negative behaviors as whining and crying. This procedure was selected because it was efficient regarding teacher time and had been shown to be effective and to have minimal negative effects. It also added another test of effectiveness to the literature.

To summarize, the procedure for change should be derived from the analysis of baseline data and should alter the client's behavioral interaction with the environment, with the emphasis usually on changing the consequences of behaviors and the delivery system of those consequences. The procedures should be easily carried out and appropriate to the setting.

The next important decision is to ascertain *who will implement the intervention procedure*; this person is the change agent. In many cases, the change agents are part of the dysfunctional interaction and will need to alter their behaviors to implement the intervention. Change agents must be taught that direct change interventions are always mutual behavior change events. The selection of the change agents depends on who controls the consequences of the target behaviors, their willingness to be involved, available time, and skill levels. Change agents should also have a high degree of investment in the client. In some instances the client will be the change agent, although consequence must be provided by others to be a valid change effort. Other considerations are discussed in Chapter Five.

Step 3: implementing intervention. Once the intervention has been selected and clearly specified and the behavior change agent identified, implementation includes training the behavior change agent in the technique, contracting for performing the technique, and monitoring the intervention. If the intervention includes a client self-modification program, the training is initiated directly with the client. If change agents such as family members or others implement the techniques, these persons must be trained. Specific procedures for *effective behavioral training* include instructions, modeling, rehearsal, feedback, and reinforcement in various combinations. Molick and others (Practice Illustration 7.4) trained family members of adult retarded persons. A combination of group didactic instruction and individual planning sessions was used to teach the parents how to contract with their children and how to provide positive consequences for their desirable behaviors. They were also taught to record data and evaluate their progress. The workers provided positive feedback for the parents' attempts to affect behavior change.

Once the change agent's training has been completed, a contract is formulated that specifies where (location) and when (time) the intervention is going to be carried out. In many cases it is unreasonable to assume that the client or supporting persons will be able to launch an initial behavior change effort over an entire day. It is better to set a specific time and location for the change effort, at least until techniques have been learned. The time and location should coincide with the highest occurrence or opportunity for the client to engage in the targeted behavior. Once satisfactory behavior change occurs within the set parameters, the contract is renegotiated to expand the time, setting, or other behaviors for intervention.

During the intervention, a feedback system is instituted to give the worker and client a method for exchanging information about the implementation and effect of the intervention. Feedback data include formally recorded information about both client and change agent behaviors or informal reports of critical events. These data are useful for helping the client and worker determine progress and any alterations that need to be made in intervention.

Step 4: evaluating intervention procedures. Data analysis enables the worker to *determine if the intervention has been applied* and further allows the specification of the nature and extent of any behavior change. If a change has occurred, then the worker and client address *whether the change has been large enough to be socially relevant.* If the intervention has not succeeded as planned, the worker examines possible competing reinforcers that inhibit intervention effectiveness or other possible sources of error. Further observation or analysis of the data may reveal other obstacles to the intervention. Generally, unsatisfactory results indicate that interventions are insufficiently intense, incorrectly timed, or in effect do not reinforce the desired behavior at a high enough rate. In short, there is a functional analysis at this time to determine any need for program revision and which specific components are to be changed. (See Chapter Two for a discussion of scheduling effects.)

If the intervention has been successful, the worker should give praise and supportive comments to the change agent and the client. Specific aspects of the change efforts should be pointed out and strengthened by positive comments. Data-collection efforts, changing previous behavior frequencies or patterns, initiating new behaviors, and relating difficulties to the worker are recognized. Even when intervention is not as successful as desired, the appropriate behaviors are praised and corrective feedback or revisions are planned.

Step 5: revising the intervention. Table 3.1 illustrates guidelines, revisions, and examples when altering the intervention plan. When changing intervention, the worker uses all available information, including the preliminary functional analysis. Revisions are planned, contracted, implemented, monitored, and evaluated.

Part of the program may be appropriate, but other aspects of the intervention may be unrealistic for the client. *Are there any physical reasons for the failure of the intervention?* In other words, does the client have any physical deficiencies—intellectually or motorically—that prevent the achievement of the targeted response? *Are there additional services that could be made available to help the client achieve the goals?*

If the change agent has not been able to arrange or deliver the agreed-upon consequences to the client, it is necessary to change the amount or type of consequences or explore *if there should be another change agent.* If the contingencies are not available to the change agent (which of course could be the client), another set of contingencies should be arranged or another change agent should be selected.

If the change agent is not altogether the problem, the worker should determine *if the behavioral targets are still relevant* (this should be determined throughout the intervention). If the target behaviors still appear relevant to the client and change agent, consider if there is a more effective intervention procedure that could be used. All this is *considered in terms of whether the client or change agent still desires change.*

Phase 3—Maintenance. The *maintenance* interviews are crucial to the long-term effectiveness of the intervention. These interviews are used to review the intervention plan and for long-term planning of the extension of treatment effects over time and into naturalistic settings. This aspect of the model is essential for increasing the probability that intervention effects will extend across settings, time, or problems. These interviews give the worker the opportunity to help the client plan ways of maintaining and, perhaps, increasing the effects of the intervention.

Maintenance procedures begin in the initial planning for interventions. The extension of intervention effects begins with

Table 3.1. Intervention Revision Guidelines.

	Question to Ask	Revision	Example
1.	Are specific behaviors not changing?	Increase reinforcement for desirable behaviors and decrease for undesirable.	Ask change agent to praise client twice as often for desired behavior occurrence.
2.	Are the interventions being implemented?	Simplify the treatment to make it more like existing behavior pattern; remove competing demands.	Change time of implementation for a task to a less frequent or more convenient time.
3.	If the interventions have been implemented, are there problems with the effectiveness of the procedures?	Determine alternate technique to achieve equivalent functional change.	Change from a token to a response cost technique (see Practice Illustration 8.1).
4.	Is the worker providing adequate support for the implementation of the procedures?	Increase worker contact, praise, or feedback.	Increase contact by inserting telephone call between visits.
5.	Does the change agent have adequate control of contingent relationships in the environment?	Increase control or use alternate change agent. Choose a different environment.	Change child behavior program from school to home setting. Change reinforcer from tokens to food.
6.	Does the client or change agent have the behavioral components of the larger behavior to be implemented?	Model missing components.	Teach parent the words and gestures necessary to praise children.
7.	Are the goals for the client reasonable?	Begin with smaller goals.	Have a caretaker praise an elderly person for putting on shirt rather than being fully dressed.
8.	Is the client able to gain positive consequences from noncontingent behavior?	1. Remove client from environment where this occurs. 2. Modify behavior or reinforcement source.	Reinforce other children in a classroom for not attending to a child's hitting; provide an activity program when child usually hangs out on street.

choosing target behaviors that are likely to be reinforced in the client's environment. Behaviors are selected to increase the client's ability to gain reinforcers or the opportunity for reinforcement in the environment over time. If the opportunity for reinforcement in the environment is not available, additional community links should be made to ensure the client's access to ongoing opportunities for reinforcement. There may be services or persons in the community that can compensate for deficits in the client's support system and be available to the client on an ongoing basis, such as daycare centers, religious affiliations, and Big Brother/Big Sister programs.

A *decision* is made as to whether all parts of the intervention need to be continued to maintain positive treatment effects. This decision varies across clients, problems, and populations.

To avoid a sudden drop of reinforcers and a concurrent loss of improvement, it is important that the intensive *behavior-consequence relationships are faded gradually to a less intensive schedule.* This is accomplished by worker and change agent planning. (This is also true for the data-feedback system.) The results of practice experience and research show that clients usually discontinue data recording following termination (Friedman, 1979). If continued data collection is essential for successful intervention, a simpler system of more infrequent measures is substituted.

Positive consequences are necessary for the long-term maintenance of target behaviors; as a result, the worker needs to determine the *consequences for maintenance of the target behaviors.* The rate of reinforcement in the natural environment is sometimes adequate for maintaining intervention effects, but for individuals whose environments are deprived or somewhat punishing, it is necessary to plan a more structured system of reinforcement of target behaviors. If the consequences are planned, it is important to decide *who will provide those consequences* and when, where, and how. Sometimes the person is the original change agent, but at other times, particularly if the change agent is the worker, it is necessary to enlist the aid of others. It is also important to plan *how the provider of long-*

term consequence will be reinforced for engaging in mainte-nance behaviors.

The following example illustrates an ongoing monitoring system, with reinforcers for both the client and the change agent. Note that the schedule for the use of procedures is reduced while the monitoring of results continues.

Mr. Jones is a fifty-one-year-old man with diabetes. Because his disease cannot be controlled by diet or oral medication, he must take daily injections of insulin. A successful prompting and reinforcing procedure is developed by using his wife as the change agent. After the procedure has been successfully adhered to for two months, two maintenance procedures are developed when the wife complains that she no longer enjoys prompting her husband. The schedule of prompts is decreased, yet adequate monitoring for the consistency of injections continues. However, reinforcement for Mr. Jones's independent injections is continued. In addition, Mr. Jones agrees to increase the Jones's nights out together in exchange for his wife's continued reminders.

Phase 4—Follow-Up. Planned *follow-up* interviews are occasions for reexamining the long-term effects of the intervention, the possible breakdown of the intervention, the causes of the breakdown of the intervention, and the success the client has been experiencing. These interviews also allow the client to return to the worker for additional consultation if necessary. For the worker, follow-up interviews are opportunities to examine the effectiveness of various interventions regarding client and practitioner goals.

Step 1: evaluating at specified times. Follow-up is worker evaluation at increasing intervals of the extension of intervention effects. For example, a follow-up schedule may include checks at one month, three months, six months, and one year after formal intervention has been discontinued. If the client has a history of chronicity, the worker may monitor the long-term effects more frequently, such as every month for six months, every two months for six months, and so forth. The worker determines *stability or changes in client behaviors* and continued use of maintenance techniques. Changes are assessed by using client self-reports, direct observation, or samples of client-recorded data. A client may be asked to reinstate data collecting for a week or so. Questionnaires and scales used in the original package are included in this follow-up evaluation.

A frequent problem is *whether the significant others increased their expectations of the client beyond the specified goals.* Expectations for change are frequently increased more rapidly than the client can improve behaviors. Concurrently, significant others may decrease the amount of attention and support of other kinds of behavior they give the client. Predictably, the client's positive behavior decreases. Or, the client may resume old behavior patterns to increase the amount of concern and attention received.

The worker assesses *whether community services are still available and used to maintain improved functioning of the client and the client's support persons.* The community services are instruments to extend the total opportunity for reinforcement, enabling the client to function at a higher level to achieve more life satisfaction.

Step 2: returning to baseline. If the levels of behavior have deteriorated over time, the worker and client reconsider the social relevance of continued work on these behaviors. If they decide that further work is needed for the reinstatement of active intervention, the worker and client return to phase 2 (redesigning and reimplementing intervention); often the steps of this process occur in abbreviated form. When reestablishing contact, alternative techniques, additional settings, additional or different change agents, and community support programs may be included to facilitate enduring change.

Step 3: terminating worker participation. To determine if the client and change agent have achieved target goals, the worker reviews the following four questions: (1) Has the client achieved the goals? (2) Has the client achieved the goals set by personal environment? (3) Will the worker be available for future consultation? (4) Are community services available that are likely to keep the client's improved situation intact?

If these goals have been achieved, the worker reviews the long-term maintenance goals with the client and the change agents and then selects a plan of action if the client should experience the same or a similar problem in the future. This plan includes review of target behaviors, consequences for maintaining target behavior, functional analysis of the overall contingency program, setting future goals and contingencies, and possible reinitiation of contact with the worker.

Determining the necessity of *community services required to implement the intervention* is a traditional job of the social worker. In this model, community services are considered procedures for increasing the client's reinforcement base with social support, material support, or opportunities to engage in reinforcing activities. An additional examination of traditional social work areas of interest, such as income, social contacts, and activities, is made at this time. Whenever possible, the worker designs the intervention to teach the clients and their significant others to obtain the desired services for themselves. The worker, then, *determines what behaviors are required to attain the necessary services.* The intervention is designed in a stepwise fashion, dividing tasks into specific achievable behaviors (Reid and Epstein, 1972). Within this model, concrete services may be implemented before, concurrently, or after other interventions.

4

◆◆◆◆◆◆◆◆◆◆◆◆◆◆◆◆◆◆◆◆◆◆◆◆◆◆◆◆◆◆◆◆◆◆◆◆

Evaluating the Effectiveness of Intervention

In the current era of scientific proof and sparse resources, the experimental components of this model assume the role of social justification for the expenditure of public and private funds. The worker is obligated to demonstrate effectiveness to the client and to society. To fulfill that obligation, social workers and practitioners need to acquire research and evaluation skills and knowledge not required of their predecessors. Many of these skills are components of systematic assessment and intervention skills, for example, specific definition of problems, goals, and intervention variables. Components of experimental control and evaluation include building a data base, experimental research designs, and clinical or practice evaluation.

Building a Data Base

Evaluating intervention outcomes requires defining and measuring relevant intervention and outcome variables. Behaviors are defined for observable responses or events. Broadly, observable behaviors encompass directly observed behaviors, behaviors reported by the client (ideally with some collateral reliability), and responses to interviews, scales, and questionnaires. Some of these measures are stronger than others; that is, they are more easily believed and command a wider audience than others. The usefulness of these measures is discussed throughout this chapter.

As stated in Chapters One and Three, it is more interesting to assess what clients actually do than what they say they do. Therefore, *direct observation* is the best index of client behavior and the most reliable source for a data base. In clinical interventions, observations are recorded by the client and/or designated observers. But before these specific observations can occur, several procedures for developing behavioral codes used in recording the data have to be followed. These procedures include anecdotal observations, self-recorded anecdotal observations, and structured diary recording. These are informal methods for determining the behaviors to be defined and the circumstances surrounding these behaviors that should be recorded. *Anecdotal observation* is looking at the client and recording both what the client does in observable terms and what happens to the client before and after the client's behavior. From these observations a pattern of critical behavior and environmental events emerges that helps the worker and the client define appropriate and inappropriate behaviors for more careful observation and, later, intervention. Anecdotal observations are usually recorded in three columns: antecedent events, client behaviors, and consequent events, with *all* client behaviors recorded in the center column. This arrangement is the basis for a preliminary functional analysis of the client's interaction with the environment and a more accurate guess at appropriate and inappropriate behaviors to be measured because it includes behaviors of both the client and others in the client's environment.

Because the client cannot usually record continuously, the anecdotal observations are scheduled at a time when problematic behaviors are most likely to occur. For example, the client who has a terminal illness complains that she wants to be treated like an adult but her mother treats her like a baby. She reports that she is frustrated by her inability to confront her mother. She might then be asked to record conversations with her mother, with her own behavior noted in the center column. This record gives the worker and the client material that will help them define the types of behaviors which occur or which the client believes should occur, such as assertive client statements, or should not occur, such as patronizing statements from the mother.

Another way of providing information relevant for behavioral definitions is the *structured diary*. The best example of a structured diary is in the works of Goldiamond and Schwartz (Goldiamond, 1974; Schwartz and Goldiamond, 1975), which discuss the integration of behavioral methods into practice. Essentially, the diary takes two forms: a record of the way the client spends the entire day and a record of critical events and the circumstances surrounding them. Although such diaries were designed as educational methods as well as for data collection, they are also excellent tools for exploring behaviors to be defined and recording in less time. The structured diary includes temporal events, specific behaviors, consequences, and other information the client may want to include. These events are particularly effective for shaping the client's observations toward specific events, a major goal of the behavioral interview. Because the diary appears more complex than it is, the worker should model recording for the client by having the client recall relevant problematic events from one day in the past week while the worker fills in the blanks. Once more the worker is shaping the client toward discussing problems as to environmental and behavioral events.

Helping the client define problems and goals for observable events is a major challenge to the worker and requires particular practice and skill. During this process, the worker accepts the client's original conceptualization of the problem as valuable and indicates that the client's feelings are important to the worker. Reconceptualizing the problem regarding topographical environmental events and behaviors is primarily a way of operationalizing the problem so that it becomes more accessible to intervention. Of course, the intervention is a failure if the client or the recipient of the client's behaviors is able to change behaviors and environmental events but is no more satisfied than before the changes. When trying to develop an observable problem definition for a positive outcome, it is useful to explore the events that repeatedly surround the client's dissatisfaction and ask the client how the situation should be; that is, ask what the desirable outcome of the intervention is. Focus on the circumstances before and after critical events. For example, ask first, "What did he say?" and then ask "What did you say?" Ask "Does this usually happen at any particular time?" and then ask "How often do you experience this difficulty? Daily? Weekly?" If it is not obvious, ask "Why do you feel so upset about this?" Most questions are difficult for the client to answer and require that the worker restate them in different ways to help the client understand and conceptualize the answer. Not all clients possess the verbal ability to do this easily, so the worker should be prepared occasionally to ask further questions, such as, "What is it that he *does* that makes you so angry?", "Is it the way he looks at you?", "Can you describe what you *do* in response to this?", and so on.

Besides being defined in observable terms, behaviors are defined and selected for excess and deficits, for occurring less frequently, not at all, or less often than desired. Less value is placed on a specific behavior; more focus is on the strength or rate of its occurrence, which is measured by frequency (how often the behavior occurs), duration (how long it lasts), latency (how long between occurrences), and intensity (how loud or assertive they are judged to be). Frequency and duration are the most useful units in practice because they are simple and more reliably measured. The client or change agent is asked to record, usually within a specific time period, each occurrence of the behavior. For very brief behaviors in which no change in duration is expected during intervention, the frequency is adequate. But for behaviors like tantrums, it is important to know that both duration and frequency have decreased following intervention.

In the Linsk, Pinkston, and Green study (Practice Illustration 7.1), it was important to measure the client's time out of bed. A simple checklist was developed for change agent (in this case the wife) to use to check if the client was out of bed for the entire hour. Hours in which the client spent any time in bed were not counted toward the total time out of bed. When asking the change agent or client to record frequency or duration, the recording method should be kept simple.

Intensity is the most difficult parameter and has been measured less frequently than the other dimensions (see Practice Illustration 6.1). When mechanical devices for measuring intensity are not available, raters can be used for research purposes. Intensity is rarely measured in practice evaluations because of the expense and difficulty involved.

Because interventions based on operant theory most frequently are designed to alter the consequences following behavior, those consequences should be defined and measured along with client behaviors. If an intervention is planned, the elements of that intervention should be coded and measured. For example, the young woman who plans to increase her assertiveness with her mother will need to record her assertiveness and her mother's response to her assertiveness.

Direct Observation. The most accurate source of data for evaluation is direct observation (Baer, Wolf, and Risley, 1968; Bijou, Peterson, and Ault, 1968; Hersen and Barlow, 1976). The measures of interest in direct observation include simple frequency counts, duration of behavior, latency of behavior, and permanent product data. Direct observations are recorded by human observers using a continuous time-sampling technique. The observer watches the client and the way the client interacts with the people and objects in the environment, noting the occurrence of the identified behavior and recording it at specified time periods, either within a time interval or at the end of a time sample. For low-rate behaviors, each event is recorded and the time of the occurrence noted. As mentioned, intensity is difficult to measure and so is less frequently recorded; also, intensity is not usually targeted as the most important aspect of behavior (McCabe and others, Practice Illustration 6.1).

Repeated observations over time provide flexible methods

that allow the discrimination of trends, level changes, and variability of a series of data points for continuous evaluation of the client's interaction with the environment. In traditional evaluative studies, data are collected before and after intervention, with perhaps a two- or three-month follow-up. Repeated measures use many data points at various intervals, including hourly, daily, weekly, and monthly.

Repeated observations over time reduce the probability that the data recorded were unrepresentative. The more observations, the higher the probability that these observations are valid and representative. In addition, generated observational data allow the worker to develop and refine the intervention technique, unlike traditional evaluative studies, which involve waiting for data on *all* cases to be collected before intervention effect can be evaluated. The individual client is not lost in means, standard deviations, and other data of the group in which they are participants. Finally, workers who use repeated measures often find that the data have a facilitative effect. Instead of "hiding" or obscuring the data from the client, as with traditional evaluations, workers often share the results with their clients, thus providing feedback. To inform clients that they decreased 14 percent on X scale is meaningless. But to inform a client of a decrease in aggressive incidents from four per day to an average of one per day is information easily understood and used by the client.

When recording frequency of behavior, a time period for the observation is selected and a simple tally of the occurrence of behavior during that period is recorded (Pinkston and others, Practice Illustration 7.3). To enhance the likelihood of reliability of low-rate behavior, the observer may also record the time of occurrence, which provides some assurance that the measures will be reliable when measured by independent observers. *Duration* and *latency* can be recorded similarly. If using these measures, it is of course important to note the time of onset and the termination of the behavior. From these data, percentage of time or a report of total time, average time, or duration of behavior can be calculated. These simple observations are used more frequently in clinical self-report observations when an observer is not available and so the client or change agent must perform that function. Permanent product data include such information as public records, grades, completed assignments, and attendance records. These data, although variable for reliability, can provide excellent collateral information for problem assessment and outcome evaluation. For instance, in the *Huntsville-Madison County Mental Health Center Programs and Evaluation* (1978), it was important to know that the community mental health statistics improved as well as the achievement of success with individual clients. Furthermore, with school children it is relevant to know both whether children achieve better and the improvement in time spent studying at home; additionally, the worker is interested in academic improvement (Polster and Pinkston, 1979).

Most empirical studies evaluating practice use measures involving very small specified time periods to increase the possibility that independent observers are recording the same behaviors. Frequently the specified time used is ten seconds, and the procedures used are *interval* or *time samples.* With interval recording, the observer records whether a specific behavior or set of behaviors does or does not occur within that time period. Time-sampling techniques require that the observer record whether a specific behavior or set of behaviors occur at a specific time or at the end of a specific time interval (Bijou, Peterson, and Ault, 1968; Hall, 1971). In both techniques, the practice of recording every ten seconds (or according to a similar time base) is a basis for calculating behavior over time and provides ratelike measures that can be reported in percentages. Thus, in an hour there are 360 behavior samples. This large number of behavior samples provides excellent opportunities for comparing the records of two independent observers for reliability. It is also a comparison of behavioral trends over time during and between intervention and nonintervention conditions, which offers the opportunity to assess and evaluate the effectiveness of the intervention.

Reliability. The reliability of direct observation is determined by comparing two independent observer records of interval-by-interval or behavior-by-behavior. The usual techniques for establishing this measure are *occurrence* and *nonoccurrence* reliability. Occurrence reliability is used for moderate to low-rate behaviors; nonoccurrence reliability is used for high-rate behaviors occurring in most intervals. The practitioner-researcher may want to calculate both occurrence and nonoccurrence reliability to ensure the most demanding measurements. The easy way to calculate *total reliability* is by comparing each interval for agreement or nonagreement across all categories of behavior. However, this method does not guarantee high reliability for each specific behavior category and can mask unreliable behaviors.

Generally, the acceptable level of reliability to most researchers is around 85 percent or above. Occasionally reliability falls below this figure; this should be accepted with reservations if the behavior under study is complex and difficult to observe. The reliability can still be reported; the reader will know that the coding is not perfect but that the data are considered important enough to report until more reliable measures can be found. Reliability should be recorded at least once per experimental condition and/or whenever there is a shift in the trend of the behavior under study because reliability sometimes varies for behaviors occurring at different rates. For example, a measure of aggressive behavior is more reliable when it is recorded at a high rate with some intensity. As aggression decreases, there is less opportunity for agreement and the topography of behavior becomes more subtle. Frequent observation therefore ensures that the observers have not drifted too far from the original definitions for reliability to be achieved.

The formulas for calculating reliability are:

$$\text{Occurrence reliability} = \frac{\text{agreement of occurrence}}{\text{agreement + disagreement of occurrence}} \times 100$$

$$\text{Nonoccurrence reliability} = \frac{\text{agreement of nonoccurrence}}{\text{agreement + disagreement of nonoccurrence}} \times 100$$

$$\text{Total reliability} = \frac{\text{agreement of total intervals}}{\substack{\text{agreement + disagreement} \\ \text{of total intervals}}} \times 100$$

Although reliability is used primarily for research studies, it is clinically useful to ascertain that both the worker and the client agree upon the defined behaviors. Observation sessions are also an opportunity to assess whether the change agent agrees with the behavioral definitions, can apply the intervention, and is able to record the data reliably.

Indirect Measures. Direct observation and self-observation are the bases for the most important direct measures of behavioral variables, but other information is used for assessing the client and the workers' evaluations of direct practice. These other data are indirectly correlated with observations and, when all else fails, are useful for expanding the audience to persons who are less interested in behavior change and more interested in the client's reports of improvement in attitudes, feelings, and perceptions of behavior change. These indirect measures are also useful for assessing clients' goals and the significant others in their lives.

Keep in mind one item regarding indirect data: These data are rarely identified as causal variables; they may or may not correlate nicely with the direct observation data. If they do not, then the researcher may be directed toward another promising area in which to hunt for possible causal variables. If a client who has experienced behavior change in a desired direction reports unhappiness or has not perceived any self-improvement correlated with behavior changed, it may be fruitful to pursue the reason for continued dissatisfaction. However, once control variables are established and the client can make the functional connection between control variables and behavior, indirect data are less important for any reason other than consumer evaluation. Indirect data come from many sources; the search for it will expand as our technology is further developed.

In social work practice, useful indirect measures are social validation procedures; problem-severity scales; pre- and post-information tests; general information questionnaires; attitude change scales; and consumer-satisfaction questionnaires. *Social validation procedures* are more formalized attempts to establish the importance of the defined problems to consumers of intervention programs (Wolf, 1978). The procedure may be simple, such as a very brief questionnaire requiring clients to check the problems they feel are most serious or the skills they feel are most important to acquire. Or it may be more formal and complex: Various societal consumers of services are asked what they feel are the most important problems. Dangel and Polster (1981) spent a year monitoring a group of parents representing a cross section of socioeconomic backgrounds, asking them to discuss the kinds of problems that should be addressed when delivering a behavioral parent training program. From these socially validated problems they developed a program that included booklets, videotapes, and direct training by social workers. Then they asked the parents to evaluate the booklets, videotapes, and so on. Not surprisingly, the parents selected many of the same problems that have always been selected in parent training programs, such as noncompliance. However, the parents did fault the researchers for inadequately handling punishment issues with children. This criticism in turn led to a complete evaluation of parental punishment of children and professional attitudes toward it (Dangel and Polster, 1981).

Minkin and others (1976) developed specific procedures for determining what members of the community thought were important behaviors for adolescents in the Achievement Place Group Home (Phillips, 1968; Braukmann, Kerigan, and Wolf, 1976) to learn. Lutzker and Martin (1981, p. 13) suggested that the three important questions to ask are: "Is the goal or behavior change something society really wants?" "Are the treatment procedures acceptable to the client, significant others in the client's environment, and consumers?" "Are the consumers satisfied with the results?"

Problem-severity scales are useful for determining which problems clients feel are important and providing a loose index of how severe the client feels the problems are. These scales are diverse and have been used in behavioral parent training (Pinkston and others, 1975; Patterson and others, 1975); marital counseling (Azrin, Naster, and Jones, 1973; Stuart, 1980); assertiveness training (Gambrill and Richey, 1975); and many others. Whenever possible, for reliability and validity it is helpful to use an existing scale. However, when practitioners are working with relatively unexplored problems and/or populations, they may need to develop a scale relevant to their own practice. Hudson (1981, pp. 130-133) formulated the following excellent axioms to help workers think about measurement and their practice:

Axiom 1.   If instruments are to have any practice utility, they must have two fundamental characteristics: validity and reliability.

Axiom 2.   For instruments to have maximum utility for social workers, they must be short, easy to administer, easy to understand, easy to score, and easy to interpret.

Axiom 3.   There are only two ways to determine whether clients have problems: Watch them, or ask them.

Axiom 4.   There are only four ways of measuring a client problem: its switch (presence or absence), frequency, magnitude, or duration.

Axiom 5.   If you cannot measure a client's problem, it does not exist.

Axiom 6.   If you cannot measure a client's problem, you cannot treat it.

Axiom 7.   If you cannot measure an intervention, it does not exist.

Axiom 8.   If you cannot measure an intervention, you cannot administer it.

Researchers have spent entire careers developing their own scales, questionnaires, and indexes. Practitioners should not assume that the measures they develop have generality to other situations; they should view them as ways to accumulate more information before, during, and after the intervention process. Mindel (1981) examined the numerous issues involved in designing and constructing instruments for specific worker needs.

Pre- and postintervention tests enable the worker to assess whether the client has acquired new information during the intervention. These measures have been used most frequently to establish the client's knowledge of behavioral principles or the steps that should be used for developing and implementing the intervention (O'Dell and others, 1981; and Linsk, Green, and Pinkston, 1981). Two such tests were employed in the Molick and others study (Practice Illustration 7.4) with the parents of adult retarded persons. The parents were tested and showed improvement on the behavioral-principles tests and the steps for establishing a contract. O'Dell noted that researchers have not found, however, a correlation between doing well on such tests and the demonstrated ability to carry out the procedures. These results were supported by Pinkston and her colleagues in their research with the elderly. Therefore, the worker should not assume a positive correlation between knowledge and skill.

General information questionnaires are directed toward acquiring specific demographic variables about clients and their environments. This information is factual, similar to that recorded by credit firms, insurance companies, or census takers. It deals with such variables as income, marital status, age, educational levels, employment, and family composition. These data do not lead to specific causes of behavior but are useful for trying to pinpoint characteristics of clients who are most or least likely to benefit from specific types of programs. For instance, parents with low educational levels may be less likely to benefit from didactic training procedures.

It is also interesting to note whether intervention results in reported *attitude changes* by clients. Hudson (1981) developed a series of measures for these data. The scales include measures of attitude toward self and others (marital partners and family members). The questionnaires have been tested on normal populations and are currently being examined in relation to behavior change. Although these scales are not measures of behavioral change, they may be valuable to the practitioner as an ongoing evaluation tool before, during, and after intervention. In many cases, these scales are sensitive to behavior change and critical events in the lives of clients (Cox and others, 1979).

Most likely, long-term findings regarding these scales will support their value as clinical tools but leave questions as to their value for measuring client improvement.

All workers are interested in *consumer satisfaction,* so why not ask clients for their opinions? *Warning!* Most clients hesitate to complain about any intervention because of the demand characteristics of the client-worker relationship: They believe that they are expected to give a positive rating, so most do. Therefore, the worker is interested in responses that report negative feelings about the intervention. These negative reports enable workers to examine various aspects of their interventions, to improve their methods or to evaluate an unpopular aspect(s) of the interventions. Consumer evaluations should be carefully administered by someone other than the worker and directed toward every aspect of the intervention process for referral through follow-up, including satisfaction with methods, procedures, and social service requirements (Friedman, 1979).

Be careful to not use unreliable indirect measures to validate direct observation. Jones, Reid, and Patterson (1975) found that mothers did not reliably report improvement; in their research, many reported improvement in their children's behavior when there was none. Parents may also report that the parent training program was wonderful, even though they still consider their child "rotten" and perceive no behavior change.

Experimental Research, Clinical Evaluation, and Systematic Practice

For the workers using scientific practice, we expect that they will be conducting at least one ongoing experimentally controlled study, employing clinical evaluation in most of their practice, and, minimally, engaging in informed systematic practice with their clients. It is unrealistic, and not particularly desirable, to assume that the worker should regard each client as a research subject. Clients are entitled, however, to thoughtful, informed, and systematic practice methods from social workers and other helping professionals. It is no longer necessary for practice to be regarded as an art. The recognition that an untested intervention should be empirically studied by using some form of experimental control is essential to this model and to knowledge building in the field of social work (Briar, 1977; Thomas, 1978). The following sections focus on the various kinds of scientific practice in this model: empirical research, clinical evaluation, and systematic practice. These methods are defined within the practice of social workers, thus providing guidelines for incorporating scientific methods into practice.

Experimental Research

Careful definition of problems and goals with reliable data-recording procedures are essential for experimental practice research. No conclusive results can be obtained without this data. To achieve this data, it is necessary to carefully define the client's problems and goals specifically and observingly and to record the occurrence of these data reliably, as described earlier in the chapter. It is also important to include clear and reliable descriptions of the intervention techniques and to record the occasions on which the intervention is implemented. In addition to ongoing data recording during baseline and intervention conditions, it is also important to record follow-up measures to determine the generality and maintenance of intervention effects. Other forms of data supplement the evaluation of outcomes, but it is the basic "hard" data that are the major source of information from which causal inferences can be made regarding the effects of interventions. Once appropriate and reliable data-recording techniques have been devised, the research-practitioner must use an adequately controlled research design before these inferences can be considered valid.

The *single-case* experimental designs lend themselves most readily to the evaluation of practice (Fischer, 1978; Gambrill, 1977; Jayaratne and Levy, 1979; and Reid, 1978). These designs are discussed at length throughout psychology and social work and can be studied in more depth in a number of texts (Hersen and Barlow, 1976; Glass, Willson, and Gottman, 1975; Polster and Lynch, 1981). This section focuses on the design's usefulness in practice evaluation and building social work practice knowledge by the individual case study. Common to all single-case designs is the collection of stable baseline data, so a major emphasis is on baselining client behaviors and environmental events to determine the existing state of affairs prior to planned intervention. All future inferences about the effectiveness of the intervention will depend upon a good stable baseline.

By "stable" we mean that the behavior fluctuates within specific limits and does not have noticeable trends in any direction, particularly that of desired change. This requirement is a major challenge to the researcher-practitioner and has been offered as a primary problem when using these designs in practice evaluations (Liberman, King, and DeRisi, 1976; Thomas, 1978). However, the payoff to the practice-information crisis in social work is high and well worth the effort. Note that the single-case methodology is not completely developed for application to all practice evaluation, but it is still the most promising methodology available. The conflict between what appear to be the immediate needs of the client and the need of the helping professional to determine functional relationships to enhance interventions with future clients is not easily resolved. No simple answer is available, so the practitioner and/or members of the clinic team must decide case by case.

In many cases it is also necessary that the worker is able to make clear causal inferences regarding the environmental variables that will benefit the client. For example, with an autistic child who appears unresponsive to most reinforcers, the worker needs to identify clearly powerful reinforcers via careful empirical evaluation. Such clients often have extremely variable baselines of behavior that require longer examination before the worker can determine functional relationships between the client's behavior and environmental events. In these cases it is important to continue recording baseline information for clinical as well as empirical reasons. Most serious problems are not transitory and have existed for some time. It is therefore not unethical or immoral to postpone intervention long enough to form a better hypothesis about an effective functional analysis and, most probably, effective intervention. Clinical demands will continue to force the worker to thoughtfully evaluate whether intervention should be delayed to facilitate a more stable baseline. Because of social demand, the worker will be tempted to try some form of intervention before adequate baseline data are recorded. Bear in mind that clinical research is designed not only to help one client but future clients.

In experimental practice research, single-case designs are used extensively to develop and evaluate techniques, procedures, and programs. The designs facilitate the intensive analysis necessary for evaluating each intervention plan and its separate components and the delivery systems for individual practice. There are two basic single-case designs: reversal/withdrawal and multiple-baseline. When one understands the logic of these designs, one can move on to a wide variety of single-case evaluations and perhaps even create new designs.

ABAB Reversal Design. It was implicit in Baer, Wolf, and Risley (1968) that the results of a successful ABAB design at least show that the experimental "variable" is functional—but the variable must be recognized as including everything the experimenter did systematically in each intervention condition. Typically, there are numerous intervention procedures, especially in applied problems. Thus, applied behavior analysis presents a problem: the multivariable intervention "package" and its subcomponents.

In some instances, it is enough to demonstrate that the intervention package was responsible for the amelioration of the problem behavior. If the components of the package are not expensive or socially inconvenient, the experimenter may decide that it is more relevant to move on to other problems. However, at other times it is of great interest to know the "(1) function of each component of the original experimental procedure, (2) function of various levels of the experimental variables, or (3) effects of other alterations of the experimental procedures" (Risley and Wolf, 1972).

In the ABAB reversal design, A (baseline) functions to establish a stable operant level of the target behavior; a comparison with B (intervention condition) shows that there has or has not been a change in the frequency or duration of the response. Return to A condition indicates a high probability that the treatment procedure was functional in changing the response. Another replication of B strengthens the evidence and appropriately leaves the client in the intervention or follow-up condition. In many cases, the addition of C, which includes fading out the intervention procedure or developing a maintenance procedure for leaving the improved response, is desirable. Given enough time, the worker may also want to reverse the maintenance condition to determine its function.

ABAB Reversal Design

Phase	1	2	3	4	5
Appropriate talking:	Base-line	Interven-tion	Base-line	Interven-tion	Mainte-nance

In the following hypothetical example of the ABABC reversal design, the client, a seventy-six-year-old woman living with her daughter's family, exhibited low rates of appropriate speech when interacting with her family and friends, especially during mealtimes and other family gatherings. During the baseline phase, data were recorded regarding initiations and questions by Mrs. L.'s family members and her verbalizations to her family or friends during both mealtimes and family gatherings. The intervention phase included a modification of the question technique evaluated by Linsk and Pinkston (Practice Illustration 8.3) for increasing appropriate verbalization with a group of institutionalized elderly women.

Family members developed a list of relevant questions to ask Mrs. L. during dinner to increase her opportunity to speak appropriately and responded to her in a warm interested manner whenever she spoke appropriately of currently relevant issues. In addition, family members introduced stimulus items to Mrs. L. to show their interest in her and to give her something to talk about. The reversal phase involved returning to conditions as they were in the baseline: normal family conversation, with very little attention to Mrs. L. A return to intervention involved a return to the question-asking procedure from the previous intervention condition. The maintenance procedure involved a gradual reduction of how often questions from the list were asked. Although the number of questions was reduced, the procedure remained as a prosthetic intervention to ensure continuation of appropriate conversation with Mrs. L.

This design therefore increased the ability of both the therapist and the family to evaluate the effectiveness of their intervention procedures with Mr. L.'s appropriate verbalizations and involvement in family conversation. From this evaluation, which included replication of effects, it was then possible to causally infer factors influencing the client's conversation.

Baer (1973) proposed that although the ABAB reversal design allows for a replication of the intervention effects on a response, the multiple-baseline design provides a replication of the technique. It is widely accepted that the intervention procedure remains constant while one of the following parameters may be varied: (1) behavior, (2) subjects, or (3) setting (Baer, Wolf, and Risley, 1968; Hersen and Barlow, 1976; Risley and Wolf, 1972).

Multiple-Baseline-Across-Behaviors Design. The multiple-baseline-across-behavior(s) design has been the most frequently used multiple-baseline design in applied behavior analysis (for examples, see Baer and Guess, 1971; Bailey and others, 1971; Barton and others, 1970; Garcia, Baer, and Firestone, 1971; Hall and others, 1970; McAllister and others, 1969; Milby, 1970; Risley and Hart, 1968; Sajwaj, Twardosz, and Burke, 1972; Salzberg and others, 1971; Schumaker and Sherman, 1970; Schwarz and Hawkins, 1970; and Wahler, 1969a). When designing these studies, the research-practitioner should carefully choose the target behaviors to ensure that they are sufficiently independent of each other. This avoids the design problem of having the intervention effects transfer to the second baseline. In addition, remember that any intervention procedure selected must be effective when implemented for all baselines.

In Practice Illustration 6.1, McCabe instituted a social-skill training sequentially across three social skills of a nineteen-year-old woman diagnosed by an intake worker as neurotically depressed. In answer to the client's complaint that the woman was unable to initiate and maintain conversations, the social worker administered social-skills training across eye contact, level of voice volume, and upper body relaxation. In each case, the behaviors involved showed improvement when social-skills training was introduced. The results of the study were further substantiated by probes for generality, in which the client's behaviors were measured while she talked with a male social worker at the agency. The client's immediate improvement upon the implementation of the intervention convinced both the client and the worker that the techniques being taught were helpful in improving the client's social behavior within the setting. However, generality to another person was shown only across eye contact and, in a limited way, voice volume. Correlated with the improvements were the client's reports that she was less depressed and changes in her scores on the general contentment scale (Hudson, 1977, 1981). Again the worker received some empirical evidence that the intervention had some direct impact on the client's behavior; that is, the client had the ability to engage in better prosocial skills. This was particularly interesting because the worker had not expected changes in the client's self-esteem based on this brief structured form of treatment.

Multiple-Baseline-Across-Behaviors Design

Phase	1	2	3	4	5
Eye contact	Base-line	Interven-tion	Interven-tion	Interven-tion	Follow-up
Voice volume	Base-line	Base-line	Interven-tion	Interven-tion	Follow-up
Upper body posture	Base-line	Base-line	Base-line	Interven-tion	Follow-up

In this study, the goal was to bring three specific social skills under the control of the intervention, to increase overall social competence. During phase 1, the baseline condition, the

operant level of responding across three behaviors was established for future comparison with the same behavioral intervention. During phase 2, social-skills training was administered
to eye contact, and improvement was noted in this behavior
while the other targeted behaviors remained at baseline levels.
This provided the first evidence that the intervention was successful in changing behavior. During phase 3, the intervention
was implemented on voice volume, and improvement followed
immediately while the baseline level of upper body posture remained at baseline levels. This provided further confirmation of
the effectiveness of the intervention. Finally, during phase 4,
the intervention was implemented on upper body posture and
showed, again, an immediate improvement, providing the final
experimental evidence that the intervention was effective, a
third replication of the effect. Phase 5, follow-up, did not offer
experimental control, but it did confirm that the client was able
to maintain the improvement in behaviors over time. This information was useful to the worker because it was experimental
evidence of the causality of the intervention and proved that
the client was able to learn and implement better social skills.
Note that the worker did not have experimental information
that the client used these behaviors in private life and the question of these behaviors' generality outside the clinic setting remained open, although the client's reports of her personal life
and her ability to conduct conversations were positive.

   Multiple-Baseline-Across-Subjects Design. Because of the
interaction that often occurs between clients in the same setting, the multiple-baseline-across-subjects design may present
difficulties; that is, the clients may interact with each other.
However, some researchers have successfully used this design or
variations (Corte, Wolf, and Locke, 1971; Panyan, Boozer, and
Morris, 1970), and it may be useful to workers within specific
settings, such as schools and institutions. The design provides
experimental control for several client interventions while an attempt is being made to modify a specific problem behavior. To
use this design the best way, the worker must have several clients. For this reason the design may be more useful for working
with clients who have specific deficits, a state of affairs often

found when working with clients with a low rate of interpersonal skills, such as the retarded or the elderly.

As discussed in Practice Illustration 9.1, Lullo and Pinkston examined self-initiated greeting behavior in three adolescents with learning disabilities. The clients were two females, ages sixteen and fifteen, and one male, age twelve, in a class for developmentally disabled adolescents. During the baseline, all three clients engaged in low rates of greetings to adults in the classrooms. The multiple-baseline-across-clients design was selected because it was thought unlikely that the clients would interact with each other about their greetings to adults. If the clients had not increased greeting as a result of interacting with other students who had that behavior, it was unlikely that there would be reactivity effects from improvement of the first client. Intervention was introduced to the first client while baseline condition continued with the other two; improvement occurred quickly following the instructions, token system (five points per greeting), and modeling. The first client showed improvement while the others remained at low levels. This effect was replicated across the second two clients. However, the result following the initial intervention varied across the three clients, with only the final client maintaining positive effects of the intervention to the end of the study. This is a good example of a procedure for checking the maintenance of intervention effects to determine possible modifications of the intervention with future clients.

Multiple-Baseline-Across-Clients Design

Phase	1	2	3	4	5	6
Client 1	Baseline	Intervention	Maintenance	Monitoring	Monitoring	Monitoring
Client 2	Baseline	Baseline	Intervention	Maintenance	Monitoring	Monitoring
Client 3	Baseline	Baseline	Baseline	Intervention	Maintenance	Monitoring

The number of clients who can be examined varies from two to five; more than five extends the baseline somewhat beyond clinical usefulness. However, more than five clients can be studied in an institutional environment where it is possible to institute intervention only in a limited number of cases at a time. In such a case, the long baseline could provide useful information without impeding clinical intervention. Again, each replication strengthens the inferences regarding the effects of the interventions, although the generality of findings is still limited by two or three clients.

Multiple-Baseline-Across-Settings Design. The multiple-baseline-across-settings design is an opportunity to test the effectiveness and generality of treatment procedures across three settings and to program generality when it does not occur (as is usually the case) or monitor it when it does. Few cases have examined this form of generality, although in clinical interventions it answers the important question, "Does this behavior have generality outside the room?" Most workers assume that if the person changes, behaviors change across setting wherever the client goes. The multiple-baseline-across-settings design is a methodology for testing this assumption.

Multiple-Baseline-Across-Settings Design

Phase	1	2	3	4	5
Institution	Base-line	Interven-tion	Interven-tion		
Home	Base-line	Base-line	Interven-tion	Interven-tion	Mainte-nance
Workshop			Base-line	Interven-tion	Mainte-nance

Although in many institutions most of the client's stay is used for diagnosis, some institutions actually provide specific interventions on specific behaviors considered helpful for the individual in naturalistic settings (Hersen and Bellack, 1978a).

Appropriate prosocial behaviors are a common target because they occur at such a low rate among institutionalized individuals, as a result of the institutional environment or because the individuals were hospitalized for that reason. In Hersen and Bellack's study, John, an eighteen-year-old man diagnosed as depressed, showed no interest in self-grooming while in the state mental institution. A program of social praise plus money was initiated for being dressed by a specific time and being on time to the group meeting. With the money, John could buy his candy, cigarettes, and paperbacks. Baseline on getting dressed and being at the breakfast table on time was also recorded at home weekend visits. Therefore, the intervention could be implemented in the home before John was released from the institution. As soon as John was released and referred to a sheltered workshop, the program was instituted, following baseline, for being to work on time and appropriately groomed. The worker planned to obtain generality of the program across two additional settings. The baseline measures at home and at work showed that the self-grooming behaviors were not going to happen unless the contingencies were also included at home and at work. The maintenance program across home and work settings included social praise for the desired behaviors, with a special bonus for an entire week of on-time behavior accompanied by good grooming. An additional step could be to gradually phase out the material reinforcers, leaving only praise for on-time behavior and good grooming.

Notice the flexibility of this design. Although this case is an imperfect use of the design—that is, the baseline in the third setting was begun at a later date, the design was quite appropriate for the clinical needs of the case, and it still allowed for replicating effects across settings and comparing baseline and intervention data. When designing experimental programs, the worker should keep this flexibility in mind. This flexibility is merely a way of altering the design to record the most systematic evidence possible. For clinical purposes, it may be desirable to develop a series of flexible single-case designs to use in practice evaluations. The following section discusses use of single-case design for clinical evaluation.

Clinical or Practice Evaluation

Clinical evaluation in social work practice incorporates structured practice with careful data recording and less powerful control designs. The initial data recording involves baseline and intervention assessment, as in experimental research, whereby the worker examines baseline data to determine specific relationships that may occur between the environment and the selected problems or goals. The research designs used in clinical and practice evaluations do not provide conclusive evidence of intervention effectiveness, but they do allow for the inference that change has occurred. The basic single-case design used is AB or baseline/intervention. By comparing intervention data to baseline data, the worker can determine whether an important change has occurred following intervention. The design may be extended to an ABB_1 or ABC design to determine whether change occurred and whether the change was maintained (baseline, intervention, follow-up). The designs discussed for clinical evaluation are based on this idea, with some additions to increase the amount of inference that can be made about the intervention.

For many clients and settings, clinical evaluation determines the effectiveness of intervention and helps the worker establish effectiveness as a criterion for using specific intervention procedures with specific kinds of problems. Three designs are often possible for clinical evaluations: intervention-reversal, multiple-replication, and clinical multiple-baseline. These designs are characterized by weak control, but they are excellent in a clinical setting.

Intervention-Reversal Design. The intervention-reversal design (BCB) is used when, for clinical or sometimes political reasons, an intervention must be made at once and it is important to have an analysis of the controlling variables. A flaw in this design is that it destroys any analysis of historical variables and weakens inferences that can be made about the original functional relationships between client behaviors and the environment. However, it does allow comparison between intervention versus no-intervention conditions.

Intervention-Reversal Design

Phase	1	2	3	4
Aggressive behavior	Intervention	Reversal	Intervention	Maintenance

Elaine, a twenty-two-year-old resident of a long-term care facility, became violent in her interactions with the staff; one staff member was taken to the hospital as a result of a physical attack. The staff became afraid of Elaine and would have nothing to do with her. A rich program of material rewards paired with staff praise was presented, based on her good time, that is, thirty-minute periods without aggressive behavior toward staff or other residents. Elaine's aggressive behavior dropped to zero. The staff remained unconvinced that her program was responsible for her improvement, stating that she was in one of her "cycles." They also complained that the extra rewards were unfair to the other residents and wanted to discontinue the rewards. To this typical institutional response, the worker suggested that perhaps the staff should remove the rewards systematically, to determine the rewards' importance to Elaine's improvement. Not surprisingly, the reversal resulted in Elaine's rapid return to high levels of aggressive behavior, and after three days the staff asked to have the program reinstated. In this case, the reversal was educational to the staff and, therefore, of clinical value to Elaine. After reestablishing Elaine's zero rate of aggression, a plan was developed to gradually reduce the frequency of material rewards while maintaining staff praise for good time. This systematic exploration of rewards gave the staff new information about their interactions with Elaine.

Multiple-Replication Design. The multiple-replication design, frequently called an AB design, is basically a comparison between baseline and intervention data. It involves a series of replications of an intervention to determine an intervention's effectiveness across clients, behaviors, or setting. The major difference between the multiple-replication and the multiple-baseline designs is that the baselines do not begin at the same time under exactly the same conditions; they begin as clinical needs dictate. In agency practice, it is unlikely that a worker will have the customary five clients referred with the same problem at the same time, so it is possible to use for practice evaluations an evaluation design that offers more flexibility. As with more controlled evaluation designs, problems, goals, and interventions are carefully defined. The intervention involves the same procedures across all replications. This design is clinically possible and useful for determining the generality across or within clients. That is, it can be used to examine the effectiveness of an intervention with the same problem across clients, with the same client across settings, or with the same client serially across behaviors. If the worker wants to study the effectiveness across several clients with an unusual problem, this can be done serially over a longer period of time as the worker is referred another client with the same unusual problem. The worker can simply hold the data from such cases until enough are accumulated to add substantially to the literature. The number of cases required for publication will vary, depending upon how much is known about intervention with the problem. With a successful intervention with a rarely solved problem, it may be important to share the procedure with the profession after a single case, although it will probably not get past a reviewing board unless the study is unusual. Therefore, it will most likely be necessary for the worker to collect three to five cases before an audience for the clinical research report can be found. If publication of the results is not possible, a report to a special interest group may be the way to disseminate the procedure. At the very least, such data can be included as pilot data in demonstration applications for research or program grants. The worst possibility is that the worker will achieve only the satisfaction of having executed elegant practice with evaluated results.

This design could be used when the worker plans to evaluate an aftercare program for adolescents following their first hospitalization experience. The program would involve a skills package for intervention within an institution followed by a family intervention in the home. Both interventions could be

Multiple-Replication Design

Phase	1	2	3	4	5
Client 1	Base-line	Interven-tion			
Client 2		Base-line	Interven-tion		
Client 3				Base-line	Interven-tion

evaluated with the design in the manner discussed, that is, by implementing the baseline and intervention at different times. The major caution is that interventions with different clients should be implemented at the same time. Although this design does not provide the same control of developmental and extraneous factors as does the usual multiple-baseline design, it does provide some control for replicating the procedures across clients and their families. The results, although not conclusive, could be convincing and provide better clinical evaluation than is usually present in clinical situations.

Clinical Multiple-Baseline Design. This design is an opportunity for good clinical evaluations of interventions with both behavioral deficits and excesses. As the worker attempts to rearrange the deployment of reinforcers to clients, it may be necessary to remove reinforcers following an excessive behavior and, once that behavior has been decreased, present the same type of reinforcer to increase behaviors occurring at a deficit rate. Using this design, baseline is recorded simultaneously, with both an excess behavior and a deficit behavior. In most cases, the first intervention is to remove reinforcers from the excessive behaviors while continuing to record baseline on the deficit behaviors. The second intervention is to present the same type of reinforcers following the deficit behaviors, to increase their rate. This provides a replication of the effect of manipulating a specified reinforcer.

Clinical Multiple-Baseline Design

Phase	1	2	3	4
Excess behavior	Base-line	Interven-tion	Interven-tion	Follow-up
Deficit behavior	Base-line	Base-line	Interven-tion	Follow-up

This strategy was used by Pinkston and others (1973) to decrease the aggressive behavior of a preschool child. Although the researchers used a reversal design to provide additional control, it is not necessary to do so in a clinical evaluation. In their study, the researchers removed adult attention from the client and gave it to the victim of the child's aggression, to decrease the rate of the client's aggressive behavior toward children. Then, after Pinkston and colleagues had determined by monitoring the baseline data that this plan did not adequately increase appropriate social interaction, they instituted praise to the client for playing appropriately with other children. These interventions resulted in a decrease in aggressive behavior and an increase in appropriate social interaction. Thus, the researchers provided a way to use extinction and differential attention to remediate behavior problems.

These clinical evaluation designs are only a few of the possible ways to increase the inferences the worker can make regarding the effectiveness of procedures. Others can be borrowed or invented to increase the rigor of these evaluations. The use of comparisons between baseline and intervention and replication across clients, behaviors, or settings are two important tools to use to show some, if not comprehensive, control.

Systematic Practice

Social work practice should involve the systematic use of practice knowledge, theory, and research findings. The minimal requirements for *systematic practice* include defining problems and goals observably and specifically, with attention to the best possible outcomes. The workers' major practice methods are also defined in observable terms. Definition of evaluation procedures can include observations, checklists, and attitude questionnaires. However, if attitude questionnaires are used, they should be considered another client response rather than strong evidence of the internal workings of the client. Some form of pre- and postassessment of clients' problems, goals, and skills is useful to the practitioner for assessing and evaluating interventions. Combined, the techniques enable the worker to formulate some well-defined assumptions regarding whether clients have solved problems, achieved goals, or developed skills. Alternatively, when the client does not have a long-term problem but needs a one-time advice consultation or the achievement of a service, workers may be more interested in evaluating their own abilities to help clients achieve these brief needs than in evaluating each client independently.

Systematic or structured practice (Smith and Glass, 1977) has been shown to more effectively help clients than unstructured approaches. To monitor their own approach to intervention, workers can be helped by developing checklists for working with specific kinds of clients. The checklists put the workers' personal practice methods into a form that can be evaluated for effectiveness. Reid and Epstein (1972), in their task-centered casework model, provided an excellent example of how this can occur. This model evolved from their years of practice experience. Once they established the practice model, they conducted a controlled series of research studies to determine its effectiveness. Pincus and Minahan (1973) developed their model from both their own and their students' practice. The more carefully workers define and structure their model, the more likely they are to contribute to the social work practice knowledge and provide methods for future research.

By defining practice methods in observable terms, the workers facilitate communication with their colleagues and future students of social work. It is also useful as a means of helping workers examine why they should or should not engage in specific behaviors when working with clients. Defining the clients' problems and goals in observable behaviors also gives the worker and the client some objective means for evaluating the progress of the intervention. Evaluating ongoing interventions with the clients give the clients opportunities to openly express their dissatisfaction with their progress or to decide that perhaps they have not really selected important goals. For instance, low rates of baseline behavior often help clients understand that specific problems are not as serious as they had thought or that some simple change in their lives would adequately ameliorate the problem. Careful assessments of various aspects of the clients' lives may provide learning experiences for the clients that will motivate them to engage in intervention procedures.

Likewise, evaluation procedures may be so informative to clients that some of the original problems are reconceptualized. Adult children may not be aware of how negative they feel toward an elderly parent until they are asked to fill out an attitude questionnaire. They may be so shocked by their answers that they are motivated to change their interaction with their parent in ways not previously considered. Or, when asked to record a diary of the circumstances surrounding his anxiety, a young man may be able to see from his recording that he always plans to do more work than possible and as a result feels anxious and afraid that he "can't cut it." If he notes this, it will be easier for the worker to suggest that he set more realistic goals and for him to give self-credit for what he does do. If he does note it on his own, the worker will be able to provide convincing feedback to help him understand how his own behavior perpetuates his problem. (Most clients do not receive adequate reinforcement for their efforts.) Diaries help some clients understand why they feel depressed and angry and give them the chance to increase more enjoyable activities in their lives. Evaluation is part of the intervention, and successful client abilities to participate fully in the evaluation effort should enable them to understand the value of the intervention.

The development of guidelines for helping clients who want a specific service, such as social security payments, is standard. The guidelines are printed in outline form for the client's use. To evaluate whether the client achieves the service, the worker need only ask the client to report back the results, that is, did they or did they not receive the service. The worker can keep a log of service delivery to determine personal ratio of success in helping clients achieve their needs.

Structured practice is not experimental research or even good clinical evaluation, but it is the first step in developing a practice methodology with minimal evaluation that can be used as the basis for future data recording and research. Researchers will tell you that their notebooks of informal observations often contribute as much as their "hard" data and lead to the discovery of new and useful phenomena. The notebook is a way of informing practice that has been used widely in social work. We are simply suggesting a bit more structure.

◆◆◆◆◆◆◆◆◆◆◆◆◆◆◆◆◆◆◆◆◆◆◆◆◆◆◆◆◆

5

Selecting and Training
Behavior Change Agents

Selecting and training change agents is the basis of successful intervention. The change agent is the person responsible for carrying out the behavioral intervention procedures. Because the selection of this person may be one of the best predictors of outcome, the worker must assess who will make the best change agent(s). Criteria for selecting change agents are relatively unresearched, although there is evidence that a variety of persons can carry out this role successfully; teachers, parents, peers, hospital staff, and others have achieved positive results with clients. In the absence of empirical research, behavioral theories and practice experience indicate that the change agent must possess adequate motivation, time, physical health, and skills for carrying out the intervention. Methods for selecting these change agents require intense study; this chapter begins with a study of the procedures.

Behavior changes often require that individuals acquire new skills and learn different combinations of skills. The worker, in the role of teacher, must develop a variety of procedures for imparting these skills. The procedures selected for training new behavioral repertoires vary, depending upon the skills to be learned and the characteristics of the change agent or client.

Specific attention should be paid to the reinforcement of the change agent. Adequate planning of consequences for behavioral change agents has not been covered in the intervention literature; the assumption is that client improvements will be adequate to maintain the change agent's behaviors. In each case, this may or may not be true, but it is certainly better to plan the consequences for the change agent than to depend on naturally occurring positive or negative reinforcement. The final section of this chapter discusses the reinforcement of change agents.

Assessing and Selecting Behavior Change Agents

Whenever possible, the change agent participates in all levels of the intervention: (1) the assessment, (2) helping design the intervention, (3) learning the necessary intervention skills, (4) implementing the intervention, and (5) the evaluation and follow-up. When the worker or the client is the primary change agent, participation in these tasks occurs automatically within the model. When others are included, however, special planning is necessary.

In client-worker interviews, both the worker and the client are part of the change effort and participate in all steps of the intervention. Each person provides consequences for the other's behaviors, either causing them to remain the same or to alter in some direction. Therefore, the term change agent here refers to a person who implements the intervention and controls most of the consequences following the client's behavior. If the worker intervenes in the classroom, most likely the individual teacher will be the change agent, although peers have been shown to be powerful reinforcers for client behaviors and have thus been used on some occasions (Chapter Six). If change is to occur in the home, one or more family members will probably act as the change agent (Chapter 7). If change is to occur in an institution, one or more of the institutional staff will probably act as change agents (Chapter 8).

Assessment. The common characteristics to consider

when selecting the change agent include the person's (1) availability and motivation, (2) access to behaviors and control of behavioral consequences, (3) educational level, (4) skill levels, and (5) adequate mental and physical health.

The change agent's availability and motivation are determined by assessing five dimensions: (1) agreement to devote effort to the change intervention, (2) relationship to the client, (3) recent history with the client, (4) possible benefit from client behavior change, and (5) adequate time to engage in the change effort.

The change agent must clearly *agree to devote a certain amount of effort* to the intervention. That amount should be specified as soon as possible. For instance, parents may agree to expand a great deal of effort on an intervention with their children, whereas a neighbor may only agree to call the client once a day to determine whether the client has remembered to take prescribed medication. Whether the amount of involvement is large or small, it should be specified before the intervention begins. If only a small amount of effort is available, the intervention must be limited to accommodate this factor or another change agent must be sought. To assess the change agent's motivation and agreement, ask the person; the answer will not always be accurate, but it is a good place to begin. If the assessment is incorrect, it has to be revised.

Examining the change agent's *relationship to the client* enables the worker to develop a better working hypothesis as to the change agent's motivation to help. Family relationship is not a guarantee that strong motivation exists, but, if the relationship is active, most likely the relative can be helpful. Clients living away from members of their family may have developed strong relationships among their friends; these ties can be part of the change effort.

Perhaps more important is the client's *recent history* with the potential change agent. It is important to determine if the change agent has an ongoing relationship with the client, that is, the frequency of personal contacts between the two, reasons for these contacts, and satisfaction with these contacts. The worker considers how much the intervention would increase the change agent's response effort; for instance, would frequency or duration of contact have to be increased? If ongoing contact is not present, it is unlikely that the potential change agent will be able to implement the intervention.

The change agent's recent history with the client is a possible motivation factor. If the change agent is the recipient of the client's undesirable behaviors and is *likely to benefit* from the client's behavior change, the agent will probably participate in the change effort. But if the client has become so aversive to the individual, the agent is unable to either spend time with the client or to discriminate any desirable behaviors to reinforce. However, if the outcome of the intervention will benefit the change agent, it may be worthwhile for the person to participate in the intervention. Finally, the change agent must have *adequate time to engage in the change effort.* If the agent is already overworked and stressed, these factors may prevent the intervention from being implemented.

To implement the intervention, the change agent must have *access to client behaviors and be able to control behavioral consequences.* Therefore, the change agent must be able to observe the behaviors to be changed or receive accurate reports of those behaviors. Resources must be available to the change agent for providing altered consequences for the client. This is particularly important when part of the intervention includes material reinforcers; a common error when designing token economies and other reinforcement procedures is to begin the intervention without adequate backup reinforcers. If material reinforcers are not available to the change agent, the worker must rely on other reinforcers, such as positive statement, attention, and privileges (assuming that there are privileges or that the change agent is a positively reinforcing stimulus). A person who does not control consequences for the behavior can *not* successfully function as a change agent.

The *educational level* of the potential change agent will either increase or reduce the variety of training procedures that can be used. Persons with lower educational and socioeconomic levels can be more easily trained to use procedures than to understand abstract behavioral concepts. They respond better to training procedures that *show* them what to do, such as direct observations of models or videotapes. Lack of education need not prevent the worker from using persons as change agents; it simply influences the educational technique. It also influences the complexity of the intervention procedures that can be developed for the client. With less educated adults, the worker should be as specific and concrete as possible when designing and implementing procedures.

To assess the change agent's *skill level,* the worker should use pencil-paper tests or make direct observations. The change agent *must* possess the component behaviors included in the intervention. If the agent does not have these component behaviors, the worker must first teach them to the agent. Once the worker determines that the change agent has these behaviors, the worker may proceed to teach the agent the necessary skills for carrying out the intervention. For example, parents frequently do not have or have discontinued using the ability to praise their children. Before a procedure such as differential attention can be implemented, the worker has to develop a repertoire of positive statements and touching for the agent. That is, the change agent may have to learn how to reinforce the client. Change agents with an education beyond high school can be taught conceptual as well as behavioral aspects of interventions, which may help them to more generally apply the procedures.

The worker should assess whether the client has *adequate mental and physical health* to carry out the intervention. This is an important assessment because implementing an intervention could add stress to a person in poor mental or physical health. Also, the intervention should be carried out consistently. If the change agent is too impaired to do so, the intervention will not successfully accomplish specific goals. Persons with recent histories of mental illness, drug addictions, or extreme physical disability are not good candidates for being change agents. It is unfair to add response requirements for them if they are having difficulty maintaining their own response repertoires in the community. The additional requirements may exacerbate their health problems and simply make their lives more difficult.

Selection. Not all change agents will possess all the characteristics listed to enable them to engage in the change effort. If certain necessary characteristics are not available, obviously the intervention cannot happen. It is important then to determine whether the agent lacks characteristics that will prevent the intervention from being carried out. When selecting the change agent, it is essential that (1) there is agreement to participate; (2) the change agent can control consequences of the client's behavior; and (3) the change agent's health is adequate for implementing the intervention. Most of the other requirements can be altered if enough time and effort can be devoted to the training. However, when it is possible to choose from among possible change agents, the worker selects the person who meets most of the criteria.

In some cases, the worker functions as the change agent by interacting directly within the client's environment; thus, in institutions, groups, or families, the worker may assume, for a time at least, the role of change agent. Whenever this occurs, it is desirable to wean persons from the natural environment into the training site as soon as possible. The worker is not a normal part of the client's life and is usually atypical of those who are. For long-term effects to be achieved, the worker must fade out gradually.

The worker may assume the role more frequently within the client interview by reinforcing the client's efforts and by praising those aspects of the client that should be strengthened to achieve a desirable outcome. This is especially functional when there is no good candidate for change agent outside the interview. (See Chapter Nine for a full discussion of these procedures.) Within the interview or session, the worker should always provide supportive statements and help the client with their change effort, but the person in the naturalistic environment will be the identified change agent.

Clients may organize and manage their own change effort, although they do not control the contingencies in their lives; that is, they cannot apply reinforcement, extinction (can you ignore yourself?), and punishments. They may decide what is likely to be an important consequence to help them in their change efforts and learn or employ the behaviors that should achieve those consequences, but they are unable to control them. To understand this concept, consider whether most starving people could deny themselves food, or how many persons who have no other source of income would tell their boss that they have not earned their salary this week and therefore will not accept it. Some people actually do both, but then the assumption is that food and money are not reinforcers to the client, a fact which may render them dysfunctional in our culture.

Educational Training Procedures

The best educational methods for training most people to intervene in naturalistic environments have not been established empirically. A number of methods achieved tentative consensus among trainers (O'Dell and others, 1981; O'Dell, 1974; Graziano, 1977; Nay, 1975). These methods were developed through efforts to train family members, teachers, and college students to be effective change agents. At times, it appears that the rule is that some methods work with some people and other methods work with other people. This is not a very helpful guideline! Fortunately, training is a very active area of research and includes a few guidelines the worker can use when deciding upon a change effort. The most carefully evaluated training techniques are (1) instructions, (2) cueing, (3) modeling, (4) rehearsal and roleplay, and (5) feedback. Most of these techniques are used in various combinations with each other to form a complete training package likely to work with a number of people.

Instructions. Because of the educational aspects of this method, instructions are included in most training efforts. Instructions include written and/or oral directions for carrying out intervention procedures. Although instructions are usually the weakest form of training (O'Dell and others, 1981), they are essential for three reasons. First, writing specific instructions for procedures helps workers define interventions clearly and specifically. Second, clients and change agents are often apprehensive during early sessions and may be unable to remember how to carry out the procedures later when the worker is not present. Third, when working through a series of interventions, the change agent may become quite skilled at implementing behavioral procedures and may only need written or oral instructions to successfully use the interventions (Pinkston and Herbert-Jackson, 1975). When possible, the third method is the most inexpensive form of training.

Instructions are usually written presentations, oral directions, or lectures. The most highly developed written instructions are set forth in parent training manuals (for review and evaluation, see Bernal and North, 1978). Typically, these manuals include sections on behavioral principles, behavioral interventions, and recording and evaluating client behavior data. Certainly written instructions are more effective than no training, but they cannot be assumed adequate for a good training program (Nay, 1975). Oral directions are the most likely procedures to be misunderstood by the client or to be inadequately delivered. They should not be used unless instructions for altering a procedure have to be delivered over the telephone. However, lectures have been used effectively in combination with other procedures for working with groups (Rose, 1977). All these instruction procedures have been effective for teaching behavioral principles but are not as effective for teaching people how to use procedures.

Cueing. A signal to indicate that the intervention should be used is called a cue. Cues may be included by (1) *adding new cues* to the environment and (2) teaching the client and change agent to *discriminate cues* already existing in the environment. Occasionally the two kinds of cues are combined and used in sequence; that is, a new cue is added to help the client discriminate the existing cues in the environment.

Herbert and colleagues (1973) demonstrated the value of cues for helping teach mothers to use differential attention procedures more precisely. The observer signaled the mothers when they should implement the intervention; the mothers increased their proficiency in presenting and removing their attention. To solve the problem of poor discrimination, the client and/or the change agent can be taught to discriminate (to respond to) the environmental cues that signal the appropriate time to start the intervention procedure. The time includes when to avoid a behavior and when to provide a new consequence. This discrimination is an informal part of all behavioral intervention; however, when the client has difficulty identifying naturally occurring cues, discrimination training should be included. When adolescents and their parents are taught problem-solving or conflict negotiation methods, they are able to improve their skills in the clinic setting but fail to use them in everyday life. This conflict occurs because probably the people become too angry before they notice the appropriate time to use their newly learned skills. But they can be taught to identify those "red flag" events that signal possible conflict. Institutional staff can be taught to identify client behaviors resulting from social deprivation and to provide social consequences for the client's positive behaviors before negative behaviors emerge full-blown. From a more positive direction, clients can be taught to discriminate cues that reinforcement is available. In the Moses and Pinkston study (Practice Illustration 6.3), verbal, audio, and visual cues indicated to the student that reinforcers were available. When clients and change agents respond to these cues, they are said to have made a discrimination.

Modeling. Procedures that include modeling as a training component are the most effective ways to teach people how to use interventions (Lutzker and Martin, 1981; Nay, 1975; O'Dell and others, 1981). The worker can illustrate modeling via in-person direct demonstration or videotapes. Both methods are used in combination with written and oral instructions, feedback, reinforcement, and cueing. These modeling procedures, developed from Bandura's (1969) observational learning procedures, work best when paired with a reinforcing consequence.

Combining modeling and other procedures is now a standard part of most behavioral training programs because it was used to train enough client populations to demonstrate its considerable generality (O'Dell and others, 1981). The question remains as to which combination of modeling and other procedures is most effective across different problems and socioeconomic groups. Various videotaped models are now on the market, and as this methodology develops, more will become available. O'Dell and colleagues and Dangel and Polster are developing and testing these models with clients of varied educational and socio-economic backgrounds. The usual sequence for using modeling in practice is to (1) describe what you are going to show; (2) model the specific behaviors (either directly or through video-tapes); (3) have the client rehearse or role play the behaviors; (4) provide positive feedback about correct imitations; (5) model behaviors the client missed or provide corrective feedback; (6) have the client rehearse again; and (7) arrange reinforcers in addition to positive feedback.

Rehearsal and Role Play. "Practice makes perfect" is not a bad guideline for teaching intervention procedures. Including rehearsal and role play in training procedures enables the worker to determine whether individuals understand the procedures and have the skills to use them. It is also an opportunity for persons to develop confidence in using the procedures and to receive reinforcement to strengthen their use of the techniques. Rehearsal is used if both the change agent and the client are present; role play may be more useful when both parties involved in the proposed interaction are not present. *Rehearsal,* often used in parent training, involves working directly with the client; *role play* is used when the recipient of trained behaviors is not present, as in assertiveness training. In role play, the worker may assume, as did McCabe and others in Practice Illustration 6.1, the role of the recipient of behaviors. Rose (1977) used these procedures extensively in his group training of children and adults. The techniques seem to work very well in conjunction with modeling and/or feedback. Rehearsal is valuable for teaching clients new behavior patterns, and role play teaches new patterns and, occasionally, teaches clients the consequences of their behaviors on others.

Feedback. Among behaviorists, feedback means providing individuals with information about their behavioral performance, with the goal of improving that performance. Feedback is usually praise of the individual's performance (thought to be a generalized reinforcer in this culture) and corrective feedback, to inform the individual of changes they need to make to meet behavioral criteria. Some practitioners consider corrective feedback punishing and therefore less useful. Feedback is an ongoing part of all behavioral interventions, both informally and in systematic training (Pinkston, Friedman, and Polster, 1981).

The procedures for providing feedback include (1) charts, (2) graphs, (3) self-observation on videotapes, (4) listening to audiotapes, (5) checklists, (6) peer verbal evaluation, and (7) practitioner verbal feedback. Generally, as we attempt to implement a reinforcement model, the bias is toward emphasizing praising or otherwise reinforcing behaviors that are completed effectively and reteaching behavior not accomplished successfully. For a worker who plans to continue to work with an individual, it is probably best to not heavily emphasize negative feedback about a client's performance. The worker should weight the feedback in a positive direction rather than eliminating corrective feedback. Therefore, feedback is presented in the following sequence: (1) positive feedback regarding correct or near-correct behaviors; (2) corrective feedback, either verbally or by once again providing a correct model; (3) positive feedback about the individuals and their attempts to engage in the correct behaviors. When behaviors do not meet stated or unstated criteria, the worker should show the person by some means how the criteria can be improved in the future. To date, there are inconclusive empirical data about the most correct way to do this. It is clear, however, that punishment disrupts ongoing behaviors, so feedback should preferably be delivered in a reinforcing rather than a punishing way. (Chapters Seven and Eight discuss providing feedback to family members and agency staff acting as change agents, respectively.)

Providing Consequences for Change Agents

Practitioners neglect providing consequences for change agents, perhaps because they assume that changes in client behaviors will be an adequate reinforcing consequence for maintaining the change agents' efforts. In some cases this assumption is true. For instance, if the change in client behaviors effectively removes an aversive consequence, this occurrence may negatively reinforce the change agent's behavior. The client's acquisition of new behaviors may add positively reinforcing consequences for the change agent's intervention behaviors. Until the client's behavior improves, reinforcing consequences may not be present for the change agent; also, behavioral improvement, once it has occurred, may not provide adequately reinforcing consequences to offset the change agent's behavioral requirements. It is therefore important to plan reinforcing consequences for the change agent as part of ongoing training and intervention.

Planning Reinforcement for Change Agents. The assessment of reinforcers for the change agent should be part of intervention planning—it is assumed that the change agent, like other people, requires reinforcement for desired responses. The worker should identify events likely to reinforce the change agent's intervention behavior. Another issue for examination is the extent to which implementation of the intervention will strain existing reinforcement. That is, will more work be required than is supported by the environment? When trying to offset the additional response requirements, adding reinforcement and fading the worker's involvement are two useful procedures.

The worker can add reinforcement by arranging social and material consequences. The worker is a potential source of reinforcement as well as others in the environment. Reinforcers under the control of the worker are usually social, that is, feedback regarding performance, praise for participating in the change effort, and verbal recognition of positive qualities the change agents possess or why they are good candidates for being change agents. In family interventions, the mother is often the primary change agent. If so, the father can be recruited to provide social and perhaps material consequences for her change efforts. If the family is more liberated, some form of mutual reinforcement effort can be arranged. Essentially guidelines for reinforcing the change agent are no different than those governing reinforcement of the client. The important task for the worker is to remember to analyze the reinforcement system at the time of intervention.

After intervention has been successful, the question is how to maintain the change agent's continued use of at least some of the intervention procedures, usually positive reinforcement. As the worker terminates with the client and change agent, procedures should be devised to help the change agent maintain an adequate level of intervention (see Chapter Nine for a discussion of extension of intervention effects). The change agent is taught to evaluate personal performance in relation to that of the client. This can be accomplished through a periodic checklist, perhaps weekly and then monthly. As the change agent successfully performs this self-evaluation and, if possible, arranges a reward contingent on continuance of the correct procedures, the worker should gradually fade out involvement, from a weekly, to a monthly, to a trimonthly schedule, until it is evident that the change agent can maintain the change effort.

6

◆-◆◆-◆◆-◆◆-◆◆-◆◆-◆◆-◆◆-◆◆-◆◆-◆◆-◆◆-◆◆-◆◆-◆◆-◆

Interventions
with Individuals

Direct practice with individuals has developed into the most common form of social work service delivery. The development of family and group intervention has relied upon individual approaches for theoretical and methodological bases (see, for example, Roberts and Nee, 1970). Similarly, behavioral intervention methods for use with families and groups were originally developed with individuals (see O'Leary and Wilson, 1975, chap. 1) and have been extensively tested (Fischer, 1978; Fischer and Gochros, 1975; Gambrill, 1977; Leitenberg, 1976; Redd, Porterfield, and Anderson, 1979; Sundel and Sundel, 1982; and Wodarski and Bagarazzi, 1979).

Implementation and evaluation considerations are part of direct practice with individuals and include contingency analysis, modifying clients' behaviors within their environments, and evaluating changes. The considerations are performed in face-to-face contacts with clients and focus on direct intervention on clients' behaviors and an analysis of the interaction of those behaviors with the environment. This method of practice is designed for direct remediation, resulting in the resolution of problems of concern to the client or others in the environment. Strategies are thus designed to help clients change their behavior, change the behavior of others, and obtain needed services.

The two intervention strategies with individual clients are direct influence by the worker or worker-management and self-management by the client. Direct influence by the worker is providing or arranging new environmental cues and behavioral consequences. In self-management, the client is heavily involved in assessing problems, designing interventions, and arranging or discriminating possible consequences for personal behavior. Do not confuse self-management with the terms self-reinforcement or self-modification, which imply that the client can control the consequences for personal behavior; this is a much-debated concept (Goldiamond, 1974). But even though clients may not be able to reinforce themselves, they can certainly learn to acquire any existing reinforcers. Frequently, in actual application the two intervention strategies are combined. Here the two strategies are considered separately whenever differentiation is likely to clarify the unique characteristics of each plan. This chapter describes direct practice with individuals according to the four essential elements of practice: (1) role and setting requirements, (2) assessment considerations, (3) intervention and the reorganization of contingencies, and (4) evaluation of intervention effectiveness.

Role and Setting Requirements

Worker. The worker is a consultant who functions as analyst, teacher, change agent, and a link between the client and the community's resources. The extent to which each function is emphasized depends upon the specific problem the worker is solving. The first responsibility of the worker is to perform a preliminary analysis to determine whether direct influence or client self-management is required. When employing direct influence, the worker assumes primary responsibility for developing, implementing, and evaluating the program. In contact with the client, the worker intervenes with clients' problems by rearranging existing contingency relationships in the clients' environments. The worker increases or decreases identified client behaviors by controlling access to reinforcers and punishers. The worker's major responsibilities are assessing and defining the problem through observation, developing a method of recording data and evaluating change, recording baseline data, intervening directly with problems, assessing change, and programming generality or maintenances of intervention effects.

The worker, assuming primary responsibility for all aspects of intervention, has a greater degree of control and is able to develop, implement, and evaluate methods more effectively than the client could. By having direct access to the client's behaviors and environments, the worker can rapidly reassess and alter unproductive methods. However, because the worker is rarely part of the client's natural environment, programming maintenance from the worker-client environment to other environments where the client interacts with other individuals can be problematic and should be included in the intervention plan.

The worker's roles in the self-management approach are as behavior analyst, consultant, and teacher. Although in the direct influence approach the worker is the primary change agent, in the self-management approach the client is taught the intervention procedures. Workers use their skills to (1) analyze problem situations with the client, (2) teach appropriate data-recording and intervention methods, and (3) consult with the client about the ongoing development and revisions of the behavioral program.

The worker assesses the client's skills and abilities to use self-management techniques and then teaches necessary skills to carry out the behavioral program. The worker should survey those community resources and services that will enhance the client's access to reinforcement. Ongoing worker availability is necessary to help the client revise and reassess the behavioral program, anticipate and reduce obstacles to program success, and recognize and develop methods that ensure the maintenance of intervention effects.

Client. The worker has primary responsibility for all aspects of program development when implementing direct influence. The client is essentially a recipient of the intervention. In the self-management approach, however, the client takes a more active role as a behavior change agent and carries out all major aspects of intervention, including data recording and implementing behavioral techniques. Through interaction with the worker, the client is taught the skills necessary to perform the functions of behavioral analysis. These skills enable the client to identify and possibly alter situational variables that are antecedents to problem behaviors. For many clients seeking social work services, the "presenting" problem is the behaviors of others. The client must modify the environment or others' behaviors and situational aspects that relate to the problem situation. Additionally, the client can be taught to identify and replace personal problem behaviors with more desirable ones, that is, those behaviors more likely to gain reinforcement. This means that the individual necessarily assumes a prominent role in developing appropriate problem and goal definitions and data-recording methods. The client collaborates with the worker to develop strategies for overcoming obstacles to successful implementation of procedures and for increasing *opportunities* for reinforcements (see Figure 6.1, p. 121).

In many forms of self-management, most aspects of intervention might be implemented by the client, with the worker serving primarily as an educator and consultant. Watson and Tharp (1972) developed a text that teaches individuals how to systematically revise their own behaviors by gradually progressing through a self-directed behavioral program. This approach is particularly useful in practice where the client experiences a problem almost totally outside the worker's access and control.

Agency. The agency provides or offers a specific type of service or resource. The agency's functions are designed to meet a need as perceived by the general community, and as such, the agency is similar to a gatekeeper, regulating the flow of clients to community services and resources (Whittaker, 1974). Agency policies, practices, and staff behavior affect practice. The agency's policies and resources may support or constrain the worker in providing social work services; they tend to "shape" worker behaviors regarding choice of approach, determination of intervention strategy, and implementation of the intervention.

The agency's responsibility is to see that services and resources are provided to clients in ways that enhance the client's
reinforcement and decrease punishment. The worker, as the
agency representative, attempts to help clients enhance behavioral functioning within the scope of the general mandate of the
agency. The worker may have to advocate for the client directly
with the agency to shape agency practices that obstruct the
worker-client intervention. Ideally, the agency's position and
power support and aid practitioners' work with clients.

To summarize, to a large extent, the specific responsibilities of the worker and the client are determined by the intervention approach selected. If the social work practitioner determines
that direct influence is most appropriate, the client assumes a
somewhat less active role than if self-management had been the
selected intervention. In addition, agency structure, policies,
and practices influence worker and client roles because they affect the type of intervention selected and the success of its implementation. Other factors are also important when selecting
the specific approach to be implemented. This chapter discusses
the choice between the two basic approaches in direct practice
with individuals: direct influence by the worker and client self-
management. How does the practitioner decide which general
strategy is most appropriate in a given case?

Selecting the Agent of Change

To a considerable degree, the choice of the change agent
determines which of the two approaches—for use with individuals—is likely to be most successful. Information gathered during the assessment should guide the practitioner in making that
decision. Whether it is the worker or client who assumes major
responsibility for implementing change procedures depends on a
number of variables, including (1) access to the problem, (2)
control of contingencies, (3) type of behavior targeted, and (4)
client and worker characteristics and capabilities.

Access. Access is the determination of who is, or can be,
part of the environment where the targeted behavior occurs. Access does not usually represent an either-or condition but a con-

tinuum of availability. Where, when, and how often a behavior does or does not occur affect the degree of access available to the worker.

Although the client has direct access to problem behaviors, decisions regarding intervention are often shaped by the degree of worker access to the problem behaviors or change environment. If the problem behavior occurs in an environment totally unavailable to the worker, or if the behavior occurs so infrequently that it is highly unlikely the worker could be present at the time of occurrence, a direct influence approach is inappropriate. Frequently these behaviors are habits and skills normally emitted away from the clinical interview, such as sexual practices, eating, and consumption of alcohol. If the practitioner cannot create an analog situation to enhance access, the direct approach is minimally useful and so client self-management is the choice. Whenever access is extremely limited, self-management is the approach; when access is great, the worker should consider carefully additional factors before selecting an approach.

Contingency Control. The worker may have access to a problem but limited control or influence over the contingencies. The major considerations here are who possesses control, what kinds of control are available, and how much control exists.

Most contingencies in the client's life are not controlled by either the worker or the client; thus the worker must examine who are the powerful people in the client's life likely to control behavioral contingencies for the client's behaviors. In the Lane and others study (Practice Illustration 9.4), clearly the workers were able to reinforce the creative response of children in the training session. However, generality of creativity in the classroom was probably under the social reinforcement control of the teachers or other students and should have been included in the intervention plan. The worker may reinforce a response in the session; however, to be important in the client's life, behavior must be reinforced outside the session. This problem can be overcome by (1) teaching clients to provide to persons in their lives appropriate cues that reinforcement is in order, (2) engaging in behaviors already reinforced in the environment, (3) asking a person who has control of contingencies to cooperate with the program, and (4) having the client arrange with another person for that person to administer reinforcers.

The degree of contingency control determines the potency of reinforcement and punishment methods. If the worker's personal ability to reinforce the individual or to prevent escape or avoidance of consequences is limited, those procedures' potency and the worker's ability to use them is minimal; another plan should be made. This plan should include naturally occurring consequences in the client's life.

Characteristics of Behavior Targeted. The characteristics of the targeted behavior include its (1) frequency and rate of occurrence, (2) intensity, (3) verbal behavior about the targeted behavior, (4) history or duration, (5) relevance to the client, (6) relevance to societal agents, and (7) relevance to significant others. These characteristics are usually considered in combination with each other to determine which approach should be used— worker- or client-managed—and they also help determine whether persons other than the work should be included in the intervention. Chapter Seven discusses families as change agents; Chapter Eight considers institutional staff. Friends, employers, or religious groups can also be solicited by either the practitioner or the change agent to aid in the change effort.

If the client's problem behavior is severe and occurs at a high rate and high intensity, the client may be unable to begin the intervention. The client may assume its management only after some improvement. Also, the client may not have analytic skills for making an accurate reality-base appraisal of the situation. Therefore, the first intervention may involve teaching analysis skills and later self-management of the intervention. Long-term problem behaviors are sometimes more entrenched and require more worker involvement. The relevance of the behavior to the client, society, and significant others is a motivating factor; relevance to the client is a major factor for self-management. Until the client regards target behaviors as important, the worker must manage the intervention, either by direct influence or by including others in the intervention. Usually, the case begins with worker influence or management and moves to self-management because of a combination of all these factors.

Client and Worker Characteristics. The motivation, commitment, and capabilities of both the worker and the client affect the choice of change agent. Individual differences in outcome may be partially the result of the change agent's inclination and ability to implement change procedures. Two general types of clients receive social work services: voluntary and nonvoluntary. Voluntary clients come willingly for service and request help with problems. Nonvoluntary clients are identified by others as having behavioral problems; these clients are required by a public agency or a court to receive services whether or not they acknowledge that a problem exists. For example, child protective services are mandated when an allegation of abuse or neglect is substantiated. It is thus important to determine who views the behaviors, or the client, as dysfunctional and in need of intervention. For a client relatively adamant about there being "no problem," a self-management approach that requires the client to be the primary change agent is not the approach of choice; instead, the worker should explain the contingencies and use direct influence to bring the client into the change effort. If the client has sought services or fully acknowledges the need for intervention, the effectiveness of a self-management approach is likely to be enhanced.

Other factors that appear related to client motivation are the client's level of current distress, amount of difficulty in carrying out behavioral procedures, expectations about the possibility that change will occur, and the value of change related to changes in reinforcers and punishers in the client's environment (Bellack and Schwartz, 1976, p. 126). When motivation is low, the client's cooperation with the intervention program and ability to function as primary change agent will also likely be low.

Similarly, worker motivation and commitment vary according to the amount of time the practitioner has to spend with the client. For example, workers in a public agency setting may have very little time to devote to direct intervention because of large caseloads and multiple responsibilities.

Worker and client skills also have an obvious effect on the use of the behavioral techniques. If the worker lacks skills for teaching certain behaviors effectively, the change agent's "power" is limited. If the client lacks personal skills in the behavioral repertoire or the capacity to implement certain procedures, the choice of change agent is also affected. A self-management approach to improve greeting skills in a profoundly retarded adult is not likely to be used; the choice will be direct influence. Essentially, the practitioner assesses whether clients' repertoires include basic components necessary to use skills designed to help them make changes. The worker does *not* attempt to teach a man to walk until he is able to stand.

Generally, selecting the change agent requires that the worker assess the degree to which both the client and worker have access, control, motivation, and capability to be responsible for intervention. It is important to note that these characteristics are not simply assessed as "fixed" and unchanging but in terms of whether there is potential for their development.

Assessment

Assessment is a complex information-gathering process that provides the data for case decision making. Upon receiving a referral or application for help, the worker begins the assessment by collecting preliminary information about the reason for the request for service. This reason points the worker in the direction of exploring and clarifying the problem behaviors and conditions that led to the service request. A preliminary analysis provides information about (1) who perceives a problem exists and why service is being sought at this time, (2) what the problem is, (3) who is involved in the problem, (4) when and where the problem occurs, and (5) what has previously been tried to alleviate the problem. This preliminary analysis gives the worker a general overview of the problem that may be the basis for further exploration and problem identification. Together, the practitioner and client attempt to define the outcome desired as a result of intervention, specify the problem behavior(s), identify available resources, and select the change agent and setting. Appropriate data-collection and evaluation methods are also chosen prior to implementing change procedures.

Defining Desirable Outcomes. Information for assessment in individual intervention is obtained from two major sources: referral sources and clients. The worker determines from the referring sources relevant information about contingencies that are maintaining the problem, potential reinforcers available to the worker for use with the client, and the sources' expectancies or client-response requirements for the individual's future behavior. Referring individuals may not have behaviorally specific definitions of the desirable outcome for the client; often their definitions are phrased for general goals or internal states, such as "increased client maturity" rather than specific behaviors.

The worker's task is to work with the referring individual and obtain a clear *behavioral* definition of desired outcomes. Questions such as "When the client is behaving appropriately, what exactly would one see?" or "What should the client be doing if help is successful?" are useful to clarifying what referral sources perceive as appropriate outcomes of service. To obtain this information, the worker conducts a client interview soon after the referral has been made, as a way of seeking opportunities to observe the identified client's behavior and the behavior of those surrounding the client as well as the environment in which the behavior occurs. The worker then returns to the referral source with some observational information and agrees upon or renegotiates expectations for service outcome. For example, Robbie, a seven-year-old boy, is referred by a teacher for individual intervention for self-stimulatory behavior. The teacher's view of desirable outcome is no self-stimulatory behavior and Robbie sitting quietly with hands folded. The practitioner observes the child and the three or four children sitting immediately around him. After recording a sample of behavior, the worker finds that all the children exhibit similar rates of self-stimulatory behavior. This information is taken back to the teacher, and the definition of desired outcome is changed from the original expectation of zero self-stimulatory behaviors and the child's remaining seated with hands folded to a more reasonable goal. The new definition only requires that Robbie exhibit behaviors which do not involve pulling on parts of the body or clothing. This preliminary observation may eliminate wasted time and help clarify the outcomes that are desired at the time of referral.

Whether a client applies or is referred for individual help, the client's view of desired outcomes is especially important. On some occasions, clients agree with the referral source about the need for service and the definition of desired outcomes. But sometimes referred clients think that there is no problem and see no need for change. In such instances the client should be informed, in a straightforward manner, of the referral reasons and consequences for nonparticipation. This alert is especially important when there is a legal mandate for intervention, although even in these cases there is likely room for renegotiation regarding the specification of desirable outcome. The degree to which the client recognizes the outcome as acceptable is an indication of the client's motivation and willingness to participate in a treatment program.

Defining Problem Behavior. Throughout the assessment, the social worker seeks to define problem behaviors. The worker begins the process by obtaining information from the client, referral source, and collaterals in the client's environment regarding individual views of the problem.

Mrs. Charles was referred to the hospital social worker by the nurses because of her uncooperative attitude. When she came to the hospital for heart problems, she caused a "management problem" on her ward. In the interview, she denied any problems but expressed unhappiness at her hospitalization and stated that the staff did not understand her. A joint meeting was set up between the head nurse, Mrs. Charles, and the social worker. Both the nurse and Mrs. Charles were encouraged to define problems from their perspective. The nurse stated that Mrs. Charles was cheating on her special diet, complained about specific staff and her roommate, and frequently asked to go home. Mrs. Charles stated that she did not have an ade-

quate explanation for the diet, that she never knew
when a treatment would occur, and that the staff
didn't talk to her except about her complaining.

Different viewpoints are the bases for negotiating an acceptable problem definition. It is recommended that problems
be defined in behavioral terms that suggest direction for change.
In other words, problems are specified as behavioral excesses or
deficits. If a behavior is a problem because it occurs at too high
a rate, a clear direction for change is suggested—to reduce the
frequency of the behavior. When possible, the worker should
develop behavioral definitions that emphasize what the client is
to accomplish rather than what the client is to eliminate or decrease.

Finally, an important aspect of problem selection is consideration of the effect of the behaviors targeted for change on
others in the client's environment. It is necessary to assess what
is different following intervention regarding specific client behaviors and how the client and others view the behavioral
changes. Behavioral changes in one individual's response affect
others' behaviors and have later reinforcing or punishing consequences for that individual.

If Mr. Goldman seeks help for ineffective assertive skills, a resultant increase in such skills likely affects others in the client's environment. If Mr.
Goldman overly asserts himself at work, it might
result in the boss perceiving Mr. Goldman's behaviors as inappropriate and punishing. The boss may
even fire Mr. Goldman to escape or avoid the punishing assertive behaviors.

Obtaining Needed Resources. The client is linked to community resources both to provide desired resources and to
strengthen various behaviors. Assessment of resource problems
includes assessing antecedent conditions, availability of resources, skills necessary to obtain the resources, and the use of
the community as the change setting. Clients do indeed have resources, but rarely are they in control of them. Societal agents

or employers often control the needed monetary resources of social work clients; personal resources are more likely friends, family, and fellow employees.

Resources are assessed to determine their availability and applicability to service provision. These resources are reinforcers and environmental supports available from either the worker's or the client's environment. Resources or reinforcers may be acquired by the worker through the agency or the community.

The worker performs a contingency assessment (described in Chapter 2) of the environment to determine available resources. Contingency analysis is analogous to the functional analysis (also discussed in Chapter Two) and includes exploring contingency relationships relevant to both client and worker behaviors. By the end of the assessment phase, information obtained by assessment of available resources suggests whether to use a direct influence or self-management approach.

For instance, a woman receiving public aid may need surgery to treat progressive blindness and may also resent her mother's failure to respect her need to be independent. Although the problems are different, the worker may determine that the woman needs to be more assertive in both cases: to obtain financial assistance from the public aid worker and more "adult" treatment from her mother. Therefore, the worker may model and then have the woman practice asserting her needs to both persons. It would be wrong for the worker to "take over" and obtain the needed resources.

Selecting the Change Setting

Besides selecting the change agent, the worker is responsible for assessing the environment in which the problem behavior occurs. Problem behaviors sometimes occur in several settings, so the worker should assess each setting. The worker then determines whether one or more settings should be the setting for change. Essentially, two broad settings are assessed: the agency and the community.

The Agency. Much social work practice occurs in agency settings, which include private and publicly funded service programs or may be part of an institutional structure. The agency is the change setting when (1) the problem behavior occurs there naturally or can be "made" to occur through analog or role-playing situations; (2) an agency worker determines that he or she will be the primary change agent; (3) it is determined that a considerable degree of control over the environment is necessary and can be achieved at the agency; and (4) it is determined that other environments are not suitable to either effect or maintain behavior change.

When the agency serves as the change setting, there is high worker control and access to the contingencies. For the worker to implement a direct influence approach, the worker must have control over reinforcers and punishers and/or the ability to reorganize environmental variables. The use of the agency as the change setting is illustrated in the Moses and Pinkston study (Practice Illustration 6.3, at the end of this chapter), where intervention occurred in a school. However, using the agency as the change setting may cause certain difficulties for the worker, principally transferring control from the agency to the client's more usual environment. Procedures for enhancing transfer and maintenance of learning are essential and must be evaluated as part of assessing any setting. Indeed, in the Moses and Pinkston practice illustration, generality across settings did not occur.

The agency as the change setting can also be used in a self-management approach. Most client behavior, especially habits, occurs outside the agency, worker access, and control; the client is the primary change agent. In the self-management approach, the skills necessary for the client to affect changes are taught and shaped at the agency; clients then use the skills and behaviors in their normal environment to change their own behavior. The agency is the place where necessary skills are taught, and the natural environment is the place where those skills are implemented. McCabe and others (Practice Illustration 6.1) and Mallon-Wenzel and colleagues (Practice Illustration 6.2) taught, practiced, and shaped negotiation and social skills in the agency that were implemented by clients in the natural environment.

The Natural Environment. In some instances, the worker

goes into the natural environment to implement interventions. In a self-management approach, the primary intervention is implemented by the client outside the agency setting. In a direct influence approach, however, this is rarely the case because access to and control over contingencies are limited.

The worker may go into the natural environment to directly observe the client's progress, provide reinforcement for the client's change efforts, and provide feedback to the client to enhance intervention effectiveness. Worker access, control, and agency support affect the worker's ability to support or be part of intervention in the natural environment.

The natural environment becomes the change setting when the worker supports the client in obtaining community resources. The worker teaches the client behaviors necessary for effectively receiving desired services. These behaviors are then performed in the community outside the worker's access and control. By linking the individual with the resource, the worker gives the client increased opportunities for reinforcement (see Chapter Three).

Selecting Data-Collection Procedures

Data-collection procedures used in the applied behavioral analysis model for social work practice with individuals are essentially those described and illustrated in Chapter Three. The primary purpose of collecting data is to obtain information about the client's and relevant others' behaviors. Data are collected on the frequencies, duration, intensity, and/or latency of problem behaviors. Several methods may be used to obtain behavioral data, including client self-report of retrospective data, observational data, and instrumentation.

Retrospective Data. Retrospective data reports are generally elicited in the first interview and may provide information about elements of who, what, when, where, how often, and how much in relation to a problem behavior. The worker asks the client to provide the desired information for the present day, previous day, day before that, and so forth. If the problem behavior occurs infrequently, such as once a week, the client may be asked to recall problem occurrence as far back as a month or more. The worker should recognize that the reliability of retrospective data is often limited (Green and Wright, 1979) and whenever possible not rely on it as the only source of data.

Observational Data. Another source of information for data collection is observation. Data are collected on client behavior by the worker, the client, or independent observers.

The interview may be used as the setting where behavior can be observed and collected. Through analog situations or role playing, the client is presented with an opportunity to engage in the actual behavior. For example, in the Mallon-Wenzel and colleagues study (Practice Illustration 6.2), short analog situations were presented to a client, and the client's responses were videotaped and evaluated.

If the practitioner chooses to apply the direct influence approach, observations are conducted at the agency, where worker access and control are the greatest. Ultimately, many behavior problems occur in the client's natural environment and so are observed there, such as interactional problems (for example, social skill deficits) and habits (for instance, eating disorders). The worker can extend observational data-collection methods to those settings by serving as an observer; going to that setting personally; training the client to observe, collect, and report data; or by using independent observers.

The worker may be the primary observer. If independent observers are unavailable, as usually happens in the public agency setting, and the client does not participate in collecting data, workers can develop methods that enable them to collect data while interacting with the client. For instance, using the direct influence approach, the worker may have to be both primary change agent and observer. The worker develops observational methods suitable for use while interacting with the client; the methods emphasize ease of application and suitability to the client problems and are relatively unobtrusive. For example, a worker applying direct influence counts the frequency of a child's out-of-seat behavior during a specified time period. To keep the count, the worker could simply put checks on a chart after each instance of behavior that occurs. The worker

Figure 6.1. Relationship of Direct Influence, Self-Management,
and Combined Approaches to One Another.

Direct Influence	Combined	Self-Management
Worker access and control maximum		Worker access and control minimum
Identified client recipient of treatment		Client is primary behavioral change agent
Worker is primary behavioral change agent		Worker as educator and consultant
Primary emphasis on worker assessment, intervention, and evaluation		Primary emphasis on client assessment, intervention, and evaluation

schedules reliability checks to ensure that the data collected is as accurate as possible.

The client is sometimes engaged to observe, collect, and report data. Clients are trained to observe in the natural environment via methods suitable to their problems and capabilities and relatively unobtrusive and noninterfering in their interaction with the environment (see Figure 6.1).

In the self-management approach, the client carries the bulk of responsibility for collecting data. Because most client behaviors occur outside the agency setting and worker access and control, the worker and client decide what kinds of data are relevant to the behavior problem and also decide observational times and intervals. Observational times are chosen according to when the problem behavior is most likely to occur; lengths of observational intervals are selected according to the nature of the problem behavior. If the behavior occurs at a high frequency, hourly observations and recordings give a sufficient representative sample of the problem. On the other hand, if the behavior occurs sporadically throughout the day or in very specific circumstances, situationally specific observations and recording are used.

Whenever the client collects data, reliability checks are performed by the worker, independent observers sent by the worker, or collaterals who are part of the client's natural environment whenever possible. Much of the data collected by the client are self-report, but structured data-collection methods that clearly describe how, when, where, and what are collected and presented to the client. Reliability checks verify the accuracy of the data reports.

Data-collection methods suitable for the client's personal resources are developed and implemented by the client. Criteria for choosing self-recording methods are ease of application, the problem, and the client's resources. Self-recording methods should be easy for the client to use during and after the problem situation and not significantly alter the situation itself.

There are many self-recording methods: checklists, interval recording, counters, and diaries. The behavioral problem defines the type of data-collection method used. For example, if the behavior consists of elements of occurrence/nonoccurrence, tallies of total behavior are helpful. Frequencies, recorded on cards, counters, or checklists, are used if the client has the necessary skills to implement them. On the other hand, temporal behaviors require the use of clocks. Intense behaviors are recorded by the client via intensity-rating scales. Clear and manageable written directions and a written recording sheet enhance the client's ability to perform self-monitoring tasks. If clients consider self-monitoring tasks aversive, they avoid or escape the task.

Data may also be collected by independent observers, who are individuals whose sole task is to collect and report data. The worker determines the type of data to be collected, when the data are to be collected, and the observational intervals (see Chapter Three).

Data-collection methods are more flexible when independent observers are used. Because the independent observer's sole task is to collect data, fairly complex methods can be used. For instance, observation in ten-second intervals is difficult for a worker interacting with the client, or for the client in her or his natural environment, but an independent observer trained to use ten-second intervals has minimal interference with completing the response requirements. If the observer is well trained and the behaviors adequately defined, data from these observers tend to be reliable and valid. As with worker- and client-collected data, reliability data are collected on the independent observations.

It is unlikely that in the public welfare setting the worker can find individuals to conduct observations because of budgetary constraints and lack of administrative support. The practitioner must turn to other methods for obtaining data. One source of data is existing records (such as school attendance records). If there is no archival information useful for measuring problem occurrence, the practitioner can use instrumentation as a source of client data.

Instrumentation. This data-collection method requires the administration of rating instruments, scales, tests, and questionnaires. Levitt and Reid (1981) discussed the application of the Rapid Assessment Instruments (RAI) for social work practice. To evaluate problem change, such instruments may be used as before-after measures of treatment administered repeatedly. Instruments are often used as adjuncts to observational data. In the applied behavior analysis model of social work practice, instruments are used alone only when direct observation or archival data are impossible to obtain. Instruments provide information about changes in and qualities of attitudes and knowledge levels about data. The series of scales designed by Walter Hudson (1977), for instance, have demonstrated usefulness to social workers. In one small study, scores on Hudson's Parental Attitude Scale appeared to correlate with child and parent behavior change (Cox and others, 1979). Although none of the scales measure behavior change per se, they do seem to pick up a more general sense of client improvement or deterioration. Other Hudson scales include Index of Marital Satisfaction (IMS), Generalized Contentment Scale (GCS), Index of Self-Concept (ISC), Index of Sexual Satisfaction (ISS), and Child Attitude Toward Mother (CAM).

Finally, surveys can be used to illustrate multiple-components problem situations.

Data Assessment

Data assessment is performed after initial data that represent the baseline or preintervention level of the behavior have been collected. Initial data assessment clarifies for the worker and client what contingencies are involved in the problem behavior and suggests direction for intervention.

The baseline data are examined for stability and trends over a series of data points. With sufficient data, the worker can operationally describe and define the problem behavior through a topographical and functional analysis. A topographical analysis is a relatively simple description, in ordinary language, of what occurs in the problem situations. A functional analysis is a specific description, in behavioral terminology, of antecedent stimuli, behaviors, and consequences that exist in the problem situation.

> John, a twenty-year-old college student, belongs to a social club and seeks help for his inability to ask young women for dates. He has avoided occasions for social interactions with women. The topographical and functional analysis might be as follows:
>
> *Topographical analysis.* Whenever John is in the presence of females and attempts to ask one for a date, he is unable to come up with what he should say, appears uncomfortable, and quickly leaves the presence of the women.
>
> *Functional analysis.* Antecedent stimuli—the presence of a female and the social club; the behavior—a lack of verbal social skills and resultant subjective discomfort of embarrassment and anxiety; the consequences—escaping from and/or avoiding social interaction with women. John, in a social-dating situation in the presence of women, exhibits a deficit of social skills and is negatively reinforced for avoiding social interactions with women.

The topographical and functional analyses describe the relationships between variables and provide a hypothesis about the situation of the client, the behavior, and the client's environment. This hypothesis is the basis for planning intervention. Collected data are graphed and, when appropriate, used with the client to show progress. Graphing enables the worker to quickly examine and assess changes in the data. In addition, examining the data allows the worker to describe the desired outcomes regarding realistic and achievable possibilities as indicated by the baseline data. Client agreement to the problem, outcomes, and contingencies involved is affirmed prior to intervention.

Selecting Intervention Procedures

Intervention procedures are chosen from a range of the behavioral techniques described in Chapter Two. Those relevant for use with individuals are reinforcement-based, punishment, and contracting techniques; they are described in this section as they pertain to the practitioner's use of direct influence and the client's self-management approach.

Many problem behaviors can be altered by either a direct influence or a self-management approach. For instance, increasing child attention and compliance behavior has frequently been accomplished via direct influence. Alternatively, a self-management approach can be used if the child is interested in changing compliance behavior.

The worker's task is to choose either a direct influence or a self-management approach, by performing the contingency assessment described earlier. In addition to analyzing access, control, type of client, and client-worker skills and motivation, the worker also assesses the appropriateness of specific behavior change strategies and the probability of generality of intervention.

Selecting Specific Techniques. From functional analyses, the worker assesses possible interventions and the degree to which the worker or the client can best use specific behavioral techniques to achieve desired change.

Reinforcement-Based Techniques. Reinforcement-based techniques have been shown to effectively alter a wide variety of behaviors. An important aspect of the applied behavioral model of social work practice is emphasis upon increasing the client's general level of reinforcement. Reinforcement-based procedures are used whenever an *increase* of a behavior is desired.

In the direct influence approach, the worker, in face-to-face contact, intervenes on identified problems by rearranging existing contingency relationships in the client's environment. When the targeted problem is a behavioral deficit, the worker attempts to increase the behavior by providing reinforcers or removing punishers that result in a low rate of behavior. If the behavior of interest occurs in excess, reinforcers are removed, with the intent of decreasing the behavior. The worker may also choose to alter the occurrence of discriminative stimuli (stimulus control of antecedent conditions). To accomplish behavioral change with reinforcement-based procedures, the practitioner can implement differential attention, token and point systems, new opportunities for reinforcement, or cueing and reinforcement singly or in combination.

Differential attention is reinforcing desirable behaviors and ignoring undesirable behaviors. The worker, having considerable access and control in the interview, is able to provide praise or physical attention for appropriate behavior while ignoring undesirable or incompatible behavior. Differential attention is basic to most interventions in the direct influence approach.

> John, who makes bizarre noises, is referred to the worker for intervention. The worker, while interacting with John, attends to and praises all appropriate child responses and ignores, by turning away, all bizarre noises.

Token and point systems can also be used in the direct influence approach (Kazdin, 1977). In these systems, tokens and points are presented following a specified desired behavior. Later, the client may exchange the tokens or points for backup reinforcers. For example, a worker who wants to increase a child's time participating in social interaction may give the child a token for each fifteen-minute interval of participation. Later, the child may "spend" the token on a desired reward selected from a menu.

Workers also increase an individual's opportunities for reinforcement. In many instances, clients exhibit problem behavior or fail to emit any behavior when they have limited opportunity to receive reinforcement. In the direct influence approach, the worker provides opportunities for reinforcement by supplying the client with the opportunity to emit behaviors. These behaviors are either punished or reinforced.

Finally, in many cases individuals possess the behaviors in their repertoire but do not know when to emit them. By cueing, through prompts, and by reinforcing the desired behavior after it occurs, the worker is able to teach the client to discriminate when it is and is not appropriate to behave a certain way.

In the self-management approach, the worker primarily uses differential attention, cueing, and reinforcement as intervention techniques to teach the client the skills necessary to intervene in personal behavior that occurs beyond worker access and control. The procedure for implementing differential attention and cueing is described later in the "Client Education" section.

Clients can implement reinforcement techniques for themselves in self-management procedures. Clients reward themselves with some desired behavior, such as watching TV, or tangible reinforcers, such as food, following the performance of the desired behavior (Watson and Tharp, 1972). The worker's task is to assess, determine, and teach the client, when, where, and how to deliver the reinforcement.

Punishment-Based Techniques. Punishment-based techniques are used whenever a *decrease* of the frequency, duration, intensity, or latency of a behavior is desired. There are three general guidelines for using punishment-based techniques. (1) Whenever possible, do not use punishment. It is preferable to increase the reinforcement rather than punishment in a client's life. (2) Whenever punishment for undesired behavior is used, pair it with reinforcement for desired behavior. (3) Whenever punishers are used, there must be no access to escape or avoid the stimuli or the efficacy of the punishment will be diminished. As with all behavioral procedures, to be effective, punishment must be administered contingently and consistently.

In the direct influence approach, the three general punishment-based techniques are positive punishment, time-out, and response cost. These methods are fully described in Chapter Two but are briefly covered now as they pertain to intervention with individuals.

Positive punishment is the presentation of an aversive stimulus contingent upon the occurrence of the undesired behavior. Positive punishment is often used, probably too often; examples are spanking, hitting, or yelling at an individual following undesired behavior. There are several potentially undesirable side effects of positive punishment: If the technique is used too frequently, the aversive qualities of the stimuli may lose some potency and the intensity of the stimuli thus has to be increased. Also, if positive punishment is not used consistently and contingently, the desired behavior may decrease. Positive punishment requires the possession of extensive control over the client's environment. It is used in the direct influence approach when worker control is high and the behaviors are potentially destructive to clients or others.

Time-out is removing the client from a reinforcing environment. For example, the worker might place a child in the corner for three minutes contingent upon the occurrence of out-of-seat behavior. Time limits for time-out should be kept to a minimum. In this technique, usually implemented with children, the period of time necessary may vary with age; one minute of time-out for each year of age is generally adequate.

Response cost is removing a privilege, reward, or reinforcer contingent upon emission of the undesired behavior. For instance, Harvey, whom the worker has reinforced with tokens for appropriate greeting responses, loses one token for each inappropriate response. In the direct influence approach, response cost is usually implemented when a token economy or point system is used. Response cost requires considerable access and control over positive reinforcers. This control is usually limited to the worker's creativity and the agency's resources. Token economies or point systems are the easiest ways to implement response cost.

When implementing the self-management approach, punishment-based techniques are rarely used for two reasons. First, clients are the primary change agents and are unlikely to punish themselves. Second, the worker has little access to or control over the behavior and little ability to prevent avoidance or escape from punishing stimuli.

Contingency Contracts. Contingency contracts are oral or written agreements between the client and worker that specify the relationship between behaviors and their consequences (Homme and others, 1969).

Contingency contracts are rarely used in the direct influence approach because the client is not likely to play an active part in assessment or intervention. The negotiation behavior required in contracting does not lend itself to the direct influence approach. When contingency contracts are used, they stipulate worker and client responsibilities and provide a clear structure for presenting reinforcement.

Contracting is used two ways in the self-management approach. First, a contract is established with the worker to present reinforcers to the client contingent upon desired behaviors:

> Ms. Grap has agreed to wanting to lose twenty pounds within twenty weeks. To provide her with reinforcement, Ms. Grap has placed in the worker's hands one hundred dollars. Contingent upon each pound loss, the worker returns five dollars to Ms. Grap.

Second, the worker teaches contingency contracting skills to clients who will establish those contracts with others in their environment:

> Mr. Brag's goal is to increase the amount of relaxation time with his wife during the week. When Mr. Brag attempted this, his wife was unreceptive in altering her schedule to fit his. Mr. Brag was taught how to contract with his wife to increase his opportunity for weekly relaxation time with her.

Modeling is used in both the direct influence and self-management approaches whenever new skills are desired. Modeling often is presented with behavioral rehearsal. Modeling is the worker demonstrating the desired behavior; behavior rehearsal is the client demonstrating the behavior as modeled by the worker (see Chapters Two and Four). Modeling gives the client an example of what the desired behavior should look like, and, when used with behavior rehearsal, enhances access to positive reinforcement. Feedback is used to shape and refine the desired behavior.

Modeling is extremely important in the self-management approach. Because the emphasis of worker intervention in the self-management approach is training clients to use skills necessary for them to intervene in their own behaviors, modeling-based techniques are essential. These methods are described more thoroughly in the "Client Education" section.

Intervention Packages. In most cases, behavioral intervention does not consist of a single procedure or technique but a "package" of techniques. For example, in a direct influence approach, Moses and Pinkston (Practice Illustration 6.3) used instruction, differential reinforcement, and social and token reinforcers to increase desired play behaviors and decrease undesired play behaviors. The Mallon-Wenzel and others study (Practice Illustration 6.2) used prompts and differential attention in a variant of a self-management approach to train in-session negotiation skills. These negotiation skills were carried out at home.

Generality. A final consideration when selecting intervention procedures is generality. In particular, the choice of approach and specific techniques is affected by the programming requirements necessary to maintain behavioral changes. Whether a direct influence or a self-management approach is used, maintenance *must* be programmed because the worker is not part of the client's natural environment.

Generality is an important concern because even though a behavior might be altered by either a direct influence or a self-management approach, the selection of a self-management approach may increase the probability of changes being maintained. Self-management tends to have a somewhat higher probability of maintenance than does direct influence by the practitioner because the learning of new behaviors is under the client's control. Despite this fact and because self-management behaviors are learned, issues of maintenance beyond worker-client contact are planned (see Chapter Eight).

The major aspects of contingency analysis for choosing an approach are summarized in Figure 6.2.

Figure 6.2. Outline of Aspects of Conducting a Contingency Analysis to Choose a Behavioral Intervention.

1. *Access*
   a. Who has access to the behavioral contingencies?
   b. Where does the behavior occur/not occur?
   c. When does the behavior occur/not occur?
   d. How often does the behavior occur?
2. *Control*
   a. Who has control over contingencies—worker, client, or "other"?
   b. What kinds of control exist—types of reinforcers, punishers?
   c. How much control exists—ability to deprive; is escape or avoidance behavior possible, and so on?
3. *Type of behaviors identified*
   a. What is the behavior being referred for?
      (1) Topographically (descriptively)
      (2) Functionally
   b. What is the definition of desirable outcome?
      (1) What will be different following intervention?
      (2) How will client view own behavior as result of intervention?
      (3) How will others view behavior as result of intervention?
4. *Type of client identified*
   a. There are two general types of identified clients:
      (1) Clients who "voluntarily" come for service and recognize and verbally state that there are problematic aspects to their behavioral functioning
      (2) Clients who are identified by others as possessing problematic aspects of their behavioral functioning
   b. It is important to understand who views behaviors as dysfunctional or in need of modification.
5. *Motivation*
   a. What skills do the worker and client need to possess to effect change?
   b. What skills do the worker and client possess?
   c. What is client motivation-commitment?
   d. What agency or community resources do the worker or client need to possess to effect change?
   e. What resources exist and are available?
6. *Type of intervention*
   a. What kinds of intervention methods based on the topographical/functional analysis appear to be useful—that is, is the intervention one the client should or would have to employ, or is it possible for the worker to implement it?
   b. Where would be the best possible environment for the intervention to occur?

Making Choices. After performing the contingency analysis, the worker chooses an approach. Although there are no formalized rules for choosing approaches, following are six basic guidelines:

1. If, based on the assessment of client, problem, and intervention, access and control are limited, a direct influence approach is likely to less effectively produce change than self-management.
2. When the client is not voluntary and verbalizes low motivation, self-management or combined approaches are difficult to implement.
3. When access and control are high, a direct influence approach can be effectively used. Generality, type of behaviors targeted, appropriate techniques, motivation, and capabilities must then be considered when deciding which approach is most appropriate.
4. If clients' repertoires lack the basic components necessary for self-management, the direct influence approach is more productive.
5. If at all possible, a combined or self-management approach is used to enhance generality.
6. The self-management and combined approaches are particularly suitable for habit and skill disorders.

It should be clear that these aspects of the assessment are not independent but highly interrelated. It is important that the worker make a careful assessment to increase the likelihood and maintenance of behavioral change.

Implementing Intervention

Client Education. Training clients is an important part of any behavioral program. When the practitioner uses direct influence, client education is minimum; the client is a recipient of the intervention programming, and training exists to the extent that new behaviors are shaped by worker activities. In the self-management approach, client education is important because the client applies the behavioral techniques independent of the worker. This section addresses client education for the self-management approach.

The client is taught to understand and analyze a problem behavior by examining antecedent stimuli and contingency relationships between the environment and the behavior, monitoring the behaviors, identifying a desired outcome to be achieved regarding behavioral decrease or increase, implementing an intervention technique, and evaluating the results of the desired outcome.

After problem behaviors have been identified, the client is trained in data collection. Data-collection methods are likely to be new to clients and should be kept relatively simple for them to implement. The most successful data-collection methods place on clients relatively few response requirements that interfere with their normal functioning. Once data collection has been taught, the client rehearses the procedures with the worker, implements the procedures, and monitors data throughout intervention.

The client is next taught to implement an intervention. Following problem assessment, self-recording, and the determination of desirable outcome, clients are taught to modify the frequency, intensity, duration, or latency of behavioral responses previously agreed upon as problematic. The worker and client select an intervention, use the behavioral techniques, and evaluate change in an ongoing manner.

The choice of specific behavioral procedures is based on data obtained through self-recording and the desirable outcome selected. The goal of intervention is to achieve the desired outcome while enhancing reinforcement and minimizing punishment existing in the client's environment.

General intervention goals are to develop skills the client lacks and to alter antecedent conditions that affect the occurrence of positive and adaptive behaviors. To achieve these general intervention goals, absent behaviors are shaped, inappropriate behaviors are reduced and replaced with more desirable or effective behaviors, and environmental manipulation is used to alter antecedent conditions.

A characteristic of intervention in this approach is the use of self-care, social-skills, and anxiety-management training packages. Often these packages are implemented by using prompts, modeling, behavioral rehearsal, feedback, and social reinforcement. Various formal packages have been developed, such as pain control and social-skills training, but informal programs tend to follow the same format of teaching skills, shaping, and reinforcement for proximate and terminal behaviors. The worker's tasks are to teach the elements of the programs and shape behaviors. After the client has learned the skills, the worker serves as a consultant, providing feedback to the client and refining and sharpening the skills learned.

In interviews with the client, the worker uses reinforcement and extinction procedures to shape the behaviors. On the other hand, strong punishers are rarely used because of the likelihood of client avoidance or escape behavior.

When the worker is attempting to educate or train a client, pieces of information about the specific behavioral skill requirements are presented. Initial (or simpler) elements of the skill are first modeled. The client rehearses the behaviors, and appropriate behaviors are reinforced; inappropriate behaviors are corrected or ignored. Closer and closer successive approximations of the terminal desired behavior are reinforced. For desired behaviors to be effectively shaped, appropriate approximations must be reinforced until the terminal behavior is successfully presented over a period of time. The terminal behavior and refinements are then variably reinforced.

An excellent outline of the components involved in shaping desired behaviors in skill training or habit alteration was developed by the creators of Achievement Place, a behavioral group home for adolescent predelinquents. These components, modified, are presented in Figure 6.3.

Finally, the client is taught to understand and evaluate data collected, to assess whether desired outcomes have been achieved, and to evaluate the efficacy of the interventions. The following section presents useful methods for evaluating intervention.

Figure 6.3. Components of Teaching Interactions.

---

1. *Initial presentation*
   a. Describe the desired/appropriate behavior
   b. Rationale for the desired/appropriate behavior
      (1) Description of consequences of inappropriate behaviors
      (2) Description of consequences of appropriate behaviors
2. *Practice*
   a. Practitioner modeling
   b. Practitioner prompts client behavior
   c. Client rehearsal
3. *Refinement*
   a. Feedback during practice
      (1) Praise for what has been accomplished
      (2) Correction of inappropriate client behaviors, *or*
      (3) Ignore inappropriate client behaviors
   b. Practitioner modeling (optional)
   c. Practitioner prompts client behaviors
   d. Request for client acknowledgment of required behaviors
   e. Client practice
   f. Praise for what has been accomplished
   g. Repeat steps a to g of refinement as necessary.

Source: Adapted from E. L. Phillips, D. L. Fixsen, and M. M. Wolf, *The Teaching Family Handbook.* Lawrence: Bureau of Child Research, University of Kansas, 1972, pp. 12-14.

Evaluation

Intervention evaluation methods useful for behavioral intervention with individuals were described and discussed in Chapter Three. Essentially, evaluation enables the worker or client to assess (1) whether desired outcomes were achieved, (2) the efficacy of the intervention technique used, and (3) the ability of the change agent to implement the technique. An overall general evaluation goal is to provide systematic feedback to the client and the worker.

The data used for evaluation are initially collected during the assessment phase. They may be observational data (from an independent observer or a client's self-report, or worker-collected) or data collected from instrumentation. These data are examined by using experimental designs, which enable the worker to assess to varying degrees what is causing the obtained changes. Single-subject designs (Hersen and Barlow, 1976; Jayaratne and Levy, 1979) are typically used.

In the direct influence approach, the worker's tasks are data collection, monitoring, and evaluating intervention. The worker uses single-subject designs (presented in Chapter Three) to evaluate the efficacy of intervention. Because worker control is considerable, the practitioner is able to choose from any design, including ABAB and multiple-baseline. The worker selects the design that gives the most information about what caused the changes observed and that is consistent with agency values and resources, the problem behavior, the needs of the setting, and the time available for intervention.

In the self-management approach, evaluation of intervention is an inherent part of the approach and is taught to the client early in the behavioral program. Client self-evaluation occurs contiguous with intervention implementation. Clients are taught to evaluate change in their behavioral performance by comparing postintervention performance to an earlier level of performance.

Self-evaluation is an ongoing process that occurs during intervention and lasts until worker-client termination. Various aspects of the intervention are evaluated: changes in behavior, the appropriateness of previously established desirable outcomes, and the effectiveness of the intervention techniques. Self-evaluation is necessary for the client to determine whether desired changes in problem behaviors have occurred. If the desirable outcomes are established in behaviorally specific terms, the worker and client are easily able to ascertain the intervention's success.

Data evaluation, based on self-reports, can be used to evaluate the appropriateness of the desirable outcome. Possibly the desirable outcomes previously established were too ambitious or inappropriate, given contingencies that exist in the client's normal environment, in which case the client and the worker then reassess and adjust the desirable outcome.

Finally, self-evaluation provides information about the effectiveness of the implemented intervention. Effectiveness of training is determined by the extent to which a causal relationship is established between techniques used and results obtained. The most effective way to evaluate this relationship is to use single-case experimental designs. Three designs are particularly suitable for evaluating the effects of self-management or combined approaches (see also Chapter Three).

The AB design allows determination of whether changes occurred but not whether the intervention was responsible for the results. Sometimes only a limited evaluation of change is possible because agency policies limit time or number of contacts. Occasionally, a worker wants to examine multiple aspects of intervention, such as training, under various setting conditions. This results in an $AB^1B^2B^3$ design, in which little experimental control is present, and the design's ability to isolate effective components is limited. Yet, when training occurs under a variety of conditions, it is important to examine whether change occurred consistently. In Mallon-Wenzel and others study (Practice Illustration 6.2), various aspects of negotiation skills were evaluated: baseline (B^1) training in session with simulated conflicts, negotiations (B^2) of conflict subjects developed in session for home practice, and unstructured home negotiation (B^3). The authors were able to examine whether negotiation changes occurred in simulated conflicts at the agency, the subject's structured negotiation at home, and unstructured negotiation at home.

A second design especially suitable for assessing self-management and combined approaches is multiple baseline. Intervention across two or more behaviors, settings, or individuals is used to demonstrate causality (Kratochwill, 1978). Baselines on two or more behavior settings or clients begin simultaneously, but an intervention is implemented at different times. Causality is established when changes occur contiguously with the implementation of interventions at the different times. In the McCabe and others study (Practice Illustration 6.1), a multiple-baseline-across-behaviors design was used to examine the effects of social-skills training. Three target behaviors were defined—eye contact, loudness of speech, upper body relaxation—and baselines taken on them. Training was sequentially implemented at various times across each behavior. The results showed changes in each behavior when social-skills training was implemented, which suggests that the training was responsible for the observed changes. The multiple-baseline design is particularly useful when several clients can be trained, over several behaviors, or under a variety of settings.

The third design useful for examining the efficacy of training in the self-management approach is changing criterion. Various predetermined levels of desirable outcomes are established; generally, these goals are to occur at equal time periods and be separated by an equal interval from one another. Causality is then determined if the successful criteria are established when predicted. This design is particularly suitable for change in various kinds of habit disorders, such as amount of calories eaten, number of cigarettes smoked, or amount of time spent studying.

> Walter wanted to decrease the number of cigarettes he smoked. Training designed to decrease his frequency of cigarette smoking was evaluated with a changing-criterion design. If, during baseline, Walter smoked on the average fifty cigarettes per day over a week-long period, level of desirable outcome over a week might be fifty, thirty, twenty, ten, and zero cigarettes on the average per day. Then, if Walter decreases smoking as predicted, the likelihood of training being responsible for the changes increases (see Hall, 1971a, pp. 27-28).

Evaluation consists of two interrelated processes: client self-evaluation and worker evaluation. An important part of self-management is the client learning to evaluate problem change. Because the primary source of data is often self-monitoring, methods for worker evaluation of intervention techniques are integrated into self-monitoring and self-evaluation. It is important to enhance client motivation for participation in more complex evaluation procedures by demonstrating that the changes observed were likely caused by the training employed combined with the client effort expended. Clients are likely to be reinforced by their own participation and successes in using the skills acquired as well as by learning skills of systematic evaluation.

Social-Skills Training for a Depressed Woman

Marcia M. McCabe, Charlotte Mallon-Wenzel,
William J. Reid, Elsie M. Pinkston

The relationship between social skills and depressive disorders may be conceptualized within a behavioral reinforcement model of depression (Lewinsohn, Biglan, and Zeiss, 1976; Lewinsohn, 1974; Ferster, 1965, 1973). Within Lewinsohn's (1974) formulation, depressive behaviors and dysphoria are viewed as elicited by low rates of response-contingent positive reinforcement. Such low rates of reinforcement may occur because reinforcing events are unavailable in the individual's environment or individuals are unable to elicit reinforcers due to a lack of necessary response repertoires. Thus, an individual who has few requisite social behaviors, such as command of the language or "acceptable style," will not attain the reinforcement that would otherwise be available (Lewinsohn, Biglan, and Zeiss, 1976). Using this model, Libet and Lewinsohn (1973) defined social skill as "the complex ability both to emit behaviors which are positively or negatively reinforced and not to emit behaviors that are punished or extinguished by others" (p. 304).

The social behavior of depressed individuals is believed relevant to their treatment in two ways (Lewinsohn, Biglan, and Zeiss, 1976). First, individual complaints about various inadequacies in social relationships suggest areas for skill training. Second, problematic social relationships are related to dysphoria, and changes in social relations are associated with improved mood.

A number of studies differentiate the social behavior of depressed persons from the social behavior of "normal" persons. Libet and Lewinsohn (1973) specified differences in behavior rates, interpersonal range, rate of positive reactions, and response latency. Ekman and Friedman (1974) compared the nonverbal behavior of depressives to that of nondepressed subjects.

Behavior therapists have developed systematic procedures for remediating social-skill deficiencies (for example, see Hersen, Bellack, and Turner, 1978; Goldstein, Sprafkin, and Gershaw, 1976; Hersen and Bellack, 1978b; Hersen and others, 1975). Social-skills training generally consists of a variety of components, including behavior rehearsal, feedback, prompting, model presentation, programming of change, and homework assignments (Gambrill, 1977). Social reinforcement is also an important component (Goldstein, Sprafkin, and Gershaw, 1976).

Despite these research studies offering evidence of the efficacy of social-skills training for psychiatric patients, there are possible limitations to this intervention approach for depression because little evidence supports the contention that changes in social behavior are associated with improved mood.

This study was designed to test the efficacy of a social-skills treatment package (instructions, feedback, social reinforcement, modeling, behavior rehearsal, and homework assignments) for remediating the interpersonal skills deficits and other depressive symptoms of a nineteen-year-old depressed woman. A behavioral measure of social skill based on standardized role-played encounters and self-report measures of depression and self-esteem were used for assessing and evaluating treatment effectiveness. In addition, probes to assess generality and durability of training effects were included. A multiple-baseline-across-behaviors design was used to evaluate the controlling effects of intervention.

Method

Client. The client was a nineteen-year-old woman who voluntarily sought treatment at a community mental health center in a large midwestern city. She was diagnosed by the intake worker as being neurotically depressed. Her depression was not recent in onset. A year prior to seeking treatment, she attempted suicide by ingesting large quantities of aspirin and alcohol but was taken immediately to the hospital by her boyfriend. The client's major presenting complaints, in order of priority, were (1) an inability to initiate and maintain conversations in interpersonal situations and (2) a paucity of interpersonal relationships.

The client had a tenth-grade education and was employed as a clerical worker. She lived with her boyfriend but was very dissatisfied with the quality of their relationship. She had a conflictual relationship with her divorced parents and had left home the previous year at her mother's request. She expressed particularly bitter feelings toward her father, whom she described as abusive and authoritarian in his interactions with her and other family members.

Setting. All phases of the study were conducted at the mental health center in a large "family" room, which was equipped with comfortable armchairs and a coffee table. The room was arranged to facilitate interaction and videotaping. A studio-quality videotape recorder was set up in the same room to record interaction during all phases of the study. The researcher-practitioner operated the recording equipment and provided the treatment.

Measures. A behavioral measure of social skill based on role-played encounters and two self-report measures—one of depression and one of self-esteem—were used for assessing and evaluating treatment efficacy.

Previous research has demonstrated that deficits in social skill can be identified according to role-played responses to a series of standard interpersonal situations, such as the Behavioral Assertive Test (Eisler, Miller, and Hersen, 1973) and the Behavioral Assertiveness Test, Revised (Eisler and others, 1975). Ten role-played scenes, developed by adapting and revising nine scenes from the Behavioral Assertiveness Test, Revised and by creating one new scene using the same format, were one dependent measure of the study. These scenes were composed of various interpersonal situations that the subject identified as problematic in her natural environment. The scenes described situations at home with her boyfriend, at work involving her boss and/or coworker, in social situations involving peers, and in public or consumer situations. For each situation, at least one scene en-

tailed positive interaction, and at least one scene entailed negative interaction, as illustrated:

> *Narrator:* You and your boyfriend are at a party
> given by one of his coworkers. Although you don't
> know anyone else who has been invited, you have
> been looking forward to meeting some of his
> friends from work and you have bought a new
> dress for the occasion. Your boyfriend introduces
> you to one of his female coworkers and then leaves
> to get refreshments for the three of you.
>
> *Role model prompt:* "I really like your dress! The
> color is perfect for you."
>
> *Narrator:* You are in the middle of watching a very
> good movie on TV. Your boyfriend walks in and
> changes the channel, as he does every time you are
> watching a good movie.
>
> *Role model prompt:* "Let's watch the football game
> instead. It should really be a good game."

In an attempt to increase the validity of the role-playing
test, the scenes were constructed to include as much detail as
possible. This strategy was adopted in light of observations (Bellack and Hersen, in press) that brief descriptions apparently
required the subject to provide personal qualifications and critical details. As a result, the subject either became anxious and/or
responded to an idiosyncratically created scene.

In a further attempt to elicit more representative behavior patterns, the trainer extended the interaction by offering up
to three counterresponses in each situation. Although this strategy was suggested (Bellack and Hersen, in press), it had not
been empirically tested.

The role-played encounters during each session of each
phase of the study were videotaped. The client's videotaped responses to the ten scenes presented during each of the three initial baseline sessions were analyzed to assess social-skills deficits.
The practitioner and an independent observer with extensive ex-

perience in behavioral analysis were the judges in this qualitative assessment. Three behaviors judged by both observers to be the most detrimental to effective interpersonal functioning were targeted for modification.

The target behaviors were defined and scored as follows:

Eye contact. The client's facial gaze should be directed toward her partner's face, with her eyes focused between the top of the partner's head and chin. The client's eye contact with the interpersonal partner was recorded in seconds from the beginning of the prompt to the end of the role-playing scene for every scene. Duration of occurrence, that is, the total length of occurrence of the behavior as a proportion of the total observation time, was determined for each session by the following calculation:

$$\frac{\text{Time of behavior}}{\text{Time of observation}} \times 100 =$$

Loudness of speech. This is the volume of the client's voice when she is speaking. The client's voice volume for each scene was determined by recording the highest volume level reached as indicated on an Ampex Corporation audiometer, which measures sound-pressure level. The scale on this meter was graduated in units of five, with an approximate range from zero to eighty. The subject's score for each session was obtained by determining the mean value over all the scenes for each session.

Upper body relaxation. The posture of the upper body should be erect, with arms and hands in a comfortable position and movement of any part of the upper body congruent with and/or supplementing verbal content. Upper body relaxation was recorded on an occurrence or nonoccurrence basis for each scene from the beginning of the prompt to the end of the role-playing scene. The client's score for each session was obtained by calculating the percentage of scenes in which the behavior occurred according to the following formula:

$$\frac{\text{Number of scenes in which behavior occurred}}{\text{Total number of scenes per session}} \times 100 =$$

Behavior during the role-playing scenes in each session of each phase of the study was observed and recorded from videotapes based on the definitions and recording procedures just described. The tapes were coded in their entirety. The practitioner, serving as the first judge, coded all thirteen tapes. The other judge randomly coded five of the tapes—one from each phase of the experiment—without prior knowledge of the experimental phase.

Self-Report Measures. In addition to the behavioral measure of social skill, two self-report measures were used. Self-report data were collected during the initial baseline phase to assess the magnitude of the client's depression and the degree to which she was experiencing a problem with self-esteem. These data were collected during the treatment and follow-up phases to determine the efficacy of the treatment package in alleviating manifestations of the depressive syndrome other than deficits in social skill. The self-report measures used in the study were:

> *Generalized Contentment Scale* (GCS)—measures "the degree or magnitude of non-psychotic depression" (Hudson, 1977, p. 2).

> *Index of Self-Esteem* (ISE)—measures "the degree or magnitude of a problem the client has with the evaluative component of self-concept" (Hudson, 1977, pp. 2-3).

> Each scale consists of twenty-five items, which include both positively and negatively worded items to control, at least partially, for the effect of

response-set biases. The score on each scale has a possible range from 1 to 100. Each scale has a clinical cutting score of thirty, which indicates that persons who score above thirty have a problem in the domain being measured and those who score below thirty do not have a problem.

Procedure. After a series of interviews in which a problem and the client's situation were thoroughly explored and assessed (see Chapter Three), the practitioner suggested that the client participate in the social-skills training program. The program's research nature and potential benefits regarding increasing interpersonal skills were explained to the client.

A multiple-baseline-across-behaviors design was used to evaluate the intervention. The study began with three sessions of baseline assessment. The initial baseline phase was followed by nine sessions of social-skills training. Probes for generality were conducted during the third baseline session and during the last training session. A follow-up session was conducted approximately two weeks after training concluded.

Baseline Assessment. The initial baseline phase consisted of three sessions extending over a three-week period. During this phase, the self-report measures were administered prior to the behavioral measure of the first and second baseline sessions. All ten role-playing scenes were administered in each of the three sessions.

The first baseline session began with a reiteration of the purpose of the training, administration of the self-report measures, and instructions regarding the role-playing scenes. After the client completed the self-report measures, the practitioner seated herself next to the client and gave the following instructions:

> The purpose of what we are going to do is to find out how you react to some everyday situations in which you might be involved. You should try to respond as if you were really in that situation at home, at work, at a store, or in any other setting described. I will describe some situations in

which you might find yourself with your boyfriend, your coworkers, your friends, or some other person. I will pretend to be the person that you are talking to in each of the situations so that it will be easier for you to imagine that you are really there. For example, after I have described a situation, I will say something to you. After I speak, I want you to say exactly what you would have said if you were really in this situation. Then we will continue to talk to each other as if we were actually involved in the described situation.

Let's practice two scenes so that you can get a better idea of what I'm talking about.

At this point, the practitioner narrated a practice scene. If the client appeared to understand the instructions and responded appropriately, the probe session proceeded as follows: (1) the practitioner presented a scene; (2) the practitioner delivered a standard prompt; (3) the client responded to the practitioner; and (4) the practitioner made another comment to which the client responded and so forth until no more than three counterresponses were made by the practitioner. This process was repeated for each of the ten randomly presented scenes. Subsequent sessions of the initial baseline phase were similarly conducted, without repeating the instructions and the practice scenes.

Training. Following three sessions of baseline assessment, social-skills training was conducted during sessions 4 through 12. These sessions were scheduled twice weekly and extended over a six-week period. Each session lasted approximately sixty minutes.

During the training phase, the self-report measures were administered at the beginning of sessions 5, 8, and 11 and at the end of session 12.

In keeping with a multiple-baseline-across-behaviors design, training was applied sequentially and cumulatively to the three target behaviors over the total training period. Specifically, during sessions 4 through 6, the subject received training directed toward increasing the duration of her eye contact with her interpersonal partner. During sessions 7 through 9, the primary focus was increasing the loudness of her voice, with a continuing focus on maintaining increased eye contact. During sessions 10 through 12, the primary focus was increasing the degree of upper body relaxation, with continuing attention directed toward maintaining improvements in the first two behaviors.

Training consisted of three components: preexercise, training in the role-playing scenes, and tasks to be completed in the client's natural environment. Three preexercises relevant to the three target behaviors were developed and conducted prior to training in the role-playing scenes. Only the exercise pertinent to the target behavior for the session was conducted. The exercises were about five to seven minutes long. The format of each exercise was designed in the following way:

> *Eye contact.* This exercise consisted of practice in staring at the interpersonal partner—during conversation and in silence. Each staring period was timed on a stopwatch, with the goal of increasing the length of staring behavior.

> *Loudness of speech.* This exercise consisted of practice in speaking at various levels of volume, ranging from whispering to shouting. The practitioner modeled the behavior and then the client attempted to replicate it. The goal was to help the client differentiate between various levels of volume and to increase the loudness of her voice.

> *Upper body relaxation.* This exercise involved paced deep breathing, with instructions to relax arms and shoulders.

The client was trained by using ten role-playing scenes presented randomly throughout the project assessment and training phases. Social-skills training specifically consisted of the following ten components:

1. The practitioner described one of the role-playing scenes and then delivered a standard prompt.
2. The client responded to the practitioner.

3. The practitioner made another comment to which the client responded and so forth until no more than three counterresponses were made by the practitioner.
4. The practitioner gave the client feedback on her performance with reference to the specific target behavior. The goals of this activity were to provide feedback to the client about her performance and to suggest ways she might effectively use this skill in real life.
5. The practitioner provided social praise contingent upon the quality of the client's performance. Although reinforcement was provided for close approximations, no reinforcement was offered when the role playing departed significantly from minimal performance standards, aside from encouragement for "trying" in early sessions. When the focus of training shifted from the first target behavior to the second and from the second to the third, praise for the prior behavior was provided intermittently.
6. The practitioner then modeled responses with specific attention to the target behavior.
7. The practitioner gave specific instructions concerning the target behavior, followed by a repetition of the role playing.
8. Rehearsal continued for a scene until the practitioner was satisfied that the criterion for that target behavior had been reached.
9. Training then advanced to the next interpersonal situation.
10. The same procedure was followed through all training scenes.

The last component of training involved tasks to be carried out in the client's natural environment. At the end of each session, the practitioner and the client formulated and agreed on a task(s) relevant to the skill being trained. The client's success in completing the task(s) was discussed at the beginning of the next session.

Generality Probes. Two probes for generality were conducted—one during the third baseline session and one during the twelfth training session. These probes consisted of brief (about five minutes each), informal interactions between the subject and a male staff member. Prior to the probes, the practitioner obtained the client's permission. The practitioner suggested that these interactions would provide the opportunity to practice "talking" with a new acquaintance. The male staff member was requested to carry on a conversation as he would when meeting a new acquaintance.

When the probes were conducted, no formal instructions were given to either participant regarding the content of their conversation. The practitioner introduced them, suggested that they talk together for five to ten minutes, and then left the room. The probe ended when the practitioner returned, at which time she asked them to finish.

Follow-Up. When training in the three target behaviors was completed, arrangements were made for a follow-up session about two weeks later. The content of this session was similar to that used during baseline. The ten role-playing scenes used throughout all the experimental phases were presented. Following the presentation of these scenes, the practitioner discussed the program's nature and results with the client. The client expressed her satisfaction with the program.

Results

Interrater reliabilities were obtained for the five video-taped sessions rated by both judges. Ratings of the three target behaviors were made during each role-playing scene for these sessions. Pearson product-moment correlations were calculated for the duration of eye contact and highest level of voice volume. The correlation coefficient for each eye contact observation was .99; the correlation coefficients for voice-volume observations ranged from .90 to .99. Dividing the total number of agreements by the total number of judgments and multiplying by 100, 100 percent agreement was calculated for each observation of upper body relaxation.

The results of training on the nonverbal components of behavior are presented in Figure 1. Data are summarized across scenes for each session. The sequential introduction of treat-

Figure 1. Multiple-Baseline Analysis of the Effects of Social Skills
Training on Nonverbal Components of Behavior.

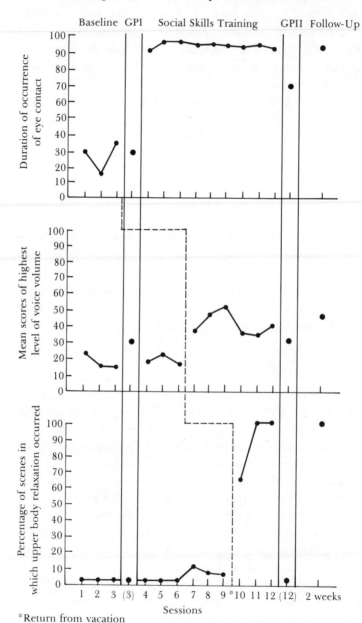

*Return from vacation

ment for eye contact, loudness of speech, and upper body relaxation resulted in sequential and marked increases over baseline levels.

The results of training for eye contact indicate marked and rapid improvement. The change in level between baseline and treatment phases is abrupt and reflects a 54 percent increase between the last baseline session and the first treatment session. The treatment-phase data were stable, following variable baseline data. The abrupt change in level and the stable treatment-phase data are convincing evidence that changes were a function of treatment despite a variable baseline. Further data points during baseline might have provided an additional basis for attributing change to the effects of treatment if the baseline had stabilized or drifted in the opposite direction. The variability of the data during baseline suggests that potentially controlling variables occasionally were in effect.

Results for loudness of speech indicate that the baseline was independent in response to treatment. Introduction of treatment resulted in sequential and positive change, although improvement was less pronounced than that for the other two behaviors. The data reflect a change in level (that is, a twenty-one-point score increase between the sixth and seventh sessions) without overlapping scores between baseline and treatment phases, suggesting the achievement of a degree of experimental control. However, variability within the treatment phase somewhat weakens evidence of the controlling effects of treatment. The upward trend of the first three data points is reversed by the fourth and fifth data points. The final data point ascends. This variability suggests occasional control attributable to extraneous variables. In fact, the reversal of the upward trend coincided with the subject's return from a one-week vacation.

The results for upper body relaxation indicate a positive and rapid change in behavior. The change in level between baseline and treatment phases is reflected by a 57 percent increase between the last baseline session and the first treatment session, which suggests that changes were a function of treatment. Initial baseline observations showed zero occurrence of the behavior. During the seventh through ninth baseline sessions, a minor increase in this behavior occurred that paralleled the introduction of the voice-volume treatment. However, the magnitude of these changes is extremely minimal (less than 7 percent), which suggests both clinical and statistical insignificance, particularly when compared to the dramatic increases that occurred when treatment was introduced for upper body relaxation. The abrupt increase following introduction of treatment appeared to stabilize at 100 percent occurrence of the behavior by the end of treatment.

Generality data indicate that the effects of training generalized to an unstructured interpersonal situation for eye contact. The data reflect a milder degree of generality for loudness of voice and none for upper body relaxation. For duration of eye contact, an increase of 41 percent occurred between the probe conducted during the last baseline session and the one conducted during the last treatment session. The percentage of eye-contact duration was higher during the second unstructured situation than during baseline sessions using role-playing scenes, but it did not reach the level obtained during treatment sessions using role-playing scenes. Identical scores were obtained for loudness of voice during the two generality probes. These scores fell between those obtained during baseline and treatment phases (that is, eleven points higher than the average baseline score and eleven points lower than the average treatment-phase score). Generality data reflect zero occurrence of upper body relaxation during both probes, indicating that training effects failed to generalize.

Changes on all three behaviors were maintained at follow-up. Follow-up data indicate that eye contact was maintained at a level exceeding 90 percent occurrence. At follow-up, the score for loudness of voice increased about seven points over the last treatment session and reached a level slightly higher than the average score for sessions 7 through 9. Follow-up data for upper body relaxation indicate maintenance of the behavior at 100 percent occurrence.

The client's scores over time on the General Contentment Scale (GCS) and the Index of Self-Esteem (ISE) are displayed in Figure 2. A fairly steady decrease over time in both the magni-

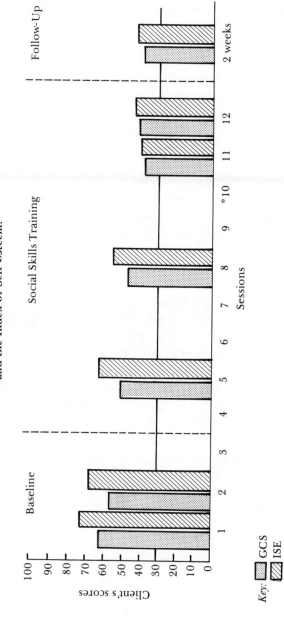

Figure 2. The Clients' Scores on the General Contentment Scale and the Index of Self-Esteem.

Key: GCS
ISE

Clinical cutting score: above 30 indicates a problem in domain measured

*Return from vacation

tude of the client's depression and the degree of her problem with self-esteem occurred throughout all phases of the study. Her score on the GCS decreased twenty-two points from the first baseline session to the last treatment session, which represents a 36 percent improvement in this area. Likewise, her score on the ISE fell thirty points from the first baseline session to the last treatment session, which represents a 42 percent improvement in this area. The self-report data indicate that the client experienced more difficulty with self-esteem issues than with depression. Initial differences in scores measuring these problems, however, were greatly reduced during the last two treatment sessions. Follow-up data indicate that improvements in problems with depression and self-esteem were maintained two weeks after the treatment was completed. The client's scores on these measures never fell below the clinical cutting score.

Overall, results of the self-report measures reflect a positive trend, although they are not clear-cut evidence for identifying the treatment procedure as the major change agent. Scores on the self-report measures administered during the first and second baseline sessions indicated a decrease similar in magnitude to those which occurred after treatment was introduced, suggesting some controlling effects of extraneous variables. In addition, the largest reduction in scores on both measures occurred when the measures were administered the week following the client's return from vacation. This factor may partially explain the magnitude of these reductions (decrease of nine points on the GCS and fifteen points on the ISE) because similar reductions did not occur during the administration of the measures over similar time lapses (average decrease of five points on GCS and six and a half points on ISE).

Discussion

This practice-research effort suggests the effectiveness of social-skills training for clinical social work with depression. Training led to marked improvements in the nonverbal components of the client's interpersonal skill. These improvements were accompanied by a steady decrease in the magnitude of the client's depression and in the degree of her problem with self-esteem.

Although treatment procedures did not focus specifically on altering depressive symptoms, such as dysphoric mood, negative expectations, and low self-evaluation, self-report data suggest improvement in these areas. A relatively steady decrease in scores on the GCS and ISE occurred throughout all phases of the study, which reflects a positive trend, although reduction of depression and problems with self-esteem appeared to be influenced by factors in addition to treatment procedures. The steady decrease over time in the magnitude of depression and the degree of self-esteem problems was accelerated between the fourth and fifth administrations of the GCS and ISE. Self-report data were collected for the fifth time during the week following the client's vacation. Upon her return, the client expressed enthusiasm about her trip and improvements in her relationship with her boyfriend. Reinforcing events during her vacation most likely contributed to a more positive evaluation of her life and increased feelings of self-worth, as measured for the fifth time on the GCS and ISE. Thus, the slight increase in scores on the sixth administration of these measures is not surprising because the immediate effects of her vacation most likely had diminished as she returned to a more routine life-style.

Self-report data indicate that the client's problems with depression and self-esteem were reduced but not totally alleviated. Although the client verbally expressed increased satisfaction with her life in general and did not wish to continue treatment after the training program was completed, she still may have been experiencing some problems in these areas. Guidelines for interpreting data obtained from the GCS and ISE are based on normative data and thus do not account for individual differences. This limits the usefulness of these scales for drawing precise conclusions about the degree to which problems still exist.

The maintenance of both behavioral and attitudinal changes two weeks after treatment terminated is an initial indication of the stability of treatment effects. However, longer term follow-ups obviously are needed to reach more definite conclusions about the durability of change.

The partial generality of treatment effects to an informal interpersonal situation may be viewed positively, given the limitations of the structure. The probe situation was quite dissimilar to the role-playing situations used during treatment in that it was highly unstructured, required interaction with a stranger, and involved more complex response requirements. Hersen, Eisler, and Miller (1974) noted that significant transfer effects are difficult to obtain even from generality tasks closely approximating the training situation. Even so, transfer of learning from role-playing situations to an informal situation occurred for eye contact and to a much lesser extent for loudness of voice. Effects of training did not generalize for upper body relaxation. Loudness of voice was difficult to modify, and upper body relaxation requires a more complex response than a behavior like eye contact. Hersen, Eisler, and Miller (1974) found that significant generality effects are hard to obtain from behaviors that are complex and difficult to modify. To ensure transfer of learning, procedures to enhance generality should be explicitly incorporated into the training program. This might be accomplished by applying training procedures to situations that more closely approximate the subject's natural environment.

The results of this study support the behavioral reinforcement model of depression in that improvement in social skill was accompanied by a reduction in the magnitude of the client's depression and the degree of her problems with self-esteem. The client also reported increased communication and improved relationships with significant others and the formation of at least one new friendship. Future research should further investigate the relationship between social-skill improvement and the alleviation of depressive disorder. Studies should also be undertaken to systematically investigate the relationship between social-skill improvement and the quality of interpersonal relationships and the amount of social interaction.

The social-skills training program presented here is an effective and time-efficient method for treating depressed clients with problem social relationships. It demonstrates a feasible method for social workers to incorporate evaluation procedures into clinical practice because the research design and measurement techniques tend to enhance rather than detract from treatment procedures. The multiple-baseline-across-behaviors design provides for the systematic treatment of each behavior targeted for modification sequentially and cumulatively, which may be particularly valuable if the client has difficulty focusing on complex stimulus inputs (Hersen and Bellack, 1978b).

Finally, self-report measures can be integrated easily into the treatment program because they require minimal time to administer and score. The practitioner can actively involve the client in treatment evaluation and planning by discussing the use of the scales and the results (Hudson, 1977). However, the possibility of social desirability response bias and the lack of precision for assessing an individual case should be considered when interpreting data. For evaluation, other sources of information may be used in conjunction with data obtained from the scales.

More effort and commitment are required from both the practitioner and client in a treatment program that incorporates an evaluative component. However, systematic evaluation is beneficial to both participants. The practitioner is able to offer services in a highly accountable manner, and the practitioner and client can participate in planning treatment and assessing progress based on data recorded systematically over time.

Negotiation: Modification of Communication Processes

Charlotte M. Mallon-Wenzel, Marcia M. McCabe,
William J. Reid, Elsie M. Pinkston

Requests for changes in behavior are a normal part of family life (Patterson and others, 1975). If family members can talk with each other about their sources of dissatisfaction and negotiate more positive changes, problem interchanges among them may be corrected. People within the family are constantly altering their interactions over time, and each change in interaction requires other family members to adjust by also changing.

Positive changes in family interactions are defined as increasing the frequency of positive or neutral behaviors and decreasing the frequency of negative or conflictual behaviors (Gottman and others, 1978). Change does not just occur; it must be planned.

Skinner (1971) stated that all social organizations can be characterized as mutual control systems, with control being exercised on, as well as exercised by, each member of an organization. The laws of adult society can be seen as components of an explicit contract; however, explicit contracts are relatively rare at other levels of society. As a system, the family requires its members to make inferences about the nature of implied contracts. These inferences can lead to confusion about privilege and responsibility and may be related to many behavioral problems. One source of adolescent problems may be the increasing ambiguity of the roles in the family.

Two approaches to conflict have been commonly used: negotiation of conflict and modification of verbal interactions. The negotiation approach centers on behavioral contracting (Patterson, Cobb, and Ray, 1973). The worker's role is as a mediator who helps family members negotiate conflicts on a reciprocal exchange basis, for example, "If I do this, you'll promise to do that." This technique has been used successfully in both marital and parent-child conflicts (Azrin, Naster, and Jones, 1973; Stuart, 1971). Whether family members comply with these requests over an extended period of time partly determines the way the family members interact.

Kifer and others (1974) implemented this model of altering verbal interactions with predelinquent adolescents and their parents. Their program focused on teaching the adolescents and parents new behaviors more conducive to negotiation, rather than only limiting problem behavior. Three questions in their study were examined: (1) Can both parents and children concurrently be taught negotiation skills? (2) Will learning these skills contribute to solutions of conflicts that are acceptable to all involved? (3) Will these negotiation skills generalize to the home environment and improve negotiation of conflictual issues in family members' daily lives? Their data showed substantial increase (from 33 percent at baseline to 100 percent for the last three sessions) in the percent of total time subjects spent applying negotiation behaviors. Five out of eight negotiated agreements were implemented by the subjects. In the final negotiation, where the dyads negotiated their own conflicts at home, the increased use of negotiation behaviors was maintained.

In this practice illustration, the Kifer procedures were refined and evaluated. Three systematic modifications were introduced: (1) Procedures were altered by adding a phase in which the subjects wrote their own conflictual situations to negotiate at home. (2) Attitude scales were administered weekly, to collect data to determine if the subjects' attitudes toward one another improved throughout the course of treatment. (3) The implementation of negotiated agreements was monitored at home over the course of treatment.

Method

Clients and Setting. The clients were a single-parent father, Mr. S. (age fifty-five), and his teenage son, John (age eighteen), who were in family treatment at a local mental health center. Structured task-oriented treatment was progressing well for the other family members, but the subjects of this research were not improving. Negotiation training was suggested as a short-term adjunctive treatment for this dyad.

Mr. S. had a different relationship with John than with the other children still living at home. He had abused John since childhood. When the oldest son reached his late teens, conflicts between father and son increased and Mr. S. consequently threw the son out of the house. The other three children in family treatment were not in this oldest son's position, and the father did not exhibit hostile behavior toward them; in fact, he was rather permissive with them and ignored their minor rule breaking.

Two weeks before the baseline session, the social worker met with the family and therapist to explain the behavioral training. Permission was obtained from them to participate in the evaluation, and all training was conducted in an office of the mental health center.

Data Collection. All intervention sessions were tape-recorded. During phase 3, when the dyad was negotiating their own conflicts at home, a tape recorder was provided so these sessions could be taped. The clients were instructed how to use the recorder; they practiced and played it back in the last office session of phase 2. Each negotiation was limited to five minutes. All office sessions were forty-five minutes long.

Two Hudson scales were also used: *Index of Parental Attitudes* and *Child's Attitude Toward Father* (Hudson, 1977, 1981); they were completed by the clients prior to the beginning of each session.

The worker kept a cumulative list of agreements negotiated by the dyad during phase 3. The clients were asked weekly if they had implemented the agreement from the prior week. Their answer was then noted on the list, and it was stressed that agreements must be implemented.

Design. A single-case design was used to evaluate the effects of treatment and consisted of the following sequence of conditions: (A) baseline, (B^1) training in session using simulated conflicts, (B^2) home negotiations of the subjects' own conflicts that had been written in session and taken home for negotiation, (B^3) unstructured home negotiation (generality probe). No follow-up sessions after termination or maintenance were built into the program. Although it lacks experimental control, this design corrects for some of the case-study method's deficiencies because the target behavior is clearly specified and repeated measures are taken throughout the A and B phases (Hersen and Barlow, 1976). Comparison between baseline data and intervention reveal any differences; attribution of the cause of those differences is limited.

Coding. Audiotapes were coded on a ten-second occurrence/nonoccurrence of the following negotiation behaviors:

> *Complete communication.* These are statements in which the individual declares what she or he wants or thinks should happen regarding the issue being discussed and asks the other person to either reply to this statement or present an alternative view.
>
> *Identification of issues.* These are statements that specify the point of disagreement in the situation. The person may try to identify differences in positions, clear up confusion as to what the other person has said, or state what he or she understands the conflict is about.
>
> *Suggestion of options.* These statements are not a repetition of the individual's first position statement but offer a plan to ameliorate the conflict.
>
> *Positive statements.* These statements are characterized by or displaying acceptance, affirmation, or praise and reinforcement. Examples include
>
> 1. Approval/praise—positive statements that indicate approval or praise, such as praise statements.
> 2. Agreement/understanding—positive statements that indicate agreement with or an understanding of the other person's position.
>
> *Negative statements.* These statements express a

negation or refusal, indicate opposition or resistance, tend to disagree with, to contradict. Examples of negative statements are:

1. Criticism—statements that are disapproving or
    pass an unfavorable judgment, finding fault
    with the other person.
2. Bossy—domineering statements which com-
    mand or request that a person change her or
    his behavior.
3. Disagreement—verbal content that identifies
    the speaker's differing point of view with the
    previous speaker's statement.
4. Defensive remark—statements that defend one's
    position or actions or replying to another per-
    son's statement that is perceived as an attack;
    can only be a response.

Neutral statements. Neutral statements are neither
positive nor negative. Examples include

1. Question—interrogative initiations or responses
    that require an answer; attempts to obtain fac-
    tual information.
2. No response—a person does not reply to an-
    other person.
3. Talk—any verbal communication that involves
    making a suggestion and cannot be character-
    ized by some other verbal category.
4. Inappropriate response—a response not con-
    nected by content with the previous initiation.

Two independent observers coded randomly chosen sessions for each of the experiment's four phases. Interrater reliability was calculated using the occurrence-agreements formula
(see Chapter Four).

Intervention

Phase 1—Home Observation. One week prior to the in-
session training, the worker went to the clients' home for the
baseline observation. The clients were asked to identify the two

most problematic situations between them at the time (Kifer and others, 1974). Any two situations agreed upon by the clients were explored and examined.

Once there was agreement about conflict situations, the clients were asked to try to reach a conclusion acceptable to them both. They discussed each issue for five minutes without interference from the worker. At the end of each negotiation, they were generally praised by comments such as "You did a good job." The worker used a stopwatch to time each five-minute segment. The clients then attempted to negotiate the second conflict for five minutes. At the end of the second negotiation, the next appointment was scheduled.

Phase 2—Within-Session Training. In the first office session, the clients were trained to use three negotiation behaviors: complete communication, identification of issues, and suggestion of options.

The father volunteered to be trained first. Each behavior was defined and then modeled by the worker. Mr. S. then practiced the behavior with John. All three behaviors were defined, modeled, and practiced by Mr. S. before John was trained. Neither subject used all three behaviors in the first simulation. They were praised for those behaviors used and reminded to use those not employed. After Mr. S. used all three behaviors in a simulation, John was trained. Training John went more quickly because he had observed Mr. S. learn the behaviors.

When both the father and the son had learned the three behaviors, a *postsession simulation* began, which followed the same format as the *presession simulation.* They were presented with a conflictual issue and a list of possible options and consequences. They negotiated the issue by using the three negotiation behaviors. The worker praised them for their attempts.

After the initial training session, all the sessions for phase 2 used the following format:

1. *Presession simulation.* The dyad was given a conflictual, parent-child issue to discuss. The conflictual situation was verbally described by the worker, and the clients role-played this issue for five minutes.

2. *Discussion and practice.* The negotiation training model
    (SOCS—situations-options-consequences-simulations)   fol-
    lowed in this research was developed by Roosa (unpub-
    lished). The clients were given a sheet (Figure 1) describing

Figure 1. Situation, Options, and Consequences Simulation (SOCS).

Situation:	You have been working all summer and saving your money. You want to spend your money on ski equipment, and your parents want you to save it for school expenses.
Options:	1. Get angry. Tell your parents it's your money, and you'll spend it any way you please.
	2. Say, "OK, I'll do it your way."
	3. Take your money before your parents can do anything and go out and spend it.
	4. Suggest to your parents that you take half of your summer earnings to spend on ski equipment and get a part-time job after school to earn the rest of the money for skis. The other half of the money can be set aside for school expenses.
Consequences:	1. Parents will get angry.
	2. Put your money in a bank account.
	3. You are angry because it is your money, and you can't do anything with it that you want to do.
	4. Your parents say they can't trust you because you spent the money before you checked with them.
	5. Your parents agree with your compromise.

the same conflictual issue role-played in the presession simulation. The worker read the situation, chose an option,
and matched it to a consequence. The father and son alternately matched options to consequences until all were
matched. Options and consequences could be added to the
list by both clients.

Each client then chose a different option to negotiate.
They practiced the negotiation by attempting to use the
three negotiation behaviors in correct order. The worker had
a cue card listing the behaviors in order, which the clients
could refer to if they became confused. After the second
training session, the card was no longer used.

3. *Postsession simulation.* The worker did not get involved in the content of the discussion but cued the clients occasionally for the negotiation behaviors. The worker gave instructions before the simulations, observed, and announced the beginning and end of simulations. The worker also gave the clients feedback in the form of praise, such as "You tried very hard." Sessions 2 through 5 were spent learning the negotiation behaviors and practicing by using hypothetical situations.

   Phase 3—Home Negotiations. When the pair successfully used all three negotiation behaviors in the presession simulations in one session, the father-son dyad and the worker wrote their own conflictual situations in session. Each client chose a situation personally conflictual. (See Figure 1 for an example.) This phase began at session 6. Both clients said that the two situations chosen were difficult topics to negotiate. The worker served as the secretary, writing the situations, options, and consequences dictated by the subjects.

   In each office session of this phase, two situations were written for each home negotiation. The clients were instructed how to use the tape recorder, practiced using it, and played it back in session to ensure that they understood its operation. They kept the tape recorder at home for all of phase 3—a total of three weeks. Each week they brought in the audiotape of that week's home negotiation and received a new one for the next week's negotiation.

   The worker reviewed the tapes at each office session and discussed the subjects' use of the negotiation skills in the previous week's tape.

   Phase 4—Home Observation. Observation was conducted in the home. The clients were instructed to follow the negotiation model learned during phase 2. Two issues that were currently conflictual to the pair were discussed. The worker signaled the beginning and end of each negotiation. The clients then negotiated, using the skills they had been taught during treatment. This observation was a generality probe of the clients discussing their own conflictual issues in their home.

Results

Interrater reliability of all four treatment phases ranged from 87 to 92 percent, with a mean of 89.9 percent for all behaviors.

The worker kept a list of agreements resulting from negotiations. The agreements were monitored for implementation: Three out of four (75 percent) agreements were implemented.

The identification of issues, essentially a discussion of the conflictual situation with no attempts at resolution, ranged from 86 percent during baseline to a mean of 49 percent during treatment (see Figure 2 for negotiation data). Suggestion of options, discussing possible ways to ameliorate the conflictual situation, ranged from 8 percent during baseline to a mean of 47.6

Figure 2. Percentage of Time Spent Identifying Issues and Suggested Options.

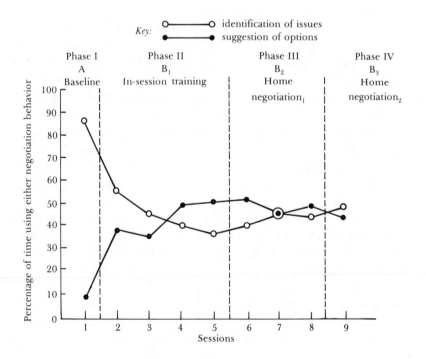

percent during treatment. At the beginning of phase 2, there was a sharp reduction in the use of identification of issues and an increase in the use of options. Across the total time of treatment, the range of the percent of time spent using these two behaviors continued to narrow. The range between the behaviors was widest in phase 1, an 81 percent difference, and continued to narrow during phase 2 to a mean of 11.3 percent. The phase 3 range narrowed further to 4 percent, and finally, in phase 4, the range was 2 percent. At the end of treatment, the clients were spending almost equal time using these two behaviors. The increase in suggestion of options represents an increase in attempts to solve their differences by presenting possible solutions to their conflicts.

Figure 3 summarizes the results of analysis of the clients' statements for positive, negative, and neutral content. Positive statements occurred 6 percent of total time during baseline. In phase 2, positive statements ranged 3 to 10 percent, with a mean of 4.5 percent. During phase 3, positive statements ranged from 6 to 12 percent, with a mean of 8 percent. In phase 4, positive statements were used 3 percent of total time; negative statements were used during 60 percent of negotiation time during baseline. Phase 2 negative statements ranged from 6 to 19 percent, with a mean of 12.2 percent. During phase 3, negative statements ranged from 16 to 30 percent, with a mean of 21 percent. Phase 4 negative statements was 14 percent. Neutral statements were employed for 16 percent of total baseline negotiation time. During phase 2, neutral statements ranged from 53 to 62 percent with a mean of 56.7 percent. In phase 3, use of neutral statements ranged from 40 to 60 percent, with a mean of 48.6 percent. In phase 4, neutral statements were used 61 percent of total time.

Negative statements decreased markedly as neutral statements increased across time during treatment. The changes in frequency of both negative and neutral statements is marked, whereas the least change was the rate of positive statements.

As an added measure to assess change, the Hudson scales were administered before each session; the results are shown in Figure 4. Both subjects showed some improvement in their atti-

Figure 3. Percentage of Time Spent in Positive, Negative,
and Neutral Communication During Sessions.

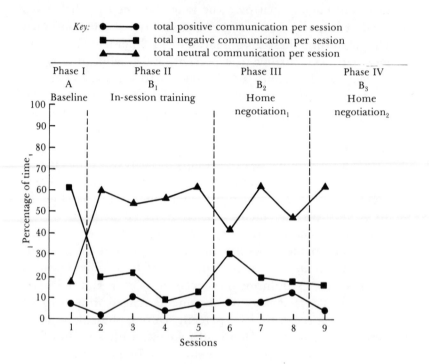

tude toward each other until session 6. The father's attitude
toward the son continued to improve throughout, but the son's
deteriorated for the last three sessions.

Discussion

There was a clinically significant reduction of the father's
and son's negative (attacking) statements, an increase in their
neutral statements, and little change in their positive statements.
Over time, the clients' percentage of time spent disagreeing, defined as a negative behavior but not essentially an attacking
statement, ranged from 5 to 7 percent and remained stable.

Figure 4. Index of Parental Attitude (Father) and Child Attitude
Toward Father (Son) Scores.

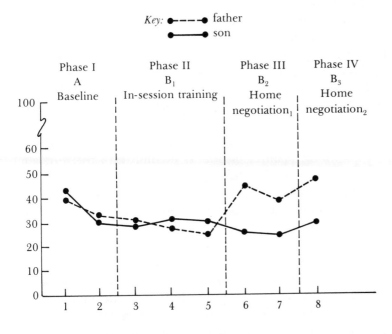

The clients were in treatment for a long time before they began the negotiation training. When this treatment was planned, neither father nor son was put in control of their relationship. They were both equally involved in developing the program and writing and planning home negotiations during phase 3. They both reported a high degree of satisfaction from transferring the program from the office to the home.

This negotiation program focused on teaching the clients to negotiate a behavior incompatible with their normal conflictual interactional pattern. The rearrangement of the consequences of their interactions was structured by using instruction, modeling, and role playing. Learning the structure of the negotiation model provided skills incompatible with chains of aversive behaviors. Before training, a conflictual situation led to arguments and screaming between the father and son. After treatment, by using the negotiation skills, they may still disagree, but they know alternate ways of informing each other about their disagreements and can attempt to find a mutually acceptable solution.

The outcome of the clients' reports of the attitudes was disappointing. Hudson suggested that the worker keep a critical incident record throughout treatment to help interpret the scales. Beginning with session 6, the son was discouraged about not finding a job. Being home all day, however, the father expected the son to carry a major portion of the household responsibility. This difference in expectation may have increased their conflict.

Future investigation of this model should address a number of questions. Maintenance must be built into the program. After learning the new skills, the clients should be taught how to maintain the use of the behaviors. For example, cues could be built into their environment to remind them to use the procedure. An increase in positive interchanges could further alter a conflictual interaction. Practitioners might evaluate alternatives that could contribute to an increase in positive communications.

This is a very efficient treatment model. Training required nine weeks of the worker's time and little equipment: a tape recorder and tapes. The cost of this treatment is very low. Because the structure of the model is flexible, allowing for differential adaptation depending on the researcher, there is wide applicability of this model to different populations, settings, and therapists.

Increasing Prosocial Behavior
of a First-Grade Boy

Carol A. Moses, Elsie M. Pinkston

School social workers often encounter difficulties when implementing treatment intervention procedures in public school settings. Minimal assistance from teachers and/or parents may not hinder traditional clinical approaches in which the practitioner works directly with the client, but a behavior modifier, who is usually the consultant in a triadic model (consultant/change agent/client) may experience some difficulty. The underlying assumption of the consultative triad is that the change agent, not the consultant, interacts with the client in the natural environment. Therefore the change agent possesses the maximum power for inducing change (Tharp and Wetzel, 1969). Quite often change agents (in this case teachers) may concentrate on the child's negative disruptive behavior. During intervention, they expect immediate behavior change and may misinterpret or misunderstand the behavioral program, even when a thorough explanation is given. Therefore, these obstacles may obviate utilization of the teacher model. In the absence of a willing change agent, other channels of intervention can be pursued. In this study, the practitioner worked with the client in a clinical setting outside the classroom because the teacher was unwilling to participate in the change effort.

As teachers, parents, and social workers focus on inappropriate behaviors, they only occasionally (and with little fanfare) notice appropriate behaviors: good behavior is the expected norm (Wahler, 1969b). Teachers and parents commonly express two misconceptions about reducing inappropriate behaviors: (1) Punitive consequences or disapproving comments decrease inappropriate behavior, and (2) rules are sufficient to decrease inappropriate behavior.

The teacher's critical comments on or disapproval of a student's behavior may reinforce and maintain noxious behavior, not decrease it. When a teacher instructs opposing or deprived children to sit down, it sometimes results in their standing up (Madsen and others, 1967). Thomas, Becker, and Armstrong (1968) found that when a teacher tries to talk to a child or suggests alternative activity to a child who has behaved inappropriately, the teacher may increase (reinforce) the very behavior she is trying to reduce.

Telling children what is expected of them, even if it is done repeatedly, does not necessarily affect their behavior (Phillips, 1968). Madsen, Becker, and Thomas (1968) demonstrated that rules alone did not effectively decrease disruptive classroom behavior and supported the finding that instructions without reinforcement have little effect on behavior (Ayllon and Azrin, 1964).

Various behavioral procedures for reducing disruptive behaviors are effective. These procedures are used to deal with disruptive behaviors by ignoring (extinction) inappropriate behaviors to decrease those behaviors and by praising or giving social attention to increase appropriate behavior (Becker and others, 1967; Madsen, Becker, and Thomas, 1968). Positive teacher response (Thomas, Becker and Armstrong, 1968); time-out and social reinforcement (Zeilberger, Sampen, and Sloane, 1968); and praise and social consequences (Allen and others, 1964) are also effective methods for reducing classroom-behavior problems.

Token reinforcement programs have also been demonstrated as effective in controlling disruptive behavior (Kuypers, Becker, and O'Leary, 1968; O'Leary and Becker, 1967; Phillips and others, 1971), such as aggressiveness, uncooperativeness, self-injury, and tantrum behavior, in a number of settings (institutions, schools). The subjects in these studies were retarded, autistic, and normal children, adolescents, and adults.

Another procedure that may just as effectively help reduce maladaptive behavior is differential reinforcement of other behavior (DRO). Reinforcement is given if target behaviors have not been emitted within a specified time period. Peterson's and Peterson's (1968) use of DRO effectively reduced a retarded subject's self-destructive behavior. When Peterson and Peterson combined DRO and time-out, as did Bostow and Bailey (1969), the effects of the procedures were more impressive. Zeiler (1970) found that a combination of DRO and punishment effectively helped eliminate behavior and that DRO reduced behavior more permanently than did extinction. A comparison of DRO, time-out, and punishment by Corte, Wolf, and Locke (1971) demonstrated DRO to be the least effective procedure for reducing behaviors. Foxx and Azrin (1973) compared DRO, response-independent reinforcement, punishment, a distasteful liquid, and overcorrection; they also found DRO to be the least effective procedure for decreasing target behavior. However, Goetz, Holmberg, and LeBlanc (1975) compared the effects of DRO reversal and noncontingent reinforcement reversal to determine response decrement and the reacquisition subsequent to response decrement. They found that DRO decreased behavior faster than the noncontingent procedure. Implementation of DRO procedure combined with other procedures by Repp and Deitz (1975) reduced aggressive self-injurious behavior; the combination could be used by the teacher. It appears that DRO, when combined with other procedures, can effectively help modify target behaviors.

The two purposes of this study were: (1) to determine whether the frequency of a normal child's undesirable and desirable behaviors could be altered in an experimental play setting by DRO procedure combined with instructions, social attention, and a token system; and (2) to see if generality to another play situation occurred.

Methods

Setting. This study was conducted in a Chicago public elementary school located in a predominantly middle-class neighborhood. The client and twenty-three other children were participants in one of the school's POD open classrooms, from which children migrated to second- and third-grade rooms for classes. The POD program helps compensate for individual differences in children's learning rates. The POD's program used a team teaching approach, was less structured than a regular classroom (that is, more physical space was available for individual activities), and emphasized individualized instruction for each child. Children grouped in this program were often double tracked in reading and/or math; that is, the course level taught was above that ordinarily for the age. Instead of skipping a child to a second- or third-grade classroom permanently, the child remained with peers (same age level) in the homeroom but exchanged classes to receive second- or third-grade-level instruction.

The intervention was conducted in a separate room of the school and contained desks and chairs. The worker rearranged the furniture to provide a large area that would facilitate playing.

Subject. Brian, a first-grade six-year-old boy, was referred by his homeroom teacher and was described as having immature relationships with other children by demonstrating lack of control. These interactions were characterized by commands to the other children and tantrums when those commands were not executed or by playing alone. He also called his classmates names, such as "stupid" or "dummy." Eight days of informal observation by the worker confirmed the teacher's report.

Observation Procedures. Brian and various male classmates selected by the teacher were observed by the social worker playing with games and/or toys in the experimental setting approximately fifteen minutes a day, three days a week. Five categories were used to define Brian's behavior: inappropriate play, isolated play, verbal commands, appropriate play, and sharing. These categories were recorded for occurrence or nonoccurrence in ten-second intervals. The worker recorded the first occurrence of each behavior during each ten-second interval. The categories of behavior were not mutually exclusive. Therefore, more than one category of behavior could occur in any interval. Also, sharing was scored as both a discrete example of appropriate behavior and sharing. The percentage of intervals scored in which Brian engaged in each behavior was calculated by dividing the total intervals scored by the total number of intervals of the session. (See Chapter Four for the occurrence reliability formula.)

Behavioral Measures. Brian's behavior was classified into

five child behaviors, which included both problem and desirable behaviors, defined as follows:

Inappropriate play includes running, skipping, and jumping around the room; grabbing toys (games, puzzle parts) away from playmates; destroying (knocking down) playmates' constructions or blocks; throwing objects around the room or at playmates; hitting, kicking, shoving, and pinching playmates; yelling, fussing, or talking loudly; getting into any situation in which Brian might hurt himself or others (such as swinging between the worker's desk and the piano); using a toy in a way that would damage the toy.

Isolated play is playing near other children (who are engaged in cooperative play) and not initiating or responding to their verbalizations; playing alone (at least three feet away from other children) and not initiating or responding to their verbalizations; engaging in no nonverbal interaction with other children for an entire ten-second interval; playing alone but throwing objects around the room or at other children; going off by himself to play with toys or other materials in the room (such as a blackboard or desk).

Verbal commands included giving orders to other children regarding what to do and how to play; appointing himself leader; bossing other children and telling other children which toys to play with (bosses other children in loud voice). Examples include "I told you to do this"; "Stop that"; "I'm captain." Excluded were "Look at this"; "Come here"; "Let's share."

Appropriate play was portrayed as handing a child an object, helping a child play a game (showing the child how to play), talking softly, adding to the same structure or construction of another child (opposite of inappropriate behavior).

Sharing is sharing or offering to use something with a child by carrying the same object, reaching into the same container for blocks or plastics, offering another child his toy, and building or bringing something for another child.

Design. A reversal design was used to evaluate the intervention in this research (Baer, Wolf, and Risley, 1968; Gambrill, 1977; Howe, 1974). The experimental conditions were presented in the following order: baseline (days 1-9), intervention (days 10-20), reversal (days 12–26), and intervention (days 27-33).

Procedures

For each session, the social worker selected two male classmates according to the teacher's evaluation of their appropriate homeroom behavior. The children were allowed to choose three games or toys that could involve one or more children (checkers, cars and garage, blocks, plastics, tic-tac-toe game, puzzles).

Baseline (Days 1-9) and Reversal (Days 21-26). During these conditions, the worker ignored both appropriate and inappropriate behavior, letting the children play as they normally would without intervention, except to prevent physical harm, for fifteen minutes each day. The worker recorded the frequency of Brian's target behaviors and gave no praise or tokens. During this time, Brian and his peers were asked to play as they did in their homeroom and to pick up toys and prepare to leave when the timer rang.

Rules for behavior were not reviewed for the children; three rules—no running, no loud talking, and no fighting—were listed on a bulletin board in the clinical room.

Instructions, DRO Using Praise and Points (Days 10-20). During the intervention, the worker instructed Brian to play appropriately during the session. Appropriate behavior was described to him in five components: (1) sharing, (2) saying, (3) talking softly, (4) playing carefully with others, and (5) handling toys carefully.

Brian was told that at the end of two minutes of appropriate behavior he would receive two points and one extra point for sharing. A timer was reset every two minutes so that he could hear the ring and see the marking of his earned points. If Brian played inappropriately during the two-minute interval, he did not receive the points.

Social attention (verbal praise and smiles) contingent on appropriate behavior was also given to Brian at the end of two-minute intervals if no inappropriate behavior occurred. Typical examples of verbal praise were "Good, Brian, you are sharing"; "That was a nice comment you made"; and "Very good Brian, you are talking softly and still having fun."

At the end of sixteen minutes, Brian could exchange points for an item on the token menu or save his points (up to eighty points) for a special lunch with the worker. The peers were given a piece of candy (Tootsie Roll) or bubble gum at the end of each session and verbal praise for playing nicely and coming to the experimental room with Brian; these peers varied on different days.

The token menu devised by the experimenter and approved by Brian was five points for one stick of gum, ten points for bubble gum, fifteen points for pumpkin seeds, eighty points for lunch with the worker. From this menu Brian chose the material reinforcers he earned.

Results

The implementation of instructions, DRO, social attention, and token reinforcers during B_1 resulted in a 43 percent increase in the appropriate behaviors, a 59 percent decrease in the inappropriate behaviors, and a 3 percent decrease in isolated play. Isolated play increased on days 11 and 12, 52 percent and 46 percent, respectively, and did not decrease significantly (1 percent) until day 13. This may have been a result of the worker's inexplicit instruction to Brian; Brian may have thought he would earn more points if he played quietly by himself. In Figure 1 (days 11 and 12), Brian was 40 percent appropriate and only 5 to 6 percent inappropriate.

Figure 2 shows the frequency of sharing and verbal commands across all conditions. In A_1 (baseline 1), Brian shared two out of nine days (three each). He gave verbal commands nine out of nine days (up to twenty-four one day). Brian shared eight out of eleven days (twelve on one day). Brian gave commands four out of eleven days (high of eight on one day). In A_2 (baseline 2—reversal), all five categories of Brian's behaviors reflect responding that is typical of extinction. Reinstatement of intervention B_2 appeared to be producing behavior changes comparable to those observed in B_1.

The number of points Brian earned and the social attention (praise) directed toward Brian for each session of B_1 and

Figure 1. Percentage of Appropriate and Inappropriate Behavior per Session in All Conditions.

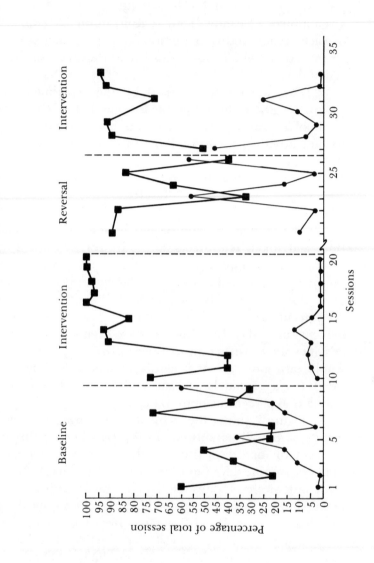

Figure 2. Frequency of Sharing and Verbal Commands Across All Conditions.

Key: ●——● verbal commands

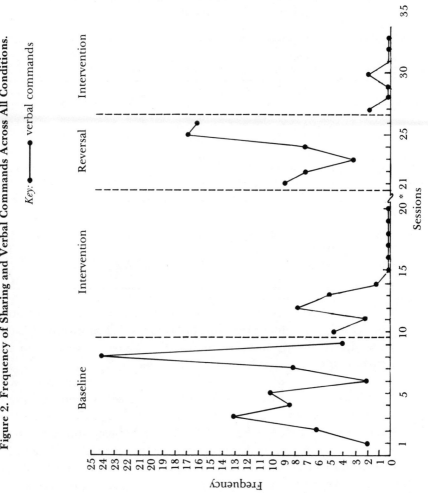

B_2 conditions are shown in Table 1. There appears to be some slight correlation between the number of points earned and the

Table 1. Number of Points Earned for Two Consecutive Minutes of Appropriate Play and Frequency of *Social Attention* Given to Brian During (Variable Interval) and at End (Fixed Interval) of Two-Minute Interval.

Points Earned Appropriate Behavior	Sharing	Praise VI		FI
B_1 (DRO)				
2	7	3	5	2
0	0	4	4	0
0	10	5	5	0
4	4	2	6	4
8	0	0	4	4
10	1	0	6	6
16	0	2	4	4
10	2	2	4	4
10	2	3	7	4
16	4	5	7	2
16	12	4	7	3
B_2 (DRO)				
4	1	7	11	4
10	1	9	17	8

amount of social attention shown to Brian. Brian received more praise when he had two-minute segments of appropriate play and shared during those segments. He received less if either occurred alone.

During two days (days 23 and 24) of reversal, Brian was observed on the playground during recess by an undergraduate student (employed at the public school). She observed the five categories of behavior and found Brian to be appropriate on an average of 74 percent for both days, whereas on days 23 and 24 in experimental setting he was 32 percent and 64 percent appropriate, respectively. Possibly more days of independent observation were needed during reversal.

The independent observer also observed Brian during days 27 and 28 on reinstatement of intervention. The percentages for these days seem to more closely correspond, even though time segments were unequal (playground observation time was ten minutes). Table 2 shows playground observations for the five categories of behavior for days 27 and 28 of B_2

Table 2. Playground Observations Compared with Experimental Setting Observations During B_2 for Days 27 and 28.

	Experimental Setting, %	*Playground, %*
Day 27:		
Appropriate behavior	51	21
Inappropriate behavior	47	33
Isolated play	4	28
Verbal commands	2	18
Sharing	1	0
Day 28:		
Appropriate behavior	90	81
Inappropriate behavior	7	5
Isolated play	2	10
Verbal commands	0	3
Sharing	1	0

compared with experimental setting observations for the same days.

Observer reliability for all behaviors across all conditions ranged between 80 and 100 percent.

Discussion

The combination of instructions, DRO, social attention, and token system effectively reduced Brian's inappropriate behaviors and increased appropriate behaviors. Zeiler (1970) commented that other behavior or superstitious behaviors may be adventitiously reinforced when using a DRO schedule of reinforcement. One possible way to eliminate other behaviors is to instruct or explain appropriate behavior to the child and define what is expected.

It is possible that students discriminate the rules but are not aware of possible alternate appropriate behaviors. Even if students know the rules, their inappropriate behaviors may be reinforced by peer attention or teacher comments.

It has been demonstrated that DRO is effective in reducing a specified response (Repp and Deitz, 1975; Goetz, Holmberg, and LeBlanc, 1975; Zeiler, 1970). However, no data show that DRO schedules do condition other behavior when they succeed in decreasing the frequency of a specified response. A potential solution to this problem is to structure the situation so that the hypothesized adventitiously reinforced response may be specified in advance (Zeiler, 1970).

To limit other behaviors, instructions (five components of appropriate behavior) were explained to Brian at the beginning of each session. Social attention, which maintains positive social behavior (Becker and others, 1967), was directed toward Brian during the interval when he was engaging in appropriate behavior. Experimenter attention reinforced particular responses. Instructions without reinforcement are ineffective (Ayllon and Azrin, 1964), so a token system was also used to reinforce appropriate behavior.

The combination of procedures used here effectively helped reduce Brian's inappropriate behavior in the experimental setting. However, generality across settings was not demonstrated. Thus, DRO procedures can be used effectively in a clinical setting.

7

◆-◆◆-◆◆-◆◆-◆◆-◆◆-◆◆-◆◆-◆◆-◆◆-◆◆-◆◆-◆◆-◆◆-◆

Intervention
with Families

Family intervention based on behavioral principles is the most promising branch of scientific intervention with families (for reviews, see Berkowitz and Graziano, 1972; Dangel and Polster, 1981; Johnson and Katz, 1973; O'Dell, 1974). Members of the family are in the most convenient position to help assess the problem, provide the resources to be used in the change effort, implement the intervention procedures, and evaluate the effects of intervention (Gambrill, 1981). For the purposes of this chapter, family members include members of foster families, two-parent families, single-parent families, and extended families. The family unit selected for change efforts depends on the nature and scope of the problem. For instance, extended family members are included because they may be part of the problem or can offer resources necessary to successfully resolve the problem. Family members are the persons most likely to maintain a high investment in the individual and are often the recipients of dysfunctional behaviors or consequences of those behaviors.

Achieving change in dysfunctional family interaction patterns is developed in four phases: (1) specifying the roles of the worker and the family member, (2) assessing the response requirements and contingencies for the change agent, (3) reviewing and selecting intervention techniques, and (4) evaluating the effectiveness and the efficiency of those techniques to produce the desired change. Several examples of clinical applications and evaluations by social workers, including families with coercive patterns, single-parent-child interactional problems, families of adult retardates, and other families, illustrate the model.

Roles of Workers and Family Members

The worker functions as a consultant and teacher and increases access to reinforcement by using direct social praise and feedback, linkage development, and the community (Thomas, 1970). The worker teaches family members techniques for analyzing and altering the frequency, duration, or latency of problems. Change agents, selected from the available family members, implement the change techniques, record data, and help evaluate how effectively the technique produced the desired change and achieved specific goals.

The worker occasionally assumes a role as a direct behavior change agent, takes responsibility for development of the intervention program, and models how to implement some aspects of the program. Family members are initially less active participants while the worker models the intervention. This alternate role offers several advantages: The worker, because of advanced training, implements procedures more efficiently and effectively than family members and can revise the techniques immediately to fit newly assessed contingencies; worker influence is enhanced; and family members can observe the behavioral technique as implemented by the worker. Thus the potential for modeling and observational learning is enhanced (Bandura, 1969). Potential difficulties of this role include: (1) family members' inability to learn the behavioral technique by active implementation, (2) lack of generality from the worker to the family members, and (3) inability of many workers to commit themselves to the amount of time required to achieve the desired outcomes. As reported in the literature, these difficulties are occasionally overridden by treatment considerations and instances where the worker in this role has demonstrated successful intervention. For example, Pinkston, Friedman, and Polster (1981) reported the successful treatment of a child who excessively threw tantrums. The worker initially took total responsibility for the program and its implementation five days a week during intervention but rapidly helped the family assume full responsibility for the successful behavioral program.

The major responsibilities (Fischer and Gochros, 1975; Thomas, 1970) of the worker and the family members in effectively altering the rates, durations, intensity, or latencies of behaviors are defined at the beginning of assessment and/or behavioral training. These responsibilities must be clearly delineated to avoid confusion and wasted effort, and obstacles to implementation should be identified, clarified, and removed.

Worker Responsibilities. The ten responsibilities for the worker in family interventions are:

1. *Assessing and defining the problems, training, and ensuring reliable data recording by the family members.* The worker's initial role is teaching the family members to reconceptualize their needs in objective, behaviorally specific, and socially relevant terms. Once these problems have been defined (see Chapter Three), family members are then taught to record information related to possible outcomes and probable interventions. The worker instructs them in recording methods. This teaching gives family members an opportunity to demonstrate their abilities to record data. To guard against observer bias, independent reliability measurements are taken periodically. Data-recording procedures are altered or simplified if there is inadequate agreement between the family members and an independent observer.

    Each practice illustration at the end of this chapter demonstrates this responsibility. A family member was selected—usually a parent—as an observer, and independent observation by an outside person was used to determine the reliability of the data and monitor the implementation of the intervention.

2. *Determining the family member's abilities to implement*

specific behavioral techniques. The potential change agent's physical, emotional, and intellectual abilities to implement the technique is part of the preliminary assessment. Techniques can be adapted to the individual change agent, or the change agent can be trained to the results of that assessment.

3. *Ensuring that family change agents have access to the problem, situations, and the client.* Change agents require direct access to the problem and potential reinforcers that exist in the natural environment. The most effective technique is totally useless if change agents never have the opportunity to implement it. For a son wishing behavioral change for his institutionalized father, the practitioner's efforts might be more efficiently spent working with staff (see Chapter Eight) than with the person who possesses limited access to the father's environment.

4. *Increasing opportunities for reinforcement following appropriate behavior.* Situations that the family members can control or in which they can implement new contingencies must exist in the social environment. For example, a mother selects her child's problem of not making his bed, but the mother herself makes the bed every morning. Access to the problem is apparent, yet opportunities for reinforcement are lacking because the mother effectively reduces the opportunities for the child making the bed by making it herself.

5. *Determining the availability of supporting resources in the community.* Links are connections between existing community resources and the family in need of these resources. Thus, links can help provide opportunities for reinforcement when opportunities are limited in the client's primary environment. If an elderly man living with his children lacks the opportunity for social interaction, links can be developed to provide for the opportunity in a day center. The worker determines if the resource exists, who provides it, whether the family or worker can provide the link, and the relationship between the problem and the link.

6. *Designing and evaluating the behavioral technique.* Using baseline observations, the worker evaluates the functional relationships between the environment and client behavior. Procedures for intervention result from this analysis and are monitored throughout intervention to determine if the behavioral technique is producing the desired outcome. This analysis answers the question: "Was there a change in the direction the client desired?"

7. *Modifying the technique or the implementation of the procedure if the technique is ineffective in producing the desired change.* If the technique or the implementation procedure is partly or fully ineffective in producing the desired effect, it is modified to produce the desired outcome. These modifications may be slight or major revisions, but they are designed with attention to the goals and desired outcomes.

8. *Enhancing the maintenance of positive change.* Family change agents are trained to use techniques which demonstrate positive effects, and the worker should plan the intervention so that desired effects will continue after the worker has terminated. This implies more than "Keep doing what you're doing." (See Chapters Three and Nine for more explicit details on the issues and techniques of maintenance and generality.)

9. *Enhancing the motivation of the family member as a change agent to apply the technique.* Many workers assume that family members are "motivated" to alter their own behaviors to affect change in another family member's behavior. Positive reinforcement for family intervention efforts should be planned as part of the intervention.

10. *Discriminating and effectively reducing potential difficulties.* Poor skills, inadequate resources, substance addiction, competing reinforcers, and inadequate stimulus conditions are potential difficulties for behavioral family intervention. If these conditions exist, it is imperative that the worker successfully recognize these difficulties. Behavioral programs can be initiated for reducing these difficulties, or the family members can be taught skills and behaviors

that may effectively reduce the potential for difficulty. Although the worker does not assume the responsibility for remediating all these difficulties, it is essential to address those competing with effective problem change.

Family Member Responsibilities. The eight responsibilities of the family members who assume the role of behavioral change agents are:

1. *Providing information regarding their problems, difficulties in solving them, and available resources.* Family members are the primary source of information for the worker and are responsible for informing the worker about their previous attempts to solve the problems. They should advise the worker of the difficulties they expect to encounter and disclose resources available for solving their problems.

2. *Collaborating with the worker to select problems and appropriate change agents.* As stated earlier, it is important for the family members to play an active part in selecting problems. It is essential that the problems selected are socially relevant to the involved family members and that as many members as possible be involved with the selection. This selection can be established by administering a structured checklist (see Chapter Four) or through less formal discussion.

3. *Recording data consistently.* Data on target behaviors must be accurately and reliably recorded to determine baseline rates, evaluate program effectiveness, pinpoint potential difficulties, and assess how well the desired procedures are being consistently and contingently implemented (see (Chapter Four).

4. *Implementing the behavioral technique consistently and contingently.* Family change agents must use interventions consistently in a newly developed program to accurately increase their effectiveness in producing desired changes. This enables further evaluation of the necessary requirements for implementing the technique and determining if another technique might be more feasible.

5. *Providing opportunities for reinforcement.* Family members provide ample opportunities for reinforcement and specific reinforcers whenever possible. Whether a reinforcer exists naturally or is developed by the worker, the opportunity for the reinforcer to be attained contingently is the family change agent's responsibility. Families are told that no program can effectively alter the rates of *any* behavior if the conditions in which the behavior naturally and normally occur are blocked or impeded.

6. *Accurately reporting those difficulties to the worker.* Confusion may occur when any new intervention is being used, and some problems are not apparent until they are attempted. Family members are informed that there are sometimes difficulties with interventions which may require revisions to the original plan. Difficulties not relayed to the worker cannot be effectively resolved. For example, a mother may be taught time-out and instructed to use the procedure for five minutes each time her son is noncompliant. However, the mother forgots the length of the time-out when she attempts the technique. It is imperative that as soon as possible the mother report her confusion or lack of results to the worker for clarification.

7. *Anticipating difficulties in providing opportunities for reinforcement, data collection, implementation of the technique or in access to the problem, client, or situation.* Potential difficulties, however questionable and tentative, should be suggested to the worker. Although the empirical relationship between the expectation and the occurrence of difficulties is unknown, it is foolish to overlook the potential of family members in depicting future difficulties accurately and precisely.

8. *Using the technique creatively and flexibly.* It is the family members' responsibility to help mold the interventions to fit their life-style. This task is facilitated by drawing on the individual and potentially reinforcing assets of the family members. They have good ideas about activities that can be used as positive consequences and are encouraged to brainstorm these assets during sessions. Ideally, persons will try

to figure out events that are reinforcing to other members of their family. Although this approach is outlined in some detail, it should be used flexibly to incorporate naturally occurring environmental events. For instance, many individuals undervalue the desire of others in the family to spend time with them in a simple activity; thus making cookies, repairing a chair in the workshop, or going to shop for plants can be turned into an opportunity for reinforcement to occur. These activities can be turned into positive events for the change agent as well as the person who has been identified as having special problems. Adults report activities that were apparently highlights of their childhood, such as having a forbidden cup of tea with their grandmother and being treated like a grown-up. Providing positive events is considerably broader than saying "Good boy," and families should be encouraged to identify their behaviors as potential positive events for others.

Assessment

Families who are referred or who seek help are often beset with numerous difficulties (Richmond, 1922; Hollis, 1974; Hamilton, 1951). In addition, they have significant and sometimes negative contributions to the maintenance of problems. A frequent example in client families is a coercive verbal behavior that apparently sets the occasion for aggressive interactions (Patterson and Reid, 1973). These contributions are modified and altered in the intervention to result in positive directions toward solving the problem. The goal of the functional analysis in problem assessment is to develop a working and yet flexible hypothesis regarding how this shift from negative to positive contributions can occur and how the worker can teach and facilitate this transfer. In the behavior analysis model, the goal of assessment is to delineate the family's goals, explore specific problems, define desired outcomes, summarize available resources, select the setting and the agents of change, and evaluate the response requirements and contingencies. The worker depicts and examines the functional and topographical relationships between the problem, the family members, and the environment. Assessment is the major building block upon which successful interventions rest.

Referral Sources. Families are referred to the worker from different sources and for various reasons. Sources include an elementary school teacher referring a family because of actual or potential child abuse occurring in the home and the physician of an elderly patient who is having considerable difficulty in the present living situation. Whatever or whomever the referral source, the family expresses interest. The referral source may or may not have specific objectives: the teacher wants the child placed in foster care, the abusing behaviors stopped, or the child to do better in school. The physician may want the elderly patient placed in a nursing home or just want someone (the physician may never say who) to come into the home once a day and visit for an hour. In the practice illustrations at the end of this chapter, the workers clarified possible agenda items prior to treatment. For example, in the Linsk, Pinkston, and Green study (Practice Illustration 7.1), the worker clarified the role of the hospital: whether the hospital would be available for medical backup, emergencies, or possible medication. It further clarified the physician's involvement in intervention.

Never assume that the family was not coerced into involvement with the change effort. (For discussions of coercion, see Goldiamond, 1975.) The degree of coercion is an issue to be explored indirectly with most families, especially the identified client. Carefully exploring the reason for the referral enables the worker to assess the family members' consent to the change effort. There is no direct correlation between client motivation and willingness to cooperate with the change effort. A mother who has been referred by a child protective service may not want to be involved in a change effort but may not want to lose her child either, and therefore she may comply with requests if she understands the potential benefits to her quality of life (Stein, 1981). This issue requires special handling and consideration by the worker as to who the client really is: the state, the mother, or her child. The involuntary client tests the fabric of ethical, social, and pragmatic considerations to a greater degree than other clients. (For a more complete discussion of this issue, see Chapter Four.) Overcoming the problems of the involuntary client or family requires more attention to presenting the rationale for change, including the possible benefits of the outcome (Budd and Baer, 1976).

Environment modification includes four steps: (1) analyzing the functional relationship between desired and undesired behavior and reinforcers in the natural environment; (2) rearranging existing resources, such as equipment, household items, or people; (3) introducing additional resources for reinforcement; and (4) reanalyzing the environment. It is imperative that the worker determine the desired role of the referral source before embarking on an intervention. Is the physician limited to medical treatment or involved in an effort to maintain the patient in the home? Will the school teacher support the behavioral program developed by the family?

Families and individual family members also refer themselves for intervention. They may recognize a problem exists and request help. The problems, as with referred families, vary and include an unwed teenage mother requesting help in learning how to parent her three-year-old child, the family who seeks advice at the social work office in a hospital about what to do with an infirmed elderly parent or spouse (see the Linsk, Pinkston, and Green illustration), and the parents who wish to decrease the stuttering (see the Rzepnicki and others study, Practice Illustration 7.2) of one of their children.

Exploring and Identifying the Problem. During the first contact, the family is asked why they are seeking help at this time or why they have been referred. The worker explores the problem—who exhibits it and who contributes to the problem— and determines previous efforts to solve the problem. The worker also solicits information about resources available for alleviating the problem.

The assessment involves evaluating the family, its strengths, its interactions around the problem, and implementing the intervention with the family as a whole whenever possible. To do otherwise is to neglect rich potential resources and reinforcers that naturally exist in the environment. One specific family member, however, may be the focus of the intervention. In this chapter, the term "client" refers to the specific family member who exhibits the identified problem behaviors. The actively interacting family members, those who will implement the technique, are referred to as the change agents. Note that to improve family interaction, the change agents' behaviors may be altered in a positive direction as much as those of the identified client.

Most problems can be assigned to one of three categories: (1) rates of behavior, (2) environmental concerns, and (3) providing links. The problems are not mutually exclusive and do not predict causality or explain how the family found itself in the present difficulty. This division does help predict what technique may effectively achieve the problem change the family desires.

Altering Rate of Specific Problem Behaviors Exhibited by One or More Family Members. Family members often identify one member who exhibits excessive or deficit problem behaviors. Parents might state that their children hang out with the wrong kids, or excessively throw tantrums. Adult children may express concern about their parents who have become isolated. When asked to identify and describe problems, many families often present the situation vaguely, without specific referents. They may state that the client does not do well in school, cries too frequently, lacks respect, or cannot take care of himself. The worker teaches the family to operationalize these problems.

Most behaviors can be operationally defined for excesses or deficits (Redd, Porterfield, and Anderson, 1979); it is better to define the problems in deficit terms so that positive repertoires can be built (Goldiamond, 1974; Schwartz and Goldiamond, 1975; Howe, 1975). Operational definitions are developed with the family, the rationale for operationalizing the problems is explained, and agreement is obtained from the family as to the definition. This process is imperative when family members as change agents are recording data on the frequency, duration, latency, or intensity of problem behaviors. For example, Mr. and Mrs. Weltman are concerned about Mr. Weltman's father, who was recently retired and is having trouble adjusting to retirement. The family lives together in a small house, and the father tends to sit all day watching television, a behavior

Mrs. Weltman finds annoying. Mr. and Mrs. Weltman are recruited as change agents and identify and develop an operational definition of two problems Mr. Weltman's father exhibits: excessive television watching during the day and a lack of activity during the day. Agreement on these definitions is reached by all parties concerned and interacting with the problem. Because the intervention is likely to include an alteration of the Weltmans' attention to the father, their attention to desired and undesired behavior is also defined. Because the behavior of the change agents needs to be reinforced, the couple is asked to record a daily log of their social contacts for possible modification.

Notice that one problem was defined as a deficit instead of an excess: Mr. Weltman's father's lack of activity during the day. This becomes the primary problem and the focus of the intervention; thus activities are defined and recorded. If the change agents are collecting baseline and intervention data, the definitions of the frequency and duration of activity are further explained and expounded to clarify misconceptions. From an intervention analysis standpoint, the definitions become the dependent variables by which the intervention is examined for effectiveness, technological development, educational value, generality, and social relevance (see Chapter One).

Environmental Problems. The modification of home environments is indicated when the physical environment impedes productive behavior (Lindsley, 1964). This category has been less frequently examined than techniques designed to alter the rate of specific problem behaviors, but it is a promising area for future investigation. The physical environment can be altered to support positive behavior. For example, environmental barriers might interfere with productive behaviors of physically handicapped individuals. Stairs may hamper the mobility of a wheelchair-bound individual because it is difficult for the person to leave the home. In this instance, a ramp might be an alternate method of going up and down the stairs. Physical disabilities often require such redesign in the home environments.

The way the environment is used may also be altered. Simple changes such as designing a special study corner with a small table lamp and chair may facilitate a home-study program (Polster and Pinkston, 1979). It is useful to ask what behaviors are desired and what physical environment is necessary to support them.

Environmental interventions also help provide cues for appropriate behaviors. Containers are a good cue: A plastic box with daily medication compartments can remind persons to take their medication; a toy box is a good cue for putting toys away. Wonderful new electronic devices are available for signaling tasks. Cooperative games are cues to appropriate social interaction. The richness of environmental opportunity for reinforcers should be used to support behavioral intervention.

Community Links. Links with community services may be used to facilitate the achievement of desired goals. The community should be used to increase the client's opportunities for reinforcement and to increase available reinforcers; thus the community is viewed as a client resource. The degree of family involvement with the community and community services is as varied as the need for such involvement. Families of impaired individuals may need to call upon the community to help share the high response cost of caring for the impaired person. In less serious cases, the community may only be a source of additional enrichment and convenience. Besides defining necessary behavioral changes, the worker evaluates the family's need for outside help with income, respite care, medical and psychological care, daily-living services, recreation, and social support. During assessment, the worker and the family should explore the available community resources. These resources are usually available through government and private agencies. Another way to start is to determine the family's religious affiliation, if any, and the possible supports available through their religious group. Other federal and private agencies may have waiting lists, so the worker should begin the search at once. The worker should find out if the client or family meet the existing criteria—usually disability and income—for delivery of the service. If formal supports are not available to the client, the worker should explore more informal resources, such as self-help groups. If these are unavailable, the worker may have to try to develop informal arrangements with concerned individuals for community aid; thus neighbors or relatives not living with the family may be brought into the change effort.

The use of links is especially viable when there is a strong community program and the targeted problem is one of low social interactions. Many times, the desired outcome of treatment is to increase social interactions, but there may not be many opportunities. The use of community links can be extremely useful for helping the worker increase social interactions.

Specifying Desirable Outcomes. The worker, after exploring and tentatively classifying the problem, helps the family specify the desired outcomes. Desirable outcomes are behaviorally specific goals describing what the family expects to be different if intervention succeeds. In family intervention, the worker elicits from all interacting family members how they view the problem and how, if the treatment is successful, each will perceive the positive change. Along with obtaining each family member's perspective of what the desired outcome is, the worker should also elicit what specific areas the family members consider satisfactory or what areas they would not want changed.

From these outcomes, additional positive behaviors are defined. The family might want a son to fight less, but the behavior he should display is also defined. The practice illustrations all concretely define some target behavior. Rzepnicki and her colleagues defined fluency and stuttering while talking and reading aloud. Molick and others (Practice Illustration 7.4) studied individual definitions with each parent of the adult retarded persons.

The unique aspect of defining target behaviors with families is that the families may have to negotiate with the aid of the worker to settle on one common statement of the problem. The worker negotiates these definitions with as many sources as possible within the family. If these multiple perspectives are difficult to obtain, the worker should obtain the definitions from both change agents and clients in as many instances as possible. The family and the worker combine perspectives and develop one overall definition of the problem or sequence of problems to be modified.

Summary of Available Resources and Reinforcers. Each family has existing resources that can be systematically used in interventions. If these resources are insufficient, the worker must initiate and develop new ones to enhance the effectiveness of the program. Additional resources should be developed to maintain the behavior change once the worker has terminated; if they are developed within the family, they should be stimuli that are supportable in the natural family environment. It is worthless to institute only reinforcers or resources that cannot be maintained independent of the worker.

In behavioral family intervention, the worker assesses the family and community resources, possible agents of change, and possible settings for that change. Each aspect is summarized, and conclusions are reached concerning the best possible alternatives with the highest possibility of achieving change.

Selecting the Agent of Change. Unless the client is living alone, daily contact with other family members is almost certain. Children see their parents daily, siblings see other siblings at home or at the playground, and an aged parent may live with children. In behavioral family intervention, the assumption is that family members interact with one another, they participate in activities together, and this interaction is quantitatively unique to the family. Selecting the agent of change from the possible array of family members is more systematic than simply choosing "who happens to be there." The worker chooses family change agents who have the greatest likelihood of success in implementing the program and ameliorating the problem. As Blechman (in press) noted, the most frequently selected family members are the mother as the change agent and the child as the target. This reflects women's caretaking responsibilities and the expected compliant role of children in our culture. The worker should not view this as *the* ideal situation and should be sensitive to this bias. When selecting change agents, the first step in determining the best possible change agent is to account for all family members and include two types of family members: those who live with the client *and* those who live away from the client. Family members who do not have to live with the client often have a significant impact on the problem. Many workers relate stories about a grandmother who sabotaged a successful intervention, an adult child who institutionalized an elderly parent, or an aunt who is always helping in the wrong way. The worker may ask the family members if they would like to be involved in the behavioral training and intervention. Often these people will support the worker's efforts and will want to be informed of any progress and take part in any major decision making, but they do not wish to undertake the responsibilities as a change agent.

At times, family members might not agree to become involved in the program. The worker might then discuss the rationale for participation and attempt to indicate potential incentives for doing so.

Once an accounting of all interacting family members is complete, the worker should identify who participates in the problem situation. If the problem behavior directly involves a specific person, that person is a logical choice for change agent. Sometimes the choices for change agents are limited. Frequently, there is only one person who significantly interacts with the problem situation and identified client, such as single parents and partners in older marital couples. However, access to the problem in the environment in which it occurs is the primary consideration for selecting a change agent.

The choice of a change agent does not have to be limited to a single person. In fact, the more change agents that are included, the greater the potential to achieve change that maintains (see Chapter Nine). Multiple change agents increase the probability of mutual support and reinforcement for program implementation, feedback on problems, and feedback on success. Although interaction with the client and access to the environment are essential to a successful program, the family members who control the contingencies (reinforcers and punishers) are extremely important. Assessing the identity of the control person is necessary; this assessment includes data on both the frequency and strength of the control.

The best methods for determining who controls the contingencies in the family are observation and data analysis. Observational data are recorded not only on the frequency and duration of the problem behavior but on the behavior of persons interacting with the problem, what that person is doing, and the frequency of the interaction.

A second source of information about who controls the contingencies are the emotions and attitudes displayed by the family members and clients. Emotions and attitudes indicate who is being punished and reinforced and who is doing the punishing and reinforcing. Family members who are extremely angry usually are being punished or having reinforcers withheld. Family members who are being reinforced generally demonstrate by verbal or physical behavior positive emotions and attitudes. It must be stressed that this type of analysis is often tenuous, inaccurate, and fraught with difficulties. It can serve as a *rough* guide if the worker recognizes its limitations.

A third source of information about who controls the contingencies in the environment may be provided by a reinforcement survey. Generally, a reinforcement survey asks the client to list potential and existing reinforcers. The survey is typically used in behavioral exchange programs, such as token economies, but it can be adapted to determine who controls the contingencies. This adaptation includes a list of possible reinforcers and punishers and asks the client to indicate who generally delivers these stimuli and for what behaviors they are contingently delivered. Again, this method is limited and is not as accurate as observation and data analysis.

When the worker has completed this initial survey of family members, their access to the problem, and who has control of the contingencies, the family members and the worker reach agreement about who is to be the change agent. The worker emphasizes the specific responsibilities of the change agent. The family change agent should possess the following characteristics: (1) access to the problem and the client who exhibits the problem, (2) control of the existing and to-be-developed contingencies operating within the family, and (3) adequate reinforcers or the ability to be taught the skills to develop the new reinforcers. Using multiple or mutual change agents within the family can enhance the effectiveness of the program and reduce sabotage, for example, in marital problems. The terminal goal of the worker's assessment is to reach a contract with specific family members about whether they will or will not accept the delineated responsibilities of the change agent.

Selecting the Setting for Change. Family members frequently do not always state where the problem occurs. It is the worker's responsibility to determine the problem sites, the frequency of the problem, and whether the problem occurs in more than one environment. If the problem occurs in only one environment, the worker's clear responsibility is to help the family alter the rates of the problem behavior in that environment. If the problem behavior occurs in many environments, the worker and the family should reach a clear contract that identifies the environments for intervention. With most families, the home is the most appropriate setting for change.

The home as the setting for change has several advantages. It is easier to develop natural reinforcers in the home, to increase the rate of those reinforcers, and to apply them contingent on specific behaviors. The home environment is the setting where the family resides and spends a good deal of time interracting. This provides opportunities for reinforcement that might not exist in other environments where the family has minimal contact, investment, or control. It is easier to program maintenance of treatment effects in a single environment than in multiple settings. Overall, the home as the setting for change offers more long-term control over the contingencies than do most environments.

The agency is almost never identified by family members as the setting for change: Families come to agencies for help in achieving change in another setting, such as the home or an institution. However, the agency may be an appropriate place for teaching the necessary skills to family members and then programming those skills for implementation in the home. Practice Illustrations 6.2 and 7.4 are good examples of intervention within the agency.

The agency may be an appropriate locus to initially achieve change because the control of the contingencies can be in the worker's hands. The control can be transferred later to the selected change agent, and programs that achieve change in the agency can be transferred to the environments where the problem frequently occurs. Procedures to transfer learning from the agency to the setting the problem behavior occurs in is essential. This transfer must be programmed and not just hoped for (see Chapter Nine).

Chapter Eight fully discusses institutions and staff members as agents of change. If the family has the time and commitment to work with an institutionalized family member, the effectiveness of the institution can be increased (Linsk, Pinkston, and Green, Practice Illustration 7.1). Family members have two routes by which to achieve change in institutions: advocacy and direct work with the client in the institution. If the family member wishes to achieve change through advocacy, the worker may direct the family toward appropriate agencies and personnel who control the contingencies within the institution. If institutional policies permit, the worker may wish to become directly involved in advocacy or may work as part of a team in advocating the change. The family members should realize the limitations of advocacy and that institutional changes are extremely difficult.

However, family members are not just limited to advocacy in the institution; they can be directly involved in intervention. Workers may wish to train the family in how to interact with institutionalized clients. If time is available, they can be taught behavioral techniques that can be applied directly to the institutionalized relative. The difficulty with this intervention is that the family does not have the control to ensure that the staff will maintain the intervention.

Not all institutions are residential. Schools offer the potential for family members to achieve change in an environment outside the home. With a time commitment and training, family members can be effectively taught to interact with their children in schools. Schools offer unique opportunities for families to learn techniques that can achieve change in one environment and then program that change to another environment. Family members, however, should be aware of existing difficulties with lines of authority, teachers, administrators, and other children.

Family members may identify the community as the locus

for the desired change. For example, families with children might cite frequent fighting with neighborhood children; criminal acts, such as shoplifting; or lack of social interactions with community members. Planned behavioral programs in the community may be difficult to implement and achieve because neither the family nor the worker can control contingencies to the extent that effective change can be programmed.

Because of this frequent lack of control in the community, the family and workers often neglect the community as the setting for the change effort. Change can be achieved in community interaction through at least three possible alternatives: (1) increasing community contact for the client by involving extended family members outside the home (respite from continual care of the client; increase opportunity for the client to interact with people other than immediate family), (2) increasing opportunities for reinforcement in the community (special classes or activities, self-help groups, daycare), (3) involving family in community social action and support programs (Parent Teachers Association, Chicago Citizens for the Retarded, for example). As in most behavioral interventions, those involving the community are directed toward increasing the total amount of reinforcement available to the client. Behavioral techniques are implemented by the family using community members and organizations as social and material supports. The family members and workers should be informed of the possibilities of change before they attempt direct behavioral intervention in the community.

Options 1 and 2 offer the most immediate source of intervention because the resources for those interventions may already be present. Extended family or neighbors may be willing to provide additional social support by daily phoning an elderly client, including a retarded child on some of their family trips, and occasionally providing weekend care for an impaired relative or friend. In some cases, option 2 will be readily available and the workers need only advise the family of available activities. Other times, family members will want to organize special activities that are not available for their impaired members or to increase the total family involvement with the community. Throughout the country, there are resources in the form of sheltered workshops, daycare, summer camps, and after-school programs that have been organized by nonprofessional family members of clients. These resources increase the positive experiences available to members of the nonprofessionals' families and friends.

Option 3 is a long-term solution and involves attempts by the families and workers to affect the development, legislation, and administration of the government's family policy. For instance, parents of retarded children are a powerful group that has affected legislation while providing mutual support for each other and their children. This involvement may enhance the amount of social support available to clients and family change agents in the local community. It is important that the workers and family members deal with persons in the community who control the contingencies and resources, such as school administrators and agency personnel, to develop more complete intervention programs.

Data Recording and Sources of Information. The fifth area of assessment is data recording and the sources of information.

The interview is a rich potential source of information. During the interview, the worker may elicit retrospective data to explore the characteristics of the problem. Family members help the worker determine the contingencies, frequencies of behaviors, settings, and typical resources. But with retrospective explorations, inaccuracy and distortion frequently occur (Green and Wright, 1979). Retrospective self-report data may be the only sources of information during the initial interview and are valid sources of initial data. The interview may be a place to record behavioral data using role playing, to have the client engage in the actual behavior, or to set the occasion for the behavior to occur.

In the Rzepnicki and others example (Practice Illustration 7.2), the occasion for stuttering and fluency to occur was set by asking the child to read from a book; the worker was able to collect data on the frequency of stuttering and fluency. If the behavior is overtly aggressive or dangerous, the worker should consider alternate methods for developing information.

The second source of information appropriate to behavioral family treatment is questionnaires, ratings, and scales. Molick and his colleagues (Practice Illustration 7.4) evaluated academic and contracting skills that were taught to a group of parents of adult retardates by using pre- and posttests.

A third source of information is observational data. Observations of the family interactions are often the most valid and reliable method of collecting essential information. Selected family members are trained to observe in the natural environment.

Family members as observers provide data on interactions without having outside observers enter the natural environment. Because the family members are often present in the setting in which the problem behavior occurs, selecting observers from the family is appropriate; thus, the change agents are often recruited as observers. Levitt (1981) reported the positive effects of recording the behavior of change agents. When the family members serve as observers, they are trained in observational techniques; the worker must ensure that observation skills are adequate. The worker, whenever possible, schedules independent reliability checks to ensure accurate independent observations by the family members. In all the practice illustrations in this chapter, at least one family member was trained as an observer. In the Linsk and Pinkston illustration, for example, the workers trained the spouse of the disabled elderly client as an observer. Behavioral family intervention, unlike individual intervention, does not rely heavily on self-reported data because the change agent and the observers are often persons other than the client. As such, the validity and reliability of the observations can be more readily verified.

Family observers tend to report observations retrospectively unless specific recording intervals are determined. For example, at the end of the day, the observer may attempt to figure out how many times a behavior occurred and the responses to the behavior. The reliability and validity of this retrospective method of observing are questionable. Finally, the observers may not actually observe. Each problem should be dealt with as soon as it becomes apparent by explaining the logic and rationale for observation, training and retraining the observers, conducting independent observation, and defining behavior adequately. In addition, emphasize positive consequences for observation through feedback.

Data Assessment

Data assessment, the sixth and final area of assessment, helps the worker determine how family interactions can be altered to affect the rate, latency, intensity, or duration of the current problem and decide the probable cause of the problem, and it helps both the worker and the family develop intervention techniques thought to ameliorate problem behaviors.

Most of the initial data assessment is based on the analysis of baseline data. The worker examines the stability, variability, and trends of a series of data points within the baseline and then examines the temporal relationship between variables and formulates a tentative and workable hypothesis regarding the client's and family's *current* situation. This hypothesis is formulated with the goal of describing how the family can alter attention, punishment, reinforcement, or schedules to provide the quickest durable change.

Using graphed data facilitates data assessment because graphing enables the worker to spot the trends and inconsistencies. Graphing also helps interpret the data to the family members. When families who previously were overwhelmed by unmanageable behaviors see the behaviors in black and white, they are often very reassured. To many, the previously elusive behavior has been nailed down and can be changed.

If it is agreed that the problem occurs as defined, a functional analysis of contingencies is conducted. This analysis includes an assessment of the behaviors considered troublesome, the family members' reactions to those behaviors, and the setting or occasion for those behaviors. The worker attempts to depict and illustrate contingencies that may be reinforcing the problem; these contingencies are interpreted to the family members, who confirm their validity. These contingencies are altered, through intervention, to produce interactions that facilitate problem reduction and the attainment of the desired outcomes.

Intervention

Family change agents are taught to alter their interactions with the goal of changing the rate, intensity, duration, or latency of the problem. Change in family interactions does not randomly occur; skills are taught to change agents who actively implement change techniques in the natural setting. Intervention is planned and systematically applied by the family members as change agents. The worker helps the family select an intervention technique that has been determined appropriate as a result of the assessment, trains the change agents to implement the technique, evaluates the effectiveness of the technique to produce the desirable outcome, and trains the family members in alternative techniques if the original technique is demonstrated unsuccessful.

Choosing the Intervention Strategy

Based on the goals and data assessment, the worker and the family members select a clearly defined technique that has a high probability of achieving the desired outcomes. Selecting the technique entails more than what looks good; it is based on past and current research.

The decision to train family members to use a particular technique depends on the characteristics of the family and the community they reside in, the time available to the worker, and the characteristics of the problem behavior. The worker initially considers the resources and time available to the family. Numerous issues should be addressed: Does the family interact with the problem? Can they alter their behavioral interactions? Does the family have access to existing reinforcers in the natural environment? Can the family increase access to reinforcement? The worker should assess whether the family has the time to interact by determining the time of the problem and competing demands. The worker assesses if resources exist outside the home. If the problem is low social interactions, the worker evaluates the family resources to determine if interactions can be increased within the family. If these interactions cannot be increased within the family, the worker examines the outside community and environment and assesses if the outside environment has potential for increasing interactions vis-a-vis a community program. If a community program does not exist, the worker evaluates close approximations to the program. The worker specifies family, problem, and environment characteristics that might impede behavioral intervention and attempts to alter the functional relationship between the family, the problem, and the environment. Given the resources, time, commitment, and access, most problem behaviors can be modified. Many techniques have been demonstrated successful when used by well-trained family members as change agents (Pinkston, Friedman, and Polster, 1981).

The type of technique selected is based on data assessment and the outcomes desired. If the goal is to establish new behaviors, the preferred intervention techniques are shaping and modeling. Shaping is teaching new behaviors by reinforcing successive approximations of that terminal behavior. Family members can be trained in shaping techniques and procedures that eventually are implemented in the setting selected for change. Modeling is presenting a behavior to the client who does not exhibit the behavior (Bandura, 1969). For example, an elderly man can be taught to learn walking with a cane by observing models ambulate with a cane, or a child can learn to reply in an acceptable manner. Both viable techniques enable the worker to teach family members and clients new skills, and they can be implemented in the home to help establish new behaviors.

A client may exhibit many problem behaviors at low rates, durations, intensities, or latencies. Family members can be taught reinforcement techniques that increase the rate of an existing behavior.

If there is insufficient frequency of contingent reinforcement, the worker can initially attempt to increase the rate in the family context, tapping its wealth of existing resources and reinforcers. If additional reinforcers need to be developed and maintained, the worker can examine if existing reinforcers can be increased or made more contingent or if other family members who have available resources can be included. Molick and his colleagues taught the parents how to use existing reinforcers contingently by teaching contracting skills and behavioral principles.

Not all families have the opportunity to reinforce positive and adaptive behaviors. If the assessment reveals a lack of opportunity to reinforce low-rate behavior, the worker can increase access to reinforcement outside the family. A parent who wants a child to interact more with playmates can consider afterschool activities that increase opportunities for reinforcement. If the child is an only child, the opportunity for appropriate social interaction with playmates may be severely limited in the home. Varied community resources are money, social activities, medical care, employment, or other preferred available activities that increase opportunities for reinforcing positive behaviors.

If the goal is to reduce the frequency, duration, intensity, or latency of problem behaviors, the worker should identify and attempt to increase incompatible behaviors. If parents want to reduce their children's fighting, the worker should also train the parents in how to increase playing together nicely. Or, if a child excessively throws tantrums, the parents can attempt to increase the child's good behavior during those occasions in which the unacceptable behavior normally occurs. If increasing incompatible behaviors is unfeasible or ineffective, the family member as a change agent can implement differential attention. The worker should be aware that differential attention has mixed results (Herbert and colleagues, 1973; Wahler, 1969a), and there is the possibility that the aversive behavior may increase. If the results indicate that differential attention is ineffective, the family members can be taught to implement simple punishment techniques like time-out, response cost, or the presentation of mild and contingent aversive stimuli. Positive techniques that increase reinforcement in the natural environment are preferred, but occasionally punishment techniques may be needed. Any punishment-based technique should be coupled with a reinforcement-based technique so the worker does not solely increase the amount of punishment in an environment. The goal is to train family members in minimal punishment, enough to reduce the undesirable behaviors to acceptable levels and to increase the family member's use of positive techniques and methods to alleviate problems.

Interventions

Many techniques are appropriate and available for behavioral family intervention. These techniques are selected for effectiveness, feasibility, social relevance, applicability, and generality. Once the data assessment has been completed and the desirable outcomes defined and established, the worker teaches the family members to apply specific techniques in the environment selected as the setting for change. These techniques are based on the operant and social learning literature and have been evaluated for effectiveness in successfully reducing the problem and achieving other desirable outcomes. The techniques are categorized into four areas with attention to behavioral family intervention.

Reinforcement Procedures. Reinforcement techniques are powerful tools for altering the rates of positive behaviors that occur within numerous families (Pinkston, Friedman, and Polster, 1981). Modifying appropriate and desirable behaviors has been demonstrated effective in a number of settings, with different types of clients and different change agents (Gambrill, 1977; 1981). The viability of family administered reinforcement-based techniques has also been demonstrated in numerous settings, with different families and with different problems. For example, parents have successfully altered such diverse problems as language deficits (Pinkston and Herbert-Jackson, 1975; Lovaas and others, 1973; Guess, Sailor, and Baer, 1977; Nordquist and Wahler, 1973); inappropriate cross-gender behavior of young children (Rekers, Lovaas, and Low, 1974); academic difficulties (Polster and Pinkston, 1979); toilet training (Azrin and Foxx, 1974); and aggressive and disruptive behaviors (Berkowitz and Graziano, 1972; O'Dell, 1974; Patterson, 1974; Patterson and others, 1975). Other problems, insufficiently researched, are likely to be amenable to family administered reinforcement.

Reinforcement techniques applicable to families are increasing contingent reinforcement, using token economies, and applying differential attention. Often it is advantageous to teach family members numerous techniques to be implemented concurrently. Change agents are taught techniques that provide positive reinforcement for adaptive behaviors which occur at low rates and are incompatible with undesired behaviors (Goldiamond, 1975). Rzepnicki taught the mother of a child who stuttered the technique of positive reinforcement of fluent verbal behavior. Differential attention reinforces an appropriate behavior while ignoring an incompatible aversive behavior. Change agents are taught to apply this technique contingently in the setting selected.

Token economies or point systems have an extensive clinical literature, and research has been conducted on the effectiveness of token economies in natural settings (for review, see Kazdin, 1977). Practice Illustration 7.3 further demonstrates the feasibility and effectiveness of family administered token economies.

For social work practice, reinforcement techniques are a humanistic basis for intervention. Change agents who selectively, consistently, and contingently reinforce desired behaviors have learned a skill that is applicable to achieving additional goals. It is therefore advantageous that change agents be taught as many reinforcement-based techniques as possible.

Increasing Environmental Opportunity for Reinforcement. The second major set of techniques that change agents can be taught involve increasing environmental opportunities for reinforcement. Often, data assessment reveals that the opportunity for clients to engage in adaptive and reinforced behavior is insufficient or lacking. For example, coercive family patterns may offer few opportunities for positive responses. It is unlikely that a husband who *demands* service from his wife will find her an enthusiastic sexual partner or even receive affection. By defining their expectations and agreeing on mutual goals, the marital partners can increase their opportunities to engage in reinforcing activities.

The worker initially attempts to increase the available reinforcers in the family setting by teaching change agents to reinforce adaptive behaviors and provide indicators that reinforcement is available. This is perhaps as simple as teaching individuals to ask for what they want. The method involves teaching family members to *notice* positive behaviors, to teach *cues* to stimulate positive activity, to *recognize* the activity, and to *reinforce* it. Teaching prompt and praise techniques increases overall opportunities for reinforcement of family members who are not identified change agents or clients.

Reinforcement of incompatible behaviors is implemented primarily to reduce undesired behavior, although it should result in increased desirable behavior. Incompatible behaviors are behaviors that cannot exist at the same time as the undesirable behaviors. For example, screaming and talking nicely are incompatible, as are compliance and noncompliance. The goal of training change agents in this technique is to discriminate the events prior to the occcurrence of undesired behaviors and to reinforce an incompatible behavior so the undesired behavior does not occur. The technique is attractive because it provides a method of reinforcing and thus increasing a behavioral repertoire and does not require using an aversive technique.

Links with the community can help provide opportunities for reinforcement that do not or cannot exist in the home environment. For example, involvement can be encouraged with an active church or community organization that has activities many nights of the week. Other examples of community programs that can increase potential reinforcers are daycare for the impaired elderly, afterschool programs for children, recreational activities during the summer, or in-home health care that might provide relief of caretaking activities so an individual family member can leave the home for short periods of time. To develop and implement the links, clear and defined goals and a specific rationale are necessary, or links to community programs might not provide the opportunity for reinforcement or may not be implemented to their fullest extent.

The family should be involved as much as possible with developing and implementing links. Community linkage implementation is a technology (Weissman, 1975), and family involvement is critical. The involvement includes decision making, investigating community programs, and assisting with application procedures. This family involvement can help the family determine whether the community program is appropriate to the problem and teach family members how to negotiate necessary social systems.

A potential advantage, yet unexplored, of using links and community programs is that it maintains the program's effects by providing the opportunity for skills and desirable behaviors to be reinforced in settings other than the one selected for change. The worker should not consider links separate and distinct from behavioral programs administered by the family; community and behavioral programs often go hand in hand, and workers should maximize all opportunities for clients to engage in adaptive behavior in and out of the change setting.

Punishment Procedures. Punishment techniques are used to decrease the frequency, intensity, duration, or latency of problem and undesired behavior. As previously stated, punishment techniques are never taught or implemented alone; any punishment technique is at least paired with the positive reinforcement of incompatible behavior. In fact, we assert that most behavioral difficulties experienced by families can be successfully reduced by reinforcement-based techniques. Thus, the use of punishment-based techniques should be minimized. However, we also recognize that in some instances punishment-based techniques should be used because not to punish may leave the client in punishing contingencies from which there is no escape or avoidance (Baer, 1970). For example, consider the autistic child who has a high rate of head banging and other extreme behavior. Positive reinforcement for keeping the head still and not banging may not be powerful enough to decrease head banging to zero. Mild and contingent punishment such as shouting "No" or making a loud noise may successfully eliminate this noxious behavior. To not punish is to punish the child by letting head banging continue or escalate to the possibility of brain trauma.

Response cost gives the family a punishment-based technique capable of altering the client's rates of problem behavior. Response cost is removing a positive reinforcer—television, toys, access to an automobile—contingent upon the occurrence of an undesired behavior. Parents, when questioned about techniques used to punish, often cite a variation of the use of response cost: They often take away television, dinner, or playtime as a result of a child's misbehavior. The task is to train the parents, if they are engaged as change agents, to use response cost more contingently and specifically to the targeted problem, with the desired goal of increasing the effectiveness of the technique. Response cost is frequently used as an integral aspect of token economies as a fine for maladaptive behavior. In these instances, tokens are removed for undesired behavior. The effects of response cost in reducing noxious behavior have been demonstrated in various settings (Kaufman and O'Leary, 1972; Buchard and Barrera, 1972; Patterson, 1974) with various change agents, including family members.

A second punishment-based technique is positive punishment, which is presenting an aversive contingent stimuli following an undesired behavior, to reduce the probability of the undesired behavior occurring in the future. Positive punishment should be considered a technique of last resort because of the probability of undesired side effects (Azrin and Holtz, 1966). Most research has demonstrated that positive punishment *can* be effective, yet the primary difficulty is that most of the research (for example, Foxx and Azrin, 1972; Bucher and Lovaas, 1968) has been conducted in institutional environments, where control is high.

The third punishment technique is time-out, which is removing a client from a reinforcing to a less reinforcing environment contingent upon the occurrence of an undesired behavior. Family members as change agents can be efficiently taught the proper use of time-out; the effectiveness of the technique has been demonstrated, primarily with the parents of children (Wahler, 1969a; Pinkston and Herbert-Jackson, 1975). Time-out is taught and used carefully and systematically because there is high potential for abuse and confusion. It is recommended that time-out be kept short (about three minutes), contingent, and consistent. This technique is easily taught, effective, and one for which the worker does not have to identify the reinforcing event that is maintaining the undesired behavior (Gambrill, 1977).

Caution is in order when using *any* punishment technique. Because many of the punishment-based techniques have been demonstrated effective in a variety of settings with family members as change agents, workers may be reinforced for training change agents in how to use punishment procedures. However, the effectiveness of the techniques does not imply that they should be freely advocated, trained, or implemented. The use of any punishment-based technique should be minimized because it does not teach a client what to do but what *not* to do. Punishment-based techniques should be considered only when reinforcement techniques such as the reinforcement of incompatible behavior, positive reinforcement, or linkage development and implementation ineffectively produce the desired change. If punishment is used, it should have constraints, checks, and be faded out as soon as possible.

Contracts. Another major intervention technique is contracting. Contracts are written or oral agreements between two or more people that delineate the particulars of the relationship between the people, their behavior, and the consequences for the behavior (Homme and others, 1969). Contracts give the family a tool for negotiating desired behaviors. Contracts have been used successfully in various settings for different problems, such as overeating (Aragona, Cassady, and Drabman, 1975); drug use (Boudin, 1972); and appropriate school behaviors (Cohen and others, 1971). Populations have included delinquents (Stuart, 1971; Stuart and Lott, 1972) and marital couples (Stuart, 1969; Patterson, 1971; Jacobson, 1977). In behavioral family treatment, contracts consist of contingency arrangements between family members (including the client) and the worker, the client, and the family members, and among family members.

Practice Illustration 7.3 illuminates the salient points of contracts. Briefly, the contract should be clear, explicit, and detailed; it should describe explicit behavior rather than issues and permit reinforcement only after the behavior has occurred (Homme and others, 1969). The development and implementation of contracts should be transferred to the family members as soon as possible. The family members learn how to recognize problem behavior, identify potential reinforcers, and develop a contract that is fair and agreeable to all parties. Manuals such as *Parents Are Teachers* (Becker, 1971) provide useful contracting procedures. As the family members and the clients become more successful at negotiation skills, most of the responsibilities for contract development and implementation are transferred to the family.

It is not assumed that family change agents have adequate contract negotiation skills. The ability to negotiate and reach agreements about a problem behavior must be individually assessed and necessary skills taught. A sample paradigm of skills to be assessed includes: (1) suggesting deals or terms of the contract, (2) making counterproposals, (3) making compromises, and (4) specifying the terms of the contract (Gambrill, 1977). If these skills are inadequate, the worker should teach them through modeling and shaping and ensure that they can be adequately performed.

In addition, contracts may be developed between family members. The worker, if involved, ensures that the family members successfully negotiate and implement the contract. Independently developed contracts, without worker assistance, are a desired goal of intervention. If family members can successfully negotiate and implement a contract independently, they have learned a functional skill that should enable them to negotiate future difficulties.

Although contracts offer a potential for successful alleviation of a problem, they are not fully developed as intervention techniques. Contracts with juvenile delinquents have been only mildly successful (Stuart and Lott, 1972). Furthermore, most contracts that have been demonstrated effective have been evaluated with marital couples or children as the client population. Finally, contracts appear appropriate with moderate to mild behavioral difficulties experienced by families, but their use has not been demonstrated with families who are experiencing severe difficulties.

Regarding maintenance, contracts have not yet demonstrated that positive effects last past the terms of the contract. If contracts can produce change only while they are in force, alternate procedures must be developed and implemented that will ensure that positive gains will maintain once they are achieved. This is an area yet unexplored.

Training Family Members in Techniques. Four specific techniques are potentially viable for educating change agents in the specifics of implementing a behavioral technique: (1) modeling and feedback, (2) cueing, (3) instruction, and (4) behavioral rehearsal. The techniques are infrequently used individually for training or educating; they are often used by the worker in conjunction with one another. For example, the worker typically instructs the change agents, then models the technique, has the change agent demonstrate the technique to the worker, and, if implementation problems exist, may cue the change agent when it is appropriate to implement the technique. A goal of training and educating the change agents is to teach how to successfully apply the behavioral technique independent of the worker. The worker first ensures the technique can be successfully implemented by monitoring performance and then ensures that the technique can be implemented independent of the cues, feedback, or monitoring.

Evaluation

Evaluation enables the worker to determine the technique's ability to produce the desired change and the change agent's ability to implement the technique. The frequency, duration, intensity, or latency of the defined problem is the outcome variable in evaluation. The technique, as implemented by the change agent in the selected setting, is the independent variable. The independent variable is manipulated by the family member as the change agent, and the worker evaluates the consequential effects on the dependent variable.

Single-subject designs (see Chapter Four for a detailed explanation and description) are applicable to evaluating behavioral intervention with families, although serious drawbacks are apparent (Thomas, 1978) when they are used in clinical settings.

They give workers and change agents advantages unavailable with alternative methods.

Analysis of Findings. The nature of scientific models for social work intervention with families enables the worker to address specific questions when evaluation reveals either difficulty or success. In behavioral family intervention, the worker examines and evaluates the relationship between the operationally defined behavior exhibited by the client and the intervention technique taught to the family member as the change agent. Is there a one-to-one relationship? Is the technique applied contingently? If the technique is not applied, what is the agent doing? If training appears inadequate, are there alternative training methods available? The rationale for evaluating implementation procedures initially is that the most powerful technique is useless unless it is applied. For example, a marital couple has successfully negotiated desired behaviors, but evaluation reveals no change. Exploration determines that the husband did not complete his requirements and the wife ceased applying the intervention technique. Or, an elderly woman has been instructed to place her husband on the toilet every two hours as a technique hypothesized to reduce incontinence. The technique was unsuccessful, although success had been demonstrated in a different setting (Blackman, Howe, and Pinkston, 1976). Evaluation and exploration reveal that the woman is unable to implement the technique because she lacks the physical ability to move her husband from the bed to the toilet. Consequently, an initial question in evaluation is whether the behavioral technique was implemented by the trained change agent in the selected setting.

A second concern is whether the technique is effective or powerful enough to produce the desired change. If evaluation reveals that the technique is consistently and contingently applied, the worker evaluates the ability of the technique to produce the desired change when applied by family members as change agents. Effectiveness is assessed by examining or eyeballing the series of data points of the dependent variable in baseline and comparing, for stability, variability, and level, the series of data points in intervention. The parents of a young child were taught differential attention and successfully implemented the technique with the identified problem of noncompliance to parental requests. Evaluation revealed no change in the frequency of noncompliance during intervention. The worker, at this junction, may propose more powerful alternate techniques. To summarize, if the technique is successfully implemented by the change agents, the worker evaluates the ability of the technique to produce the desired change.

The third question addressed in the analysis of evaluation data is one that may affect either the power of the technique to produce the desired outcome or the effectiveness of the application procedures. The worker evaluates competing demands and obstacles that interfere with either the application or effectiveness of the technique. Marital discord does not cause behavioral problems in children, but it can escalate the competing demands. Consequently, the effectiveness and efficiency of the intervention may be reduced. If evaluation reveals that competing demands and obstacles are extreme, the worker may wish to focus, for a limited time, on a program for those difficulties. For example, the parents of a ten-year-old child attempted to reduce the child's fighting. The parents were trained to use time-out and contracting, but the techniques were only moderately successful regarding application and effectiveness. The worker's evaluation revealed severe marital discord. The worker suggested that the intervention program for the child's fighting be postponed and that intervention initially focus on the parental fighting. When the parents agreed, the worker conducted a brief, three-session training based on contracting (Stuart, 1969). Once the parental fighting was reduced, the worker reinitiated with the family solution of the child's fighting.

During evaluation, the worker assesses the change agent's ability to implement the technique, assesses the ability of the technique to produce the desired outcome, and evaluates competing demands and obstacles. Once a difficulty is apparent, the worker retrains the family member as change agent or uses an alternate technique that might be more effective in producing the desired change. This process of evaluating and reevaluating application and intervention techniques is continued until the desired outcome is achieved.

Most single-subject designs are applicable for evaluating the effectiveness of intervention conducted by family members as agents of change. As described in Chapter Three, selecting the appropriate design depends upon a number of variables. The minimal design available to evaluate change in the applied behavior analysis model for social work intervention with families is AB. Variations on AB designs, multiple-baseline designs, changing-criteria designs, and others can be used and are appropriate, depending upon the degree of control available in the family, the setting selected, and the particular question addressed in intervention and research.

The practice illustrations provide examples of the different designs for clinical application. Pinkston and others used multiple-baseline and ABC designs to test the effectiveness of the parent training. Molick and others used AB designs that were replicated across the parents of the adult retardates. Rzepnicki and others used a multiple-baseline-across-problems design. Linsk, Pinkston, and Green used multiple-baseline-across-problems and AB designs. Each set of authors proposed a series of questions, evaluated the outcome of the intervention, and answered the questions by using different single-subject designs.

Home-Based Behavioral Social Work
with the Elderly

Nick L. Linsk, Elsie M. Pinkston, Glenn R. Green

Although family liaison and consultation are established components of gerontological social work (Brody, 1974; Lowy, 1979),
there are almost no practice methods to assist families when
older persons develop behavior problems. Despite an increasing
focus on "alternatives of institutionalization" (Kaufman, 1980;
Morris, 1971; Tobin and Lieberman, 1976), elderly persons still
face the risk of having increased physical or mental health problems interpreted as the need for long-term care. When the family or other involved care givers are willing to provide help, they
may serve as change agents to ameliorate behavioral problems.
Objectionable or insufficient activities may be viewed as skill,
opportunity, or discrimination deficits. In such cases, the social
worker examines behavior problems by analyzing behavioral
contingencies and existing resources. Interventions are implemented to improve the life situation of both elderly and support persons by (1) teaching or reteaching relevant skills, (2)
providing resource links, and (3) developing feedback mechanisms to sustain family support.

Previous efforts to apply behavior analysis methods to
the problems of older persons have been limited to institutional
settings. Target problems have included self-care activities (eating, dressing, continence, and locomotion) and social and verbal
behaviors. Reinforcement, token systems, and stimulus control
procedures have all been used successfully. (For reviews, see
Hoyer, 1973; Rebok and Hoyer, 1977; Tobin, 1977). Behavior analysis with families of the elderly has not yet been presented in the practice literature or evaluated in the research
literature.

Results of research that combine the uses of behavior

analysis with the institutionalized elderly with the development of behavioral family training programs are reported as part of a developmental research project to generate and evaluate techniques useful for behavioral social work with families, including older relatives with behavior problems. This Elderly Support Project (ESP) has as its objectives developing means to maintain older persons in support. The case study reported here investigated the use of behavioral procedures with a depressed elderly man.

Method

Client. Mr. Kent was a sixty-nine year-old retiree who was referred while he was an inpatient in a geriatric psychiatry unit. At the time of hospitalization, he was living alone with his wife, who was his major support in day-to-day activities. In addition, he had five children, all of whom lived within the city. Mr. Kent retired as a railroad worker five years before he was hospitalized. After efforts to find part-time maintenance work were unsuccessful, he began a series of psychiatric hospitalizations after attempting suicide. In addition to multiple hospitalizations, he had a five-year history of multiple psychotropic drug usage, and he lived for a time in a group home. Additional, actual, or suspected health problems included tardive dyskenisia, emphysema, possible Parkinson's disease, dental problems, recurring boils, and constipation.

Mr. Kent's clinical diagnosis at time of referral was psychotic depression. Prior to retirement, he had been reported as a gregarious individual, with multiple friendship, church, and family contacts. Besides a previous active work life, he reported a number of former leisure-time interests (playing cards, sports, spectator events, out-of-town vacations, and church and club membership). At the time of referral, presenting problems suggested by hospital staff included increasing activities, decreasing cigarette smoking, and reducing reliance on the wife for personal needs.

Mrs. Kent was a sixty-four year-old woman who was retired at the time of referral to the project. She previously had engaged in office and organizational work, although her major occupation had been caring for her family. Mrs. Kent was eager to participate in the program, expressing willingness to learn ways to help her husband. She also complained about his lack of cooperation and general paucity of activities.

Settings. The major setting for intervention was the home of the client and support person. They lived in the house Mr. Kent had lived in all his life, a well-cared-for bungalow-style home full of conveniences and a variety of memorabilia of their married life together. Other family members lived on the block, and the Kents' church was within two blocks of the home. Both, however, expressed concern about the ethnic changes in the neighborhood, stating that the local bar and other businesses were no longer available to them because the clientele had changed.

A secondary setting was the hospital where Mr. Kent was living at the time of referral. The hospital is arranged in traditional long-corridor/patient room/nursing station fashion. While at the hospital, he lived in a two-bed room with a roommate; his treatment included medication management, milieu treatment, and individual and group therapy.

Procedures

Staff. Workers for the study included two collaborators: a behavioral social worker with a master's degree in social work with the elderly and a Ph.D. psychologist with expertise in human development and behavior analysis. In addition, research assistants participated by recording direct-observation behavioral data for reliability purposes.

Referral. Mr. Kent was referred after he had been in the hospital about seven weeks and initial trial home visits had begun.

At the time, he was participating in a research protocol to test the effects of antidepressant drugs with the elderly. The protocol included diet and smoking limitations. Staff reported minimum activities, except for improved eating, staying in bed, requests for cigarettes, and attending weekly group meetings.

Hospital staff expressed concern regarding Mrs. Kent's tendency to do everything for her husband, thereby increasing dependency.

Assessment. The initial assessment occurred in both the hospital and during preliminary predischarge home visits. Structured assessment instruments for both the subject and his wife were administered, accompanied by a discussion of problem behaviors with the client, his wife, their adult children, and the hospital staff.

Target behaviors were identified from the hospital treatment plan and Mr. and Mrs. Kent's concerns about activity levels. Initial behaviors included: (1) cigarette smoking, due to the need to decrease frequency because of possible drug-tobacco interactions and lung disorders; (2) cigarette requests, because of Mrs. Kent's concerns about his repeated requests, threats, and demands; (3) hours not in bed, due to concern that Mr. Kent spent excessive time in bed; (4) hours out of house, because of his previous low levels of out-of-home activity; and (5) visitors, in an effort to monitor family involvement and social interaction. After one week, Mrs. Kent was asked to monitor her own activity out of the home.

Recording Baseline Data. Mrs. Kent was taught to use a daily checklist to monitor the five behaviors. Data recording was taught by written and verbal worker instruction and feedback during home visits. Mrs. Kent learned to use hourly interval samples to monitor whether her husband was in or out of bed, out of the house, whether visitors had been present, and whether Mrs. Kent left the home each hour. In addition, continuous recording of the number of cigarettes smoked each hour was included. Initial baseline periods included two predischarge weekend home visits.

In a later phase, additional behavior records were developed, taught to Mr. and Mrs. Kent, and recorded daily. Mrs. Kent completed a daily checklist of self-care and housekeeping tasks and communication and recreation activities. Mr. Kent learned to self-record in-home and out-of-home activities, chores, and cigarettes smoked per day. Instructions and feedback were also used to teach Mr. Kent to self-record, although initially daily feedback and prompts were needed.

Reliability checks, using direct observations and intersubject comparison, were computed for each treatment condition. Low occurrence of several target behaviors during observation times limited the frequency of behaviors available for independent reliability comparison. Reliability scores including both occurrence and nonoccurrence of behaviors were computed (see Chapter Four). Overall reliability for spouse/observer observations was 90 percent agreement. Scores for specific categories ranged from 67 to 100 percent.

Research Design. The independent variables for this study were a series of task assignment contracts followed by feedback from the worker at least weekly. The independent variable consisted of a multicomponent service package that included: (1) specification of reported problems into behaviors which could be measured; (2) data collection, which included the client and support person recording frequency of these behaviors; (3) weekly interviews to formulate and review tasks; (4) specific written contracts, with a copy left with the client; (5) midweek prompts to remind Mr. and Mrs. Kent of both the contract and the time of the next visit; (6) reviews that included attention to the data, interpretation of trends and patterns, praise for adhering to a task, reformulation of contracts when their goals were not achieved, and development of new contracts. Tasks consisted of specific recordable events that were familiar activities to both Mr. and Mrs. Kent. For example, a task might include smoking two or less cigarettes per hour or going outside at least every other day. In addition, each interview included an opportunity for both Mr. and Mrs. Kent to express their opinions about the contract, report important events that had occurred the previous week, and report on their general emotional state. A further treatment component was an effort to identify and implement community links for both Mr. and Mrs. Kent. Because no specific links were implemented or completed, these were not analyzed as part of the independent variable. Finally, a didactic behavioral-principles training course for Mrs. Kent was included after other behavioral objectives had been achieved.

The dependent variables for the study were the levels of Mr. Kent's daily activities. Specifically, a number of variables were measured: time in bed, time out of home, drying dishes, taking out garbage, and social activities.

A multiple-baseline-across-behaviors design was used to evaluate the impact of the program. Baseline data was collected on activities, taking out garbage, and drying dishes, with contracting and feedback as the major treatment procedure. Also, a changing-criteria design (Hall, 1971a) was attempted to demonstrate the effects of contracts regarding cigarette smoking.

Maintaining and Extending Treatment. General procedures for maintenance include transferring program design and monitoring responsibilities to the subject and support persons and implementing specific maintenance procedures. For Mr. Kent, a self-recording procedure was implemented after the seventh week. This technique removed some of Mrs. Kent's recording responsibilities and further involved Mr. Kent in his own program. In addition, the Behavioral Family Instruction program, including three sessions of structured instruction in behavioral principles to Mrs. Kent, was designed to enable the family to continue behavioral analysis and programming following termination with the workers.

Results

Several intervention procedures were developed and implemented throughout the first thirteen weeks following discharge, including:

Prompt and Praise for Adherence to Cigarette Schedule. Mrs. Kent was instructed to prompt Mr. Kent at designated periods that it was time for cigarette smoking, to praise him for adhering to the schedule, and to ignore intervening cigarette requests. The program combined prompt, praise, and extinction procedures. Using modeling, behavioral rehearsal, and feedback as training techniques, Mrs. Kent was taught to offer a cigarette on a scheduled basis and to ignore intervening requests for cigarettes. Results are presented in Figure 1. Following discharge, Mr. Kent increased his cigarette smoking, particularly when the criterion was changed from one cigarette per two hours to one per six hours at the hospital's suggestion at discharge. Following

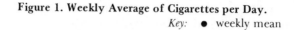

Figure 1. Weekly Average of Cigarettes per Day.

Key: ● weekly mean

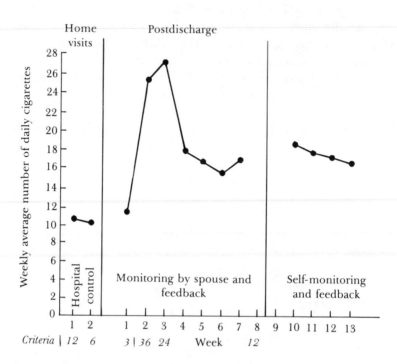

this, medication was discontinued and criterion was changed. By the sixth week, cigarette frequency decreased to one per hour and Mr. Kent took over responsibility for dispensing cigarettes and monitoring their use. Both the frequency of cigarette smoking per day decreased, as indicated by the weekly means, and the variability between days diminished, as shown by changes in standard deviations.

Contracting and Feedback for Out-of-Bed Time. Mr. Kent agreed to maintain his hospitalization out-of-bed schedule in the home setting. Experimenters provided weekly feedback regarding the number of hours he was not in bed. This feedback was accompanied by verbal praise for maintaining or increasing the number of hours he was not in bed. Results are presented in Figure 2.

Contracting and Feedback for Activities. Going out of

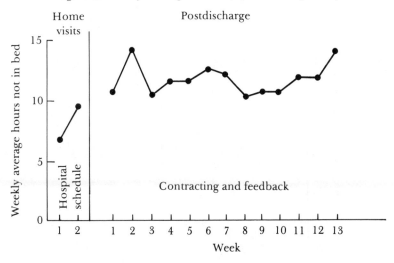

Figure 2. Weekly Average of Hours Not in Bed per Day.

the house, participating in activities, and household-chore contracts were developed, implemented, and accompanied by feedback. Following discharge, workers contracted with Mr. and Mrs. Kent that he would go out of the house each day. Figure 3a presents the results of this procedure. Frequency of trips per week increased from 0 during baseline to a mean of 2.4 trips during the contracting procedure. This frequency increased further to a mean of four trips during a self-monitored maintenance procedure. Similarly, duration outside per week increased from a mean of 1 hour per week during baseline to 5.2 hours during the initial contract to 9.8 hours per week during a self-recording phase. Mrs. Kent's out-of-home activity increased from eleven to an average of twenty-three hours per week. Her pretreatment report was that she could not leave him alone. These results were discussed with Mr. and Mrs. Kent during weekly sessions, with the worker providing verbal praise for positive results.

During this time, baseline data were recorded on other activities, and no activities were reported. A contracting procedure to increase activities was initiated in the sixth week when Mr. Kent reported playing cards with his son. He agreed to engage in at least one activity per day and record these activities

Figure 3. Number of Activities

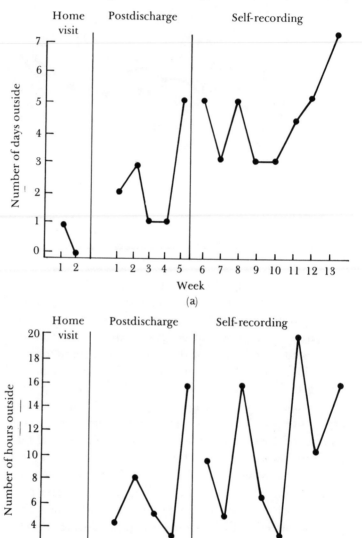

Week
(a)

Week
(b)

and Tasks per Week.

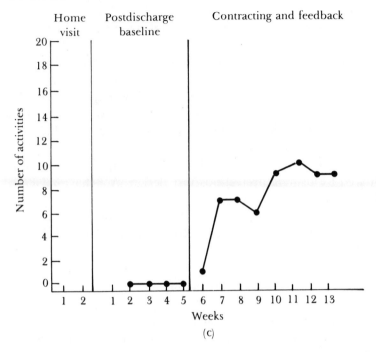

(c)

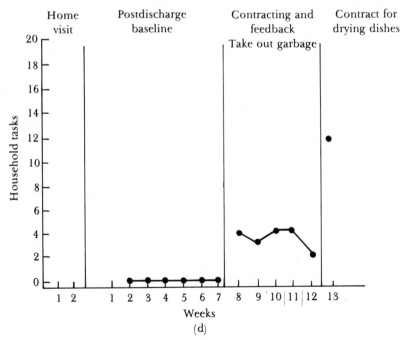

(d)

(Figure 3b). He was given weekly feedback to review between sessions.

Mr. Kent's self-recorded housekeeping activities were monitored after the fourth week following discharge. After four weeks of no occurrence of household tasks, Mr. Kent initiated requests for taking out garbage. Household tasks completed increased to four per week. After the twelfth week, a contract for Mr. Kent to help dry dishes once per day was implemented. This resulted in an increase of tasks to over ten per week. These results are presented in Figure 3c.

The outcome of the behavioral principles training was evaluated by using a pretest-posttest design. A Behavioral Principles Knowledge Inventory was adapted from O'Dell (1974) and administered both before and after the program. Results suggest minimal changes in Mrs. Kent's knowledge of behavior procedures.

Discussion

In this study, both an elderly individual and his wife participated in efforts to clearly specify and quantify their behavior. Such specification is important because frequently behavior problems are used by social workers and other professionals, as well as the aged and their supports, as criteria for institutional placement. Once quantified, at least one major problem in this study was reformulated into a minimal problem area: excessive cigarette smoking. When cigarette smoking was viewed as one of Mr. Kent's few remaining reinforcers, the need to eliminate the behavior became less pressing; in fact, elimination of incompatible medication became a more viable response. It was in response to a desire to buy his own cigarettes that Mr. Kent began his out-of-house activities. Clearly, the ability to teach clients to specify and record problem behaviors is a useful technique available to the social worker, particularly when the nature and frequency of the behavior in question are unclear.

This study also illustrates how a more reinforcing environment can be constructed from simple daily activities. During the course of this research, Mr. Kent added activities serially to his daily functioning. First, his wife was taught to reinforce him for engaging in existing responses, as examples, getting out of bed, limiting his smoking, and not requesting cigarettes too often. Later, Mr. Kent was given the option of selecting social activities, which included daily walks, watching television, and playing cards. These behaviors had previously been in the client's behavioral repertoire and were available when desired. This information was reported to the worker by both Mr. and Mrs. Kent in early interviews. Most of the specific activities were chosen by the Kents for themselves, which added to the interventions a measure of self-management that could be maintained after termination.

Although data on learning of behavioral principles did not show substantial conceptual learning, the procedure did communicate Mrs. Kent's ability to use the behavioral procedures on her own. Further research is needed to evaluate such teaching and to reveal how effective such efforts are for this population.

Finally, a number of procedures implemented during this study were interrupted by illness. In each instance, although Mr. Kent reported discomfort, this was initially discounted by his wife, his doctor, the worker, and even Mr. Kent himself. In almost each case, a treatable malady developed and intervention continued after medical treatment. This problem suggests an ongoing concern that needs to be incorporated into behavioral social work with the elderly: ongoing participation with medical personnel. Physical ailments can certainly interfere with the effective delivery of reinforcement or the potency of discriminative stimuli for specific behavior. Often conditions that are considered untreatable medically are responsive to behavior analysis, but ongoing medical consultation is crucial.

The results of this case provide preliminary support for the use of home-based behavioral procedures for treating the impaired elderly. These procedures are especially valuable because they act to change the total environment for the elderly person in ways that increase the amount of positive support they receive from their family and/or friends. The procedures, including prompts, praise, contracting, and instruction, increase the elderly person's rate of reinforcement and opportunity to receive reinforcement. The behavioral social worker can directly teach behavior analysis to involved relatives, friends, or to the elderly person. This program tended to increase the opportunity for reinforcement of support persons, thereby increasing the probability that the older person will continue to remain in familiar surroundings.

Treating Stuttering by Using Parental Attention and a Structured Program for Fluency

Tina L. Rzepnicki, Matsujiro Shibano,
Elsie M. Pinkston, Wendell H. Cox

Stuttering is a problem experienced by many people, but until recent years, there was no generally effective intervention for remediation (Beech and Fransella, 1968; Ingham and Andrews, 1973). Successful approaches to this problem include the metronome procedure (Barber, 1940; Fransella, 1967; Jones and Azrin, 1969), in which the stutterer learns to speak in a steady rhythm, and the habit reversal procedure (Azrin and Nunn, 1974), in which the speaker uses a combination of interrupted speech at moments of anticipated stuttering and at natural pause points and regulated breathing, preparation, and relaxation procedures. The use of natural stop points for pausing in speech (juncturing) to yield a more natural speech pattern was first reported by Goldiamond. The procedures used in this study are adapted from those currently being used in Goldiamond's fluency laboratory.

The four factors emphasized in this study for fluent speech were (1) preparation, (2) juncturing, (3) breathing, and (4) voice projection. Direct manipulation of stimulus conditions is implied by the emphasis on these factors. Goldiamond has demonstrated that stuttering is a learned behavior and can be modified the same way as any other operant behavior (Goldiamond, 1965). Furthermore, this behavioral approach, developed by Goldiamond and associates in the Behavior Analysis Research Laboratory at the University of Chicago, allows the stutterer to develop self-control once the client has discriminated the stimulus conditions controlling the nonfluency.

In this case study, the consequences maintaining stuttering

were not apparent, so an approach that required only the manipulation of consequences was not suitable. For this reason, the client was taught a new response pattern that was incompatible with stuttering and that also focused on the antecedent conditions immediately preceding stuttering.

In this particular approach to the treatment of stuttering, the cooperation of another person in the stutterer's environment was enlisted to help modify the client's nonfluent behavior. The practitioner decided that a behavioral mediator (the client's mother) would be especially useful for several reasons. First, the mediator would learn the procedures for fluency along with the client and could practice them with the client between training sessions, thereby enhancing generality from the treatment situation to everyday life. Second, if there was a need to reinstate training after treatment ended, the mediator would know how to proceed. Finally, because the client was young (ten years old), it was believed that initial reliance on self-control procedures alone would not sufficiently and successfully decrease stuttering. His mother was with him much of the time and was the logical person to provide positive consequences for fluency.

Method

Clients and Setting. The two clients in this study were a thirty-five-year-old woman, Mrs. P., and her ten-year-old son, Joe. Recent emigrées from Russia, they had lived in the United States for approximately one year. During that year, Mrs. P. had divorced and moved with her son from New York to Chicago. They were referred to the Single Parent Project by the school social worker because of the boy's stuttering. There was a speech therapist in his school, but she worked only with children whose speech impediments were caused by physical causes.

Joe's stuttering greatly interfered with his ability to communicate effectively in Russian or English and was a source of constant frustration for both him and his mother. According to Joe's mother, his stuttering began even before they left Russia. She associated its beginning with surgery for the removal of his adenoids that she stated was conducted without anesthetic. He received treatment from a therapist in Russia, but Mrs. P. stated that it did not help.

Joe could speak English and continued to improve during the study. He frequently read and was at an age-appropriate level in school. Because of his stuttering, however, he was embarrassed to read in front of his classmates.

Although Mrs. P. was able to communicate, her vocabulary was less extensive than her son's. When she did not understand something said to her, it was not always immediately apparent to the speaker. Thus, the therapist kept communication and instructions simple and relied on repetition, modeling, and guided practice to convey the behavioral procedures to mother and son.

Sixteen sessions were held weekly with the therapist in the home to teach both clients skills for fluent speech. The rationale for treatment in the home was to enhance setting generality and for the convenience of the parent. Because Mrs. P. was employed full time, her daily practice sessions with Joe were usually held soon after she got home from work in the evening.

Data Recording. The data sources were audiotapes from recorded daily reading and conversation sessions of mother and son. The tapes were fifteen to forty-five minutes long. From these tapes, rates of stuttering and parental use of technique taught during the training sessions could be determined.

Throughout the first month of the study, Mrs. P. observed and recorded frequency data for her son's stuttering during a daily reading session. An independent judge listened to the tapes and recorded frequencies of both Mrs. P.'s and Joe's relevant behaviors.

Each baseline tape included approximately fifteen minutes of reading from one of Joe's own books, which was of the same reading level as the training book that was to be used. Joe subscribed to a monthly club in which he received a series of Walt Disney books; these books were used for the baseline data and "nontraining book" reading sessions. He had not read any of them previously, and there was a continual supply of new reading material, all on the same reading level. Using these books helped control for improvement in reading due to familiarity with the material or differences in level of difficulty.

In addition, each daily baseline tape contained approximately fifteen minutes of conversation between Mrs. P. and Joe because conversational stuttering was also a concern.

During treatment phases, the audiotapes contained an average ten- to fifteen-minutes reading session using the training materials, ten to fifteen minutes of reading from another book of the same level that was used for the baseline data and not marked (unlike the training book), and ten to fifteen minutes of conversational training. However, at that point in treatment, Mrs. P. was frequently unable to spend the time required to engage in conversation with her son; therefore, these data are missing from a number of the tapes.

Coding Procedures. After the practitioner defined the target behaviors and baseline tapes were collected, two independent judges listened to the first tape and discussed and clarified the specifics of each target behavior, to make sure that the definition of each behavior was precise and comprehensive. Adequate definitions enabled the judges to discriminate between behaviors based on the quality of information available on the audiotapes.

One child behavior and two parent behaviors were recorded over time:

> *Stuttering:* Inappropriate repetition of a vowel or
>   consonant while speaking
> *Parent positive verbal attention:* Praise for child's
>   fluent speaking
> *Parent negative verbal attention:* Verbal attention
>   directed toward child to stop child's speaking

The judges used the first and second tapes for practice coding. They listened to five minutes of tape and tallied a frequency count of each behavior. Percentage of agreement was calculated. If the percentage was low, the judges discussed their disagreements and refined the definitions. They repeated this process until they attained 80 percent or more agreement in two consecutive trials.

Once acceptable interobserver reliability was achieved on all the defined behaviors, the judges tallied the frequency of occurrence for each behavior on every tape. Individual activities (reading and conversation) were timed so frequencies could be converted to behavior per minute. Interobserver agreement was calculated on all the audiotapes.

Reliability. Interobserver occurrence reliability with the mother's observations of stuttering ranged from 31.3 to 100 percent, with a mean agreement of 67.1 percent.

A second judge was also used to obtain reliability estimates on the data from the audiotapes. The judges coded the tapes independently. Occurrence reliability between the two judges for these tapes ranged from 66.7 to 100 percent, with a mean agreement of 92.0 percent for the stuttering behavior and 100 percent for mother's contingent attention. Attempts were made to encourage Joe to self-record stuttering behavior during his daily reading sessions; this goal was achieved only sporadically.

Intervention Procedures

Baseline. A baseline period of nine days was followed by the initial training session with Mrs. P. and her son. During all training sessions, the practitioner gave Mrs. P. verbal instructions for and modeling of the techniques so she could carry them out when the practitioner was not present. In addition, a large portion of the session was devoted to mother and son practicing the speaking and parental attention skills, with the practitioner coaching them.

Throughout the intervention period (sixteen sessions), the general procedures just described were implemented with some variation, depending on the teaching material used. The treatment goal was to teach Joe to speak fluently by introducing the techniques into his reading and gradually intervening in conversation. Speech training on advanced, new material occurred only when 98 percent fluency was achieved on the activity developed in the previous training session.

Training 1 (Session 3). Joe was taught by the practitioner to read phrases presented on flash cards by using the procedures of preparation (reading the phrase silently to himself) and breathing (inhaling and then speaking while exhaling, projecting his voice across the room). The phrases were two to four words long, a comfortable length to say in one breath. All phrases were taken from a book of his reading level that was used for training throughout the intervention. His mother was instructed to praise him each time he read a phrase without stuttering and to have him repeat each card he had trouble with after she had first gone through all twenty-five cards. She provided no attention for instances of stuttering. She continued to have him repeat the remaining cards until he had gone through all the cards at least once without error. By the end of the seven-day period, he was able to implement the speaking techniques and not stutter on any of the cards. It was evident that Joe could use the procedures and, when he did, had no difficulty speaking fluently. This observation led to the addition of a cue for the mother to remind him in the next training session.

Training 2 through Training 5 (Sessions 4-8). Joe and his mother were given chapters from a book in which phrases were marked with slashes. He was instructed to read these phrases as he had the flash cards. His mother continued to praise him for every fluent phrase; she cued him by inhaling loudly when it was evident that he forgot the "rules": (1) read silently before reading the phrase out loud and (2) exhale while speaking. She provided no critical remarks when he stuttered; she merely provided the cue for him, and he repeated the phrase using the rules. As Joe mastered each section of the book (98 percent fluency), he was assigned new chapters with increasingly faded marks separating the phrases.

Training 6 (Sessions 9-11). Joe began conversational training while he was still receiving chapters from the training book. Conversation rules were presented as an extension of the rules (procedures) he was trained to use in reading. The initial stimulus conditions (setting and procedures) for conversation varied little from reading; the objective was to transfer learning from reading to normal speaking conditions. This was facilitated by teaching Joe and his mother how to develop a story outline and then scripting the story using complete sentences that were broken down into two- to four-word phrases. Mrs. P. then asked

Joe questions about what he wanted to tell her, and he read from the script. Mrs. P. and Joe continued to practice these procedures daily with new topics as well as the reading material.

Training 7 (Session 12). The practitioner taught (instructed, modeled, and practiced) Joe to outline his story using keywords only and then engage in dialogue with his mother as he had before, using the keywords as prompts for speaking. Preparation now consisted of looking at the keyword, silently constructing a sentence, and then speaking in phrases using the breathing technique he had learned. His mother praised fluent speech and continued to cue him when necessary.

At this point, the marks in Joe's reading material had been totally faded, so that he now read the training book, using the learned techniques without any visual cues.

Training 8 (Session 13). In the last session during which new material was presented, Joe implemented the fluency techniques without using any outline at all.

Experimental Design. Evaluation of treatment effectiveness was achieved by using a two-tiered multiple-baseline-across-behaviors design (reading and conversation) (see Figures 1 to 3). Although both behaviors are verbal, they were hypothesized relatively independent. The antecedents and consequences of these behaviors are likely to be different (for example, discriminative stimulus for reading is a visual cue and a verbal cue for conversation).

The practitioner intended to have a nine-day baseline period for reading and a forty-day baseline for conversation. The long baseline for conversation was the result of the program's structure, which required that the client achieve a certain criterion level of fluency in reading before continuing the training. Mrs. P., however, stopped taping conversation from day 14 through day 40, so there are only the first thirteen days of baseline data for conversation (Figure 3).

Trend Bar Graphs. Bar graphs have been used to summarize the data (see Figures 1 to 3). The top of each bar is sloped to approximate the general direction of the data for a particular phase. The trend line for each set of data was determined by dividing the data points in half for both the baseline and interven-

Figure 1. Stuttering per Minute on Nontraining Book and Mother's Positive Attention for Fluency.

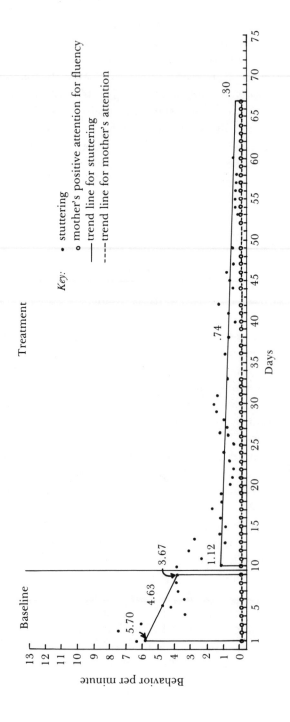

Figure 2. Stuttering per Minute on Training Book and Mother's Positive Attention for Fluency.

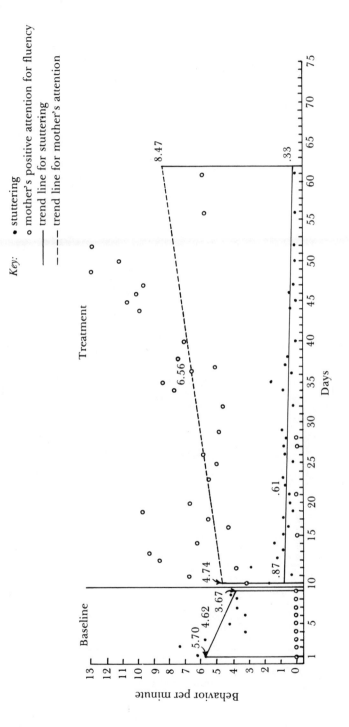

Figure 3. Stuttering per Minute and Mother's Positive Attention for Fluency.

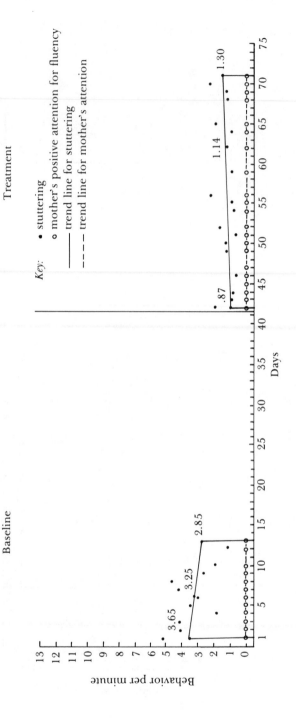

tion periods and then calculating a mean for each half of each phase. A line was then drawn between the two points to illustrate the trend of the data. The mean for the phase is designated on the trend line.

The treatment phase includes all data collected during the course of training, but outside the training sessions themselves. These data were collected during Mrs. P's and Joe's daily practice sessions, without the practitioner present. Included were all reading data collected after day 9 and conversation data collected after day 41.

Because of the varying lengths of the audiotapes and the high frequency of behavior, stuttering and parental attention for fluency were measured in occurrences per minute.

Results

Joe showed an increase in fluent reading from a mean of 4.62 stutters per minute during baseline to .74 stutters per minute on the nontraining book during intervention (Figure 1). It is evident from the bar graphs that this improvement followed a descending baseline trend in which progress had already begun. It is reasonable to conclude that the decrease in stuttering during the treatment phase was caused by more than a continuation of the baseline trend, especially because the change was so marked. The change appears to be even greater on the training book; however, it must be remembered that the data used for baseline purposes were from the nontraining material (Figure 2). The mean rate during intervention was .61 stutters per minute when Joe read from the training book. The rate of stuttering for reading continued to decrease throughout intervention on both the training and nontraining books.

Mrs. P., who had never provided negative attention for Joe's stuttering, learned to use positive attention contingent upon fluent reading. Although Joe's improvement carried over to the nontraining book, his mother's use of differential attention did not. On the training material, his mother provided no positive attention for fluent reading during baseline. In the treatment phase, however, she provided an average of 6.56 positive statements per minute contingent on fluency. This trend increased over time. On the nontraining material, Mrs. P. never used positive attention during baseline or after, even though she had been instructed to do so. Nevertheless, Joe's fluency in reading improved.

Although Joe's conversational fluency increased from a baseline mean rate of 3.25 stutters per minute to a mean of 1.14 stutters per minute during intervention, it is difficult to draw firm conclusions regarding intervention effectiveness because there is a large block of data missing from the baseline (Figure 3), due to a lack of conversation data on tape. Mrs. P. stated that because of her busy work schedule during that period, it was extremely difficult for her to devote the time and energy to taping conversation with her son. She reported that the language problem created an additional burden that made her reluctant to initiate unstructured conversation. Once the training sessions for conversation began, she said it was less stressful for her to participate because the conversations were carefully structured.

Mrs. P. did not use praise for fluent speaking during conversations with Joe, although she had been trained and could do so. She indicated, however, that she cued him when she noticed that he was having difficulty speaking fluently. These data were not coded because the cue (inhaling) could not be reliably detected on the audiotapes.

In addition to taping practice sessions, Mrs. P. observed and recorded frequency of stuttering on nontraining reading material during baseline and two weeks into the intervention phase (see Figure 4). Her data were very similar to those coded by the judges and followed the same trend. Not surprisingly, she generally observed the problem as worse during baseline than had the judges and better during training.

Discussion

There was a clear improvement in Joe's fluent reading and speaking. Mrs. P. and Joe were able to use the recommended procedures, as evidenced by the training sessions and data re-

Figure 4. Mother's and Coder's Frequency of Stuttering on Nontraining
Book in Practice Sessions.

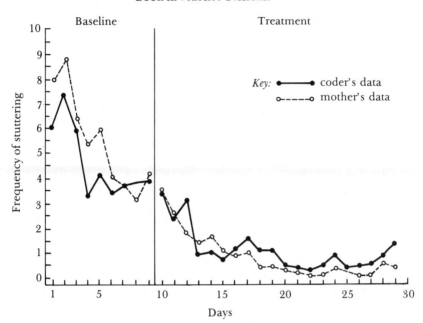

corded on the audiotapes. However, Mrs. P. had difficulty using
the techniques in the nontraining book sessions and in conversations when the practitioner was not present. The juncture marks
in the training book not only served as a discriminative stimulus
for Joe's use of speaking rules, but they also seemed to cue his
mother's use of praise as a consequence for fluency.

Language barriers presented a problem in training and implementing procedures. Instructions and data-recording techniques necessarily remained very simple. The mother's language
deficiencies resulted in her discontinuing the recording of conversation data during baseline. She resumed data recording during intervention because the interactions recorded were structured sequences; therefore, it was easier for her to participate.
Although the practitioner suggested that she and her son con-
verse in Russian to make the situation less stressful for her, Joe
was not willing to do this.

Joe stated that practicing the speaking rules gave him new

skills to think about rather than worrying about his stuttering and what others might think. In addition, he was apparently not punished by others for the use of the speaking rules and said, in fact, that he sounded better. Unfortunately, there are no data from school regarding his rate of stuttering in the classroom because Joe was very opposed to the worker contacting the teacher and involving her in the intervention. Therefore, no evidence that the stuttering was affecting his academic performance was available. Joe reported that he implemented the procedures in school, more successfully in reading than in speaking.

Overall, there was a reduction in Joe's stuttering. It is not apparent how much of this was the result of Mrs. P.'s participation and how much was the result of Joe's independent work outside the practice sessions. His mother's participation fluctuated, possibly because of her work schedule, how tired she was, and how aversive she found his stuttering at that particular time. Additional supportive calls from the worker might have increased her participation. Providing positive consequences for parents for engaging in change efforts for their children should be explored in future research.

This study provides evidence that this structured program for fluency can be effective. In addition to providing the client with self-cueing procedures and social reinforcement, this program supplied him with new behaviors incompatible with stuttering. The intervention emphasis on both stimulus conditions and consequences may have led to more positive results than reliance on either factor alone. This study thus additionally supports the usefulness of behavior analysis in social work interventions.

Intervention for Coercive Family Interactions

Elsie M. Pinkston, Richard A. Polster,
Benjamin S. Friedman, Mary Ann Lynch

The design of behavioral programs often provides counseling for emotionally disturbed children in therapeutic settings. Such programs frequently involve sessions with a mental health professional in an office or clinic (Ebner, 1967; Patterson and Brodsky, 1966). But research reports indicate that the initial effectiveness is sometimes short-lived: later follow-up reveals incidents of truancy, fighting, drug addiction, alcoholism, and suicide attempts as frequent as before the children received counseling. Thus, focus is shifted from mental health institutions to community agencies and persons within the children's immediate environment. Parents, teachers, siblings, and peers are used to encourage prosocial behaviors of targeted children. Subsequently, the concept of parents as active participants in their children's therapy is widely accepted and pursued extensively by behaviorists (Berkowitz and Graziano, 1972; Johnson and Katz, 1973; O'Dell, 1974).

Several areas of supporting literature contribute to the present design of parent training: currently accepted behavioral intervention procedures for children (Christophersen and others, 1972; Herbert and others, 1973; Pinkston and Herbert-Jackson, 1975; Wahler, 1969a, b: Wahler and others, 1965; Wetzel and others, 1966); investigations of parent training in the home (Bernal and others, 1968; Budd, Pinkston, and Green, 1973; Hawkins and others, 1966; Levenstein, Kochman, and Roth, 1973; O'Leary, O'Leary, and Becker, 1967); intervention with children and parents in clinical settings (Bernal, 1971; Budd, Pinkston, and Green, 1973; Hanf, 1968; Henderson and Garcia, 1973; Pinkston and Herbert-Jackson, 1975; Pinkston, Budd, and Baer, in press; Russo, 1964; Zeilberger, Sampen, and Sloane,

247

1968); and parent training in community mental health settings (Becker, 1971; Miller, 1975; Patterson, 1971; Patterson and others, 1975; Pinkston and others, 1975).

The Parent Education Program was designed to alter coercive interactions between children and their parents. Patterson and others (1975) studied the behavior patterns of families of aggressive children and found that, with the exception of fathers, all members of these families were more coercive than families of nonaggressive children. The purpose of this program is to use behavioral principles to design brief interventions for altering these patterns by focusing on reinforcement procedures paired with systematic negative consequences. The program is designed for children between the ages of three and twelve years with acting-out behaviors at home and/or school. The clients were referred by a public school social worker. Procedures for training parents to intervene with their children are presented here, followed by specific procedures to be used with the children. Following a description of the program, a sample case study is presented.

Parent Training Procedures

There is an integral relationship between the techniques used to teach behavior management skills to parents and the procedures applied by the parents to change their children's behaviors. Training of precise intervention procedures for specific target behaviors enhances parental success in managing deviant child behaviors. Didactic parent training procedures included combinations of verbal instructions accompanied by one or more of the following three procedures: modeling, behavioral rehearsal, and reading of an instructional manual. Each technique is now briefly described.

Instructions. A standardized explanation of behavioral principles, for example, reinforcement, punishment, and shaping, is presented to the parents during initial clinic interviews. Parent trainers cover items from a checklist and whenever possible provide examples pertinent to the parents' child management problems. Parents are encouraged to ask questions and provide their own examples of home-based behaviors to illustrate their grasp of behavioral principles. Instructions also accompany demonstrations of specific child behavior change procedures and are continued in home training sessions when needed. Standardized sets of instructions of behavioral principles and basic change procedures facilitate a clear, structured approach to altering specific child behaviors by precise procedures.

Modeling. Direct or videotaped modeling is reported by parent trainers to teach parents child management skills (Hanf, 1968; Patterson, Cobb, and Ray, 1973; Russo, 1964). Modeling serves two purposes: The parent observes the procedure applied correctly, either with the child or a stand-in, and the child becomes aware of the procedures that should be used contingent on specific behaviors. Modeling is used in both clinic and home settings. Verbal praise and feedback are frequently applied following parental engagement in modeled behaviors. Cues or nonverbal signals from the trainer to the parent (Herbert and others, 1973) are used to instigate the appropriate use of change procedures when parents are unable to follow the model.

Behavior Rehearsal. Overt behavioral rehearsal is frequently included in behavioral group work and was defined by Rose (1977) as "an enactment by the target client of the desired behaviors in a simulated situation" (p. 114). Parents demonstrate their abilities to apply change procedures via their children (or a substitute worker playing the role of the child) without modeling the parental responses. Behavioral rehearsal often occurs for behavior previously contained in the parent's repertoire but infrequently used, such as praise, or in simulations of new events within a chain of procedural responses, for example, awarding points and praise.

Manuals. Parent training manuals are used as adjuncts to training and learning behavioral principles for parents (Becker, 1971; Patterson, 1971; Patterson and Gullion, 1971; Patterson and others, 1975) and professionals. A recent survey of parent training manuals by Bernal and North (1978) concluded that "the more circumscribed the child's problem, the more likely it is that a manual for parents will be useful" (p. 541). Parents are given a copy of Becker's *Parents Are Teachers* (1971) and requested to read it as a source of increasing their knowledge of behavioral principles and their application to child management. The workers give individual families copies of instructions for how to apply specific interventions to target behaviors.

Treatment Procedures

Borrowing from Goldiamond's constructional approach to behavior (1974), the focus is on providing positive consequences for those attractive child behaviors incompatible with deviant ones. Because the mediator of positive attention and material reinforcers in the home is the parent, parent attention and access to home-based positive consequences comprise the focal point of intervention. Reinforcement of desirable child behaviors is accomplished by applying contingency contracts including specific behaviors. Parents are recommended to present positive attention and award points contingent on appropriate child behaviors. Extinction, or ignoring undesirable child behaviors nondestructive to other persons or the home, is the first course of intervention to reduce behavior. A short (three minutes) time-out is suggested for aggressive behavior or behaviors that did not decline under extinction. Following is a brief description of contingency contract procedures and time-out.

Differential Attention. Differential attention is the contingent and frequent application of parents' attention following desirable child behaviors and the removal of attention following undesirable actions (Herbert and others, 1973). All parents are taught to use their attention discriminately—for example, reinforce appropriate behavior and ignore negative behavior—in conjunction with other intervention procedures. The function of attention for a variety of child behaviors is carefully analyzed, and, during training sessions, demonstrations with the child include a focus on the parents' verbal attention (positive, negative, and silence). For example, workers observe parents using an excessive number of instructions or nagging remarks in an attempt to influence their children's behavior. Therefore, ignoring is demonstrated for the parents and practiced by the parents during home visits. The careful, discriminative use of differential attention may alleviate some of the stress and frustration reported by parents regarding their children's problem behaviors and may be used as a maintenance procedure after the withdrawal of contract/point systems.

Contingency Contracts. The positive contingency contract (Homme and others, 1969) enhances the learning of appropriate behavior in a framework mutually agreed upon by the parent and child. In the home visit following parent training, the children's desires are incorporated into the reward menu of the contingency contract within the parents' means. Access to daily events, watching television and playing outdoors, and weekly rewards, that is, attending a movie or special event, are built into the contingency contract between the parents and children. Alterations to the contract's terms or weekly schedules focus on shaping behavior and include the substitution of a variety of reinforcing events. Parents are able to alter contract contingencies on their own or by telephone with the worker.

Time-Out. Time-out is removing the child from a reinforcing situation contingent on undesirable behavior (Bostow and Bailey, 1969; Wolf, Risley, and Mees, 1964) and may be effective when applied intermittently (Clark and others, 1973). When time-out is recommended to Parent Education Program (PEP) parents, the procedure with the child is demonstrated, a specific time-out area is designated, and a precise statement of the conditions for application are completed before the procedure is instigated. A written agreement for the parents to record their use of time-out for no more than the agreed time per occasion is signed by the parents and worker.

Overcorrection. Overcorrection (Foxx and Azrin, 1972, 1973) is a period of practice of appropriate behavior contingent on undesirable actions. The overcorrection procedure is used sparingly, as are all punishment techniques, because the sequence of events required to implement the techniques and the time involved are not practical for many participating families.

Implementing Intervention

Step 1—Initial Contact. Following referral, a social worker contacts parents by telephone and briefly explores the problem with a parent, usually the mother, to determine the relevance of the program to family needs. Workers then describe the Parent Education Program. If the parents agree to participate in the program, they are mailed a questionnaire covering the child's interactions with parents, siblings and peers, household chores, and school behavior. Parents are also asked about their child's strengths and what kinds of consequences are provided for both positive and negative behavior. Besides yielding assessment information, home questionnaires help identify language or educational problems and probe parents' readiness to commit time and effort to family problems. The worker uses checklists for implementing the program as a reminder to cover all points.

Step 2—Orientation to Educational Approach to Intervention. After the questionnaires have been completed and returned, families participate in orientation and parent training is videotaped in a clinical media laboratory. Goals for orientation interviews are (1) extending parents' knowledge regarding educational and behavioral approaches to family therapy, (2) defining the social worker's and the parents' responsibilities during the program, (3) specifying and defining target behaviors, and (4) instructing data-collection procedures for baseline assessment. At the beginning of the interview, workers explain to parents that they will be taught skills that will help them with current problems and be useful for handling future problems. Training emphasis focuses on discriminating and modifying problems early so parents can work independently after a relatively short time. Avoiding as much as possible behavioral and technical jargon, the worker discusses how children may learn to get what they want in ways not always reinforcing to parents and that parents often learn punitive and aversive methods to make children behave. PEP is presented as a vehicle for helping families learn to interact appropriately through more positive means. Social workers' responsibilities are defined as teaching parents data collection and procedures for independent intervention with future child-interaction problems, helping implement school interventive programs if necessary, and being available for consultation by telephone or home visits. Parental responsibilities include attending two clinic sessions, collecting data on their child's behavior, reading Becker's *Parents Are Teachers* (1971), and carrying out negotiated interventive programs.

Step 3—Defining Target Behaviors. Using the home questionnaire responses, workers explore problems and help parents specify behavior listed as troublesome or needing improvement. Specific descriptions of behaviors are written on an observation form, preserving much of the parents' language. Typically, a positive and a negative behavior are selected for baselining, plus three or four desired chores.

Step 4—Data Recording and Baseline. Once behaviors and chores have been defined, instructions are provided specifying the daily use of data-collection forms and audiotaping a fifteen-minute dinner conversation between the child and at least one parent several times a week. A frequency count of targeted behaviors is recorded by the parents during a one- to two-hour period in which the problems are most likely to occur. Occurrence of chores is recorded at the end of the day. The data are telephoned to the answering service for daily monitoring by the worker. These data then provide a baseline rate of behavior for future comparison following intervention.

Step 5—Reliability and/or Revision of Behaviors. Following the initial interview, an observer visits the home, with four goals in mind: (1) to record independent data on parent and child target behaviors, (2) to determine whether the correct behaviors have been defined, (3) to compare independent observer data with parent-recorded data to determine reliability, and (4) to answer any questions the parents have regarding the data collection or the program.

Step 6—Training Behavioral Principles. Following the collection of two to three weeks of baseline data, the parent training session is scheduled. The goals for this interview include (1) presenting operant principles, (2) examining family communication issues, (3) reviewing parent and social worker responsibilities, (4) teaching contracting rules, (5) exploring available reinforcers, (6) training in child management techniques, (7) specifying behavioral targets for intervention, and (8) developing home point systems. Operant principles are taught mainly by example; jargon is avoided. For instance, when discussing reinforcement, workers remind parents of how they contribute to their child's early walking and talking by praising the child and calling each other's attention to these marvelous new responses. Family communication is addressed regarding its relationship to parent-child interaction. Workers emphasize the importance of parents presenting a united front—that is, agreeing on behavior appropriate for their children and the consequences for both appropriate and inappropriate behavior. The suggestion is made that disagreements frequently result in children receiving different and confusing messages from parents. Parents are also told that analysis of family communications often reveals that children pit parents against each other to avoid negative consequences for inappropriate behavior and are puzzled about appropriate ways to obtain positive consequences.

Step 7—Setting Up Home Intervention System. Parents are introduced to a set of contracting rules that include the following six steps: (1) Set aside a block of time to talk with the child. (2) Select one behavior and define it in observable terms. (3) Describe all important aspects of the behavior (for instance, how often it should be done, when it should be done, and who will demonstrate and teach it). (4) Agree on a reinforcer for performing the behavior. (5) Decide who will determine whether the behavior was completed. (6) Note all this information in a written and signed contract.

Because the success of the program relies heavily on reinforcement, parents and workers devote considerable time to identifying immediate and backup reinforcers. This process begins when parents are asked to list reinforcers already existing in their environment: television, free time, trips, and movies, for example. Whenever possible, workers suggest that parents engage in a positive activity with the child as a consequence for appropriate behavior.

Major child management techniques discussed with the parents are differential attention, shaping, time-out, and overcorrection. Techniques are again described by examples, usually drawn from the parents' own experience. Workers stress that time-out and overcorrection procedures should be used only with predefined seriously negative behavior, such as hurting another person, and that punishment is most likely to be successful when combined with differential attention and shaping of positive behavior.

Decisions regarding the selection of target behavior for home intervention are based on baseline data. In most cases, highly visible behavior and actions that occur frequently are selected. Occasionally, a behavior is dropped because parents no longer consider it a problem or it occurs at such a low rate that it provides limited opportunity for parents to learn to treat it. Home point systems are jointly negotiated with parents and children until agreement among all involved family members is obtained, with the most difficult behavior receiving the most points. Point systems are developed for the target child's siblings when desired by parents or requested by the children.

Step 8—Modeling and Rehearsing Intervention. During the final segment of the parent training interview, workers model differential use of parent attention, monitoring of point systems, time-out, and overcorrection procedures. After modeling, parents are asked to rehearse each procedure with their child and are provided reinforcement and feedback from the trainers following their performance. If they are unable to carry out a procedure, parents are given positive feedback on some aspect of their performance and additional instructions. If parents still have difficulty with a procedure, workers praise specific performance aspects and again model the procedure. Workers cue the appropriate use of procedures until the parent has performed each step.

Step 9—Feedback and Reliability. Application of material covered in training sessions is facilitated by home visits. Here, workers record independent data on targeted behavior; make necessary revisions in the data-collection procedures; discuss with the children any difficulties with the point system; help the parents rehearse praise, ignoring, awarding points, and contracting; show them how to use punishment procedures; and review all intervention procedures. In most cases, only one visit is necessary; however, if the data fail to reflect improvement in parent-child interaction, additional visits are scheduled.

Step 10—Termination and Follow-Up. The Parent Education Program terminates when parents and children have achieved a stable interventive effect for three weeks, children have been removed from the original home point system, and control of the point system has been transferred to the parents. At this time, parents are given data-collection materials for developing home point systems should other problems occur and are asked to complete an evaluation form. Parents are also told to call workers if their child has further problems they feel need our assistance.

Two to three months following termination, parents are called and asked if they are presently recording data on any behavior. For affirmative responses they are asked to describe the behavior and any interventive program being used. They also rate the program and describe its effectiveness in remediating deviant child behaviors. Similar follow-up calls are repeated at six-month intervals for two years.

Assessment and Evaluation

Perhaps the most important contribution that behavioral social workers and other mental health professionals have to offer family treatment is their ability to target problems, devise behavioral measures for assessing those problems, and design the evaluation outcomes. Although the technology for accomplishing these ends is not complete, development of it continues to extend promise. Assessment and evaluation are not external to behavioral treatment but an integral part of the amelioration of family problems. Absence of these variables would certainly decrease the effectiveness of the treatment and, it could be asserted, decrease the possibility that the parents can become skilled behavioral change agents for themselves and their children. Therefore, emphasis is placed on the counting and collection of data by the parents and its use by workers to make more objective decisions. Although data recording has been cited as a deterrent to using behavioral procedures, it is possible to assume that parents who cannot or will not count behaviors are not sufficiently motivated or able to alter their interaction patterns with their children. The analysis of data enables the worker to determine the extent of the problem and the effectiveness of the treatment program and provides a tool the parents can use to determine the effectiveness of the procedures.

Basic Data Sources

The parent training program, as detailed here, is aided by the recording and use of a number of data sources. The most important source is the recording of data by the parent during the program's baseline and treatment phases. They record a simple tally of the number of times the targeted behaviors occur in a specified time frame (usually one to two hours) each day. Daily these data are then reported by phone to the worker or worker's automatic phone recorder, to enable the worker to monitor progress and continued participation by the parent.

The observer who visits the home for the probes or reliability checks records additional data. This home visit is scheduled for the period when the parents usually record data; the observer records data that will establish the reliability or accuracy of the parent-recorded data. The observer's data can be compared before and after treatment to note whether it reflects behavioral changes similar to those found in the parent-recorded data.

More subjective data regarding the program are provided by a consumer evaluation form, which is mailed to the parents one to two months following termination, to determine the parents' opinion of the program's effectiveness. This is supplemented by periodic telephone interviews with the parents to solicit their perception of the long-term value of the program and the behavioral procedures they were trained to use.

Case Example—Daniel

The data in Figure 1 describe the frequency of temper tantrums of Daniel, a ten-year-old fifth grade student. Temper tantrums included yelling insults, crying, and stomping off to his room. Daniel frequently engaged in tantrum behavior con-

Figure 1. Number of Temper Tantrums per Session.

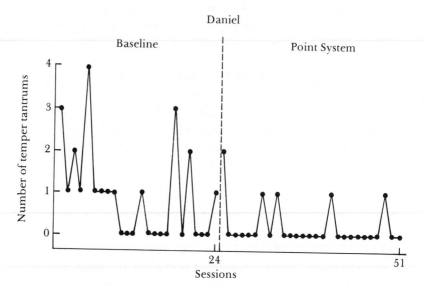

tingent on a parental instruction of interactions with his two sisters, aged four and twelve. Daniel's mother especially found it difficult to control his outbursts.

During the baseline condition, Daniel's temper tantrums occurred approximately once a day, with a range of zero to four. Although occurring at an ostensibly low rate, Daniel's temper tantrums upset his parents and sisters. At least one tantrum occurred on thirteen of the twenty-four days of baseline, or 54 percent of the days.

In the treatment condition, Daniel earned points contingent on appropriate behaviors. Household duties and behaviors that the parents were interested in developing, such as returning home to dinner at a specific time, were included in the list of target behaviors, along with responses incompatible with those in the chain of behaviors that resulted in temper tantrums, such as settling arguments with sisters or asking for a parent to mediate in Daniel's disputes with them. His older sister participated in a similar point system. Daniel earned a minimum number of daily points that could be exchanged for activities of his choice. Points earned beyond the daily minimum were used to purchase special treats at the end of the week, such as movies, trips to museums, and ball games. Additionally, daily points earned an allowance paid weekly. The parents assumed responsibility for altering target behaviors, point values, and reinforcers.

Temper tantrums continued below an average of one per day during treatment, with a range from zero to two. Only one tantrum occurred on five out of twenty-seven days of treatment, or 18 percent.

Follow-up interviews indicated that although there was an occasional problem with Daniel, the parents continued to regard the program as successful and the referred child's behavior as considerably improved. They also reported that he had continued to help around the house and was better at getting home on time, although they had discontinued the point system. Although causal relationships can be inferred carefully, these data are perhaps even more important than data showing decrease in deviant behaviors.

Discussion

Clearly, parents can be taught, by instructions, contracts, modeling, rehearsal, and feedback, to alter their children's inappropriate aggressive behaviors using contingency management procedures. In the case presented here, child behaviors were altered in a positive direction when the treatment package that included differential attention, contracts, point systems, and time-out was instituted by the parents.

Although the length of the cases studied ranged from 80 to 139 days, note that the training procedures for the parents were confined to the initial interview and the parent training interview and that effects were seen in the child's behavior almost immediately.

The program was designed to teach parents who could benefit quickly, with a minimum investment of time from both parents and the social worker, and was flexible enough to provide additional training when the parents were unable to implement the procedures. Daniel's troublesome behaviors were eliminated during the PEP point system condition, and the parents did not wish to work on additional positive behaviors.

These procedures, based on reinforcement theory, can be taught relatively easily to parents to enable them to act as change agents for their children's inappropriate behaviors. They are a positive alternative to aversive control and can be modified to fit the specific problems presented by a variety of families.

The most important aspect of this research, from both an economic and humanitarian point of view, is that it is an alternative to excluding children from normal interaction with their families. It can be used in community agencies and provide clinical services to families or children with serious behavior problems. Essentially, the research is most valuable in situations in which inappropriate communication and contingency management are major factors in the family.

Group Training Parents
to Negotiate Behavior Change
with Their Mentally Retarded Adult Children

Ronald Molick, Brian T. Love,
Paul D. Henderson, Elsie M. Pinkston

Results from available research indicate that behavioral techniques can be effectively applied to children's problem behaviors by training their parents (Allen and Harris, 1966; Berkowitz and Graziano, 1972; Bernal, 1971; O'Dell, 1974; Pinkston, Friedman, and Polster, 1981; Zeilberger, Sampen, and Sloane, 1968). The literature also suggests that parents can be successfully trained in group sessions and that the sharing of their diverse problems and therefore treatment procedures might actually give group-trained parents an advantage over individually trained parents (Galloway and Galloway, 1970; Howard, 1970; Rose, 1974, 1977).

More specifically, it has been shown that training parents of mentally retarded children in groups as behavior modifiers of their own children's behavior has been successful with a wide range of behavior problems (Jeffords, Danzig, and Fitzgibbons, 1971; Rose, 1974, 1977; Rose and others, 1972). The question raised in this research is how effectively a parent training program enables parents of mentally retarded adolescents and adults, still living at home, to deal effectively with problem behaviors involving family interactions. Because of the numbers of sheltered workshops and daycare facilities for the mentally retarded, there are increasing numbers of adolescent and adult mentally retarded persons living at home with their parents instead of being institutionalized. Therefore, it is crucial that these parents be given the necessary skills to deal effectively with problem behaviors that may arise at home.

Because one goal of this particular program was to encourage the parents to see their mentally retarded daughters and sons as adults, it was decided to stress the use of contracting as the major model for problem intervention. Several parent training programs suggest the contracting approach with older children (Becker, 1971; Patterson and Gullion, 1971); the contract model would be behavioral change using an "adult" form of interaction. The program was thus designed to provide behavioral training with a special emphasis on contracting with parents of mentally retarded adolescents and adults and to evaluate whether that training produced changes in the behaviors of the parents and/or the mentally retarded children.

Methods

Clients. The clients were parents of employees at the Shore Training Center (Skokie, Illinois), a sheltered workshop and work-activities center for the developmentally disabled. These parents ranged in age from late forties to early seventies and represented a variety of ethnic and religious backgrounds; all were economically in the middle class. The parents expressed diverse concerns about their daughters and sons, but most wanted to see greater independence in daily living skills, such as making lunch, showering, and shaving. Other behaviors of concern to parents were less easy to put into convenient, specific categories, such as excessive talk of death and constant nagging. The sheltered workshop staff also considered these behaviors as either being problematic to work-related behaviors or hindering competitive job placement.

The sons and daughters of these parents ranged in age from twenty to thirty-five years and had lived with their parents for most or all of their lives. They had been clients of the workshop from between five months to six years and most were diagnosed as brain damaged and/or mildly retarded. IQ scores ranged between 58 and 87, depending on the type of IQ scores used: verbal, performance, or full scale.

Recruitment. During the annual parent conference with the Rehabilitation Coordinator of the sheltered workshop, twelve of the parents spoke of home-based problems with their children. These parents were sent a letter describing the proposed parent training program. Eleven responded positively and came to an intake interview. At the intake interview, the home-based problems were stated in specific, behavioral language, and the parents were given a general outline of the project. If the parents were satisfied with what was being offered, a contract was signed that (1) gave permission for information to be used in the research project; (2) committed the parents to attending each of the four evening sessions, collecting appropriate data, and allowing home visits by the authors; and (3) stated $7 as the cost for the materials involved in the instructional component of the program. Eight families agreed to the program and signed the contract; the other three families did not participate because of family sickness or lack of available time.

Procedures and Materials. The treatment package for the Parent Training Program was designed to instruct parents in operant and social learning theory through large group sessions. This training was to be reinforced by pinpointing desired new behaviors and implementing a program for the acquisition of these new behaviors via the use of small groups, each led by one of the authors. Home visits were also made to further individualize and "concretize" the theory and daily operations of any program that had been designed. The overall goal of the program was to help each parent develop a behavioral contract that would result in the positive experience of at least one modification of their child's behavior. It was hoped that this process would thus provide a model which the parents would then turn to in the future when trying to deal with behavioral problems.

Instruction. The first component of the Parent Training Program was four weekly, one-hour sessions of instruction in operant and social learning theory. All the parents met together for these sessions at the workshop. The first evening discussed behavior as observable and countable phenomena and explained the importance and value of collecting baseline data. The second session concentrated on reinforcement and contracting principles. A special emphasis was placed on the power of social reinforcers for appropriate behaviors in the home. A checklist of steps for behavioral contracting was also handed out and discussed. The parents were each given a copy of Wesley Becker's book *Parents Are Teachers* (1971) and asked to read it for further clarification of social learning principles at home. Any questions the parents had concerning Becker's book were answered at later sessions. The third and fourth sessions discussed the principles of stimulus control, chaining, and punishment. Reversal of treatment was encouraged wherever possible in the programs developed by the parents to show the parents that they did, in fact, have control over the previously problem behaviors. These principles were taught by minilectures, videotaped examples, and general discussion.

Small Groups. For the second hour of the four evening sessions, the parents were divided into three small groups (randomly assigned). Each group was led by one of the workers and its task was to individualize that evening's instruction in the opening session. A checklist was developed for each evening to ensure that each group leader was following the same procedures. The first session enabled the parents to choose one specific behavior and define the behavior so that baseline data could be taken. Each parent was also helped to establish a specific method for data collection and a specific time when data collection would take place each day. During the second session, the baseline data were analyzed by the small group, and the parents individually or collectively developed a treatment program that they could then take back to their child as a proposed contract. The last two sessions fine tuned the programs in progress, planned for other behaviors that might be tackled, and discussed the possibility for a reversal of the treatment procedures being used.

Home Assignments. The parents were requested to do a variety of tasks at home. Before the first evening session, they were sent a questionnaire requesting specification of a target behavior and examples of its occurrence. During the first week of the program, they asked to record baseline data on the behavior specified in the first small group session. In subsequent weeks, the parents were responsible for continuing to record data and implementing the provisions of the contract agreed upon with their daughter or son. Parents were also asked to read

Becker's book and bring any questions they had to the weekly large group sessions.

Home Visits. Home visits by workers were used to gather reliability measures on the parents' data recording and to reinforce the parents' change efforts at home. During these visits, an attempt was made to further individualize the instruction and intervention program. The leader of the small group was present during the first negotiating session between the parents and their son or daughter, not to negotiate for them but to be sure that the model they were using was an appropriate approximation of the one given to them during the instructional session. Home visits were made weekly during the Parent Training Program and gradually reduced in frequency after the formal learning sessions had been completed.

Measures, Reliability, and Research Design. Three measurements were used to determine the effectiveness of the training program. The parents were given a pre- and posttest on both academic skills in social learning theory and contracting skills. The parents took a sixteen-question behavioral principles test before the first and after the last session concerning general behavior modification theories. They were also asked to role play the solution to an imaginary problem with their daughter or son before being taught the behavioral contracting model and again asked to solve a behavioral problem in a role-playing session after the training program had been completed. The performance on these role-playing sessions was evaluated by the group leaders, using the six steps to successful contracting as the scoring factors (Homme and others, 1969). The parent could score from zero to six points on the role-playing test. Finally, the change in behavior of the daughter's or son's behavior was used as a measure of effectiveness. If the parent was able to use new skills to produce positive changes in the son's or daughter's behavior, the program would be considered successful.

Reliability measures on the first two measurements were made by having at least two of the authors score one test from each group to see if they did in fact score the tests and role-playing situations the same way. Home visits were used for reliability checks on the parents' data collection during each phase (baseline, treatment, and reversal—if appropriate) of the program. The group leader would take data simultaneously with the parent(s) and then compare the two scores. Reliability on the academic and role-playing tests was consistently high (90 to 100 percent). Reliability between the parents' and group leaders' data was also high (85 to 100 percent).

With as many behaviors as possible and where parents' willingness and the nature of the behavior allowed, an ABAB reversal design was used in the intervention procedures. When this was not possible, it was hoped that the parents would contract on more than one behavior, thus providing a "simulated" multiple-baseline design. If the model worked on successive behaviors that previously had been a problem, it could be concluded that it was the model which was responsible for behavior change. When neither of the first two designs was possible, a simple AB design was used. The reversal and multiple-baseline designs were considered more desirable options not only for research but as instructional tools for the parents; that is, parents learned that they did have control over behaviors which had previously seemed uncontrollable. The research design used with the parents' behaviors was AB. Parents' knowledge and skill levels in behavioral principles and behavioral contracting were evaluated before the program and at the end.

Results

Figure 1 shows the results of the academic pre- and posttests. These tests were graded with a high criteria for language accuracy. Unless the specific behavioral language was used to answer a question, it was marked as incorrect. The test results may therefore underestimate the parents' level of understanding of social learning theory. However, every parent who took the posttest (two were absent due to illness during the fourth evening session) showed an increase in the number of correctly answered questions. The group mean on the pretest was 6.7 correct answers out of a possible 16, and on the posttest the group mean was 11.6 correct answers. Several parents actually doubled or tripled their academic scores.

Figure 1. Academic Pre- and Posttest Scores.
(Asterisk denotes subject was not present during a testing session.)

Subject	Pretest	Posttest	Gain
Mrs. Arnold	5	12	+7
Mr. Bach	6	12	+6
Mrs. Bach	7	10	+3
Mr. Church	5	9	+4
Mrs. Church	6	10	+4
Mr. Day	8	12	+4
Mrs. Day	5	13	+8
Mrs. Elson	9	12	+3
Mr. Ford	6	12	+6
Mrs. Ford	8	13	+5
Mrs. Grant	9	*	*
Mr. Horn	9	13	+4
Mrs. Horn	7	*	*
Mean	6.7	11.6	+4.9

Figure 2 shows the results of the role-playing tests on contracting skills. Once again, parents showed a marked increase in skills after they completed the parent training program. The group mean score on the pretest on contracting skills was 6.7; the group mean score on the posttest was 11.6.

Figure 2. Role-Playing Contracting Skills Pre- and Posttest Scores.

Subject	Pretest	Posttest
Mrs. Arnold	1	6
Mr. and Mrs. Bach	5	6
Mr. and Mrs. Church	2	6
Mr. and Mrs. Day	3	6
Mrs. Elson	1	5
Mr. and Mrs. Ford	2	6
Mrs. Grant	2	5
Mr. and Mrs. Horn	3	6

The eight families involved in the program completed a total of eighteen behavioral contracts. The behaviors chosen covered a wide range of daily living skills, interpersonal skills, and bizarre problem behaviors. Each behavior was brought under control by behavioral contracting between the parents and their son or daughter. A graph of the frequency of each behavior was provided as feedback to the parent. Definitions of the behavior, criteria for success, and the actual reinforcers used are now described.

Mrs. Arnold wanted to reduce the amount of nagging her son Abel did about future events once a decision about that event had been made. The goal was to reduce nagging to a zero level. The contract called for social praise from Mrs. Arnold for every twenty minutes free of nagging comments by her son. To help reduce the amount of nagging, decisions about future events were tape-recorded, and Abel was referred to the taped discussion if he had any questions. During periods of excessive nagging, Mrs. Arnold would simply leave the room for one minute. Abel's nags decreased from an average of 6 episodes per day to 1.6. Parental disapproval decreased from 2.6 to 1.6, and approval statements increased from an average of 4 to 16 per day.

The Bachs contracted with Bob on three behaviors. The first contract was designed to increase Bob's verbal initiations. Each day at the workshop Bob was given a note that he was to share with his family during dinner. If he did initiate a conversation by using the note, Bob received a dessert of his choice. When the contract was in effect, Bob earned the reinforcer daily. A reversal brought the number of initiations about work back to zero.

During the fourth week of training, Bob and his parents contracted on his self-shaving. If Bob was able to shave successfully by himself in the morning, he was allowed to watch television while waiting to go to the workshop. He was able to earn his reinforcer every day during the treatment procedure.

The final behavior involved the number of times Bob would use the bathroom. There were no medical reasons for his excessive use of the bathroom, so a contract was negotiated that would result in social praise for Bob if he used the bathroom only once in the morning before going to the workshop. Criterion was met from the first day of treatment on.

Mr. and Mrs. Church were concerned about their son Chris's constant talk about death during meal times. The contract gave Chris the privilege of eating dinner with his parents as long as he did not talk about death. If any death statements were made, he was to be sent to his room and later would have to make his own supper. If he refused to go to his room when sent away from the dinner table, his bicycle was to be impounded. The correspondence between the parents' attending statements and Chris's death statements during baseline was an average of 44.2 death statements to 25.2 parental statements. Once the contract was implemented, death statements dropped to a frequency of zero and fluctuated above that only twice, on those evenings Chris's brother came to visit.

The Churches also contracted for making lunch. Chris was to be provided all the materials he needed but was to make his own lunch. If he made the lunch, he would have one to eat. If he did not make the lunch, he would not have one to take to work. Chris missed making his lunch only one day during intervention.

Dave Day's severe epilepsy made it crucial that he take his medication. Dave was promised one poker chip for each time he took his medication independently or with an indirect prompt; these chips could then be cashed in for a variety of events (movies, baseball games). He consistently self-administered the medication after intervention began. Although there are no data available, the Days reported that they were able to negotiate with Dave on two other daily living skills (making his bed and his lunch) and began a program to help Dave stop drooling.

Mrs. Elson wanted to decrease the amount of time it took her to get her daughter Edith out of the family car and into the workshop. During baseline this process took up to twenty-five minutes. If Edith got out of the car and entered the workshop in less than three minutes, she was allowed to go on an afternoon bicycle ride. Edith was able to meet criterion performance on the second day after the contract was negotiated and maintained performance, with one exception, consistently after that.

The Ford family concentrated on their daughter Faye's increased daily living skills. In their first contract, Faye would be taken out to a favorite hamburger stand if she set the table with only one prompt on five out of seven days. Faye met criterion every day, with one exception during treatment. Faye and her parents had also contracted for five other daily living skills. In each case, some special event in Faye's life was made contingent upon meeting criterion performance. Eventually special events were phased out as reinforcers and social praise was used to take their place.

Mrs. Grant wanted her son Gary to improve his personal appearance by taking a shower daily. If Gary took a shower for seven days, he was then to receive a prime rib dinner. Once the contract was negotiated, Gary consistently took his shower each evening and earned his prime rib dinner.

The Horns wanted Hank to make his bed in the morning. If Hank was able to make his bed for seven days, he would then receive a pineapple upside down cake. To help him reach his goal, Hank's parents were to give him social praise whenever he made his bed correctly. Hank consistently made his bed each morning before leaving for the workshop once the contract was implemented.

Along with the behavior of the mentally retarded daughter or son, the workers were also interested in the behavior exhibited by the parents before, during, and after contracting procedures were implemented. Data on parent behavior were kept by both Mrs. Arnold and the Churches. These data are included with their sons'. The remaining families did not actually record parent behavior, but all the parents reported that they did in fact carry through those behaviors required of them in the contracts. The authors decided to accept the parents' self-reports as evidence that their behavior did change as a result of the contracting procedures. Their sons and daughters also reported that the parents had followed through on the contracts.

Discussion

The results of this program indicate that in a short time parents of mentally retarded adolescents and adults were able to bring behaviors which had been problematic, for years in some cases, under control and to begin producing more adultlike behavior which previously had been nonexistent. The excitement that this program generated in the families was certainly rewarding for the workers.

Although the data are not as concrete as the worker would like, it was nevertheless very clear to both the parents and the workers who made home visits that the parents now had a model which could be used on a wide variety of behaviors that would either reduce household tension or increase their son's or daughter's independence. Many of the parents began making plans for future behaviors for which they would contract.

Another side benefit of the training program was that the parents became familiar with the language of behavior modification and began to understand more fully the general concepts of behavioral principles. Because these concepts are the backbone of the programs implemented within the workshop setting for increasing work skills, it is advantageous to have the parents acquire a better understanding of and appreciation for the methods used by the workshop personnel. Programs in the workshop now make more sense to the parents who have been through this training program. Also, these parents can now be used more effectively as backup reinforcers for programs being used in the workshop.

The greatest difficulty encountered for research was recording data on the parents' behavior. Many of the parents had been out of school for a long time and felt very uncomfortable taking academic tests and participating in the role-playing sessions. The workers also had difficulty getting parents to record data concerning their own behavior in response to their son's or daughter's behaviors. It would be helpful in future research if better means of recording data and obtaining reliability on parents' behavior could be developed and implemented.

The parents' enthusiastic response to the invitation to participate in the program (eleven out of twelve responded; eight families participated throughout the program) affirmed the authors' suspicion that there is a strongly felt need by parents of mentally retarded adolescents and adults to deal more effectively with behavior problems. The results of the program indicate that teaching behavioral skills with a special emphasis on behavioral contracting does give these parents an effective model for modifying both their own behavior and their son's or daughter's in ways which will provide maximum harmony within the family and maximum independence for the mentally retarded person.

8

◆▶◀▶◀▶◀▶◀▶◀▶◀▶◀▶◀▶◀▶◀▶◀▶◀▶◀▶◀▶◀▶◀

Intervention in
Institutional Settings

The social worker's functions vary within specific institutions;
thus a practitioner may be involved in interdisciplinary planning, program development, staff training, or evaluation. In all
these functions the worker may aid other staff in their roles as
behavior change agents, consistent with the social work tradition of team participation (for a review, see Compton and Galaway, 1979). Consultation on special problems is not a new
role for the worker. For example, in school settings social work
practice includes components of direct observation, teacher
consultation, and intervention evaluation (Polster and Pinkston,
1979). These multiple roles are also present in behaviorally
based psychiatric programs (Dahl, 1973) and residential programs (Linsk, Howe, and Pinkston, 1975), where the social
worker acts as counselor, administrator, or staff trainer. In other
instances, such as group work or recreational programs, the
worker often assumes overall responsibility for the program.
This chapter includes cooperative work with staff as the direct
change agents.

The scientific approach in this chapter may be used with

both professionals and nonprofessionals involved with clients (teachers, nurses, care-giving staff, other social workers, or volunteers). Criteria for selecting appropriate staff change agents are developed, along with guidelines for selecting specific intervention settings appropriate to problem remediation. The resources and restrictions of staff as change agents are considered, including their skill levels and personal qualities. Competing staff demands and the degree of administrative support necessary for intervention are also discussed, along with techniques for work with staff. Finally, training and evaluation methods appropriate for staff, including methods to enhance generality and maintenance of the intervention effects, are discussed.

Role and Setting Considerations

In this model, one role of the social worker in cooperation with other staff is as a *behavioral analyst*. The worker participates in (1) analyzing behavior, (2) formulating intervention plans from baseline data, and (3) evaluating those plans within the client's environment in or out of institutions. In addition, the worker may teach and monitor staff performance of the skills and behaviors necessary to implement the behavior program. The worker also often takes major responsibility for data analysis, providing feedback, reinforcement, and support for the staff efforts in the behavior change program (Fischer and Gochros, 1975).

Other staff members typically act as *behavior change agents,* participating in *problem assessment* by providing background information and anecdotal data and completing preliminary and ongoing observations. The staff assumes responsibility for *data collection* in their work settings, including classroom, activity areas, or living quarters. *Specific interventions* are designed to change certain staff behaviors as well as those of the client. Examples of altering staff behavior are changes in reinforcement patterns, modeling, or stimulus cues (such as instructions); these modifications alter client behavior. The major tasks of staff behavior change agents are learning the techniques and consistently performing the interventions. The staff provides the reinforcement and support necessary to initiate and maintain client change. Their reports of other events in the client's environment and observations regarding unexpected changes in the client's functioning are valuable data for planning and evaluating the intervention.

Although many referrals for the development of behavior change programs come from other professionals, the worker cannot assume these people are eager to learn behavioral techniques. Often the referral may follow failure to help the client (which may be viewed as a skills deficit) and may reflect the prospective staff change agent's major frustration. Instead of expecting help in changing the environment and contingencies relevant to the problem, the other staff may expect the worker to repair the problem or confirm the impossibility of repair. In other instances, the referral is necessitated by administrative requirements rather than a genuine understanding of behavioral services. In recognition of these possibilities, specific agreements are made to provide for shared work.

An adequate *structure* to support these roles is a prerequisite for an effective behavior change program. The basic structure for implementation often exists within staff meetings, team meetings, or client staffings. The worker regularly participates in this structure, screening referrals, training staff in procedures, and presenting findings. Individualized consultation models involve regular meetings between the social worker and specific staff persons involved in the behavioral intervention. Successfully developing a change program sometimes depends upon a regular structure for training and communication and written guidelines for worker and staff.

Assessment

Assessment procedures are vehicles for exploring the referral staff's desire to participate as change agent in the intervention. An initial evaluation period gives both the worker and the prospective change agents time to assess their own capabilities to provide an intervention for the client.

Staff engage in cooperative efforts with the worker for

several reasons: (1) for intervention or consultation regarding a specific behavior problem; (2) to help design a class, floor, or unitwide program, such as a token economy; (3) to provide workshops designed to increase general staff knowledge of behavior analysis procedures; (4) to relieve staff frustration regarding behavior problems; or (5) for administrative purposes, such as to increase accountability or develop a research component for an ongoing program.

Defining Desirable Outcomes. Assessment information in staff-based programs is derived from various staff persons as well as clients and their families. When working with staff to define desirable outcomes, a number of specific techniques are useful. Formative evaluation techniques (Rutman, 1977), where various individual assessments of staff goals are determined, may contribute to the formulation of program objectives. Brainstorming meetings, where a number of staff meet with the worker and propose many possible outcomes, may also be used. Informal discussions with various staff members about possible changes may be included. These discussions may focus on the behaviors of clients or staff members that need most to change. (Remember that this is a reinforcement approach—drinking coffee and socializing are useful formats in which to collect informal data.)

To obtain information from clients, the worker may conduct structured or semistructured interviews. The initial interview format suggested in Chapter Three may be adapted for an institutional setting. Semistructured interviews with clients may be particularly helpful for identifying current behavior, previous behavior, and individual goals. For example, in our work with the aged, we used reminiscence (Pincus, 1972) to identify previous activities and current reinforcers and determine desirable outcomes.

To avoid a common pitfall of defining problems in institutions, the worker should meet with direct service staff as well as the administrative staff. A multitarget approach that includes staff who have direct contact (and who may well control the direct contingencies of the client) is most important and decreases resistance to or confusion about proposed plans. Of course, such multilevel assessment of client problems has long been part of the diagnostic approach in social casework (Richmond, 1917) and has been incorporated into all major social work treatment models (for a review, see Roberts and Nee, 1970). The emphasis in the behavior analysis model is on identifying target behaviors for change and the related reinforcing or punishing environmental contingencies.

Summary of Available Resources

Selecting the Agent of Change. Selecting the change agent is an important determinant of intervention success. Although the referring staff member is often viewed as the most likely change agent, analysis of key variables may provide data indicating that other options may be more feasible. Several considerations are crucial for positive results; one is the *availability* of people to work on the problems. A written list of potential staff for direct behavioral intervention is useful; this list includes both professional and nonprofessional staff, volunteers, or other clients in the setting. A general guideline for preparing such a list is to include the staff persons who have frequent contact with the identified clients, receive reinforcement from their work with the clients, and have *access to* or *control of* the contingencies that require modification.

As an example, in work with residents in homes for the aged, we find a diverse array of staff that could be available to intervene with behavior problems. In an effort to increase participation in social activities, an obvious behavior change agent might appear to be the group leader. To test this possibility, some systematic anecdotal observations are completed. Observations of the ongoing activities to encourage group attendance demonstrate that the leader is busy with preparing and announcing the group session. Apparently, the leader will not be a good resource for increasing participation, and the observational analysis may suggest alternatives (see McClannahan and Risley, 1974). A number of other persons may have an effect on participatory behaviors, including the charge nurse, who may schedule conflicting appointments; family and volunteers, who may reinforce other kinds of visiting during this time; aides and orderlies, who may facilitate or limit the resident being fed, dressed, and clean; and other residents, who may reinforce or punish participation in activities. A team approach may be necessary to train all involved individuals in ways to enhance activity participation. An analysis may show that the charge nurse has the greatest control of contingencies and competing events and so should be viewed as the primary behavior change agent. Or, the aides and orderlies may control the contingencies necessary to prepare the person for participation. Finally, the worker may select other residents as behavior change agents; the residents may be taught to reinforce each other or an identified client for participation. Final selection of behavior change agent(s) depends on situation-specific variables.

This example suggests a number of considerations about resources for potential behavior change agents. The prospective behavior change agent's current and potential skills should be evaluated. Several questions to consider are: Is the agent sufficiently literate to complete the data-recording procedures? Does the individual have the necessary physical capabilities for carrying out the intervention? Does the agent have biases against the client's capabilities or the behavior analysis approach that would require more training than is available to effect the change? Does the agent have special skills that may facilitate successful implementation of the technique? Is the agent particularly adept at conversation with the client? Does the agent have knowledge of physical or educational components of the intervention? Has the agent participated in successful behavior change programs in the past? A final consideration in choosing an individual to be a change agent is the quantity and type of competing demands placed on the prospective agent. For example, does work schedule allow the time and activities necessary to complete the behavior change program, or do demands made by other clients preclude participation in the change effort?

Given these factors, the worker determines whether there is a staff person available with the appropriate resources to act as primary behavior change agent. Occasionally the worker discovers that no such person exists. In such cases, it is tempting to begin to develop a program that minimizes the response demands on staff in the setting, but this decision involves a risk. If the worker begins a program knowing there is potential staff inconsistency, discontinuity, and lack of cooperation, there is a risk of program failure being blamed on the intervention rather than the staff or institutional limitations. In such cases, staff may say in the future that "Behavioral analysis programs do not work here; we've tried them before." The outcome may damage the potential of future programs more than if no effort at all were attempted.

An alternate model to use when the appropriate behavioral change agents are not available is to develop a worker-executed program with sufficient maintenance procedures. If the practitioner has the necessary resources (time, in particular), a more positive outcome can be achieved than by attempting a staff-implemented program with insufficient resources (see Chapter Six for procedures). This demonstration may provide data to generate resources for future programs. A further alternative is to negotiate with the agency's administration to modify the staffing procedures to facilitate the program.

The worker should consider administrative support before initiating any program. Hersen and Bellack (1978a) emphasized the role of agency politics in successful behavioral programming. The tendency of an agency to add or remove reinforcers for staff-member participation in a behavior change program appears to be an important predictor of outcome. The staff members should not be asked to increase their rate of responding without increased reinforcers; thus an analysis of staff requirements should be shared with supervisors. Efforts can be facilitated by ascertaining that the administration has sufficient information regarding the nature and advantages of behavioral programming. An individual who controls staff practices may not be supportive, although a program has general administrative support. Staff training and short-term contracting are useful techniques for fostering consistent backing. After considering all these factors, if an appropriate change agent is selected and sufficient reinforcers and resources are made available to ascertain participation, the worker can then initiate further assessment and intervention procedures.

Selecting the Setting for Change

Selecting the change setting is simpler with staff as behavior change agents than with individuals or families. Generally, a client is referred to the worker because of problems that occur in specific places. As examples, a student may be referred because of lack of on-task behavior during classroom work time or aggressive behavior in the classroom; a child in a residential center may be referred because of antisocial behavior in the dormitory; an older person in a hospital setting may be referred because of excessive complaining whenever a staff person enters the room. In these situations, other settings may be specified as part of the identified behavioral problem.

Preliminary observations occur in the problem setting(s). As target behaviors and potential change agents are identified and baseline rates of behavior recorded, a setting for intervention is selected. Within an agency or institution, multiple settings are usually available. Whenever possible, data should be recorded on an ongoing basis in as many settings as possible to evaluate generality of intervention effects. For example, intervention can be applied serially across settings in a multiple-baseline design to determine experimental control of intervention effects. The data recording may also extend outside single institutions: Home-based data or data recorded in a community setting may be used to supplement the institutional data.

The actual choice of the change setting should be based on the same general guidelines as those followed for choosing a change agent. Frequency of the target behavior in the setting is an important determination. In order for intervention to occur and be evaluated, the behavior must occur frequently enough before and during intervention for a difference to be noted. If the worker is confronted with a behavior occurring at a very low level during baseline, it may be difficult to demonstrate change unless plans are to increase the behavior. The change agents available in the settings should have the resources to affect behavior change programs. The contingencies operating in the change environment should suggest some potential change possibilities, sufficient reinforcers should be available in the change setting to maintain the behavior after intervention, and the setting should be representative of the client's usual environment to facilitate transfer of learning.

Response Requirements and Contingencies

Institutions are often viewed as far more controlled environments for effecting treatment than community or home settings (Goffman, 1961). From a behavioral viewpoint, this assumption implies that the expectations and discriminative stimuli are clearer in an institution and that the contingencies affecting the client's behavior are under administrative control. An institution may control, to some extent, the dispensation of food, privileges, time, and interaction with others. Controlled distribution of reinforcers may be used to encourage or discourage behaviors. Who actually controls the occurrence of reinforcement may vary considerably among and within institutions. Control over reinforcers is ultimately the responsibility of the administrators. Although various staff persons can control reinforcers in different ways, the ultimate control of reinforcers is provided indirectly by administrative support or lack of support for staff behavior. These reinforcers are then, in some form, passed along to the clients.

The worker analyzes functional relationships between reinforcers and behaviors in the change setting and offers data-based suggestions about how changes in these relationships can affect identified problem behaviors. The worker, in consultation with staff, considers how the proposed changes may effect other behaviors of interest in the setting. For example, in a residential setting for the retarded, a reinforcement system is set up for individualized eating training by floor staff. A side effect is that ongoing socialization with other residents may decrease during mealtime. The worker and the staff should consider possible consequences regarding other behavioral reactions to the intervention.

Data Recording

Data-recording procedures with staff change agents are based on the methods discussed in Chapter Four. The general strategy is to record data on both the behavior of the identified client and the behavior of relevant staff.

Observational data are useful in areas of staff-client interaction, for example, classrooms, activity areas, dormitories, or work settings. Initial *informal observations* may include observations by the worker to assess the characteristics of behaviors of interest and their environmental antecedents and consequences. Staff may also be asked to observe their own interactions with clients for a specified period to facilitate agreement on objective definitions of behavioral targets. Each staff observer is asked to record what happens before, during, and after behaviors of interest. For example, sheltered workshop staff contact a worker regarding a depressed client and the worker requests a log of their observations of depressive behaviors in an effort to clearly specify what they mean by depression. These observations are supplemented by the worker's observations and interviews with the prospective client.

The first step in observation and eventual intervention is to define relevant behaviors for targeting. These behaviors may be selected for one client or multiple clients. Multiple clients provide possibilities of simultaneous observation and intervention. In a classroom setting, one student, several students, or all students may be included. The practice illustrations presented at the end of this chapter discuss behavior definitions for both individuals and groups. Banzett (Practice Illustration 8.4) and Green and Pinkston (Practice Illustration 8.1) describe behavior codes for individual subjects. The studies by Linsk and Pinkston (Practice Illustration 8.3) and Dougherty, Friedman, and Pinkston (Practice Illustration 8.2) present behavioral definitions and codes for a large number of subjects (thirteen and fifteen). Whenever possible, behavior codes should include both excess and deficit behaviors, or desirable and undesirable behaviors. These illustrations include behaviors to be increased or maintained as well as behaviors to be decreased. When possible, both staff and client behaviors are defined and observed by using codes that permit measurement of both independent and dependent variables. For example, Banzett, in a residential setting for disturbed children, measured both inappropriate client questioning and staff acknowlegment; Green

Effective Social Work Practice

included a range of client behaviors and tracked staff behavior
regarding points dispensed; Dougherty, Friedman, and Pinkston
included teacher fines, points given, praise, and negative attention as teacher behaviors in a school setting while measuring
subject aggression, disruption, and refusals.

Direct observation involves decisions about who will observe, when observations will occur, and what kind of sampling
procedures will be adapted. In a staff-based program, the choice
of observers may include the worker, the staff change agent, the
client, or other observers. The most controlled observations of
both the change agent and the client are done by the worker or
a noninvolved staff member. Change agents may frequently be
taught to record their own observations; these procedures are
discussed later in this chapter. For example, in the Green and
Pinkston study, teachers in the special day school were taught
data-recording methods. Clients may also be taught to record.
In ideal circumstances, observers may be hired or recruited for
data collecting and used throughout the institution. Finally, a
combination of the methods may be used. For example, Dougherty, Friedman, and Pinkston (Practice Illustration 8.2) illustrate the use of teacher-recorded fines and time-outs and
worker-recorded behaviors. The choice of who records is dependent on available resources. Where the behavior analysis
methodology is being taught to clients or staff, those who are
learning should assume at least part of the recording responsibilities; staff inclination, training time, and capabilities need to
be considered when making this decision. The worker will generally do some recording for training, code development, reliability, and validity purposes.

Recording periods are scheduled to coincide with times
when behavior is likely to occur, although staff convenience
may be a major factor in determining observation time. For
example, Doughterty, Friedman, and Pinkston (Practice Illustration 8.2) chose the "most disruptive time of day" for observations, whereas Linsk and Pinkston (Practice Illustration 8.3)
observed during the appropriate activity sessions. The sampling
procedures (see Chapter Four for a discussion of observation
sampling methods) are dependent upon behavioral frequency,

environmental factors, and competing observation demands. Generally, preliminary observations indicate approximate frequency, and a reasonable time unit can be developed. In the practice illustrations, time samples ranged from five seconds (necessary to record individualized data in group observations) to longer intervals of one to three hours. Often, ten-second time samples are used (Bijou, Peterson, and Ault, 1968) because they give observers more time to make coding decisions.

Reliability is a critical component of data recording, especially when observers also serve as behavior change agents. Reliability checks are crucial for ruling out observer bias. Procedures outlined in Chapter Four may be used to check reliability. Although the worker often serves as a reliability observer, when possible, other people such as volunteers, other workers, or noninvolved staff, or even peers of the client, are also used to check reliability.

Problems with achieving acceptable reliability may occur with group, multisubject, or multibehavioral codes. With many subjects or behaviors, an 80 percent reliability criteria may be difficult to achieve. Often the worker may consider collapsing categories or examining overall or nonoccurrence reliability. Use of lower reliabilities is often discouraged because of research standards, but they may have clinical consequences as well. When reliability is 70 or 75 percent, however, it is exceedingly difficult to demonstrate treatment outcome. If errors occur one-fourth of the time, and a 20 to 30 percent improvement occurs in the target behavior, it may hard for a worker to prove a change occurred. To control such problems, clear codes, sufficient observer training and practice, and multiple measures should be used. However, if severe problems need attention, treatment is not delayed to await satisfactory reliability.

Questionnaires and scales may also be used to explore and rate attitudes and behaviors. Tests of staff and change agents' attitudes toward the client, or assessment of behavior or work performance, help discriminate possible difficulties. Health and mental statuses may be evaluated by professional staff using structured questionnaires, and clients' attitudes, perceptions, opinions, and feelings may be assessed. Questionnaires and scales may be administered at preintervention, post-intervention, or during follow-up and provide additional data to complement or supplement the direct observational data (Cox and others, 1979; Hudson, 1977).

Data Assessment

Reviewing the data with the change agents is an essential part of collaborative behavior change efforts, and a structure for reviewing data and intervention planning is an ongoing component of behavior analysis with support staff. Data may be reviewed by interpreting graphs to staff (the interpretation may be posted or included in the client's official record or chart). An alternate approach is to show staff audio- or videotapes that reveal change and help them understand the purpose of the behavioral data. The graphs and tapes are used to confirm or revise previously stated expectations. Discussing the data points out the client's interaction with environmental factors (other persons who reinforce or punish behaviors, the physical setting, critical events in the environment that may influence behavior change efforts). In Practice Illustration 8.3, Linsk and Pinkston showed both a videotape and graphs to the group worker-change agent and discussed possible interventions with her. Dougherty, Friedman, and Pinkston (Practice Illustration 8.2) and Molick and Pinkston (Practice Illustration 8.5) reported the use of joint meetings between experimenters and teachers to discuss treatment decisions.

Intervention

The range of techniques for use with staff as behavior change agents is similar to those for use with individuals or families; see Chapters Two and Three for a full description of the theoretical and practical applications of these techniques. This discussion reflects previous and potential applications specifically for staff persons as behavior change agents; there are application guidelines for four techniques: reinforcement, punishment, modeling, and contingency contracting. Finally, this chapter presents guidelines for choosing a program in a staff setting, training the behavior change agents in how to apply techniques, maintaining positive results, and evaluating the interventions.

Specific Techniques

Reinforcement-Based Procedures. A major task for the social worker is to increase the total numbers and the frequency of reinforcers, to enhance the likelihood of clients' positive behavior. Staff reinforcement techniques include individualized reinforcement programs, programs to organize and structure group-based reinforcement (token systems), and programs to increase reinforcement. Reinforcement tends to characterize all client-staff interactions, but the degree of staff awareness and the systematic use of contingent reinforcement varies considerably. For example, a teacher may be very adept at giving praise, compliments, prizes, or awards to a student or a class of students for successive progress in paper-and-pencil work but be relatively unaware of the inadvertent reinforcing value of her attention when reprimanding a child who hits other children. The teacher may assume that reprimands and instructions to stop hitting will lead to decreased aggression. If this conduct is not effective, the teacher may conclude that the child has inherently serious socioemotional problems. However, a functional analysis may reveal that such reprimands are the child's major source of attention from the teacher and so teach the child that aggression gets attention. A similar phenomenon may occur with a youth worker who seeks out and counsels youths who seem alone and isolated. The reinforcing nature of the worker's attention may limit rather than increase the client's interaction with peers. Staff may also be unaware of the role of attention for enhancing positive behaviors in their interaction with clients. The housekeeper in the nursing home who makes a point of complimenting those residents who are fully dressed for meals may be unaware that these friendly gestures contribute to residents' continuing social skills. Methods for retraining staff and reinforcement principles are considered later in this chapter.

One approach to increasing reinforcement is to *increase the overall opportunities for reinforcement in the environment.*

The physical and social setting are modified in an effort to increase the occurrence of positive behaviors and decrease the occurrence of negative behaviors. For example, a worker may be consulted regarding the operation of a group home for retarded children. Following the behavioral analysis model, the first step in work with the home is assessment. Observation of both the physical and social elements of the program, as well as initial exploration interviews with residents and staff, indicate there are very few pleasurable and reinforcing activities for the clients. The environment is unattractive and sparse, there are few toys or games available for play, no music, the only television is in a very small lounge with room for only three or four viewers at a time (which causes frequent arguments), and there is no access to the outside because the group home staff is concerned that the residents will wander throughout the neighborhood. There are several rules that result in punishment (restricted time out of room, limited menu, isolation) but no structured ways for residents to earn special privileges. It is observed that the staff does not compliment or praise the residents; they communicate with the residents mostly through instructions and criticism.

Although this example seems extreme, at least portions of the descriptions apply to most settings. Such settings lead to a deprived range of environmental intervention possibilities that require minimal expenditure, staff training, or individual resident focus. These possibilities include redecorating the facility to make it more pleasing, developing a structured activity schedule with behavioral criteria for participation, teaching staff to observe positive behaviors that are already occurring and attend to them, moving the television, setting up an accessible area outside the facility, asking outside groups to come to the facility to increase social contacts and entertainment, or setting up a gameroom and library area. Such efforts may not be immediately viewed as behavioral interventions—they may seem like a milieu or socialization approach—but the behavioral element includes the positive reinforcing value of such changes and making staff aware that they *can* serve as positive behavior change agents by performing such modifications. Introducing such modifications may necessitate orienting staff and residents, selecting from a stepwise priority list, and emphasizing what will be most reinforcing to the staff.

A structured way to increase overall reinforcement in the environment is by sharing behavioral data with staff. The worker develops a data-observation code that samples reinforcing behaviors and events at predetermined times. For example, in the group home for retarded children, several reinforcers may be identified: praise to residents for activity and/or appearance, resident engaged in solitary activity (television, reading), resident engaged in group activity (game), and staff efforts to increase resident activities (bringing television or games into room or suggesting an activity to a resident). Three fifteen-minute periods are identified each day for observation, and the worker used a Pla-Chek method (Doke and Risley, 1972) to assess several specified areas in the home (see Chapter Four). After observing for four days, the worker shares the findings with the childcare staff. Data may show that none of the five behaviors or events occur more than 8 percent of the time. The worker then teaches staff, through modeling, shaping, rehearsal, and cues, to engage in one or more of the behaviors. Weekly data sharing gives the staff feedback on changes in reinforcement patterns. Through feedback, the rates of staff behavior may increase to an acceptable criteria of reinforcement. (It is also useful to collect simultaneous data on problem behaviors and note any corresponding changes in negative behaviors.)

Thus, several methods to increase access to reinforcers are physically modifying the structure of the environment, modifying the social schedule of reinforcing activities, introducing equipment (games) that lead to opportunities for reinforcement techniques, and giving staff data-based feedback on their positive behavior.

A more structured intervention technique for increasing reinforcement is *token systems.* There are two kinds of token economies for behavioral social work interventions: individualized and group-based. Most of the literature's attention to staff-implemented procedures focus on group-based systems, which use a general medium of exchange, the token, as reinforcers for one or more behaviors. Accumulated tokens may be exchanged for material items, social reinforcers, or activities. Token systems have four components: the target behavior, the token, backup reinforcers, and specific contingencies (Kazdin, 1977).

Steps in developing a token system include (1) assessing target behaviors, (2) assessing reinforcement, (3) developing contingencies, and (4) implementing the system. Data recording, staff training, and target orientation are necessary components of a staff-operated system to achieve satisfactory results.

The first step in developing token systems (as with other interventions) is to *assess target behaviors.* Interviews with staff and clients and direct observation contribute to a formulation of behavioral targets and desirable outcomes. Behavioral targets may include increasing self-care activities, positive social interactions, or completion of academic problems. Targets may also include decreasing inappropriate behaviors, such as pouting, complaining, aggression, or bizarre speech. (Ayllon and Azrin, 1968; Dougherty, Friedman, and Pinkston, Practice Illustration 8.2; Green and Pinkston, Practice Illustration 8.1; Kazdin, 1977, are examples of the results of token systems for decreasing inappropriate behaviors.)

The second step in developing token systems is to *assess the reinforcers.* Often a menu of alternate reinforcers is constructed for clients' use; examples include material reinforcers, activity reinforcers, and social reinforcers (Tharp and Wetzel, 1969). The menu of backup reinforcers should be diverse enough to include reinforcement potential for the full range of clients involved in the program and to ensure continued potency of reinforcement over time. Reinforcement inventories (Tharp and Wetzel, 1969) are used to personalize reinforcers and may lead to useful and potent interventions. The medium of exchange (points, chips, or coupons) is selected, and values of reinforcers are determined. If these criteria cannot be achieved, do not implement a token economy because it will not be effective!

The third step is *contingency development.* Developing realistic contingencies requires attention to staff information about the individual clients, observational data, and principles of reinforcement (Ferster and Skinner, 1957). The initial contingencies that are programmed should facilitate the reinforcement of existing positive behaviors. An effort to involve staff (and clients) in planning the token system will enhance the system's acceptability and effectiveness.

Similarly, there are both staff and client considerations when *implementing* the token economy system. Worker interventions vis-a-vis staff members include concern for knowledge of behavioral principles and procedural abilities. The worker ensures that staff is taught and accepts the implementation of the token economy by teaching behavioral principles, assessing knowledge through paper-and-pencil inventories and experiential testing, use of examples, and rehearsal. (See "Training Behavior Change Agents" section later in this chapter.) Little empirical research has demonstrated the relationship between the need for discussing the rationale and theory that underlie a token system and accurate learning of procedures, but ensuring understanding may contribute to staff investment in the use of the system and minimize resistance to the program's implementation (Kuypers, Becker, and O'Leary, 1968).

Procedures are taught by instructions, modeling, rehearsal, and feedback. The staff learns the structure of the system, the equipment involved (tokens, records, signs), and the rules. Possible training techniques include using hypothetical or real examples, role playing so the staff may experience the system from the client's perspective, and rehearsing procedures within the system. Rehearsals begin with routine situations and proceed to anticipated problems that may arise from using the system. Teaching guidelines include:

1. Include staff in the planning of the system.
2. Include the rationale of the system in staff orientation.
3. Clearly specify, in both oral and written instructions, the procedures for using the system.
4. Teach the staff to use the procedures.
5. In the learning and implementation phases, give the staff feedback on both reinforcing and corrective methods.
6. Teach staff to look for naturally reinforcing events as the system is implemented.

Clients also must learn the purposes and operations of the token system before it is implemented. The exact format of orientation into the system must be individualized to the client group. The intellectual sophistication of the clients may determine whether orientation is to be didactic, experiential, or a combination of each style. Visual cues, whether in the form of written reminders, pictures, or signs on a blackboard or bulletin board, help ensure that clients have ongoing access to information about the token economy. Staff help determine the method of client orientation as well as who will orient the clients. Staff members who operate the system explain it to clients, although occasionally the worker will assist in such explanations. The clients are appraised that tokens which can later be exchanged for desirable goods or activities will be introduced into the environment as consequences for appropriate behaviors.

Once the system has been explained, preferably by using multiple formats, *the tokens must be potentiated as reinforcers.* The first step in making a token reinforcing is to provide the token at the same time a reinforcer is introduced. For example, if providing food is a potent reinforcer for children sitting still in a discussion group, a cookie and a token coupon may first be given simultaneously. After several sessions, when the group is comfortable with the tokens, the coupons may be given alone with the statement that they will be exchanged for cookies later. Initially, the time span between token and cookie may be very short, perhaps only one minute or as soon as after all children receive the coupon. However, later the time span is gradually increased as the token in itself becomes reinforcing. For a token economy to be effective, the tokens must be given as reinforcers *more often* than reinforcers were available previously. If overall reinforcers decrease at this juncture, we can predict that positive behavior will also deteriorate. Finally, staff may *rehearse* the use of tokens with clients; this practice is especially effective in early stages of client orientation.

After the token system has been in use, it is necessary to evaluate it. Often such evaluation can be made directly from the collected data. If positive behaviors increase and negative behaviors decline, effectiveness is noted. The worker and the staff also look for additional effects or side effects, both positive and negative; attendance or length of sessions may be such a side effect. Complaints or positive comments about the tokens are usually presented by clients and the staff. The ongoing reinforcing qualities of tokens and exchange choices must be monitored and evaluated. Inclusion of alternate procedures within the system may be viable. (See Practice Illustration 8.2.) The Green and Pinkston study (Practice Illustration 8.1) examines procedures for using token economies, including recording forms, program guidelines and rules, and evaluation results.

Finally, the token system may be faded. Fading may include the simple gradual withdrawal of the worker/consultant from the system or the disbanding of the entire system if it is no longer needed. With either fading procedure, special care is given to maintain the quantity and quality of reinforcement in the environment. If tokens are no longer to be used, social reinforcement may be sufficient to maintain behavior. This may be tested by careful attention to the data when the tokens are not in effect. For example, the entire system or a component may be removed for a week or so and then reinstated (as Green and Pinkston show in Practice Illustration 8.1).

The individual token system exemplifies the third reinforcement technique: *individual reinforcement program.* Staff-administered individual reinforcement programs are similar to the family administered reinforcement programs discussed in Chapter Seven. Practice Illustration 8.5 is an excellent example of an individualized reinforcement system. Individual analysis was completed regarding behavioral and reinforcement patterns for an adolescent girl. After baseline data were recorded, staff were asked to contingently increase reinforcement to specific behaviors in a serial manner. A minimum amount of actual staff training was necessary for this intervention, although consultation with staff was necessary to initiate and affect such changes.

Other *staff-based* reinforcement techniques include differential reinforcement, in which staff is instructed to reinforce a targeted behavior (see Chapter Two). Practice Illustration 8.4 is an example of differential reinforcement of low-rate behaviors. That study illustrates how low rates of asking questions contingent upon a one-minute interresponse time were reinforced. Teachers were asked to use a clock to determine if a minute had elapsed between responses and to acknowledge questions only under this contingency.

Additional techniques may include use of the Premack principle (Premack, 1965), where a low-rate behavior is reinforced by providing access to high-rate activity. For example, an activity worker may be taught to give participants an opportunity to run contingent upon participation in a five-minute discussion period. Staff behavior change agents also use prompting or cueing, which often are accompanied by reinforcement. An opportunity for reinforcement prompts an appropriate behavior that is contingently reinforced by staff. In the Linsk and Pinkston study (Practice Illustration 8.3), a cue signified a response opportunity to individually directed questions. Appropriate answers were reinforced by contingent social praise from the worker.

These examples only begin to suggest the possible use of reinforcement for staff persons. The advantages of using reinforcement-based techniques are: (1) The potential reinforcers are derived from existing staff behavior; (2) reinforcers do not have side effects of avoidance or escape behaviors; (3) they increase interactions; and (4) they have a high likelihood of being maintained. Staff engage in designing or choosing reinforcers, as can certain clients.

Punishment-Based Procedures. Punishment-based procedures are used to reduce the frequency of inappropriate behaviors, particularly those with severe consequences to the client or to others. Punishment in a group setting may include escape and avoidance behavior as side effects. The effect of both individual and group punishment must be considered. Both may lead to punishment of appropriate behavior of group members if they are not applied correctly. In its milder forms, punishment may be the technique of choice when reinforcement proves ineffective or when the behavior must be decreased quickly despite potential side effects.

The risk of punishment is well documented (Azrin and Holz, 1966; Johnston, 1972), but staff members unsophisticated in the complexities of behavior analysis often tend to equate behavior change with punishment. In a recent case conference at a psychiatric facility, we observed staff locking an individual out of the bedroom in an attempt to encourage activities. This action was labeled a "behavioral technique." Punishment is certainly a behaviorally relevant action, but the lack of analysis and contingency planning revealed the general confusion about the approach. The fact that the client involved spent the majority of time sitting in a chair isolated from other patients suggests a lack of analysis.

Punishment used by staff behavior change agents requires functional analysis of contingencies, clear procedures that are systematically applied, cautions that will protect the client, and simultaneous consideration of increasing reinforcement opportunities. Two mild forms of punishment are discussed in Practice Illustrations 8.1 and 8.2: response cost and time-out.

Response cost is systematically removing a reinforcer contingent upon the occurrence of a targeted behavior to be decreased. For example, in a classroom setting, a teacher may use a ten-minute early dismissal as a reinforcement for completing problems. In addition, any shouting or hitting during work time may be punished by a five-minute decrement in early dismissal. The decrement is referred to as a response cost. For response cost to be useful, reinforcers must already be earned or be potentially available.

Response cost may be most applicable in a token system where opportunities for reinforcement occur frequently and tokens may be contingently removed. Both the Green and Pinkston and the Dougherty, Friedman, and Pinkston studies (Practice Illustrations 8.1 and 8.2) discuss the use of response cost. Both studies found that the use of response cost enhances the token system.

Time-out, an alternate punishment technique, is removing the client who exhibits a target behavior from the available reinforcers. The technique is often used with children by removing them from the room, from access to peers, or from activity area when misbehavior occurs. This technique effectively eliminates an inappropriate behavior. Dougherty, Friedman, and Pinkston (Practice Illustration 8.2) evaluated the relationship between time-out and response cost.

Contingency contracting can be used for decreasing or increasing behaviors. Individual contingency contracts can be developed within a multiclient setting, with the staff as contingency managers. Staff is taught to specify contingencies, negotiate with clients, and develop a mutual contract. For example, a nurse may contract with a patient to take her outside for a walk if the patient completes a portion of the treatment regimen. Molick and Pinkston (Practice Illustration 8.5) demonstrated the use of a number of other possible reinforcement contingencies.

Group contingencies may be used in a multiclient setting to reinforce or punish either individual or group behavior. Group contingencies are consequences that affect an entire group. For example, teachers and activity workers often use trips or special activities as contingent reinforcers for positive group behavior. An agreement that if everyone finishes an assignment the group can go on a field trip is an application of a group contingency. A group contingency may be individually based: For instance, club group members get extra snacks if all members do not act aggressively toward one another. Peer group pressure is used to decrease the likelihood of the group provoking an aggressive act.

Modeling. A final intervention technique in staff-based programs is modeling. Teachers, therapists, nurses, and care-giving staff all model appropriate behaviors as a part of their ongoing activities to teach new behaviors. An interesting example of a staff-implemented modeling procedure is the Blackman and Pinkston study (Practice Illustration 9.2). Staff was taught to model appropriate eating behavior by using a guided practice method: The clients were taught how to use utensils by staff assistance in actual self-feeding. As this study illustrates, simultaneous use of modeling with reinforcement techniques maintains the new or restored behavior once it has been taught.

Choosing an Intervention Program. Intervention techniques offer a range of possibilities for behavior problems. A decision regarding techniques to be used is made in consultation with the staff behavior change agent, and at individual or group staff meetings the appropriate intervention techniques are selected. Decisions about techniques include assessment of the nature of the behaviors, staff interest and commitment, and the resources and time available. Criteria for selecting the best treatment procedure are now outlined:

Criteria for Choosing an Intervention in Staff Settings.

If	*Then*
It is desired to develop new behaviors	A modeling or reinforcement of successive approximations is useful.
The worker wants to increase an existing behavior	Reinforcement procedures should be selected.
The worker wants to eliminate an inappropriate behavior	Reinforcement of incompatible behaviors and differential reinforcement are the first procedures to consider. In extreme situations, punishment may need to be considered.
The program is for an individual client	Client observations will be helpful for determining an intervention strategy. Individual reinforcement, modeling, punishment, or token systems are all considered.
Staff and/or worker time is very limited	A staff consultation or training model may be the only option. A special structure may need to be set up, including appropriate administrative support.
Several clients are involved in the behavior problem	Environmental design, token economy, or group contingency contracts may be considered.
Staff is highly motivated to participate in the program	Staff may be taught to design, assess, and implement the relevant programs.

Two additional criteria should be reviewed when selecting the appropriate intervention. First, review the criteria of optimizing the amount of positive change possible while minimizing the demands upon staff time. This involves accurately assessing available staff and staff reinforcers. As Tharp and Wetzel (1969) pointed out, the best technique maximizes staff involvement and reinforcement. Second, consider the social relevance criteria (fully discussed in Chapter One). The relevance of the behavior change to client functioning is the overriding consideration when selecting an intervention plan. The worker assesses, with the staff and client, what the client will be able to do or achieve for the program to be successful. Besides relevance to staff and client, consider the institution and the community.

Training Behavior Change Agents

One of the most crucial components of a staff-based behavior change program is assurance that the staff member applies the program correctly (Kuypers, Becker, and O'Leary, 1968). When the intervention includes other staff, two behavioral interventions must occur to effect client behavior: The behavior of the staff or the environment must be changed, and the behavior of the client has to be modified. Staff modification programs include functional analysis of contingencies, provisions for reinforcer maintenance, and maintenance of learning.

Components of staff training include training staff (1) in general behavioral principles, (2) to collect behavioral data, (3) to formulate interventions, (4) to apply interventions, and (5) to maintain interventions; evaluating staff training is the final component. When considering staff training, the worker reevaluates the individual nature of the setting, the staff, and the clients to be served. Institutional schedule, competing demands, and staff interest in the program all may affect the success of training. Staff may say that they are interested in the training program, but insufficient time and reinforcers for participation will reduce the success of the program. Consequently, the training program must be designed to match available resources and needs.

General Behavioral Principles. A frequent component of behavior social work consultation is group staff training. Workshops and classes for staff members involved in behavior change programs may teach general principles or program techniques for ongoing implementation. Behavioral principles training packages have been developed for staff persons without prior behavioral training (Becker, 1971). Texts may be combined with didactic presentation of theoretical material, structured exercises to enhance learning of material, and between-session assignments. Training is frequently supplemented by out-of-classroom observation by trainers to assess the generality of learning. Research evidence indicates that classroom training is an effective setting for learning principles of behavior, skill-acquisition role playing, and feedback, but direct experience with clients is more effective (Gardner, 1972).

Group training may also complement institutional in-service models, increase reinforcers for the staff-learners, facilitate early development of a relationship between the worker and direct service staff, and provide a reinforcing exchange of ideas about issues and procedures not always available when training staff persons individually. Group training ensures uniformity of training when large numbers of staff implement the same techniques, such as a token system. Provisions to ensure mastery of material should be included in group approaches.

Stein (1975) warned about the risk of superficiality when behavioral training is limited to such a group effort. When open workshops and training sessions are offered to professionals, many come seeking a set of techniques to add to their standard operating procedures. The danger is in the misapplication of procedures, which may lead to potential client harm. Another consequence of misapplication is the lack of effect caused by inappropriate use of techniques, inadequate data base, inability to appropriately analyze data, or behavioral inconsistency. Within the limits of structured training sessions, direct practice efforts may be incorporated to offset these problems. Stein (1975) suggested that sessions be used for analysis of observational data collected between training sessions by participants. Programmed texts should be used as adjuncts to individualize training and identify deficits in participants, and experiential analogs such as behavioral rehearsal should be incorporated.

Workers cannot assume that each nurse, teacher, or house-parent can successfully incorporate techniques into day-to-day interactions. Although the integration of behavioral intervention and other approaches has been attempted (Saleebey, 1975; Wachtel, 1977), no systematic integration has yet been highly developed or empirically tested. What is generally compromised is the analysis components of behavioral treatment, and unsatisfactory outcomes are often attributed to inherent weakness in the technique rather than the application.

Group training should be planned and paced realistically,

with ample opportunity for feedback from participants via discussion, role playing, and structured exercises. The worker uses modeling, shaping, and corrective feedback as teaching devices. Videotapes, audiotapes, and experiential exercises may be included. Group training may be supplemented by written training materials. Materials for training persons in behavioral principles may include theoretical explanations, case examples, or structured written exercises. Programmed material that paces the learner individually is available. Prospective change agents often request reading material to become familiar with the intervention approach. Hall (1971a to c), Reese, Howard, and Reese (1978), and Sulzer and Mayer (1972) developed materials that give an overview of the behavior analysis approach that is useful to staff.

Behavioral training occurs individually as well as in groups. When only one staff person is involved, the training may go into more depth and be less complex to administer. Tutorials may be a less cost-effective use of the worker's time and sacrifice the benefits of group learning. The support of one's peers may not be available if only one staff person is learning the principles at a given time. Particular attention should be paid to the available reinforcers for the learning.

A third kind of training involves using staff to train other staff. This approach is referred to as a "pyramid" model of training and has been tested in a number of studies (Fremouw and Harnatz, 1975; Beard, Cox, and Pinkston, 1977; Jones, Fremouw, and Carples, 1977; Whalen and Henker, 1971). In the pyramid model, one group (tier 1 of training) is trained; the group then trains another group (tier 2 of training). Using direct staff as trainers contributes to the incorporation of behavioral programming into an agency practice. Training should incorporate ongoing consultation opportunities and monitoring of results to ensure program continuation.

Recording Behavioral Data. Behavioral data recording is usually a new behavior to introduce into the staff person's routine. The worker should include efforts to minimize the additional demands placed on the change agent. Forms are designed to maximize simplicity, observation periods are fit into existing routines, and existing permanent products are used whenever possible. The general procedure for any staff-collected data procedure is: (1) define behavior, (2) share definition with staff member, (3) rehearse data collection, (4) implement data collection, (5) monitor data collection, (6) reinforce and give feedback, and (7) correct data collection as needed.

Many investigators have considered the problems involved in improving staff data collecton (Welsch, Radicker, and Krapfl, 1973). For example, in a nursing home, a social work consultant may be asked to collaborate on programs to increase (1) self-care and (2) resident social interaction. Initial interviews with staff on the unit and observation may indicate that staff inconsistently helps residents dress and use washrooms; staff is charting and watching television in afternoons rather than talking with residents. Staff seldom praise residents for being dressed or talking to another person, except when special activities or parties occur. The worker sets up a two-session general orientation to the applied behavioral analysis model, which includes emphasis on observing behavior and reinforcement. In a third session, three behaviors are defined collaboratively with staff: resident dressed, resident used washroom, and resident talking. The following definitions are agreed upon by the eight staff persons involved in the study:

> Resident dressed: Resident is observed with street clothes (that is, dress or shirt and pants, socks or hose and shoes) appropriately on and fastened (buttoned, zipped, or tied).
> Resident used washroom: Resident is observed going into or out of washroom.
> Resident talking: Resident sat or stood within five feet of another person (staff or resident) and spoke at least one audible word.

An observation system is established involving a two-minute frequency count of each behavior six times per day. Staff is asked to select times at least one hour apart that are convenient for them. Observation schedules are matched to staff and resident schedules: (1) when A.M. staff person arrives at unit, (2) immediately after breakfast, (3) immediately before staff person goes to lunch, (4) when P.M. staff person arrives at unit, (5) immediately after resident's dinner, and (6) following the 7:30 P.M. medication. Four staff members per shift select two residents to observe simultaneously. Instructions, definitions, and a data-collection form are prepared and reviewed. Data collection is rehearsed in a fourth training session, and a videotape of three two-minute observations of residents is used. All staff members simultaneously complete the data-collection forms. Reliability is then computed on each members' observations, and definitions are further clarified. The process is repeated until the criteria of 80 percent reliability is reached. A direct observation is used for practice purposes. The following day, direct data collection is instituted, with the worker present for consultation and reliability checking. A fifth training session is then used to report reliability and praise the staff for their data collection. A certificate of completion (a reinforcer) of data-collection training is awarded. If necessary, appointments with individual staff members are set up to review the procedures. Subsequent meetings are devoted to intervention planning.

Formulating Interventions. Intervention formulation is taught by data analysis, determination of desired outcomes, and selection of techniques. Initially, the worker may assume responsibility for choosing interventions; as staff become adept in applying and collaborating in designing interventions, they may be taught to select their own interventions.

After stable and reliable data have been collected, it is shared with the staff change agent. The desired direction of the change in target behavior is confirmed. An intervention is selected based on the criteria discussed earlier in this chapter. The major role of staff in selecting the intervention is to help create an individualized program based on knowledge and preferences. For example, a reinforcer may be suggested by the change agent for an incompatible behavior. In work with a retarded boy, a recreation worker suggested access to the phonograph as a potential reinforcer for academic work.

Applying Interventions. Intervention training consists of (1) describing the intervention, (2) reviewing a written intervention procedure, (3) rehearsing the intervention, (4) applying the intervention, (5) evaluating the intervention, and (6) reinforcing and giving corrective feedback about the intervention.

In the nursing home example described earlier, a review of baseline data shows that residents are dressed in 60 percent of observations, and both washroom and talking behavior occur at average rates of less than 5 percent. Staff-identified goals are increasing washroom use and increasing conversation. After reviewing possible techniques, a prompt and reinforcing procedure is selected. A multiple-baseline-across-subjects design is used, and two of the eight subjects are initially selected (others may be added serially). A written procedure like the following is developed and incorporated into a checklist:

_____ Resident is asked if wanted to go to washroom
_____ If agreeable, resident is taken to washroom
_____ Resident is asked
                1.   If family has been heard from recently
                2.   What resident planned to do today
                3.   Other individualized question
_____ Resident is praised for cooperating in toileting
_____ Resident is praised for talking to staff person

Date _____ Time _____ Staff _____

A different staff member, other than the observer, is assigned to each subject, and intervention is implemented at the same time as observations.

The procedure is reviewed and practice sessions are developed by using role-playing procedures. After 100 percent accuracy on each step of the procedure has been achieved, the intervention is introduced. During the first day, and periodically thereafter, the worker collects reliability data. The change agents are praised and given corrective feedback for applying intervention. For each agent, a letter of commendation is sent to the staff member and the director of nursing.

Checklists specify the steps and the completion of the procedure for each period. The checklist is designed to provide a format for uniformly implementing the procedure, the independent treatment variables. Ongoing review of checklists may prevent or redirect drift between original intervention and subtle changes that may occur because of the change agent's interest level and learning history.

Giving Staff Feedback and Reinforcement. The use of feedback and reinforcement is an important component of staff training. Generally, the worker meets regularly with involved staff members, giving them information about behavior changes and sharing relevant data. These meetings should be as positive as possible. The staff is helped to interpret the data regarding whether the techniques are being applied as designed and whether the expected effects are occurring. This review may indicate additional training procedures for staff, changing the intervention procedures, or strengthening existing procedures. The presence of correct intervention applications and expected client change is a powerful reinforcer for staff as behavior change agents.

Staff feedback has received increasing attention in the behavior analysis literature. After the program has been initiated, a frequently reported problem is maintaining staff performance in change efforts. Alternate approaches to ensure staff continuance have included praise by supervisors (Monteger and others, 1977; Pomerleau, Bobrove, and Smith, 1973); publicly posting staff performance data; instructions, workshops, and administrative directives. A number of studies have demonstrated that publicly posting staff data in multistaff settings is preferable (Greene and others, 1978; Kreitner, Reif, and Morris, 1977; Panyan, Boozer, and Morris, 1970; Patterson, Griffen, and Panyan, 1976; Quilitch, 1975). Other studies have favorably evaluated the effectiveness of public posting used jointly with other approaches (Greene and others, 1978; Pommer and Streedback, 1974). Andrasik and McNamara (1977), in a quasi-experimental study comparing seven staff motivation techniques, found that feedback to staff or to their supervisors increased staff accuracy in administering a behavioral token program and increased innovations such as changing recording forms and administrative changes in contingency systems. This study asserted that an effective method to modify staff behavior is to alter client behaviors. Changes in client-related contingencies also alter staff functioning.

Reinforcement systems for staff should maximize available opportunities for reinforcement and reduce competing demands. Often, this involves careful analysis of reinforcers and demands through interviews and observation and work with supervisors and administrators.

Perhaps the most important staff reinforcement is accurate and honest feedback about their performance in the behavioral program. Staff performance in behavioral programs improves steadily when shaping is used. Concrete reinforcements may also be provided: awards, commendations, monetary incentives, and expressed thanks for participation. Access to privileges or time off may also facilitate cooperation. Finally, sharing data with related staff is reinforcing. For staff persons unfamiliar with behavioral data, the ability to quantify their work achievements may provide needed support. For those persons with scientific training, the behavioral data may be reinforcing and be incorporated into their own recording systems. The most important consideration in the ongoing success of staff-worker collaboration is that the levels of reinforcement remain high.

The literature includes a number of staff reinforcement procedures. Supervisory verbal praise has been shown to increase staff-resident interactions (Monteger and others, 1977). Schinke and Wong (1978) combined reinforcement with role playing, practice feedback, cueing, and contracting in a training program for staff in a group home setting. Financial incentives have been used as reinforcers for performance and patient improvement (Pomerleau, Bobrove, and Smith, 1973; Katz, Johnson, and Gelfand, 1972; Pommer and Streedback, 1974).

In numerous settings, reinforcement may need to be modified or applied indirectly. Supervisory feedback and praise are useful for reinforcing appropriate levels of staff. Paraprofessional and direct care-giving staff may respond to direct or written supervisory commendation. Written commendations may prove especially effective with professional colleagues. Privileges, schedule options, or task options may be arranged contingent upon staff performance. With professional staff, participation in professional conferences with shared authorship and presentation may act as reinforcers. Certificates of completion of training courses may reinforce, and salary advancements or continuing education credits can be incorporated into workshops or classes. An alternative strategy includes agreeing to engage in tasks as a reinforcer for program participation. The worker may assist in group activities, relieve the change agent of certain responsibilities, or give special attention to a client for whom the change agent has insufficient time. These alternatives are viewed as exchanges as well as reinforcers, and the attention and time directed by the worker reinforce the staff member.

Attention and discussion with staff members often provide reinforcement for program participation. The opportunity to discuss caretaking, scientific, or professional issues is frequently not available to staff working with persons experiencing behavior problems. The worker's interest may often reinforce the change agent's efforts. An opportunity to discuss agency or administrative problems with a less involved staff person may reinforce. Clearly, the best choice of reinforcement for staff depends on an accurate assessment of their work situations. Often, the best way to find reinforcers is simply to ask the staff person what might be a positive consequence of program participation.

Evaluating Interventions

Methods to evaluate programs where staff members act as behavior change agents are the same as those used to evaluate practice where the worker, the client, or the family serves as primary change agent (see Chapter Four for a full discussion). In this chapter's practice illustrations, intrasubject or reversal designs are used frequently. Individual client case studies using reversal or intrasubject replication designs include the Molick and Pinkston study (Practice Illustration 8.5), the Banzett study (Practice Illustration 8.4), and the Green and Pinkston study (Practice Illustration 8.1), which modified the design to study contrasting components. Two group case studies used reversal designs (Linsk and Pinkston, Practice Illustration 8.3 and

Dougherty, Friedman, and Pinkston, Practice Illustration 8.2). In reversal or withdrawal designs, particular care is necessary to interpret these designs to staff. Staff should understand that the design is useful for clinical evaluation and for demonstrating to worker, client, and staff that the intervention is effective. Staff should understand that evaluation results in a more effective intervention, which leads to greater client improvement and maintenance of improvement.

Intersubject replication is used extensively in staff-based programs because different subjects or settings are often available for multiple baseline and application of treatment (Levitt and Pinkston, 1979). The Blackman and Pinkston study (Practice Illustration 9.2) discusses the use of multiple baselines across subjects.

In addition, consumer evaluations and posttest measures are useful adjuncts to the evaluation of the intervention. As noted in earlier chapters, consumer evaluations can supply information about unobserved changes, emotional reactions, and client's and change agents' opinions about the program. Consumer evaluations are often used to evaluate training programs in institutional or agency settings. Subjects frequently participate in these evaluations, providing information on the format, timing, and subject's suggested improvement in the program. These evaluations can give the worker both critical feedback and reinforcement.

Generality and Maintenance

Planning and assessing program generality and maintenance is a vital component of the worker's task in a staff-based setting. Because of multiple staff, staff turnover, administrative demands and changes, a principle of work with staff is to try to leave as much of the program as possible within the setting. When possible, work rules, evaluation formats, and ongoing inservice programs need revision to incorporate data collection and intervention evaluation. The worker can consult, serve on committees, and draft suggestions to effect such agency changes.

Chapter Nine discusses programming generality and maintenance. Probes for generality and maintenance are included in both the Linsk and Pinkston and the Banzett studies (Practice Illustrations 8.3 and 8.4). Follow-up probes and possible programming should be a component of all programs when staff serves as the change agent. Practice Illustration 9.2 is an example of programmed transfer of learning with staff change agents.

A Response-Cost Token Economy: Effectiveness and Side Effects

Glenn R. Green, Elsie M. Pinkston

Children with behavior problems in the classroom are frequently referred to social workers for individual treatment. In these cases, teachers may think that treatment means psychotherapy or, in the best case, they expect some counseling from the worker on how to treat the child differently. In the worst case, the teacher may believe that the problem lies within the child, and if the child is somehow "fixed," the problem will no longer occur. In this study, the teachers cooperated with the worker to alter the contingencies within the classroom. Here we discuss how to include a response-cost procedure in a token economy without producing harmful side effects.

Researchers have systematically explored the effectiveness of response cost within the token economy and the nature of any side effects. Response cost is "A procedure to decrease the strength of behavior by removing a reinforcer, contingent upon that behavior" (Reese, Howard, and Reese, 1978, p. 23). Results have shown that response cost is equally effective to time-out procedures (Iwata and Bailey, 1974) and that negative side effects are not present in the classrooms using these procedures (Kaufman and O'Leary, 1972). Further exploring the use of free tokens and response cost, researchers have found that removing tokens following a response can reduce the response, even though there are no backup reinforcers available (Hall and others, 1972). This is a surprising finding and requires further confirmation.

This study examines the effectiveness of an intervention package encompassing free tokens removed contingently upon the occurrence of an undesired behavior and analyzes positive or negative side effects of this intervention. The research includes

307

analysis of three aspects: components of the treatment package, the effectiveness of feedback within this package, and the experimental manipulation of the value of the tokens. The rate of behavior and side effects are examined across all experimental conditions.

Method

Client and Setting. The client was a nine-year-old boy who was placed in a self-contained classroom in a special day school for children with behavioral difficulties. According to the teacher's reports and preliminary observations, the child engaged in a high frequency of pouting, crying, noncompliance, and teasing. The child, as of the beginning of this research, had attended the school for four months. Testing revealed that the child had a near-normal IQ and age-appropriate academic abilities.

The client was placed in a primary behavior-disorders classroom with seven other children, all of similar age and difficulties. The classroom personnel consisted of a special education teacher, certified in behavioral and learning disorders with one year of teaching experience, and a classroom aide with five years of experience. At the time of the research, a global token economy already existed in the environment. Specific behaviors were reinforced or punished by presenting or removing tokens contingent upon the occurrence of specific behaviors. The definitions of the reinforced and punished behaviors within the global token economy are presented in Figure 1. The upper part of the figure refers to those behaviors that are contingently reinforced; the lower part refers to those behaviors contingently punished.

Observation and Reliability. Observations, using the teacher and the aide as observers, were made throughout the entire research project. The observers independently observed and recorded the frequency of the behavioral targets of whining, pouting, or crying, defined as follows:

> *Pouting:* sticking out or stretching the lower lip past the upper lip, usually accompanied by facial grimaces

Figure 1. Definition of Student Behaviors.

Positive warmth: A person gives/receives clear gestural or verbal approval to/from another individual for appropriate interaction. Must include some clear indication of positive interest or involvement. Includes "strokes," compliments, empathic response, and understanding.

Compliance: A person immediately does what is asked; can be used in tough situations or for special requests of tasks.

Disapproval: A person gives verbal or gestural disapproval of another person's negative behavior in a socially appropriate manner.

Ignore: Person A has directed behavior at person B and person B appears to have recognized that the behavior was directed at him but does not respond in an active fashion and/or "minds his own business."

Initiation: Attempts an appropriate interaction with persons or materials when it is unprompted.

Cooperate: Agreeing to go along with someone else's suggestion (without any implied authority) with another student, including sharing and possible negotiation skills.

Work/play: Engaging in activity independently with minimal supervision.

Physical negative: A student physically attacks or attempts to attack another person: hitting, pinching, tripping.

Destructiveness: A student destroys, damages, or attempts to damage any nonhuman object: The damage need not actually occur, but the potential for damage must exist.

Stealing: A person is caught stealing or in possession of anything where ownership cannot be substantiated by the person.

Noncompliance: A person does not initiate or do what is asked of her.

Dependency: Person A asks help in doing a task that he is capable of doing himself, and it is an imposition on the other person to fulfill the request.

Pestering: Inappropriate physical interaction with another student. Directed toward another individual: interrupting, poking, or annoying.

Swearing: Verbal expressions or nonverbal gestures that are inappropriate in a school setting.

Threat: Expression or gesture that indicates possible intent of harm to person or property.

Disruption: Verbal or nonverbal behavior directed toward class or no one in particular, resulting in the teacher discontinuing a lesson. The classroom climate is affected. Includes shouting, yelling, or talking loudly.

Tease/humiliate/zaps: Verbal behavior to another person that indicates disapproval or displeasure.

Source: Adapted from G. R. Patterson and others. *A Social Learning Approach to Family Intervention.* Vol. 1: *Families with Aggressive Children.* Eugene, Ore.: Castalia, 1975.

Whining: complaining about a task in such a manner that it produces a shriveling or nasal utterance, occasionally accompanied by the slamming of objects or fists

Crying: the act of bringing tears to the eyes, without physical reason, or sniffling without a cold or other medical illness

The teacher and the aide were given a copy of the observation code to refer to while performing the frequency counts.

Frequent and random reliability checks were performed during each phase of the research. These reliability checks were performed independently by third observers, either the authors or a graduate student, and calculated by the percent agreement between the person doing the reliability check and the mean of the observers' observations. (See Chapter Four for formula.)

Procedure

The intervention was a variation on response-cost techniques used in token economies. The intervention has several components; each is now discussed separately. These components are the basic requirements as described by Kazdin (1977).

The Token or Medium of Exchange. The token used in this intervention was a book of coupons measuring approximately one by two and a half inches. Each coupon could be easily torn from the book without harming the remaining coupons. Each coupon was typed: "This coupon gives _____ permission to pout, whine, or cry one time." The coupon book held twenty-five coupons. A cover for the coupon book was provided.

Backup Reinforcers. Backup reinforcers consisted of a menu of activities that are high probability behaviors (Premack, 1959; 1965). Observation and teacher interviews with the worker indicated that the following activities were high frequency in nature: playing games, putting puzzles together, riding a bike, playing with Lego blocks, and shooting baskets.

Specific Contingencies. The child was given a book of twenty-five free coupons at the beginning of each day. The book was attached to a piece of yarn, and the child wore the book around his neck. When the child engaged in a response class behavior, the teacher and aide were taught by the worker to remove a coupon from the coupon book and asked to point out to the child that he had engaged in crying, whining, or pouting and to tell him the number of remaining coupons. At a predetermined time each day, backup reinforcers were made available for a specific length of time that was determined by the value and number of remaining coupons. At approximately 2 P.M. daily, reinforcement was made available contingent upon the number of remaining coupons.

Experimental Design

The research design is that of a single subject, $ABABBC_1$ $BBC_2 BBC_3$, where A is baseline and withdrawal, B is the implementation of the coupons without backup reinforcers, and BC is the use of the coupons with the backup reinforcers of different potencies made available. The subscripts in BC refer to the different manipulations performed on the independent variable to increase or decrease the potency of the coupon.

Baseline (A). The teacher and the classroom aide conducted frequency count of crying, whining, and pouting. Both the aide and the teacher had been trained by the worker in observing and the observation code, and their tallies were kept independently. The procedure used for frequency counts was used during all phases.

Coupons (B). The child was introduced to the coupons. No explanations about the purpose of the coupons were stated, and all verbalizations concerning the coupons were held constant across all phases. The quantity of coupons remained the same: Twenty-five were given to the child each morning.

Withdrawal (A). The child was not given the coupon book, and the only explanation given was that ". . . the coupons will not be used today." Frequency counts continued.

Coupons (B). The child was reintroduced to the coupons and no backup reinforcers were made available.

Reinforcement (BC_1). The reinforcement menu was introduced. Verbalizations concerning the coupons explained the contingencies: It was explained that menu items were contingent upon the remaining number of coupons at the end of the day. At the beginning of the day, the teacher told the child the number of coupons in the book and the value of each coupon. The teacher's explanations were: "Today, your coupon book contains twenty-five coupons and each coupon will buy one minute of your choice from the reinforcement menu." The general format of these explanations was held constant across all BC phases.

During this phase, the value and quantity of the coupons remained the same for each day. This manipulation maintained the potency of the coupon at the same level throughout the five-day interval.

Coupons (B). The coupon book was maintained in the environment, coupons contingently removed, but the backup reinforcers were withdrawn. No explanations were given as to why backup reinforcers were withdrawn.

Reinforcement (BC_2). Backup reinforcers were reintroduced. The potency of the coupon was enhanced by increasing the value and cost of the individual coupon 50 percent (one and a half minutes from the reinforcement menu per coupon) and maintaining a constant number of coupons given each day. Note that the new price of the backup reinforcers was explained daily by the teacher.

Coupons (B). This phase is exactly the same as the previous B phases.

Reinforcement (BC_3). This phase is exactly the same as BC_2, except that the value of the coupon was decreased in value by 50 percent and the number of coupons remained the same. The coupons during this phase were worth one-half minute of time from the reinforcement menu.

Results

Reliability between the observers was calculated two ways. Pearson showed that the reliability between observers was .88. Because the frequencies were collected hourly, agreement was also calculated by dividing the fewer number of behaviors, as recorded by one observer, by the larger number of behaviors, as recorded by the second observer. A mean reliability was calculated by summing the reliabilities and dividing by the number of intervals. Reliability, as determined in this fashion, was 84 percent for the entire research project. Frequent and random reliability checks were performed; these checks were calculated by the percent agreement between the third observer and the mean of the observers' observations. The checks produced an overall mean agreement of 91 percent.

Figure 2 shows the mean hourly frequency of the behav-

Figure 2. Mean Hourly Frequency of Pouting, Whining, and Crying.

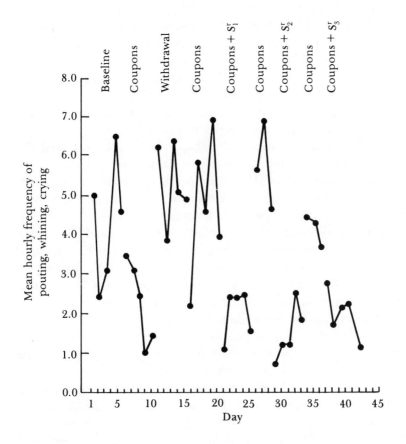

iors during each research phase. Baseline measures showed a highly variable rate of pouting, whining, and crying, with a mean occurrence of 22.4 per day. The introduction of the coupons, without backup reinforcers, decreased the rate of behavior. The mean daily rate during this phase was 12.0 occurrences. During withdrawal, the frequency of the behaviors increased to an average of 28.1 per day. When the coupons, without backup reinforcers, were reintroduced, an interesting phenomenon occurred. During the first day of this phase, the frequency of the behaviors decreased to a level comparable to that of the first coupon phase. After the first day, the rate of pouting, whining, and crying increased and maintained at a level approximate to that of baseline and withdrawal. The introduction of backup reinforcers (BC_1) reduced the mean daily rate of pouting, whining, and crying to 10.5. A return to coupons, without reinforcers, increased the mean daily rate to 26.3. When backup reinforcers were reintroduced in BC_2 (an increase in coupon potency), the mean daily rate decreased to 8.0. A return to coupons, without backup reinforcers, increased the mean daily rate to 20.3 occurrences. During BC_3 (a decrease in coupon potency), the behaviors decreased to a mean daily rate of 9.6.

The coupons, without backup reinforcers, decreased the rate of pouting, whining, and crying during the first six days of the initial two phases. Using the mean occurrence of pouting, whining, and crying during withdrawal and baseline as a base, the coupons reduced pouting, whining, and crying 24 percent, 32 percent, 64 percent, 79 percent, 71 percent, and 67 percent for each day, respectively. On the seventh day of the coupons (day 2 of the reintroduction of the coupons), they became ineffective. The effectiveness of the coupons was maintained through the final days of that phase and in all subsequent coupon phases that did not include backup reinforcers.

When the coupon phases were combined, both positive and negative side effects could be analyzed by comparing the coupon phases to the combined baseline and withdrawal phases. The frequency of fines—noncompliance, swearing, threatening, and disruption—was tested for randomness. Also tested for randomness was the frequency of prosocial behaviors—compliance, cooperation, and work/play—in each of the combined phases. Thus, if the frequencies of the positive and negative behaviors were random, the coupon phases had little, if any, effect on those behaviors. Using chi square for between-phase significance and as a test of randomness, a nonsignificant value was obtained for the absolute frequency of fines ($\chi^2 = 5.05$, $df = 3$, $.20 < p < .10$) and for the absolute frequency of pro-social points earned ($\chi^2 = 1.66$, $df = 2$, $.50 < p < .30$). It can be concluded that the frequencies of positive and negative behaviors were random in each of the combined phases and that the coupons, without backup reinforcers, did not significantly influence the frequencies of fines or prosocial behaviors.

Clinically significant main and side effects of the program are shown in Figure 3, which is a detailed presentation of the means and standard deviations of the variables. The mean frequency of the variable is a good descriptive statistic because the program's main and side effects can be compared between phases. The standard deviations are excellent descriptive statistics of the

Figure 3. Means and Standard Deviations of Side Effect Variables During Each Phase. Note That the Means and Standard Deviations Are Calculated Daily.

Phase	Points earned under global token economy		Frequency of pouting, crying, whining		Points lost under global token economy		Prosocial points earned	
	Mean	St. dev.	Mean	St. dev.	Mean	St. dev.	Mean	St. dev.
Baseline	28.8	4.97	22.4	12.3	15.0	12.75	3.0	2.34
Coupons	39.2	3.76	12.0	5.90	11.0	14.75	5.4	3.57
Withdrawal	32.8	5.67	28.1	6.30	17.0	22.50	2.4	2.20
Coupons	35.2	5.12	20.0	8.70	13.0	13.50	3.8	2.30
Coupons + S_1^r	35.2	4.40	10.5	4.06	12.0	5.70	6.2	2.17
Coupons	25.7	6.51	26.3	10.1	16.7	24.66	3.3	1.53
Coupons + S_2^r	41.8	4.55	8.0	3.5	15.0	9.35	5.6	3.51
Coupons	43.0	4.36	20.3	2.3	15.0	10.00	3.7	2.31
Coupons + S_3^r	40.8	3.03	9.6	4.1	7.0	5.71	4.2	2.95

stability within each phase of a variable. The contention is that an intervention which stabilizes a variable, as shown by a decreased standard deviation, can be legitimately described as a positive main or side effect.

Comparing baseline to the introduction of coupons, the means of points earned increased and the standard deviation decreased for the points earned under the global token economy. This is a positive side effect because the client was more successful under the global token economy regarding exhibiting more positive behaviors with less day-to-day fluctuations. Withdrawing the coupons decreased the mean of points earned and increased daily fluctuations. The reintroduction of the coupons and the introduction of stable backup reinforcers had little effect on the points earned and their daily stability except for an increase in the mean of points earned over the baseline mean. The last three phases had little effect on the mean of points earned under the global token economy. The only significant clinical difference was in the BC_3 phase: The standard deviation was at the lowest point and the mean of points earned was high as compared to baseline.

The points lost under the global token economy—fines— showed both positive and negative side effects. The mean of fines decreased as the coupons were introduced and reintroduced. The standard deviations during each initial four phases showed that fines markedly fluctuated daily. They also showed no discernible pattern. The coupons had the positive side effect of decreasing the means of fines but had no effect on the stability. When the backup reinforcer phases were introduced, the reverse occurred. The mean of fines during these phases remained at approximately the same level as the previous four phases, but the stability increased greatly. The most significant positive side effects occurred during BC_3 because both the mean and the standard deviation of the fines were at clinically low levels as compared to the previous phases.

Discussion

The results clearly show that the addition of backup reinforcers was effective and that manipulating the potency of the cost had minimal differential effect on this child's pouting, whining, and crying. In all the phases that the potency was altered, the means and the standard deviation of pouting, whining, and crying are very similar. Because all three phases equally reduced pouting, whining, and crying, one possible variable to consider is feasibility. The maximum time that could be earned during BC_2 was 37.5 minutes, as compared to BC_3, in which 12.5 minutes could be earned. The difference of twenty-five minutes could possibly be a major variable for the worker with limited time. The intervention should be further evaluated for main and side effects. The coupon phase that had decreased potency of the backup reinforcer (BC_3) appears to have the least negative side effects and the most positive side effects. During this phase, the points earned under the global token economy were high, with few daily fluctuations, and the frequency of the fines was low and stable. This phase is even more powerful considering the desire of many clinicians to increase the frequency and intensity of reinforcement. These facts, combined with the feasibility variable, heavily point toward the use of minimal cost as the most desirable punishment procedure. A further reinforcing aspect is that it is of minimal cost and easily taught by workers to institutional staff.

The coupons, without backup reinforcers, presented unique results. The coupons initially decreased the behaviors, yet rapidly decreased in effectiveness. When the coupons are viewed as a limited degree of feedback, this result is not surprising. The question that needs to be addressed is why they were initially effective. There are a number of alternate reasons that were not empirically studied in this project but might be the basis for future research. One reason may be that the cost procedure itself was initially effective. Just the fact of giving the child the coupon book and then contingently removing the coupons acted as a punishment procedure. A second reason, in conjunction with the first, might be that the child responds as if punished but this child needed time to learn the contingencies, the rule for responding, and the potency of the procedure. The main concept to consider is that this procedure, as used, was relatively ineffective.

One concept investigated in this paper is that increasing

the potency leads to an increase in aversive side effects. The results suggest that this was generally the case. Increasing the cost led to an increase in the mean of fines and their standard deviations. Points earned under the global token economy show that the increased potency phase (BC_2) slightly increased the points earned. Conversely, a more systematic evaluation should be conducted regarding stability. The most stable, for points earned under the global token economy, is the decreased potency phase (BC_3). When considering prosocial points earned, the statistics that should be dealt with are standard deviations because the means are so similar. In this case, the standard deviations show that the increased potency phase is the most unstable. The data directly confirm Kaufman and O'Leary's concept (1972) that the increased potency of the cost leads to more aversive side effects. These results are limited because of the limited series of points in each phase.

The results suggest that various common procedures used in token economies should be reevaluated. One commonly used procedure is to increase the magnitude of the punishment so as to decrease the frequency of aversive behaviors. This concept was empirically studied by Buchard and Barrera (1972), who found that a higher magnitude of response cost led to a greater suppression of behavior in all but one subject. Although this study used differing methods and procedures, the effect was generally supported, but the effect of increasing the punishment was negligible for reducing the frequency of pouting, whining, and crying. Furthermore, side and main effects need to be considered. Instead of increasing the magnitude of the punishment, perhaps a more realistic approach is to develop token economy procedures that have minimal side effects yet are potent enough to decrease the undesired behavior, or to reevaluate the contingencies. This concept needs to be further evaluated as a clinical practice in light of the results.

There are many benefits of using a similar coupon program. The most powerful is that it is simple to use and operate. The coupon program makes it difficult to inadvertently increase punishment. The procedures can be easily taught. A further consideration is that there are two ways to increase the potency:

manipulating the number or the value of coupons. Another major benefit is that the coupon program has a data system built into the program and the worker's major concern with data can be focused on the contingencies. Expanding this point, the worker should explore the consistency with which the program is being implemented by performing spot reliability checks.

The results clearly show that for effectiveness, side effects, and main effects, the most desirable response-cost procedure is one just potent enough to decrease the undesired behavior. Theoretically developing a hierarchy of potency procedures, the least potent procedure is losing tokens when no backup reinforcers are made available. The difficulty is that this procedure may not effectively decrease the undesired behavior. The next most potent procedure is using free tokens contingently removed upon the occurrence of the undesired behavior. The most potent procedure is removing previously earned tokens. Workers can move up the hierarchy until the procedure is effective and can be fairly assured that the procedure will have *minimum* side effects for that specific potency.

In this research, a free token was removed contingent upon the occurrence of pouting, whining, and crying, the value of backup reinforcers was systematically manipulated, and the results on the dependent variables were studied. An analysis demonstrated that workers should develop token economies for effectiveness and positive and negative side effects. Because of the widespread use and power of token economies, further research into positive and negative side and main effects and generality is needed.

An Analysis of Time-Out
and Response-Cost Procedures
in a Special Education Class

Richard Dougherty, Benjamin S. Friedman, Elsie M. Pinkston

Time-out and response-cost procedures have been frequently used to reduce disruptive behavior of children in classrooms (Kazdin, 1972; MacDonough and Forehand, 1973). Although both time-out and response cost have been shown to effectively reduce deviant behavior (Birnbrauer and others, 1965; Bostow and Bailey, 1969; Buchard, 1967), many of the variables relevant to the individual effectiveness of the two procedures have not been investigated (Kazdin, 1972; MacDonough and Forehand, 1973). Furthermore, the increasing attention to the ethical issues involved in using time-out procedures in the classroom and institutional settings (Anderson and King, 1974; Wyatt vs. Stickney, 1974) has further heightened the need for evaluative research into the parameters of time-out (MacDonough and Forehand, 1973) and alternatives to time-out. Few investigations in the literature have reported a systematic comparison between time-out and response cost (Buchard and Barrera, 1972). This present study is an attempt to extend these findings and to demonstrate the value of research in an applied setting for programmatic problem solving.

Time-out procedures, as employed extensively in various settings, typically follow the criteria set forth by Leitenberg (1965) in his review of the experimental literature. According to Leitenberg, "The essential feature of time-out is a period of time in which positive reinforcement is no longer available" (p. 428). Buchard and Barrera described the typical forms of time-out in applied settings as being the discontinuation of the administration of reinforcement for a specified period of time, or the removal of the subject to "a restricted, allegedly less-rein-

320

forcing environment" (1972, p. 271). Both Leitenberg (1965) and Kaufman and Baron (1968) suggested that the functional aversiveness of the time-out may vary depending upon the background conditions. Tallon's (1976) research with retarded adolescents demonstrated that the effectiveness of time-out is directly related to the frequency of reinforcement. Further research is needed to understand the conditions under which time-out may function as a positive reinforcer (Steeves, Martin, and Pear, 1970).

Response-cost, or fine, procedures are also effective when presented contingent upon the emission of specified undesirable behaviors. Kazdin defined response cost as referring "to a procedure in which a positive reinforcer is lost or some penalty is invoked" (1977, p. 69). Response-cost procedures can be of special benefit in token economies, as in the present study, because both "reinforcement and punishment can be administered along the same reinforcer dimension" (p. 70). Response-cost procedures have been compared with token reinforcement programs with generally equivalent, although mixed, results.

In a study that compared time-out and response cost, Buchard and Barrera (1972) showed that there is a functional relationship between response suppression and the magnitude of response-cost and time-out duration. Additional research is needed to determine the persistence of this effect. The results demonstrate relatively similar effects between the response-cost and time-out conditions, although there are problems with each condition. One advantage of response cost over time-out is that the individual is not removed from the opportunity to engage in desirable behaviors which would be rewarded. Time-outs may frequently result in physical confrontation between staff and students, requiring further exercise of control. A disadvantage of response-cost procedures, noted in the study, was that the client might be unwilling to control his own behavior and that the accumulation of fines might be reinforcing (Buchard and Barrera, 1972, p. 280). Removing the child from the ongoing situation was recommended in these instances.

The present study was developed in response to problems in the time-out program in a special education classroom. Teachers expressed concern with the disruption and frequency of time-outs and an increasingly large number of times in which physical force was necessary to administer the time-outs. Teachers had requested assistance from a social work consultation unit with the management of their classrooms, and there was also a growing concern with the ethical issues associated with time-outs and physical punishment. (See Anderson and King, 1974). In light of Buchard and Barrera's (1972) findings and Walker and Buckley's (1974) recommendations for response cost over time-out, an alternative program was developed. The evaluative goal included an assessment of the comparative frequency of time-out or fines, as in the previous studies (Buchard and Barrera, 1972; White, Nielson, and Johnson, 1972). Direct observation measures were compared with frequency counts to control for possible confounding effects resulting from the differences in the administration of the two procedures. Effectiveness of the procedures on student behavior was assessed as major evaluation criteria. In addition, the ethical implications of the two procedures were analyzed. The goal was to develop a less restrictive punishment program with an improved or equivalent level of effectiveness to be accepted by staff and implemented in the facility.

Methods

Students. The students were all thirteen boys in one classroom. Ages ranged from ten to fourteen years, and approximately half the students had varying degrees of learning disabilities. The students' presenting problems were predominantly aggression against the teachers or other students or "hyperactivity," such as the inability to pay attention or sit still. Approximately five students had records of previous residential placements in a psychiatric setting; one was receiving psychotropic medication.

During the course of the study, the classroom faculty consisted of two full-time special education teachers who implemented and assisted in the evaluation program. A student teacher also helped run the class. In the middle of the study, the internship of one of the student teachers was completed; that teacher was replaced by another student.

Setting. The study with these students took place in their regular classroom at a private school for children with learning disabilities and behavior problems. All the students had been excluded from the public school system in Chicago or its suburbs. There were approximately 120 children in the school divided among ten classrooms. Each classroom operated on a point system combined with time-outs contingent upon inappropriate behaviors.

The classroom was a large room, approximately twenty-five by thirty feet. Students' desks were arranged in a semi-circle, with the open end toward the blackboard at the front of the room. Two tables for group activities or games were at the back of the room. Records of point earnings were kept on a large grid on the blackboard. Rules were posted in full view of the class, above the blackboard.

Experimental conditions were in effect the entire school day for this classroom, under the supervision of one of the teachers in the actual classroom. During lunch and while in the halls, students were subject to the general rules, which consisted of time-outs for rule violations. Teachers were instructed not to change their lesson or activity plan during the course of the study. Occasional field trips and outdoor activities occurred during each phase of study. Data recording did not occur during this time.

Procedures. The *point system,* or programmed environment, in which the study took place was divided into three categories, as outlined in Table 1. Student earned points for com-

Table 1. Categories in the Point System.

	Earnings	Spendings	Savings
Assignment	Three assignments per day	800 pts. = 15 min free time	In time-out conditions, if less than 800 points, then may be saved
	900 possible pts.	400 pts. = in-class free time	
Attitude	Excellent = 300 Positive = 200 Neutral = 100	900 = 15 min extra 600 = 10 min extra 300 = 5 min extra	Not saved
Bonus	Intermittently awarded in various amounts	Menu in free room Menu in classroom store	Saved, if not spent

pleting assignments and for their attitude during these assignments, and they were intermittently given points for other positive behaviors, such as ignoring someone's teasing or getting to work quickly. There were three different assignments or activities during the day, in which students could earn up to 300 points per assignment. Smaller amounts were awarded for partial completion. Assignment points (800) could then be used to buy fifteen minutes of time in the free room. The free room was a large activity room with a snack shop, pool table, Ping-Pong, air hockey, table games, television, and so on. These different items and activities could be purchased with bonus points or savings. Attitude points were used to purchase extra time in the free room. Only the assignment and bonus points might be saved, with the following qualification: During the time-out phases of the study, children must have reached the 800-point criterion for free room to save their assignment points. To ensure the values of points that fell below the criterion, as a result of fines, in the response-cost conditions any number of assignment points could be saved or used in the class store.

The program of time-outs ran concurrently with the token system. Time-outs were given to students contingent upon any of the behavior described in Table 2. Time-out duration was three minutes, and location was in one of the nonisolated corners of the classroom. A student's failure to take the time-out when instructed resulted in an increase in time-out length to five minutes. Further refusal, or any aggression on the way to time-out, would result in a five-minute time-out in the hall. Students often had to be physically taken to time-outs when they refused to go, resulting in a considerable degree of classroom disruption. Refusals also resulted in the loss of free room privileges for that day.

Another important aspect of the classroom program was "reminder status." Students who had gone for four days without refusals or leaving school were placed on reminder status, which meant that they were entitled to one reminder, or warning, for each category of inappropriate behavior, except aggression. Refusing a time-out while on reminder status would result in the loss of that privilege. Reminder status remained a constant condition throughout the course of the study.

Table 2. Inappropriate Behavior Definitions.

1. Inappropriate language
   a. Talking without permission
   b. Loud talking or noise
   c. Insulting or threatening
2. Inappropriate locale
   a. Out of seat without permission
   b. Leaving class without a pass
   c. Going into cabinets or others' desks without permission
   d. Returning late from the free room or pass
   e. Free room card not signed
3. Aggression
   a. Fighting
   b. Hitting, kicking, biting, shoving, spitting, or throwing objects
   c. Physical threats
4. Distractions
   a. Making sounds or performing actions that disturb others
   b. Eating in the classroom
   c. Running in the halls
5. Noncompliance
   Not following an explicit direction from a teacher or other staff member
6. Damage to property
   Marks, scratches, spitting on, or breaking the property of others
7. Stealing
8. Violation of smoking rules

Fine conditions consisted of fines for all behaviors listed in Table 2, except for aggression, damage to property, and stealing. Those behaviors received time-outs in addition to a fine. Fines were subtracted from the assignment or bonus points if there were no remaining assignment points. There was no limit upon the number of fines a child could receive, but if a child ran out of points, he had to have a conference with the principal to determine whether he should remain in class. Students were warned that fines would continue if disruption did not end after the first fine. Fines could be made up by completing short (five to ten minutes) drill sheets which equaled fifty points.

Teacher Training and Participation. The study was initiated at the request of teachers and administration, following a pilot study in another classroom within the school. The social work consultant took the role of experimenter in the study, actively involving the teaching staff in all phases of the project.

During the baseline period, teachers were requested to gather additional data from the token and time-out system. Furthermore, the experimenter observed the classroom, as specified below, in an effort to develop program recommendations for the teachers.

Following the baseline conditions, a meeting was held to discuss an alternative system of behavior management. Various alternatives were discussed, and a response-cost system was chosen as the most appropriate given the existing token system. It was decided that some of the inappropriate behaviors, such as aggression, continued with time-out and fines because of their seriousness. Time-outs were designed to remove the child from the conflict and seemed to match the level of the child's inappropriate behavior. Teachers also hesitated to discontinue the full time-out system, presumably because of their prediction of lessened control over the class. The decision was made at this meeting to set the amount of a fine at fifty points, allowing two fines, assuming maximum earnings, before free room privileges could be lost. Overall, the worker actively involved the teachers in all phases of the research by using a consulting and problem-solving approach. The various types of data were recorded to control for any bias introduced as a result of the teacher's knowledge of goals and procedures.

Behaviors Observed—Dependent Variables. Two types of data were recorded for the evaluation. First, teachers kept records of the number of time-outs or fines they had given the students. Second, the worker directly observed the students and teachers. The direct observation measures were undertaken to supplement the teacher-recorded data because the rates of time-outs versus fines conceivably could be a function of the relative ease with which fines might be administered as compared to the time-out procedure.

Teacher-recorded data included the number of time-outs or fines given to the students as well as refusals and isolation for each student. Teacher recording took place from 9:00 until 12:00 each day. The afternoons were excluded because there was often only one teacher in the room, while the other was administering a refusal in the hall, making recording difficult. On day 18, halfway through the second phase, the teachers agreed to record the number of confrontations between the students and the staff. A confrontation was defined as the use of physical force on the part of a staff member to restrain a student, who was usually refusing a time-out. The addition of this measure at this point in the study, resulting in a BAB withdrawal design, helped assess the two procedures based on ethical and staff time considerations.

Worker observation took place every school day at 1:15, after the students had eaten lunch and gone to the free room, if they had earned it. During this time, the students worked on math or reading assignments, for which they earned bonus rather than assignment points because the students had already gone to the free room. This was also one of the most disruptive times of the day because the point system did not seem to have very great control then. Observation began when a no-talking direction was given by the teachers and students were to begin working on their assignments. Students were instructed that they were not to interact with the observer during this time. The observer sat at the back of the class, at one of the activity tables, in a position in which all the students could be seen.

Data for both students and teachers were recorded in ten-second intervals. One-minute sampling procedures were used, in which the students were observed during the first minute followed by observation of the teachers. During the baseline conditions, the teachers did not know that their behavior was being recorded. The measures obtained through this observation were group measures; for example, disruption was coded in an interval if any student engaged in this behavior. Teacher behaviors were recorded to measure the stability across conditions of possible competing variables that might influence the children's behaviors. The occurrence/nonoccurrence was noted in each interval, and each interval could contain two or more types of behavior for teachers. During this time, the observer also recorded the frequency of time-outs and fines and refusals. These were simple frequency counts, computed on a group basis. Behavioral definitions are indicated in Table 3.

Table 3. Behavioral Definitions.

Student Behaviors

Disruption (D): Disruption is to be coded in an interval in which any of the students are observed to be:
    Talking without permission
    Engaging in excessively loud talking or noise that disturbs others
    Using threatening or insulting language
    Being out of seat without permission
    Performing other actions, such as physical teasing, which disturbs others

Aggression (A): Aggression is to be coded in any interval in which fighting, or any physical contact of an angry manner is observed. Aggression is characterized by physical abuse toward another student, a student's belongings, or school property. Thus damage or abuse of property, throwing of any objects, slamming or kicking desks, and so on, are included in this category.

Teacher Behaviors

Praise (P): This category includes intervals that contain positive value statements regarding a student, his behavior, or his possessions. These statements are to be coded only when spoken in a normal conversational voice. Praise is to be coded when it involves assignment work or the students' behavior. If points are being awarded, praise is to be scored only if the teacher verbally indicates the students who are receiving the points.

Negative Attention (NA): Intervals containing any negative value statements from the teacher regarding the behavior of a student or the class is to be coded in this category. This is to include statements or commands for a student to stop behaving in a certain fashion and requests for a student to behave or act differently, if this follows some sort of off-task or disruptive behavior. This category excludes all interaction that occurs during time-outs.

Reliability. The worker assessed the reliability of a teacher's observation by intermittent spot checks at least once during each phase. The worker both observed and recorded instances concurrently with the teachers and checked records after time-outs or fines were observed at other times. Agreement was defined as concurrence between teacher and worker as to whether a time-out occurred, for which student, and for which rule violation. (See Chapter Five for occurrence reliability formula.) Reliability figures for these checks ranged from 75 to 100 percent across conditions, with an average of 95 percent.

Reliability measures of worker observations were recorded

at least twice during each phase of the study. The reliability observer was a substitute teacher in the school, familiar with the rules and the children.

Training consisted of memorizing the definitions and practicing for several days until 80 percent criterion was met. Both observers sat at the rear of the room, one slightly in front of the other to obscure their recording. An agreement was scored if both coders had marked the same behavior in the same or immediately adjacent interval. Occurrence reliability for disruption was 83 percent; aggression was 60 percent, with a small number of intervals; praise, 78 percent; and negative attention was 65 percent. These figures are for occurrence; figures would increase substantially if nonoccurrence was included. Reliability for observed time-outs was 91 percent; for fines, 86 percent; and for refusals, 67 percent. These low reliabilities for refusals may have resulted from insufficient training in observation techniques for the reliability coder and difficulties in accurately observing the group as a whole.

Design. The design utilized in this study is a modified form of the single-subject reversal ABAB design (Baer, Wolf, and Risley, 1968). The baseline conditions (A) were the ongoing time-out conditions described above, paired with the token program. The specific variable to be manipulated was the time-out system, while the token program remained constant, except for the changes noted above. The B (experimental) conditions were the response-cost, or fine, procedures, as outlined above.

Lengths of the different phases were intended to be two weeks for each phase, to allow a long enough interval for stabilization. Decisions to change conditions were made, however, when trends in the data seemed consistent and stable and when changes seemed clinically advisable. The baseline phase lasted approximately three weeks, although data are excluded for several days because of teacher absences and special activities. Data are reported for eleven days in phase 1, twelve days in phase 2, ten days in phase 3, and eleven days in the final phase. Graphs are presented for standard lengths, with points excluded for those days in which a special activity or early dismissal precluded data gathering.

Results

The data recorded by teachers each morning are shown in Figure 1. Of the thirteen students in the classroom at the start of the study, three were excluded from the data, where possible, because of sustained absences due to suspension for two students during the reversal condition and because one student was placed in residential care. Note that it was not possible to exclude these students from the direct observation data because of the group nature of these data. The reduction in the number of time-outs per student achieved with the new system is illustrated. The average number of time-outs decreased from 1.8 during baseline observations to .25 in the first implementation or time-out. When fines were reviewed, during the return to baseline, the average number of time-outs increased to 1.5, within the initial baseline range. When the response-cost condition was reinstated, time-outs again decreased to an average of 13 per session and remained at a stable low level. In both response-cost treatment conditions, time-outs occurred at levels about 80 percent less than in baseline conditions.

It appears that when using response-cost procedures, day-to-day variability in frequency was greater than when using time-out procedures, which suggests that during response-cost conditions there were days when a smaller number of overall control procedures were needed. There were also two periods of extremely high numbers of fines. The average number of time-outs in the four phases was 1.8, .25, 1.5, and 13. The number of fines, although slightly higher for average number, showed both a higher and lower range than time-outs. Days 21, 22, 41, and 42 had extremely high numbers of fines. Days 21 and 22 were the second and third days that a new student teacher was in the classroom. Days 41 and 42 were immediately following the return of one of the more disruptive students; on these days, many of the fines seemed to occur in bursts or strings of fines as compared to time-outs.

One of the more interesting findings related to the point accumulation across the different phases: 77 percent of the students, on the average, reached the 800-point criterion during

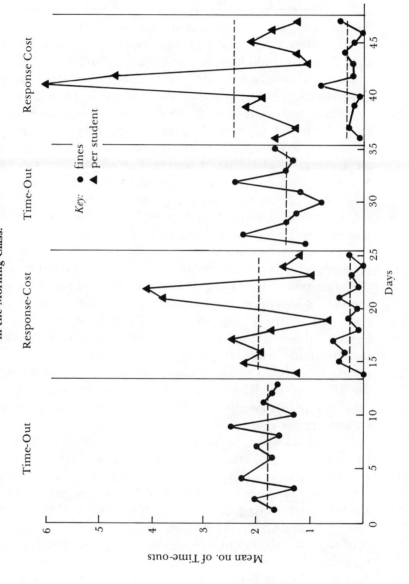

Figure 1. Mean Number of Time-Outs and Fines per Student as Recorded by the Teacher in the Morning Class.

the first phase, 78 percent made it during the fine conditions, a surprising 92 percent made it during the reversal phase, and 69 percent reached criterion in the final fine condition. It is unclear why the earnings increased so markedly during the reversal, unless there was a possible teacher bias as a result of their desire to continue with the fine procedures.

Data from direct observation of the students are presented in Figures 2 and 3; they show a slight suppression of both disruptive and aggressive behavior in response-cost conditions that correspond to the slightly higher frequency of control procedures. This suggests that the afternoon may have come under greater control of the point system. This assumption is substantiated by the decreases in observed time-outs and fines in phases 2 and 4 as compared to phases 1 and 3 (see Figure 3a). The reduction in the number of refusals during the afternoon period is also substantial for the fine condition (Figure 3b).

Figure 4 presents rates of teacher praise and negative attention across the conditions. There is a general stability across the conditions, with a slight depression during several days of the second baselines. The rates of negative attention seem more stable across the phases of the study. The depression in the levels of praise during withdrawal condition with a rise in the point earnings lends support to the possibility of teacher bias during withdrawal. Teachers reported anxiety in returning to the time-out conditions. Possibly reduction of praise and increases in points awarded resulted from overcorrection and evaluation apprehension.

The rates for the number of refusals and the number of confrontations in Figure 5 are some of the most relevant data to an understanding of the ethical issues associated with the two conditions. These are teacher-recorded rates, refusals being recorded solely during the morning hours, with confrontations being recorded all day. These rates excluded absent or suspended students. The number of refusals decreased markedly during the fine conditions but did not return to baseline levels in the withdrawal. Referring back to Figure 2 (which represents afternoon observations on refusals), note that from day 26 to 31, most refusals occurred during the afternoon. The rate of confrontations

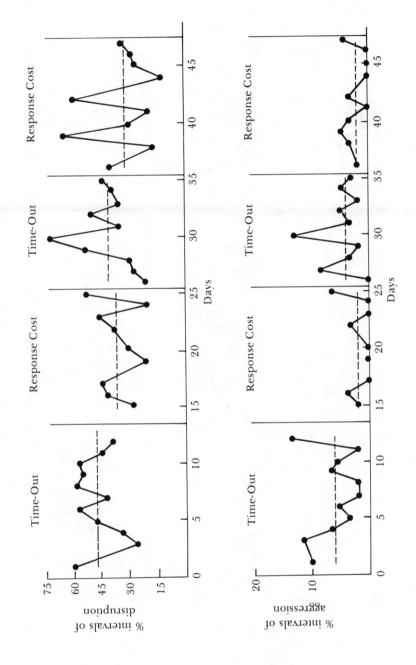

Figure 2. Aggressive and Disruptive Behavior in Afternoon Class.

Figure 3. (a) Number of Time-Outs and (b) Refusals per Minute.

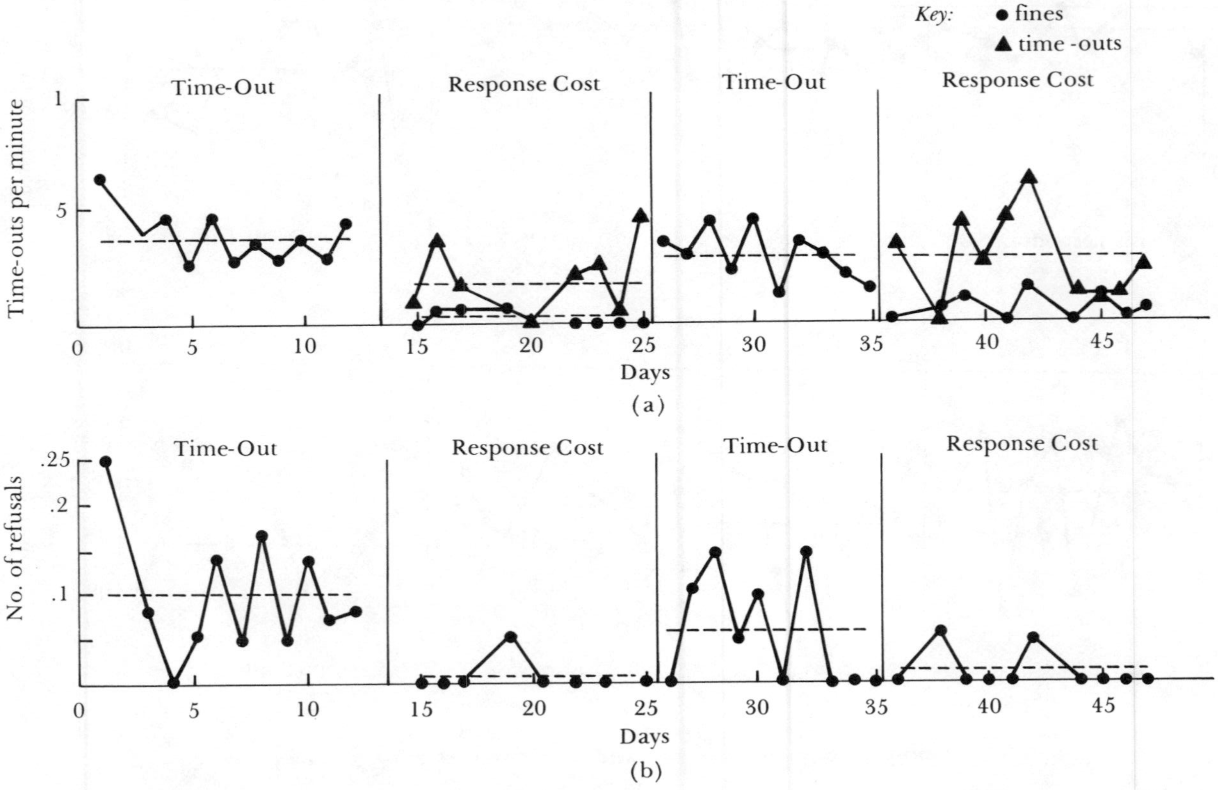

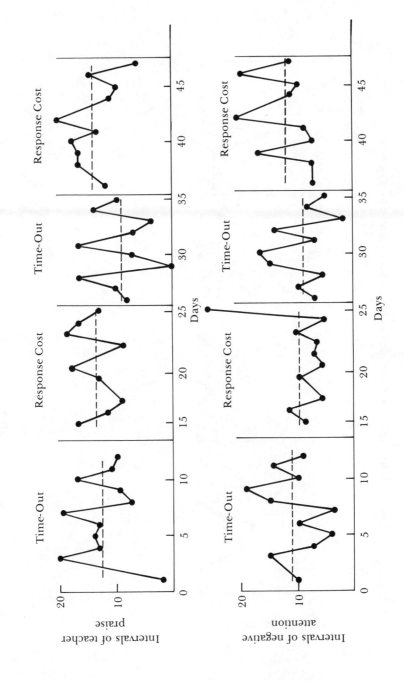

Figure 4. Intervals of Teacher Praise and Negative Attention.

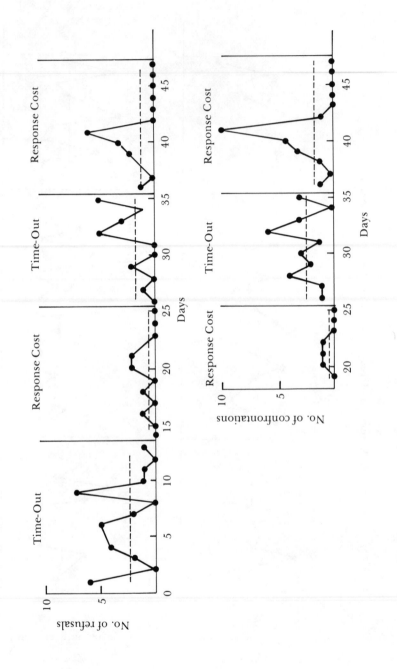

Figure 5. Intervals of Refusal and Confrontation Recorded by Teachers.

shows an increase during the withdrawal period, with a decrease in phase 4. Note that day 41, return of one of the more disruptive students and a trip to camp (as below), had ten confrontations, the highest point in the study. However, the percentage of total observed days in the last three conditions, with no confrontations, was 57 percent, 10 percent, and 50 percent, respectively. During baseline, there were five isolations: one during the response-cost condition, four in reversal, and eight in the final phase. During days 41 and 42, six isolations occurred. As mentioned, it was felt that the return of one of the students who had been excluded from the data had a contagion effect on the other students. The data seem to suggest that there is less aggression between students and students and students and staff in the fine conditions, despite increases on individual days.

One further result relates to the change in the consequence for leaving the classroom without permission. During the baseline phase, none of the students left the class. However, when the consequences were changed, two of these students, who were excluded from the analysis because of extensive absences, left on three different occasions. Two other students left once and twice, respectively. The former two students, who left so many times, finally ran out of points and were suspended. It was difficult to get them back to school because of family problems. During phase 3, there were no instances of this kind; after returning to the fine condition on day 40, three of the students left again. Generally, the same children left without problems for the others in the class.

Discussion

Generally, the response-cost program functioned equivalently to time-outs. Fines occurred at a slightly higher rate than time-outs, yet disruption during the observation session decreased slightly. The fine condition was associated with less aggression regarding the number of isolations and confrontations between staff and students. Conclusions with regard to the rates of aggression during the observation period must take into account the *addition* of the fine to the time-outs. The teacher-recorded data on the types of rule violations did not yield any differences across the phases.

Teacher-recorded data on the number of time-outs versus fines showed a slight increase of the incidence of punishment. There are at least two alternate explanations for these differences. First, the fines may be less effective in response suppression because of the low value of the fines. Differences in aversiveness would seem to be supported by the increase in the number of students who left the class during the fine conditions. A second reason for the increases might be that the teachers responded to the changes in administration of punishment and they may have punished more inappropriate responses. Buchard and Barrera (1972) controlled for this type of teacher expectancy; their results indicated that there were a slightly greater number of fines at the low value than time-outs.

A possible reason for the decrease in disruption observed in the data was that the point system was restructured to allow assignment points to be saved. Those students who had not gone to the free room or who did not have enough points to go still had an incentive to continue working during the fine conditions. An alternate possibility relates to the addition of makeup assignments. During the observation time, many of the students were completing makeup assignments during the fine conditions. During time-out phases they were given work to do, yet it seemed that they did not want to do this work as much. One final comment about the quality of the data: The type of measure that was used did not seem sensitive to many of the changes in the room. Both the teachers and the observers subjectively felt that the students' behavior during fine conditions was much better than the data indicated. For example, disruption would be coded in an interval whether one student or four had been disruptive. The inclusion of some form of measure of appropriate behavior, such as on-task behavior or individual data, would have helped to answer some of these questions.

One major source of the high rates of fines recorded by the teachers was a high number of response bursts, in which the student continued to receive one fine after another. Unfortunately, it was not possible to isolate these bursts from the data.

Buchard and Barrera (1972), however, demonstrated that response bursts were particularly associated with the low value of fines. During the high fine-value conditions and during time-outs, bursts were considerably lower. Fines in the present study were worth approximately one and a half cents for backup reinforcers in the classroom and free room. At this low rate, bursts were not particularly aversive. As Buchard and Barrera (1972, p. 280) stated that the control conditions in fine situations are more realistic because the student is allowed to control himself, rather than be controlled, as in time-out conditions. In the present study, in these instances the subject was often asked to talk to one of the teachers or leave the room with one of them. Additional evaluation is necessary to determine the most effective means of controlling the frequency of these bursts. One effective way to decrease these bursts may be to increase the value of the fines, with an equivalent increase in the value of the makeup assignments. This would probably affect those students with large numbers of fines, without excessively increasing the aversive qualities for the students who are doing well.

An attempt was made to examine the relationship between the reinforcement rate (token earnings) and the frequency of punishment (time-out and fine conditions). The importance of this relationship was discussed by Buchard and Barrera (1972) and functionally demonstrated by Tallon (1976). Unfortunately, records of points earned were recorded after fines had been subtracted, reducing the comparability of earnings figures between phases. Furthermore, the aversiveness of the time-out conditions must also be understood regarding the location of the time-outs, within the room and often with social reinforcement from peers, and the possible reinforcing efforts of time-out under certain conditions (Steeves, Martin, and Pear, 1970). Solnick, Rincover, and Peterson (1977) demonstrated the importance of the background conditions on the effectiveness of time-out. That time-outs may have functioned as reinforcement for several students seems possible, given the extinction type of behavior demonstrated during the fine conditions. Suspension did result for several students during the fine conditions, and yet teachers reported progress for these students upon return. "Testing" limits is a frequent occurrence following changes in the reinforcement contingencies.

Changes in the token program may have been responsible for some of the changes in student behavior during the observation period. The extent of these changes, however, remains an empirical question. Analysis of the data with regard to the relative effectiveness of the two programs suggests equivalence. The ethical implications associated with time-out and response cost, however, favor the use of response cost based upon the lower rates of physical confrontations that occurred between students and staff, the relative ease with which response-cost procedures can be implemented, and the equivalence between the two procedures for response suppression. The fine program also encouraged students to do extra work to make up for any lost points. A source of weakness in the present study was the lack of control over variables, such as vacations, camping trips, and warmer weather. The experimenter sought, however, to emphasize the practical value of research in an applied setting.

Further investigation seems necessary to determine the most effective value of response cost. Buchard and Barrera (1972) demonstrated the relative degrees of response suppression associated with different values of response cost. The decrease in the number of bursts at the higher value of fine is particularly significant for future modifications in the present setting. An economic analysis seems particularly relevant here. Although longer time-outs have also been shown to increase response reduction (Buchard and Barrera, 1972; White, Nielson, and Johnson, 1972), the ethical issues become even more important with the longer time-outs. Another area of inquiry into the present system might be an investigation of the effects of a weighted fine system, in which differing values of fines are given for various degrees of disruptive or aggressive behavior. The relationship between the token system and the function of fines needs to be specified and measured more closely. Individual data are essential in this analysis to determine the relationship, if any, between earnings, appropriate and inappropriate behavior, and spending patterns, as in an economic analysis.

A particularly noteworthy aspect of the present study

was the use of a single-case withdrawal design for program evaluation. The design permitted the comparative analysis of two treatment "packages" to demonstrate their relative effectiveness. The school subsequently adopted the fine system in lieu of the overly restrictive time-out program. Traditional evaluation research approaches do not consider this design (Weiss, 1972; Cook and Campbell, 1979), and yet the benefits are clear. Withdrawing interventions involves some ethical issues, but in this case it provided important findings that helped programmatic decision making.

The use of research methods as an integral element of social work consultation proved valuable in the present study. Although research controls and designs must often be compromised in an applied setting, the use of research data for decision making can be invaluable. It is the authors' contention that social work practice, whether consultation, direct services, or administration, must increasingly utilize research data to support policy decisions. In this instance, the use of research techniques resulted in changes in the school program and assisted in the implementation of the program changes. The use of a withdrawal design permitted both a quantitative and a qualitative analysis of the two programs by both teachers and the school administration. Recommendations from the social work consultants were empirically grounded, which added to their impact and utilization. Program consultants should increasingly utilize research methods and evaluate program modifications to help with program-change techniques.

Applying Behavior Analysis to Social Group Work with the Elderly

Nick L. Linsk, Elsie M. Pinkston

Social work in long-term care facilities is frequently concerned with developing or improving group programs. Often the goal of these programs is to increase resident participation and interaction within the facility. Behavior analysis methods have been used to refine and evaluate interventions designed to enhance residential behaviors (Berger and Rose, 1977; Frankel and Glasser, 1974; Lawrence and Sundel, 1972; Rose, 1977). Studies of methods designed to increase interactions have used verbal behavior as the primary dependent measure (Hoyer and others, 1974; Mueller and Altas, 1972).

Group programs may be useful methods of intervention with behaviors of multiple individuals with communication deficits. Lindsley (1964) suggested that aged individuals, having experienced possible sensory or cognitive losses, may require more highly specified or intensified cues for behavior. Such cues as speech, announcements, or television may need amplification or expansion to enable reception and response. In addition, reinforcement systems for elderly should be individualized. The alternative to predictable engagement with the environment includes a slowdown of body processes, muscle atrophy, and loss of social relationships (McClannahan and Risley, 1974). The environment of the older person may require specific modification to create opportunities for socialization.

This practice illustration evaluates the application of behavior analysis to social group work; it examines the effect of direct task-related questions on individual members of a group of highly impaired elderly women. The procedures were developed from a behavioral functional analysis of group meetings the women participated in.

342

Intervention and Evaluation Methods

Agency and Staff. The study was conducted in a thirty-three bed unit of a large urban home for the aged. A variety of staff were assigned to the unit, including a full-time social worker with a medical social work background who served as the group leader. The social work consultant was a graduate student with knowledge of both social group work and behavior analysis.

Clients. There were thirty-one female residents in the unit. Their mean age was eighty-five, ranging from sixty-eight to ninety-five. The clients had a variety of physical and mental impairments. Nine of the women were able to leave the unit independently for meals; the rest were confined to the unit unless directly supervised because of physical impairments or confusion. Therapeutic activities included occupational therapy, religious services, current-events discussions, cocktail hours, remotivation classes, reality-orientation classes, and sheltered workshop activities.

Social Group Work Activities. Three ongoing weekly group activities—a newspaper activity, a folktale activity, and a residents' meeting—were selected for the study because they were conducted at the same early afternoon time on different days of the week, and observational analysis showed that they had similar format and participation levels. In the newspaper and folktale activities, the worker read short stories to the residents, pausing occasionally for comments or questions. In residents' meetings, the worker read a series of announcements, occasionally pausing for questions and discussion. All residents were invited to participate in these activities, although generally less than half the residents in the unit attended.

Determination of Desirable Outcomes. Consultation with the group leader occurred prior to any formal data-collection activity. She reported her desire to learn behavioral group work methods and improve the group activities. Problems specified were recruiting residents to attend activities, maintaining resident attention, encouraging resident verbal participation, and selecting material to interest the mixture of impaired and more able residents. Desirable outcomes were specified as (1) increasing the number of residents who attended the group, (2) improving resident attention span, and (3) increasing relevant comments by residents regarding subject matter. Less specific goals were to improve the residents' orientation, provide social stimulation, and involve residents in the day-to-day operations of the home through resident self-government.

Behaviors for intervention were selected based on the leader's requests and the worker's preliminary observations. During preliminary *anecdotal observations,* it was found that the leader spent much time transporting residents to the meeting, attended frequently to residents who were exhibiting behaviors unrelated to the activity, and spent considerable time reading to residents. The leader made few attempts to listen to residents or solicit their opinions. Residents were seldom oriented to the group leader or to other residents, some slept during meetings, and some made requests unrelated to the group activity. A comprehensive code was developed; the code is described fully in Linsk, Howe and Pinkston (1975). The behaviors selected for observation and analysis included:

> *Leader behaviors.* Questions, statements, and positive or negative comments directed to group or individual residents; listening behavior; participation in activities; and attending to external events

> *Resident behaviors.* Appropriate and inappropriate verbalizations, verbal behavior related to environment, appropriate attention, appropriate activity, and inappropriate activity

Data Collection. Direct observations of group meetings occurred three times per week. Observers used a five-second sampling procedure to serially record the behaviors of ten residents once each minute and the behavior of the leader twice each minute. In effect then, a one-minute time sample was used for resident group members and a thirty-second time sample for the leader. Observers coded the behavior of each member in sequence. A number of the residents were observed simultaneously by both observers each session. The observations were compared for reliability computations. Reliability for worker behavior was recorded in every session; in sessions in which there were fifteen or fewer residents present, reliability was recorded for five resident behaviors. Occurrence reliability was computed (see Chapter Four for formula).

In addition to behavioral observations, videotapes were recorded at least once per session per condition. The tapes were used as descriptive data, to make more specific measures of behaviors, for analysis with the social group worker, and for training observers.

A reversal design was used, with the following conditions and procedures: baseline, intervention, baseline, intervention, and follow-up.

Baseline. The group leader was asked to conduct the group as she normally did. She was informed that the experimenters were developing and testing some behavioral measures for the group and that the findings would be discussed at a later date.

Intervention. Following baseline observations and prior to the first intervention session, the worker arranged an interview with the group leader. At this time the group's objectives were discussed and a videotape of a recent session was viewed. The leader and worker agreed that residents' participation should be increased. The worker showed the leader current data on both her activities and residents' behaviors. After discussing alternatives for increasing the residents' participation, the worker and leader decided that frequent questions related to material being discussed would be used as the intervention procedure. The leader directed these questions to individual group members, and as many members as possible were asked each session.

After this meeting, the intervention was implemented. A written contract between the group leader and the worker was developed that specifically detailed their individual activities. Throughout this condition they met prior to each session to review the directions for the condition and the data from previous sessions.

Baseline. After twelve sessions, a reversal procedure was

implemented. The worker and group leader met and reviewed data which indicated that participation had increased. To ensure that this increase was a result of the leader's questions, the leader agreed to ask fewer questions in the next group session and to conduct the meeting as it had been originally, with a low rate of questions to individual group members. This procedure was written into a contract, and pregroup meetings to review procedures and data continued.

Intervention. After ten sessions, the worker and group leader met and determined that the relationship between questions and increased appropriate verbal participation of residents had been established and that the leader would now return to the question-asking procedure. This was written into the contract, and the leader implemented the intervention in ensuing sessions. Pregroup session meetings were also continued during this condition.

Termination and Follow-Up. Following thirteen treatment sessions, the worker and group leader decided that sufficient data had been collected for purposes of the study. The progress of the group was discussed generally and specifically according to the data. Individualized data were made available to the group leader for her use in the agency, and she was given copies of the group graphs. The leader agreed to continue conducting the group for several weeks until follow-up data were collected. No intervention contract was in effect in these meetings.

After five weeks, or fifteen additional group sessions, observers returned to record follow-up data. No pregroup interview was held with the leader before this group meeting, and the worker agreed to conduct the meeting the way she had in previous weeks following the termination of the contract.

Results

Interobserver reliability measures were computed for social group worker behavior, group member behavior, and behavior categories of interest. Mean percentage of interobserver agreement for the group worker's total behavior was 88 percent. Mean scores on specific categories of behavior for the group leader ranged from 69 to 90 percent. Mean percentage of inter-observer agreement for all resident behaviors was 85 percent, ranging from 60 to 83 percent.

Figure 1 illustrates the measurement of the group leader's behaviors. The data represent percentages of the total group

Figure 1. Questions, Statements, and Listening by Group Leader as a Percentage of Total Intervals in the Session.

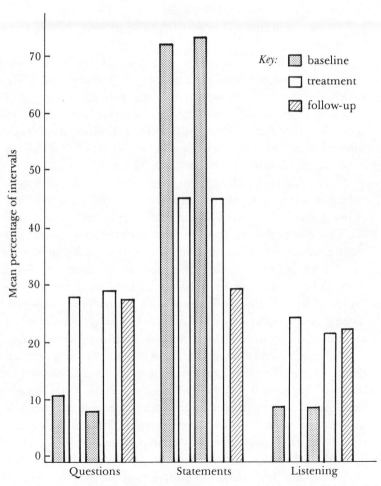

Source: An earlier version of this figure appeared in Linsk, Howe, and Pinkston, 1975.

leader's behaviors for specific behavioral categories. The first set of bar graphs shows the percentage of questions to individual residents for each session. This was the independent variable for the study. The percentage of questions to individual residents was substantially higher during treatment conditions than during baseline and reversal conditions. The mean percentage of questions to individuals for treatment conditions was 16.1 percent of total leader behavior, compared to a mean percentage of 3.8 during baseline conditions. Follow-up measurement indicated that the leader asked questions as 20 percent of her behaviors, which was slightly higher than the mean of treatment conditions. Similar patterns of behavior were found for total questions.

Other leader behaviors, not part of the treatment contract, also changed similarly to changes in questions. Listening, which increased in a positive relationship to questions, indicated that increasing questions decreased statements and increased listening on the part of the group worker. Follow-up observations showed that the treatment levels of the leader's behavior had been maintained on these three behaviors.

In Figure 2, changes in two measures of resident verbal behavior show the rate of appropriate verbal behavior for the entire group per minute. Mean rate of appropriate verbalization for the group during the baseline and reversal conditions was .19 behaviors per minute. The mean rate of appropriate verbalizations per minute during treatment conditions was .44, more than double the rate of behavior during nontreatment conditions. Means during follow-up were considerably higher than means of any previous condition (.57), suggesting that rate of verbalization continued to increase following treatment. Further analysis demonstrated an increase in the number of residents who verbalized appropriately per session. Results during baseline indicate that the percentage of the total number of residents who verbalized appropriately ranged between 8 and 36 percent, with a mean of 21 percent. With implementation of treatment, the range of verbal participation increased to between 27 and 64 percent of the residents present, with a mean of 46 percent. This shows that the proportion of the group participat-

Figure 2. Resident Rate of Appropriate Verbalization.

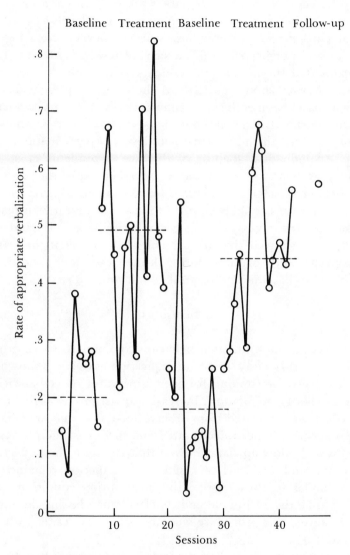

Source: An earlier version of this figure appeared in Linsk, Howe, and Pinkston. 1975.

ing verbally during the treatment condition was twice that of baseline. During the second baseline condition, the range was 7 to 40 percent of the group members present, with a mean of 13 percent. Reinstatement of treatment returned levels of resident verbal participation to previous treatment levels, averaging 44 percent and ranging 26 to 67 percent of residents present. This indicates that the number of residents participating in meetings increased from about one-fifth of the residents present during average baseline meetings to almost one-half of the residents present during treatment conditions. Follow-up data showed maintenance of the higher treatment levels of participation.

An individual analysis of the twelve residents most frequently present was completed as a further test of the relationship between leader and member behaviors and to determine if these procedures could be applied to individual treatment plans. These reflected day-to-day changes in participation. The individual analysis showed that 67 percent of the residents increased appropriate verbalization during leader question conditions, compared to baseline and reversal conditions.

Conclusions

Asking questions is a behavior common to social group workers. In this study, *systematic* question-asking was shown to be an effective technique for increasing rates of verbalization with an elderly population. Increasing questions as a treatment procedure was indicated from observational data and knowledge that older people need decelerated and specific stimuli to make responses. Follow-up data showed that the individual question technique and the level of resident participation remained at levels similar to those during the intervention condition, suggesting that the technique and its effects had lasting duration. Significantly, this procedure was simple for the leader to learn and control.

Although this study did not directly assess the benefits of such increased participation, these benefits may include a more active group experience for residents, more opportunities for residents to become socially engaged with other residents, meetings as an improved source of information about both upcoming events and other residents' reactions to previous events, and meetings as a setting that provides opportunities for expressing opinions and getting recognition for participation. Elderly people often become isolated and noncommunicative in institutions; techniques for increased participation provide opportunities for communication and general engagement with the environment. The increased time the leader spent listening during treatment conditions indicated that residents had more opportunities to contribute in these sessions.

Further analysis of data showed that, as the study continued, attendance at meetings increased and that the length of meetings was considerably longer during treatment conditions than in nontreatment conditions. During later treatment conditions, meetings were attended by residents who previously had never participated in a group activity, residents who previously had never participated in a group activity spoke appropriately, and residents who previously had remained silent spoke appropriately. Although these aspects of the group meetings were not directly manipulated in the experimental design, the absence of other changes in procedures for notifying residents of meetings or changes in the format of the activity shows that the increased length and size of group activities may have been caused by increased participation levels.

The social group leader was able to use behavioral data for formulating and implementing treatment intervention. The leader regulated her behavior by using daily data examinations as feedback. She received considerable assistance in data analysis from the worker, a system that may be useful in social group work evaluation, supervision, and training. A social worker with specific training in behavioral approaches to social group work and direct observational research may be able to record and analyze data independently. This approach works toward a data-based practice of social group work, but additional research is necessary to further develop techniques of intervention analysis.

Future interventions could include worker verbalizations and tangible reinforcement for specified behavior, either individually or by group; individualized intervention based on data recorded for individual residents; varying the amount of leader listening and repetition; using amplification equipment for leader or residents; or systematically varying the seating arrangement of residents.

The present study is a base for establishing and validating both an observational technology and a treatment procedure that may prove useful to social group workers. Applications to other settings with other client groups would necessitate different defined and observed behaviors and different treatment interventions. The use of empirical data as a tool for intervention planning and evaluation has several advantages for social group work: increasing accountability, measuring behavior changes of group members, comparing individual behavior at different stages of treatment, and analyzing social work training and supervision. Each advantage is evident in this study.

Differential Reinforcement of a Low Rate of Behavior in an Applied Setting

Lorelle K. Banzett

High rates of inappropriate behavior lead to three kinds of consequences for institutionalized clients: (1) They are ignored because interacting with them is so unpleasant; (2) they receive concerned attention as members of the staff try to discuss their problems with them, often following the inappropriate behavior; or (3) they are punished intermittently for their behavior. Predictably, none of these procedures effectively decreases the client's inappropriate behavior, so the clients, if they leave the institution, leave with the behaviors intact. This study is an application of a reinforcement principle to decrease the rate of inappropriate questioning of an institutionalized child. Differential reinforcement of a low rate of responding (DRL) has been investigated extensively in the animal laboratory but rarely as a procedure applicable to human problems in applied settings.

Ferster and Skinner defined differential rate reinforcement as "reinforcement (continuous or intermittent) which depends upon the immediately preceding rate of response. This may be the reciprocal either of the time elapsing between the reinforced response and the immediately preceding response or of the time required to execute three or more responses" (1957, p. 725). In a DRL specifically, "reinforcements occur only when the rate is below some specific value" (Ferster and Skinner, 1957, p. 726). Most of the existing research specified an interresponse time after which the first response is reinforced (Kramer and Rilling, 1970). According to Ferster and Skinner's terminology, this is a "CRF DRL" schedule, but through common usage in the literature it is termed simply a DRL.

Deitz and Repp (1973) used differential reinforcement to decrease mental retarded students' rate of talking-out behavior

353

and off-task talking. The students were reinforced with free time or candy at the end of a fifty-minute class period if the rate of the target behavior was equal to or less than a specified number of responses during that period. In one experiment, the specified limit was gradually reduced to zero responses. Both individual and group contingencies were used, and in all cases the students were informed of the contingencies of reinforcement. Results show a systematic decrease in rates of responding corresponding to the upper limits set by the DRL procedures.

Deitz and Repp scheduled differential reinforcement based on a specified number of responses over an elapsed time period because they predicted this would be more feasible in a classroom situation. As noted, however, most of the literature pertaining to differential reinforcement of low rates has scheduled reinforcement contingent upon a specified interresponse time. This study was an effort to test the generality of this form of DRL to human problems and its feasibility in a applied setting. The DRL schedule, if shown to be effective, would seem to be a particularly appropriate intervention for cases in which an otherwise desirable behavior is defined as maladaptive or inappropriate due to frequency of occurrence rather than topography or function. In these cases, the DRL may be a needed alternative to extinction or punishment.

Method

Child. A ten-year-old boy diagnosed as a borderline childhood schizophrenic was the focus of this study. He had been referred to the center for differential diagnosis by a local community service bureau and was submitted ten days prior to the beginning of the study. His dosage of medication (Dexedrine) was changed several times during the weeks over which these data were collected: no medication (sessions 1-4); fifteen milligrams per day (sessions 5-8); no medication (sessions 9-12); twenty milligrams per day (sessions 13-17); twenty-five milligrams per day (sessions 18-25); and ten milligrams per day (follow-up). None of these modifications, however, coincided with a change in experimental condition.

The boy asked an unusually high rate of questions, and it was the impression of the worker and childcare staff that this was his primary mode of initiating interaction with adults. Although his questions were, for the most part, relevant to the situation or valid requests for information, the high frequency with which they occurred was aversive to the adults in his environment. In addition, the child would often repeat questions that had already been answered and engage in episodes of questions emitted in rapid-fire succession. As a result, anecdotal observation and comments made by staff indicated that counselors tended to ignore the child, express displeasure with his behavior, or answer tersely in the hope of avoiding further interrogation. Counselors requested that the social worker suggest an intervention when these methods failed to decrease the boy's questioning to a socially acceptable level. The worker was a graduate student in social work assigned to this institution as a second-year field placement.

Setting. This study was conducted in a short-term, residential, diagnostic and treatment center for children. The child attended school at the center and lived in a dormitory with four to six other boys, ranging in age from four to eleven years. All observations were recorded in the dormitory. Each boy had his own area containing bed, dresser, and shelves on which his personal belongings were kept. The childcare staff consisted of six counselors and one coordinator who occasionally worked in the dormitory. Staff members were between twenty and thirty years of age, and each had at least two years of college. Counselors had some prior exposure to the principles and application of behavior analysis because the worker had served as consultant to the dorm five months previous to this study. Normally, there were two counselors on duty closely supervising the children during their nonschool hours. There was one change in counseling personnel during the study, and for seven of the observation sessions, one of the two counselors on duty was not a regular member of the dorm staff. All counselors new to this dorm during the intervention conditions were informed of the procedure before data were recorded.

Design. Research was evaluated using a withdrawal design,

involving the following sequence of conditions: Baseline 1 (no intervention), Intervention 1 (differential reinforcement of a low rate of questioning), Baseline 2 (counselors instructed to suspend differential reinforcement), Intervention 2 (reinstitution of the differential reinforcement procedure), generality, and follow-up (intervention condition maintained with no further instruction to staff).

Behaviors. One child behavior and one counselor behavior were recorded according to the following definitions:

> *Question.* Any interrogative sentence or phrase directed by the child to a counselor, including one-word questions but not including incomplete questions

> *Acknowledgment.* Any response to the child's question by the person to whom it was directed; consisted of a direct answer to the question, verbal or nonverbal recognition that a question was asked, or nonverbal compliance to the question

Observation and Recording. All recording was scheduled during free time, reportedly one of the child's worst periods of the day with respect to the target behavior. Children were permitted to choose a toy, game, or whatever at the beginning of this period and then expected to play quietly alone in their areas. After each boy had chosen a toy, counselors typically stayed in a central position to monitor their activities or interact briefly with individual children in their areas. Talking between peers or between child and counselor was usually discouraged, except as initiated by the counselor or necessitated by general dormitory rules (for example, requests for other materials).

Data were recorded by the worker using a stopwatch, clipboard, and recording forms. The worker sat approximately six feet away from the child's area and recorded every occurrence of questions and acknowledgments. Each occurrence was recorded in the corresponding ten-second interval to indicate the timing of the behavior. Each repetition of a question was recorded as a separate question.

Data were recorded twenty-five times over a period of fifty days, plus one day of follow-up a month later. Observation sessions averaged twenty-five minutes in length.

When scoring the data, a series of questions was defined as three or more questions occurring within one ten-second interval or in consecutive intervals. Questions were scored as congruent with the DRL contingency if (1) there were no questions recorded during the preceding minute or (2) two questions were recorded within two consecutive intervals and the first question was preceded by one minute of nonquestioning. An acknowledgment was scored as congruent with the DRL contingency if it occurred in response to a question congruent with the DRL contingency.

Reliability. Reliability was obtained in each condition by comparing observations made by the worker with those recorded by an independent observer. An agreement was scored if both observers recorded a behavior in the same interval. A disagreement was scored if only one observer recorded the behavior. Because more than one occurrence of a behavior could be recorded within one interval, each occurrence was scored separately. Percentage of interobserver agreement was calculated by dividing the number of agreements by the number of agreements plus disagreements times 100 (see Chapter Four for a discussion of reliability).

Procedures

Baseline 1 (Sessions 1-2). The child and counselors were observed under normal conditions. Counselors were aware that the worker was recording data on the child's questioning but were unaware that the counselor's acknowledgments were also being observed.

Intervention 2 (Sessions 3-10). The procedure applied was differential reinforcement of a low rate of behavior. Acknowledgment of the child's question, in the form of a direct answer, was made contingent upon a one-minute minimum interresponse time between questions.

Counselors were given the definition of a question, an oral explanation and clarification of the procedure, and a written description that included the rationale of the procedure and the following instructions:

1. The child's questions are either to be answered or totally ignored. Do not acknowledge questions by any means other than a direct answer.
2. The child's question is to be answered if he has not asked any for approximately one minute. Your answer and attention are contingent upon at least one minute of nonquestioning.
3. The one-minute requirement starts over if the child asks another question before a minute has passed. There must be a full minute of nonquestioning before he is again eligible for reinforcement.
4. Estimate this timing as accurately as possible. Use a clock when one is available.
5. When the child is eligible for reinforcement, answer no more than two questions in a row (that is, no longer than a ten-second pause between questions).
6. Never answer a question that has already been answered once.

The DRL procedure was applied at all times when the child was in the dormitory. He was informed of these contingencies on the first day of treatment. Counselors were instructed to initiate a brief, positive interaction with the child at least once every half-hour. This was intended to supply reinforcement for other interactive behaviors by offering counselor attention unelicited by a question from the child.

Baseline 2 (Sessions 11-14). Counselors were instructed to discontinue the intervention and return to their former pattern of responding to questions. The child was inadvertently informed of this change on the first day of the reversal condition.

Intervention 2 (Sessions 15-19). Counselors were instructed to resume differential reinforcement of a low rate of questioning. The child was also informed.

Generality (Sessions 20-25). Following ten days of observer absence, the child and counselors were observed but no feedback or reminders were given regarding the procedure until session 25.

Follow-Up (Session 26). The child was observed one month after session 25. No instructions or reminders were given to counselors or child, and they were not informed of the purpose of this observation.

Results

Interobserver agreement on the child's questions was 89 percent in each condition. Interobserver agreement on counselor acknowledgments averaged 85 percent, ranging from 75 to 91 percent across conditions.

Only two counselor-subject interactions unsolicited by a question were observed, although this component was presented to the staff as part of the intervention package. Possibly the frequency of interaction initiated by staff increased during periods when the observer was not present, but observations during free time do not support such an assumption.

As shown in Figure 1, the child averaged 1.7 questions

Figure 1. Number of Questions per Minute.

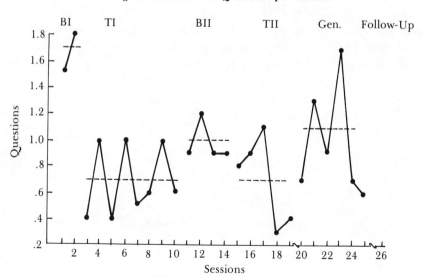

per minute in the first baseline phase (B1). This rate decreased immediately upon institution of the DRL procedure (2) to an average of .7 questions per minute. The second baseline condition (B2) resulted in an increase in rate of questioning to 1.0 questions per minute. Reinstitution of differential reinforcement (3) again reduced the rate of questioning to .7 per minute. Following this phase of the study, no data were recorded for ten days. At the end of this time, recording was reinstituted (session 20). This was not discussed with the counselors until session 25. Thus, although counselors had not been instructed to discontinue the procedure, the data from sessions 20 through 24 represent the last ten days of a twenty-day period during which counselors received no further instructions, feedback, or reminders regarding use of the DRL procedure. Data recorded during this generalization condition show an increase in questioning to a mean of 1.1 question per minute, ranging from .7 to 1.7. Data from session 25, when the procedure had been again discussed with the staff, reveals a rate of .6 questions per minute. At follow-up one month later, this rate was maintained with no further discussion with staff.

The frequency of question series (three or more questions in a row) shows a similar variation across conditions (see Figure 2). Under the first baseline condition, the child emitted an average of .19 series per minute. This decreased immediately under the intervention to a mean of .04 per minute. Similar to rate of questioning, the frequency of series per minute did not regain

Figure 2. Number of Question Series per Minute.

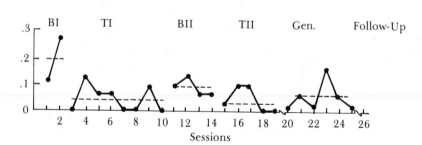

baseline levels under the withdrawal conditions but did increase somewhat to .09 per minute. Under the generality phase, there was an average of .07 question series per minute. At session 25, this decreased to .03 per minute and at follow-up showed a rate of .07.

The mean percentage of questions acknowledged by a counselor during each observation session showed a gradual decrease from 57 to 42 percent over the duration of the study. Changes in the percentages of questions acknowledged were slight and did not correspond systematically with changes in experimental conditions. This supports the assumption that differential reinforcement rather than extinction led to observed changes in the independent variable.

Further analysis of the data shows that there was a change in the temporal spacing of questions, as expected under a procedure which specifies a particular interresponse time. The percentage of questions asked was congruent with the DRL contingency, that is, eligible for reinforcement according to procedure. These data also show a systematic variation according to the experimental conditions in effect. During baseline 1, a mean of 35 percent of the child's questions were timed appropriately with respect to the contingencies later applied, that is, a one-minute interresponse time. This percentage increased to 49 percent under intervention 1, dropped to 38 percent under baseline 2, increased to 54 percent upon reimplementation of the DRL, and decreased to 43 percent during the generalization phase. At session 25, 53 percent of the child's questions were preceded by at least one minute of nonquestioning, and at follow-up, 42 percent were spaced in the same manner.

The percentage of counselor acknowledgment congruent with the DRL contingency was variable across conditions. Variations in the mean percentages for each condition generally corresponded to the variations observed in the child's timing of questions: 26 percent (baseline 1), 52 percent (intervention 1), 29 percent (baseline 2), 42 percent (intervention 2), 36 percent (generalization), 43 percent (session 25), and 25 percent (follow-up).

Discussion

The DRL procedure effectively reduced the child's rate of questioning to a level no longer aversive to the adults in his environment without ever extinguishing appropriate questioning. These results were obtained despite the staff's relatively low rate of proper use of the procedure. Contrary to reports of human performance in highly controlled settings, the child did not approach a high level of efficient responding; thus he did not achieve a high percentage of possible reinforcements. Under the DRL contingencies, he could have been reinforced for two questions per minute (two in a row provided that the first question was preceded by at least one minute of nonquestioning). The disparity between the child's performance and an optimal level of responding under the DRL contingencies may have been a function of (1) relatively low probability that an optimal rate would be reinforced because of his overall tendency to ask isolated questions rather than two or more in a row, and (2) the absence of clear cues caused by the inconsistency of counselor reinforcement.

The partial reversal evidenced under baseline 2 conditions is consistent with the DRL data from the animal laboratory, which show a gradual return to the baseline level under extinction conditions. A longer period of withdrawal in the present study might have shown a more complete recovery of the baseline rate of responding.

Data recorded during the generality phase support the conclusion that response generality was not achieved under the previous intervention phase. Without intermittent prompting and feedback, counselors' use of the DRL contingency decreased to level below that of previous intervention phases. Observation subsequent to another reminder to the staff (session 25) suggested that this had at least a temporary effect on counselor and child behavior. Anecdotal observations indicated that by this time, a few counselors had forgotten about the procedure and others were uncertain as to whether they were expected to continue using it. Additional data, however, would be necessary to substantiate the assumption that simply the worker's prompt was sufficient to effect response generalization. The design of this study does not allow for an analysis of the effect of instructions.

The desired reduction in rate of questioning was achieved without the use of punishment or extinction procedures. In the modification of an appropriate class of behavior, such as question-asking, these procedures could result in the suppression or extinction of an adaptive behavior. The DRL procedure has the advantage of maintaining reinforcement while simultaneously modifying the rate of occurrence. The behavior is thus maintained in the child's repertoire while the frequency is decreased to a level acceptable in his social environment.

The present study demonstrates the feasibility of implementing a DRL schedule in an applied setting. Childcare workers who had limited experience with behavioral intervention programs were able to carry out the requirements of the DRL without disrupting their normal duties and with enough proficiency to effect a change in the target behavior. This was possible despite the relative complexity of a schedule of reinforcement on a specified interresponse time.

For staff who are reinforced by seeing patients emit appropriate behavior, implementing a procedure designed to decrease such behavior may be particularly difficult. The DRL establishes an important distinction between topography and frequency which may enhance the probability that change agents will in fact use the procedure. Inherent in the DRL is a discrimination between the inappropriate element of the subject behavior (frequency) and the appropriate element (topography). As such, it may well offer change agents a palatable method of decreasing inappropriate rates of behavior. For the same reason, future research may indicate that although a DRL schedule can be equally effective in decreasing the rate of inappropriate behaviors, it may not be the method of choice for intervention with maladaptive behavior in applied setting.

Using Behavioral Analysis to Develop Adaptive Social Behavior in a Depressed Adolescent Girl

Ronald Molick, Elsie M. Pinkston

A number of behavior therapists have proposed that depression results when a discriminative stimulus or reinforcer for a behavior is removed; this hypothesis links depression and the amount of social reinforcement available. In one conceptualization of depression, Lazarus (1968) assumed depressed persons to be on a weak schedule of positive reinforcement, and intervention was designed to increase the amount of positive reinforcement received by the depressed person. In another conceptualization (Libet and Lewinsohn, 1973; Lewinsohn, Weinstein, and Alper, 1970), the emphasis was on the absence of demonstrated social skills as an important antecedent condition for the occurrence of depressed behavior. Social skills are the emission of behaviors that elicit positive reactions from other people, for example, social interaction or self-management. A new social environment is provided through intervention with a depressed person whose behavioral difficulties are identified objectively and where new and more efficient patterns of interpersonal behavior can be acquired.

These conceptualizations are complementary, Lazarus's dealing with responding behavior and the others' with initiating behavior; furthermore, they may be used sequentially when working with a depressed person. This study presents a series of systematically applied positive reinforcement programs for developing socially adaptive and culturally important behaviors for a young woman labeled as catatonic schizophrenic; her behaviors were considered depressed by institutional staff. The worker found it helpful to regard the client as a person with low rates of appropriate behaviors and to engage staff as change agents to alter the antecedent and consequent events in the institutional environment.

A series of four reinforcement procedures were designed to improve problem situations with the client during a nine-month school year. A behavioral social work staff consultation approach was employed within a psychodynamically oriented psychiatric hospital. Contingent praise, prompts, contingency exchanges, and client praise were used to modify the social environment as well as the client's behaviors.

Method

Client. Mary, a 15-year-old high school freshman, was referred to a children's residential diagnostic center. She was diagnosed as catatonic schizophrenic with depressive behavior, a diagnosis that was changed to depressed following these interventions. When initially observed by the worker in the center's school, Mary exhibited a number of behavioral deficits that could be associated with depression. She engaged in infrequent speech and deficient and low rates of social interaction. On her first day of class, when asked to choose a place to sit, Mary chose a corner of the room with her back to the class. During preliminary observations and baseline, she moved slowly and sluggishly, a style most readily apparent when complying with teacher requests for behaviors requiring her to leave her seat. The most notably sustained operant behavior she performed in school was tracing her academic work over and over. During code development and baseline conditions, she infrequently responded to teachers' verbal initiations; when she did, she typically refrained from eye contact and her speech was barely audible to the teachers. The only occurrence of sustained physical and/or vocal responding to the teachers during baseline followed the presentation of strong aversive consequences when she was held back from a field trip because of an incomplete assignment. She responded by repeatedly cursing the teachers, stiffly walking back and forth, and saying that no one cared about her.

Settings. The settings for this research were a hospital

school classroom with two teachers and from nine to thirteen students and a hospital dormitory that included six roommates and two counselors. The classroom was programmed for response-reinforced contingencies. In this classroom, the teachers were positive regarding reinforcing a completed task, although their ability to shape higher rates of behavior in Mary was low. Mary easily disappeared in the classroom. The day before baseline data recording began, the position of Mary's desk was changed so that she could more easily see and be seen by the people in the room.

Dormitory counselors were warm and accepting but had little understanding of contingent reinforcement of desirable behavior. Data recorded for another study indicated that the counselors made few positive statements about behavior and usually communicated with the subject using multiple instructions.

Observation and Recording. Mary was observed most school days at 9:30–10:00 and 11:00–11:30 in the morning. The first half-hour of the observation was vocabulary class, and the second half-hour contained both math class and free time. Both Mary's and teachers' behaviors were recorded in the classroom; they are listed in Table 1. Observations were recorded by the worker in 10-second intervals using a stopwatch, clipboard, and data sheets. Occurrence of each behavior was recorded during each interval in which it occurred. Reliability was measured through observation by a second observer, in this case a social work student intern. Reliability estimates were calculated on the agreement of occurrence between the observers using the occurrence formula (see Chapter Four). Reliability was recorded once per time base in each experimental condition.

During intervention 3, the exchange intervention, points were recorded by the teachers and counselors as they were administered. Points, rather than client behaviors, were recorded in this intervention as a way of monitoring Mary's reinforcement and because it was a simple evaluation technique to be used by staff with limited time.

Design. Reversal designs were used in this study in interventions 1, 2, and 4 to both control intervention effects and as

Table 1. Behavior Definitions.

Teacher initiation (TI)	p—teacher moving to and stopping within an arm's length of the subject, with head or body oriented toward subject, for example, standing behind subject and looking over her shoulder.
	v—teacher vocalization directed to subject.
	+—the occurrence of positive or praise words during a teacher vocalization directed to subject.
	0—the absence of positive or praise words during a teacher vocalization directed to subject.
Mary's response (MR)	v—a vocalization, audible to observer, following a TI and directed to the initiating teacher.
	e—eye contact following a TI, directed to the initiating teacher.
Compliance to instructions requesting out-of-seat behaviors by Mary (C)	The subject following a specific instruction requiring out-of-seat performances.
Contingent teacher attention following (C) (x)	Praise or positive words directed to the subject following the subject's compliance and within the same ten-second interval that the compliance behavior is recorded.

a way to demonstrate to the staff the importance of their behavior in relation to Mary's prosocial behavior. Using multiple replications of treatment, the reversal design used in intervention 3 enabled the staff to intervene on specific behaviors first and then determine whether continued exchanges were necessary to continue the same level of performance. It also offered multiple opportunities to observe quick improvement in the client following intervention. It did not provide experimental control, although the repeated replications support worker confidence in the procedure.

Intervention 1—Responses

The intervention was designed to increase Mary's responses to teachers. During baseline conditions, the teachers were asked to behave as they normally did with Mary. They were told that both their behaviors and Mary's were being observed. They were not informed of the specific categories being observed.

During this intervention, the teachers were asked to increase their positive statements when initiating conversation with Mary, make eye contact with her whenever possible, and praise her contingent on her appropriate responses to them. Because the teachers had the necessary skill to do this, no special training was involved. The result of this intervention was an increase in Mary's response rate from an average of 41 percent in baseline condition to an average of 92 percent in the final four days of the intervention. Teacher attention varied systematically across baseline and intervention conditions, maintaining a level of approximately 15 to 20 percent of total intervals during the final intervention. This was not an essentially different rate from baseline levels. Reliability scores averaged above 90 percent on all behavior throughout the study.

Intervention 2—Initiations

Instructions during baseline were the same as in intervention 1. To increase Mary's initiations to teachers, the worker and teachers developed a four-component intervention: (1) praise at the onset of statements from Mary; (2) instructions on when and how to make appropriate initiations; (3) written cues, such as stars; and (4) checking specific points in her work to enable her to initiate to teachers how far she had progressed.

Figure 1 displays the frequency scores of both Mary's initiations and the teachers' application of procedure components. Data from the two thirty-minute recording bases are combined. During baseline, Mary averaged just above two initiations per day. The first data point during intervention is isolated because this day was to have been a baseline day, but following a team discussion and approval of the proposed intervention plan, Mary's teachers immediately used elements of the procedure. The next four days, 23 to 26, are also separate. They represent a procedural development phase in which the teachers used dif-

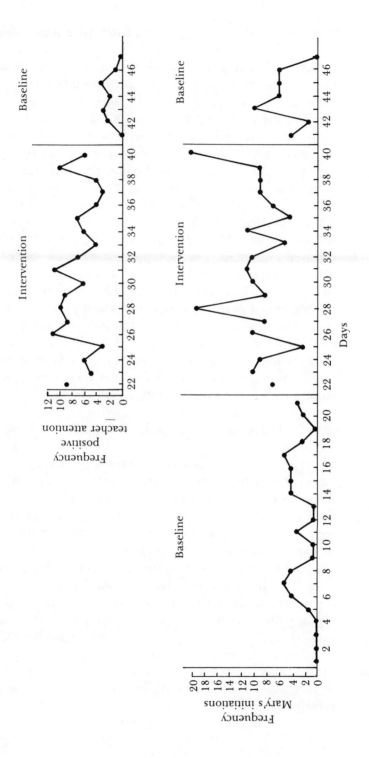

Figure 1. Upper Graph: Total Frequency of Teacher Implementation of Intervention Procedures.
Lower Graph: Total Number of Imitations by Mary.

ferent combinations of operant techniques to empirically determine the intervention package most conducive to Mary's initiations. During this phase, Mary averaged 7.8 initiations per day.
The data indicated that the highest initiation rates resulted from
initial praise at the start of a verbal episode, plus oral instructions on when and how to make initiation, and finally, contingent praise for initiating. This became the intervention package,
with one addition. Mary's initiations became dependency
oriented, centering around requests for help with academic
work. The teachers added the written cues, such as stars and
checks, to give Mary discriminative stimuli for achievement-
oriented initiations. For example, a start at the end of a row of
math problems would cue Mary to raise her hand after she
thought she had correctly completed the problems, giving
the teachers a chance to praise her. During this formal intervention phase, the rate of Mary's initiations rose again to 10.5 per
day; during reversal she averaged 4.5 initiations per day. The
teachers were unable to completely refrain from using the procedure during reversal, explaining that these techniques had become a part of their teaching style with Mary.

Intervention 3—Negotiated Behavior Exchange

A series of contingency exchanges were implemented.
Mary, her teachers, her dorm counselors, and her mother all participated in these exchanges. Except for the verbal initiations of
earlier interventions, all target behaviors exchanged by Mary
were responses that had been extremely resistant to acceleration
or improvement during her previous 6.5 months at the hospital.
The responses can be classified as classmate interactions, test
scores of some academic subjects, grooming behaviors, and laundry duties. In exchange for these behaviors, Mary earned access
to such reinforcers as the phonograph, paid clerical work with
the hospital's nursing and accounting departments, and the
most powerful reinforcer, time away from the hospital—over
the weekend with her favorite relatives or during her mother's
weekly visit. The social work consultant served as monitor for
these exchanges.

Figure 2 displays the results of the first five exchanges. Each column of graphs represents an exchange, and each graph is a behavioral component of that exchange. The broken line above and parallel to each abscissa is the performance criterion. The terms of each exchange grew in detail, but all nine graphs show that (1) Mary performed at or above every criterion and (2) she generally ceased to perform when the exchanges were no longer in effect.

Following these five exchanges, a continued multisetting use of exchanges was negotiated directly between and monitored solely by Mary and her teachers, counselors, and parents. The duration of these exchanges ranged from a week, a day, or a single activity. These exchanges were made by this technique to teach Mary to function reciprocally by learning to offer to engage in specific behavior and to specify what she wanted.

Intervention 4—Positive Staff Feedback

After intervention 3, there was to have been a follow-up on earlier interventions. The combination of surprisingly low rates of teacher praise and total verbalizations to Mary plus the shared team concern that Mary learn to assert herself in a positively reinforcing way prompted intervention 4. In this research, workers examined the extent to which Mary could influence teacher behaviors, specifically praise and total verbalizations toward her. Mary was taught to use the positive feedback of saying "thank you," a social skill elementary but heretofore nonexistent in Mary's repertoire. The worker cued Mary to say "thank you" once during both thirty-minute time bases for all but the final two days of the treatment condition, during which she thanked the teachers without being cued. Worker rewarded this novel behavior by giving her chewing gum. Two "thank yous" a day was only a fraction of the number of times Mary could have thanked the teachers.

The upper graph of Figure 3 shows the percentage of total teacher verbalizations to Mary during one of the time bases. Data for the first three days of procedure application showed increases in both behavior categories. Mary's occasional positive

Figure 2. Points Earned by Mary During Five Consecutive Contingency Exchanges.

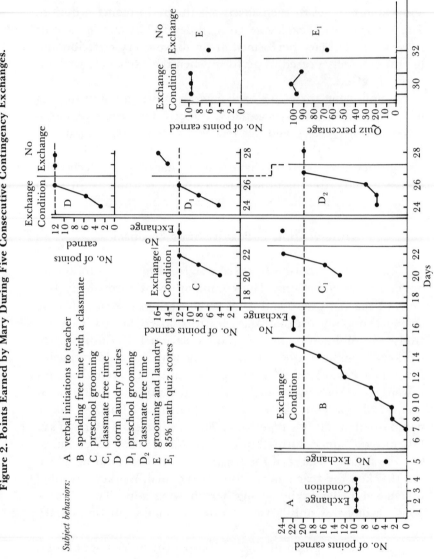

Subject behaviors:

A verbal initiations to teacher
B spending free time with a classmate
C preschool grooming
C_1 classmate free time
D dorm laundry duties
D_1 preschool grooming
D_2 classmate free time
E grooming and laundry
E_1 85% math quiz scores

Figure 3. Percentage of Total Verbalization by Teachers to Mary
as a Function of Total Intervals (Upper Graph) and Percentage
of Positive Verbalizations by Teachers to Mary as a Percentage
of Total Intervals (Lower Graph).

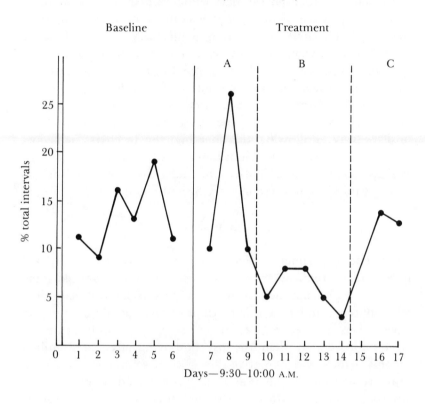

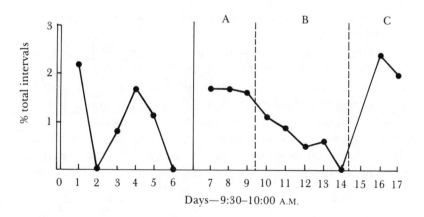

feedback seemed to desirably influence the teachers' behavior. Then something occurred that seemed to have a greater effect on the teachers' behaviors to Mary: a team meeting in which the discussion focused on Mary's aberrant behavior and which took on a negative depressing tone concerning Mary's functioning. Following the team meeting, while Mary continued to say "thank you" twice a day to teachers, both total and positive verbalizations by the teachers dropped to levels below baseline. The worker asked the team consultant, a psychiatrist, to modify the tone of the next team discussion to emphasize Mary's prosocial behaviors and to generally interpret her behavior in a positive way. Following this meeting, the teachers' behaviors abruptly increased to previous baseline levels. The psychiatrist's positive feedback apparently influenced these teachers' behaviors toward Mary more than Mary herself could.

Discussion

The experiments demonstrated that systematically applied positive reinforcement regimens effectively modified some of the identifying behaviors of a person labeled catatonic schizophrenic and that this method of treatment for these behaviors was decidedly more effective in demonstrating behavioral improvement than the psychodynamically based milieu therapy which was operative during all baselines and reversals. Concurrent to the behavioral procedures was a daily chemotherapy treatment of Thorazine. Although this medication undoubtedly established an altered psychological state, the extent to which it affected positive behavior change was not experimentally determined.

These findings suggest that it is most profitable and useful to develop treatment procedures for those labeled severely disturbed on the basis of functional relationships similar to those of people considered relatively normal. The new behaviors in Mary's repertoire, including higher rates of receptive and expressive speech, reciprocal exchanging of reinforcers, improved self-care, and the beginnings of social skills, are all behaviors that will likely avail her to a greater degree of reinforcement from her environment than was the case before operant conditioning.

The final intervention regarding the effect of positive and negative staffings was not adequately measured or experimentally controlled. It should, however, elicit some thoughtful evaluation on the effect of ongoing staff meetings discussing the implementation of planned interventions.

◆▸◆◆▸◆◆▸◆◆▸◆◆▸◆◆▸◆◆▸◆◆▸◆◆▸◆◆▸◆◆▸◆◆▸◆◆▸◆

9

Extending Intervention Effects: Procedures for Maintaining Positive Change

The decrease of problem behavior and the acquisition of new skills are important aspects of the intervention process, but the ultimate test of the success of intervention is the stability and permanence of desirable change once intervention has ended. This issue is considered from the first worker-client contact throughout assessment, intervention, and termination. The maintenance and stability of change after termination is referred to as generality or generalization (Baer, Wolf and Risley, 1968; Stokes and Baer, 1977). Generality is the term preferred to generalization because it is more clearly synonymous with planned extension of intervention effects. There are three types of generality: (1) temporal, which is maintaining change after the termination of the intervention; (2) setting, a transfer of behavior change from the setting in which intervention occurred to a situation or setting in which no intervention occurred; and (3) behavioral, a change in one behavior leading to change in related behaviors. Temporal and setting generality are frequently joint goals to extend change beyond worker-client interviews and maintain change beyond the conclusion of intervention. Behavioral generality is an explicit goal of intervention rather than an unprogrammed by-product to be left to chance. In developing this model, generality is an ongoing concern of the worker. Primary emphasis is on temporal and setting generality, and, to a lesser extent, behavioral generality is considered.

Temporal and setting generality are two of the least studied aspects of change efforts. Research attempts clearly have not kept pace with the necessity for extending intervention effects. Expectations, the ability to learn new concepts, and the acquisition of skills can be conceptualized as key predictors of potential for change and generality. Research evidence regarding these predictors is inconclusive. Clients, staff members, and family members who exhibit these abilities appear most changed during intervention but may quickly revert to their old dysfunctional patterns either outside the clinical interviews or after worker-client termination if their learning has been incomplete or incorrect.

The following discussion is a framework for understanding generality and stimulus discrimination. Strategies are proposed for enhancing the probability that these phenomena will occur during the course of intervention, and the reasons for failure of generality are also discussed. The chapter closes with three research illustrations of generality programming and evaluation.

Learning as a Result of Intervention

Learning occurs according to specific and defined universal laws of behavior that affect the way family members, staff members, or individual clients learn particular behaviors. Practitioners use these laws to program initial change *and* to extend intervention effects. They assume that learning occurs during intervention and that changes apparent during interviews carry over to real life. There have been few investigations of extrainterview carry-over; the topics of maintenances and transfer of intervention effects are not even found in most books devoted to social work theory and practice, reflecting the view that clients change rather than learn.

Theories of learning are relevant to social work practice. When defining personality change, Hollis stated that change has occurred "whenever a new response or behavior has been sufficiently incorporated into the personality to enable the individual to respond consistently in a changed way to repetitions of the same event or its equivalent" (1970, p. 60). The concept of learning is also present in Perlman's view of problem-solving casework. She stated that the objective of problem-solving casework is to help individuals cope or resolve current difficulties in ways that enhance competence. The by-product of this process "is learning a way by which tomorrow's (or next year's) difficulties and decisions may be dealt with" (1970, p. 139).

Workers can not assume that the transfer of change from the interview to the client's natural environment automatically takes place. This transfer of change must be programmed according to the rules that determine which learned behaviors are transferred and maintained. There are several useful conceptualizations regarding the way in which learning takes place. Thorndike and Woodworth (1901) developed a theory of "identical elements." Based on the results of several experiments, Thorndike concluded that when there is a facilitative effect of one behavior on another, the behaviors share elements. For example, the facilitating effect of the skill of walking affects learning to run. An extension of this theory is that transfer takes place as a result of learning a general principle which can be applied in a variety of situations. The theory consequently predicts that transfer of learning from the intervention to the nonintervention situation occurs either as a result of (1) similar events in the nonintervention situations cueing and maintaining a response developed during intervention or (2) applying general principles learned in interviews to nonintervention situations.

Based on these conceptualizations, transfer of learning is a function of three factors (Goldstein, Heller, and Sechrest, 1966). First, similarity of the situation or the stimulus condition from intervention to extraintervention settings is relevant in programming temporal and setting generality. Second, the degree of original learning is also extremely important. To facilitate generality, original learning taking place during intervention interviews should be thorough. Teaching, for example, should continue over more trials and more situations than necessary to merely produce initial changes in behavior. Several stimulus conditions are important; if training continues over only one situation, such as the clinical interview or with one individual like the worker, discrimination (between situations) rather than generality is likely to develop, with minimal carry-over to nonintervention conditions. Third, some general modes of responding may be acquired that make it possible for individuals to improve their capacity to acquire certain kinds of behaviors. Under a particular set of circumstances, individuals may gradually improve their ability to meet a variety of difficulties, developing a set of behaviors that is functional for several situations. Little is known about the conditions that contribute to the development of these behaviors, but practice seems to be sufficient.

These learning theories are a rationale for behavioral programming developed to enhance generality to nonintervention situations. For instance, conducting the intervention in the home environment where the client's problem typically occurs is one method used to program generality. Intervening directly in the environment in which the problem occurs minimizes or eliminates problems of setting generality. Also, similar stimulus conditions are presented to cue and maintain the new and more adaptive behavior, to maximize the probability of transfer of learning from the intervention to nonintervention conditions. Many other programming techniques that enhance generality are available to the social worker; they are described further in this chapter.

Reasons for Generality Failing

The failure to achieve generality of behavior change can be explained as a large discrepancy of events and conditions between the clinical situation and the client's natural environment. The client discriminates distinct contingency settings with different antecedent stimuli and consequences. For instance, the worker may socially reinforce appropriate behavior at each occurrence, whereas the client may be reinforced less frequently for the same behavior in the natural environment. The abrupt shift in the reinforcement schedules between the natural environment and the clinical interview results in a lower rate of the behavior outside the intervention setting. In addition, the worker is quite different from persons the client typically encounters. Even if workers have similar characteristics to these persons, they do not provide the variety of experiences the client encounters in everyday life.

A final reason for failure is that targeted behaviors socially relevant to the client's natural environment are not chosen. Those behaviors selected to be decreased may be reinforced outside the clinical session, and behaviors to be increased may not be supported; instead, they may actually be punished. As an example, the worker helping a student in a classroom for behaviorally disturbed children may identify a child's problem as physical aggression toward other children. The intervention goal is to reduce aggression to zero and to increase the behavior of playing nicely with other children. Most likely this goal will be difficult to achieve unless the inappropriate behavior is not reinforced by the students *and* the appropriate behavior (playing nicely) is. Both these consequences are difficult to program because the appropriate behavior might be reinforced by the teacher, but peers, who are likely to be a more potent force, can easily undo the positive effects.

In sum, lack of response opportunities and competing reinforcers maximize the likelihood that transfer of learning will fail to occur. However, planning generality as part of the intervention program increases the probability that behavior change will extend to the client's natural environment and be maintained after termination with the worker.

Applied Behavior Analysis and Generality

Introduction to Programmed Generality and Research. According to operant behavioral principles, a behavior is maintained as a function of its consequences, if the consequences are withdrawn and the behavior declines. Using this relationship as a basis for planning maintenance and transfer of learning by the client, specific contingencies must remain in effect either outside the clinical session or in the client's natural environment. The contingencies need not be continued indefinitely for maintenance and transfer to take place; however, it has been found that unless programming toward generality is incorporated into intervention, the problem behavior has a higher probability of reverting to preintervention levels.

Investigators are systematically looking at and recommending various techniques to promote generality after termination and transfer of effects to other settings. Studies that include programmed generality procedures focus on observable change in behavior as data indicative of problem change. The generality of intervention effects has been investigated with various client populations, such as autistic and psychotic children, delinquents, institutionalized adults, parents, and teachers, and with different problems, including aggression, classroom behavior, verbal behaviors, social interaction, mealtime behavior, and child management.

One major finding arising out of this research is that generality does not automatically occur (Stokes and Baer, 1977). In several studies, if generality did occur without being programmed, there was evidence of deterioration (Jackson and Wallace, 1974; Koegel and Rincover, 1974; Wahler, 1969b). Fischer (1976) and Mullen and Dumpson (1972), in their review of outcome studies, suggested that this is an issue of great relevance to the field of social work. The research demonstrates that the generality of intervention effects can no longer be taken for granted; they must be carefully considered in both intervention planning and evaluation.

Kazdin (1977), who reviewed research conducted on token economies, and Stokes and Baer (1977),who reviewed the generalization literature, can be given much of the credit for initially defining and describing many of the categories of behavior programs presently being used to enhance generality. The following text proposes strategies and incorporates these strategies into the intervention method. Within this model, generality is treated as an ongoing concern from the initial interview through termination. The issue of extending treatment effects is considered when the problem is defined, the change agent and setting are identified, the intervention is developed, and the termination procedures are designed. Generality then is considered in four major categories: assessment, intervention, termination, and unplanned generality. The strategies most appropriate for each stage of treatment are identified, and guidelines for implementing them are included.

Generality and Assessment

Efforts to enhance maintenance and generality begin during the first interviews. When workers make correct choices and judgments during assessment, their job of planning for lasting change is easier during the intervention and termination stages. This section builds upon that recognition by describing five considerations, without reference to importance of order, to be used during assessment that are believed to effect generality once intervention has successfully produced the desired outcomes. Each description ends with specific practice guidelines germane to enhancing generality.

Selecting Behaviors Likely to Be Maintained in Natural Environment. The most dependable generality technique is to target for change behaviors that are likely to be maintained outside the intervention by naturally occurring consequences. This is called "behavioral trap" (Baer and Wolf, 1970). It may develop when behaviors initially maintained by artificial reinforcers in the natural setting come under the control of naturally occurring contingencies and trap the client in new positive behavioral interactions with the environment; this is a goal of every intervention that programs generality. In this chapter's three practice illustrations, behaviors to be increased that were likely to have positive consequences were chosen. In the Lullo and Pinkston study (Practice Illustration 9.1), a self-initiated greeting was considered likely to be reinforced by a social response from other individuals. The second behavior (Blackman and Pinkston, Practice Illustration 9.2), eating with utensils, was chosen as a self-help skill that would be supported by peers and staff in the dining room. Playing nicely with siblings in Practice Illustration 9.3 (Shibano and others) illustrates a behavior that is likely to be maintained naturally once the mother was trained to praise this desirable behavior. In addition, the appropriate parent behaviors, as responses, are likely to be reinforced by the child playing nicely with his brother. This selection of behaviors likely to be maintained in the environment does not ensure that those behaviors will maintain after termination; rather, it increases that possibility. Workers, particularly when conducting assessments, are aware of several reasons why generality does not occur after termination, even after the "behavioral trap" has been set.

Any intervention is intrusive into the lives of clients and, directly or indirectly, into their environments. An intervention may provoke inappropriate behavior, anxiety, or anger in the clients or the recipients of their behaviors. Behaviors that were previously reinforcing to clients are hard to extinguish; therefore, it is important to arrange contingencies so that clients are reinforced for new desirable behaviors. Intervention then is focused not only on decreasing behaviors that are undesirable but on developing reinforcers for new incompatible behaviors. This dual effort minimizes negative emotional reaction by replacing something that has been taken away from the client with something that is also rewarding.

The natural environment is frequently considered a discrete, single situation when, in reality, the clients exist in many environments. School or home settings, often sites of behavior change, are actually complex, multiple-stimulus conditions, each of which controls behavior differentially. It is difficult to predict specifically the environment in which behaviors will occur or to measure behaviors in these environments. The child who lacks social skills with peers may learn to interact more appropriately with siblings at home, but interactions with classmates are unaffected if intervention is not extended to the school. Even though intervention *is* implemented at school, social skills may not generalize to other students or teachers not involved with intervention who present novel stimulus conditions.

Seldom are behaviors consistently reinforced in the natural environment. Although most appropriate behavior is reinforced only occasionally, it maintains for most people on these intermittent reinforcement schedules. The five practice guidelines for enhancing generality during assessment, by selecting behaviors likely to be maintained in the natural environment, are:

1. Select for increase behaviors that already exist but are occurring at low rates in the natural environment.
2. In addition to behaviors to be decreased, select for change behaviors that include those incompatible with negative behaviors to be increased.
3. Select for change behaviors that are easily altered before attempting to change more complex and difficult behaviors.
4. Select target behaviors that occur in one environment prior to selecting behaviors that do not occur in any environment, to ensure opportunity for reinforcement.
5. Select for change behaviors that are compatible with a client's social system, values, and goals.

Availability and Scheduling of Reinforcement. During assessment, the worker determines the quantity and quality of reinforcement available for programming needs. This enables the worker to program an increase of available reinforcers if the client is deprived or to transfer existing contingencies to promote and assist behavior change. An important goal of intervention, based on this assessment, is the presentation of reinforcement immediately following the occurrence of the desired behavior, to establish the behavior firmly in the individual's repertoire. Once the behavior is established, it is possible to delay presenting the reinforcer with minimal declines in performance. The distinguishing feature is that a reinforcer is provided for each occurrence of a behavior, but the presentation of the reinforcer is not usually immediate. The increasing delay of reinforcement is introduced gradually to make the transition as smooth as possible. This technique builds upon the assessment of available reinforcers and the rate with which they occur. Through careful and detailed assessments, the worker then avoids flooding clients with reinforcers that cannot be supported in the natural environment or that are insufficient to provide durable change.

The five practice guidelines for enhancing generality by the assessment of reinforcer delivery are:

1. Determine existing reinforcers available for future programming needs.
2. If insufficient reinforcers exist in the natural environment, increase natural reinforcers before attempting to use artificial reinforcers.
3. If artificial reinforcers are used, pair them with natural reinforcers and, as soon as feasible, fade the artificial reinforcers while leaving the contingent natural reinforcers intact.
4. If sufficient reinforcers exist, assess the possibility of using existing reinforcers for programming.
5. Avoid flooding clients with novel reinforcers unlikely to be maintained independent of the worker's or change agent's efforts.

Self-Management. Clients use self-management techniques for the administration of consequences (see Chapter Six) to intervene with their own behavior and to learn skills and procedures to make changes in a number of different settings, enhancing transfer of intervention effects outside the clinical session and over time. Using these techniques, the clients monitor and evaluate their own behavior and determine the most effective consequences and amount of reinforcement. Use of self-management does not mean that the environment lacks reinforcers to maintain behavior; it lets the client arrange for contingent environmental reinforcers. Shibano and colleagues (Practice Illustration 9.3) taught the mother to use both self-praise and tangible reinforcers to maintain her child management skills after training.

Self-control programs have worked as well as administration of rewards by others; it has been suggested, however, that clients may become increasingly lenient with themselves over time (Felixbrod and O'Leary, 1974; Frederiksen and Frederiksen, 1975; Polster and Pinkston, 1979). A few investigators have successfully corrected for this tendency by having an outside observer randomly check the accuracy of self-monitoring and present reinforcement for accuracy in applying contingencies (Drabman, Spitalnik, and O'Leary, 1973; Kazdin, 1977; Turkewitz, O'Leary, and Ironsmith, 1975). One more concern of self-administration of consequences is voiced by those who are reluctant to accept the notion of self-reinforcement (see Chapter Six for a discussion of this issue). Even though long-term effects of self-administered contingencies have not been evaluated, this approach to behavioral maintenance and transfer holds promise, especially if occasional reinforcement by others is incorporated into the program to help prevent leniency.

It is apparent that the worker, prior to using self-management techniques, has many considerations to address during assessment, including the client's maturity and skills. Because self-management can be worked into programs either during intervention or when approaching termination, the worker can assess the potential for self-management training by following these five guidelines:

1. If the client has major skill limitations, consider alternate approaches that use existing skills for behavior change rather than attempting to teach many new skills.
2. If skills are increased during intervention, teach self-management skills as a supplement to an implemented program.
3. Program for rapid initial change to engage the client, and then incorporate self-management as a final component.
4. If assessment reveals that the potential for change is equal to comparable programs, select the intervention program most compatible with self-management.
5. Self-management should be enhanced with complementing procedures when additional change agents are available.

Removing Cues That Lead to Undesirable Behavior. It is possible for clients to avoid situations that precipitate the occurrence of the problem behavior rather than control them in response to the problem. For instance, individuals with problems of anger outbursts learn to discriminate those situations that lead to this volatile behavior. To make this discrimination, clients will need to note which antecedent events, settings, persons, and consequences most frequently are associated with their anger. This information will help determine the probable cause of the anger and design an intervention that will alter the control of the anger. If these cues are assessed as highly predictable and as controlling the occurrence of positive or negative behaviors, the worker has a potential intervention with a high probability of successful change and maintenance. The four guidelines are:

1. Remove behavioral cues that prompt undesirable behavior.
2. Assess behavioral alternatives that have a high probability of obtaining the same reinforcer as the problem behavior.
3. If there is less than a one-to-one correspondence between the environmental cues and the problem behavior, assess all situations associated with same behavior.
4. Removal of cues may be insufficient to maintain the desired behavior. Assess potential reinforcers that can be used to strengthen the more positive behavior.

Involving Significant Others in Supporting Client Change Efforts. Individuals in the client's environment can be involved in assessment and intervention to enable the client to transfer change to the relevant situations (see Chapters Seven and Eight for a more complete discussion of using collaterals as behavior change agents.) It is helpful to clients to have collaterals involved in the assessment and intervention. Collaboration of significant others with the worker provides an atmosphere that is supportive of client change; indeed, they are in the best position to provide social and material resources. They are also in the best position to prevent positive change from occurring. Collaterals may be initially skeptical about accepting and supporting change efforts or even agreeing about the problem definition. However, the worker encourages significant collaterals to support the intentions of the client to change. Once support persons have cooperated with assessment and intervention and change has occurred, an evaluation of change by the relevant others in the client system is made. Sometimes change is so conspicuous that the significant others do not need assistance observing the results. This often occurs when altering discrete behaviors, such as a child's increased eating when mother praises him when he tries new foods. In other cases, change is not as easily defined and observed, so the worker provides assistance interpreting information about the consequences of behavioral change.

Ongoing contacts with collaterals help the worker verify client change. The supportive relationship with the worker can increase the likelihood of the client attempting to please the worker by exaggerating the degree of change. Consultation with collaterals to monitor client progress and maintenance thus provides valuable feedback and enhances generality.

The three guidelines that enable the worker to assess significant others and their impact are:

1. Assess the current interactions between the significant others and the identified client by determining who should change which behaviors for intervention to be successful.
2. Actively and formally involve significant others from the initial contact.
3. Assess available reinforcers for the significant others to ensure that they remain involved and active participants in intervention.

Generality and Intervention

Each step of the intervention phase includes attention to techniques for extending treatment effects. The worker uses data collected during baseline to note when and where problem behaviors occur. From this information, the worker determines the most appropriate persons and settings for the change effort. Techniques are selected that are likely to maintain the extension of intervention effects. Evaluation of intervention includes results of training and current or potential generality. Throughout intervention the worker considers: (1) Is the intervention likely to enhance generality? (2) Can the intervention be maintained over time? (3) Is there an alternate intervention more likely to maintain effects and if so, when should it be implemented?

Here we present four specific strategies to maximize extension of change: (1) methods to extend relevant stimulus conditions, (2) methods to schedule intermittent reinforcement, (3) worker support of client change efforts by promoting opportunities for practice of behavior analysis skills to solve future and similar problems, and (4) combinations of techniques to ensure maximum effectiveness.

Extending Stimulus Conditions. This strategy takes advantage of common stimuli so that a shift from the intervention condition to the natural environment is less abrupt and discrimination of the two settings is less likely to occur. For example, a school social worker may use the same academic material in sessions as is used in the child's classroom. Institutions and residential treatment centers should be designed with an interior decor familiar to the resident, such as incorporating home furnishings, and they often have staff wear street clothes rather than uniforms. If carefully selected, the stimuli can be made functional and aid generality. This effect is also accomplished by increasing the number of individuals who administer reinforcement or introducing various environmental components into the treatment session. Including in sessions people the clients will encounter in situations relevant to the performance of their new behavior has been part of behavioral interventions with children. This may mean that, for example, peers are brought into the session to administer reinforcing contingencies (Rose, 1977). Parents may be taught to use systematic attention to reinforce their child's appropriate behavior and extinguish undesirable behavior, as the practitioner did in their family sessions (Pinkston, Friedman, and Polster, 1981). The use of two or more practitioners or a worker with another behavior change agent to teach new behavior to the client is likely to enhance the generality of the behavior to persons not involved in the training (Stokes, Baer, and Jackson, 1974). In addition, when the client learns in several settings (office, classroom, and home), the new behavior is more likely to occur in a variety of situations. The number of practitioners or settings sufficient for desired generality varies widely, but a survey of studies using this method indicates that frequently no more than two exemplars are needed (Stokes and Baer, 1977). Greater diversity may be inefficient; too much diversity of presented stimulus conditions or not enough variety may make potential gains disproportional to the investment of training effort.

Although this approach to programmed generality looks promising, there is as yet very little research concerned with its development and evaluation. Lullo and Pinkston (Practice Illustration 9.1) used different intervenors (teachers) in two classroom settings for each client with mixed results. Blackman and Pinkston (Practice Illustration 9.2) also used multiple intervenors. The practitioner first implemented the maintenance procedure (prompt and praise for eating with utensils) at lunch. Later, in phase 2, two other staff members alternately introduced the same maintenance procedure during dinner each day. The extension of stimulus conditions should be introduced while the main intervention is still in effect, to provide a smooth transfer of behavior from the clinical setting to the natural situation. Kazdin (1977) suggested that once the desired behavior is performed in a few settings or in the presence of several people, the probability that the behavior will be performed in a variety of new situations is increased.

The worker-client sessions are held in the environment in which the targeted behavior occurs (for example, in the home, school, or other setting away from the worker's office). This method is frequently used in family interventions when sessions are held at home (Shibano and others, Practice Illustration 9.3; Linsk, Pinkston, and Green, Practice Illustration 7.1; Rzepnicki and others, Practice Illustration 7.2) and with clients who are not functioning adequately in an institutional setting (see Blackman and Pinkston, Practice Illustration 9.2; Lullo and Pinkston, Practice Illustration 9.1; Linsk and Pinkston, Practice Illustration 8.3).

The four guidelines that specify ways the therapeutic setting can be made to resemble the natural setting and the stimulus control can be expanded are:

1. Incorporate physical stimuli from the natural setting into the therapeutic setting.
2. Incorporate individuals from the natural setting into the therapeutic setting.
3. Incorporate multiple practitioners or multiple settings in treatment.
4. Incorporate intervention into the natural environment.

Scheduling Intermittent Reinforcement. Intermittent reinforcement is a consequence that follows only some occurrences of a specified behavior and results in an increase in the probability of that behavior being emitted in the future. Research on token economies and other behavioral programs has demonstrated that the use of intermittent reinforcement can postpone extinction of the appropriate behavior quite successfully. Kazdin and Polster (1973) provided an illustration of the differential effects of scheduling. They looked at the maintenance of treatment effects in two withdrawn adult retardates. Both adults developed social interaction skills while on a token economy; however, one was on a continuous reinforcement schedule and the other on an intermittent schedule. During the final extinction period (after withdrawal of the token economy), the client who previously had been reinforced intermittently maintained a high rate of social interaction throughout the five-week follow-up period, while the client on the continuous schedule returned to the pretreatment level of interaction. These findings suggest that manipulation of scheduling can be very useful for delaying extinction. However, there were only two subjects in this study, and the short-term maintenance of behavior in one subject may reflect only differing rates of extinction. Unfortunately, there are still very few studies investigating the effects of scheduling on people.

Intermittently reinforced behaviors are more durable than behaviors on continuous schedules possibly because occasions to be reinforced cannot be easily discriminated from occasions not to reinforced. Delayed reinforcement seems to have the same effect.

The two general guidelines for implementing intermittent scheduling (Kazdin, 1977) are:

1. Develop the desired behavior quickly with a continuous re-
    inforcement and schedule, then gradually reduce presenta-
    tion of reinforcement on an increasingly large intermittent
    schedule until all reinforcement is eliminated.
2. During intervention, utilize intermittent rather than con-
    tinuous reinforcement.

Strengthening Out-of-Session Behaviors. During the intervention phases, the change agent uses a number of techniques
to maximize the likelihood that setting generality will occur.
Various methods have been designed to help clients generalize
their behavior changes: practicing desired behaviors, learning
cues for desired behaviors, or contracting with the worker to engage in out-of-session behaviors. Using these methods, the client
learns cues in the environment that signal or elicit the occurrence of specific behaviors or preclude other behaviors learned
during intervention. The worker must foster the client's acquisition of the necessary skills for performing behaviors out-of-session. Intervention training may include planning for predictable
performance difficulties and techniques for modifying intervention if necessary.

For example, in McCabe and others' intervention (Practice Illustration 6.1), the client role-played a number of realistic
vignettes to practice out-of-session behaviors. In Practice Illustration 9.1, Lullo and Pinkston describe the use of modeling
within sessions to teach school-age children social behaviors.
Blackman and Pinkston (Practice Illustration 9.2) depict prompting and guided practice as methods to help clients learn and
maintain eating behaviors. Finally, Shibano and colleagues
(Practice Illustration 9.3) used behavioral rehearsal in intervention sessions to strengthen target behaviors over time. The following four guidelines are useful for strengthening out-of-
session behaviors:

1. Include opportunities for clients to imitate and practice
    skills during intervention sessions.
2. Let the client practice the behavior in a safe, noncritical
    environment.

3. Give clients cues for appropriate behavior, both within and out of session.
4. Use specific contracts to initiate out-of-session use of recently acquired behavioral abilities.

Training Basic Behavioral Analysis Skills for Future Problems. As general preparation for changing circumstances, the practitioner can encourage the client to actively collaborate in the problem specification and resolution process. The client can also participate in gathering data, analyzing the cost benefits of alternate solutions, selecting and implementing a problem-solving action, anticipating and planning obstacles to alleviate problem(s), and evaluating the effort. Participating in these activities enables the client to learn a general problem-solving methodology. Perlman, in developing the problem-solving approach for use in social casework, viewed the treatment process as having two goals: alleviation of the individual's problems is learning a way by which tomorrow's (or next year's) difficulties and decisions may be dealt with (Perlman, 1970, p. 139). Recently, there have been a number of investigations into the possibilities of clients learning behavior analysis skills in treatment (Blechman, 1974; Spivack, Platt, and Shure, 1976; Weiss, Hops, and Patterson, 1973). Our practice experience has shown that clients learn behavior principles best when illustrations can be directly drawn from their own current experiences. When each behavioral program is developed, the clients can be taught the basic principles being used. As data-recording contracts are developed, the client can be taught the importance of quantifying problems for evaluation and becoming aware of behavior-environment interactions. Evaluation can be taught as a function of changes in treatment phases. Then, during an intervention such as differential attention, the clients may learn the principles of reinforcement and extinction. The worker can use praise, attention, and discussion as reinforcers for the client's understanding of principles. Often the client can specify the functional relationship between behaviors and their consequences and antecedents.

Although originally clients may not know they are performing a functional analysis, cues, feedback, and praise are effective teaching methods for shaping this behavior. Whenever possible, the client is given opportunities to make choices among interventions, settings, and behavior targets. If choices expressed by clients are inappropriate, the principles used in the program design may be explained and taught. As choices do seem appropriate, the worker may use these opportunities to praise these client responses. A number of self-teaching materials (Becker, 1971; Tharp and Wetzel, 1969) are available to teach clients behavior principles. This material can provide out-of-session reminders and additional information interesting and useful to the clients. Specific training sessions for clients on behavior change principles are used as methods for summarizing the information taught previously or to present information as to "why" the programming has been effective. Although research is inconclusive as to the effectiveness of such efforts (O'Dell and others, 1981), these methods are often used, particularly when clients are other service staff. (See Chapters Seven and Eight for more discussion of educational sessions for clients and staff.) Many of the findings suggest that this "hoped for by-product" may, in fact, be a reality if planned into the intervention package.

The six guidelines for training in basic behavior analysis skills are:

1. Use the ongoing intervention as opportunities for client training.
2. Encourage the client's understanding of behavior principles.
3. Let the client make intervention decisions whenever possible.
4. Give clients reading materials on relevant behavior principles.
5. Let clients take more and more responsibility for use of principles as the program proceeds.
6. Use specific training sessions individually or by group.

Generality and Termination

In this model of social work practice, termination is the ending of worker behaviors directed toward shaping specific client behaviors. Successful intervention programs continue beyond termination. As the behavioral program draws to a close, workers examine the cause of intervention. They assess the degree to which methods for maintaining client behavior change incorporated earlier during the assessment and interventions phases are sufficient or whether additional methods need to be added. Termination is a period of planning maintenance.

Described here are methods for enhancing maintenance of intervention effects that are implemented near the end of the behavioral program. Although these methods are implemented at the end of the program, planning for their use begins earlier.

Instructional Control. Simple instructions are useful for maintaining behavior change when the client has the necessary skills and environmental supports. Studies suggest that when delivered early in intervention, instructions facilitate behaviors in extraintervention situations (Margholin, Siegel, and Phillips, 1976). Generality can be achieved by specifying explicit expectations; this technique has been under used in clinic settings. Why not say, "Now that you've developed these excellent skills, try them the next time you talk with your mother."

Generalizing behavior change can be directly reinforced. School teachers frequently do this when, after illustrating a particular principle by use of example, they encourage students to apply the principle with a similar example. There has been very little research, however, into the technique of instructing "to generalize." Studies most frequently examine generality to other behaviors rather than to settings (see Stokes and Baer, 1977, pp. 31-33). Many instructional techniques are not implemented independently; they are included as methods of fading reinforcement. When there are many reinforcers controlling the target behavior, the probability that the behavior is maintained in a variety of situations in the natural environment is increased. A combination of instructional techniques is used for optimal effects.

There are four practice guidelines for structuring termination to increase the probability of temporal and setting generality:

1. Use instructions early in intervention and continue to use instructions through termination.

2. State instructions consistently and accurately; allow ample time for feedback from the client.
3. Provide clear and understandable instructions and ask the client to repeat them and to present other examples of when they might be relevant.
4. Divide instructions into short and direct small steps for accomplishment of behavior.

Substituting One Program for Another. A number of investigators have shown that substituting one program for another in a particular setting or extending a program to several settings are ways of increasing the probability of maintenance and transfer of treatment effects. O'Leary and colleagues (1967) intervened in a youngster's aggressive and hyperactive behavior by providing candy, tokens, and social approval for appropriate behavior. The child's mother was taught the systematic use of differential attention to reinforce the desirable behavior and extinguish the undesirable aggressive behavior in the child's home. This illustrates how significant others can be trained and used as mediators in the client's natural environment to continue some aspect of behavioral intervention after the practitioner leaves.

Intervention programs have been designed in which artificial reinforcers (that is, a token economy) are paired with natural reinforcers. Once the target behavior changes, the arbitrary reinforcers are withdrawn, leaving the naturally occurring reinforcers such as attention, social approval, or praise to maintain the change. The intervention described by Lullo and Pinkston in Practice Illustration 9.1 shows program substitution designed to maintain self-initiated greeting responses in three students.

Practice guidelines for extending a program from one set of environmental circumstances to another include:

1. Pair artificial reinforcers with natural reinforcers; thus, include naturally arising contingencies such as praise, affection, and privileges that are available in the client's environment.
2. Incorporate as many contingencies as possible from the personal environment into the intervention environment.

3. Start the program in the second environment *while* maintaining program in the intervention environment.
4. Then fade contingencies in the intervention environment.

Enhancement Generality While Terminating. In the successful change effort, clients give up the support of the worker and agency and are able to continue on their new course without the practitioner's direction or advice. For this transition to take place, ending contact is a gradual process. This is useful if the client has not had much opportunity to try out new behaviors or behavior change procedures (self-management in everyday life). Increasing the interval between sessions enables the client and practitioner to obtain feedback regarding the maintenance of change and/or the effectiveness of the techniques being used. Independence from the worker can be encouraged by focusing on positive achievements and by limiting the focus on problems or affect-laden topics. As termination approaches, the worker develops more informal contacts with clients. This procedure is similar to the fading techniques previously described: Attempts are made to avoid an abrupt change in contingencies from the clinical session to the client's natural environment.

Guidelines for using termination to enhance maintenance include:

1. Terminate gradually.
2. Specify criteria for termination as far in advance as possible.
3. Terminate once behaviors are stable.
4. Increase intervals between sessions as termination approaches.
5. Avoid working on new problem areas as the end of contract approaches; if they are serious, do not terminate.
6. Praise autonomous behavior and maintenance of behavioral performance during final sessions.

Modifying Termination and Maintenance Contingencies. Another procedure used in behavioral interventions to help increase maintenance of change entails gradually changing the cues and reinforcers that have been used to effect behavior change. This decrease in the strength or the frequency of reinforcers or cues is called fading. The client is much less likely to discriminate slow and subtle removal than an abrupt end to the program and is also less likely to return to former behavioral patterns. This technique is particularly important in parent-child interactions. The child's misbehavior continues to receive parental attention more often than does desirable play behavior. Gradual fading of specific parent attention learned during intervention can help regulate attention to maintain appropriate behavior. Another illustration of this kind of programming is the multilevel token economy often used in residential treatment programs, such as Achievement Place, where the long-term objective is to return individuals to their own communities. The social worker uses a fading procedure by decreasing the density of specific reinforcers. For example, a worker instructs Mrs. Jones to reinforce only two out of every three occurrences of appropriate child behavior rather than each occurrence. Then, once the behavior has stabilized, the worker asks Mrs. Jones to reinforce the appropriate behavior only 50 percent of the time.

Although the fading of contingencies in the token economy has been used extensively, very few investigations have conducted follow-ups regarding long-term maintenance. Nevertheless, the fading procedures are useful with interventions that incorporate arbitrary reinforcers. Gradual changes in contingencies serve as transitions to the natural contingencies present in the client's life, in which consequences are unsystematic and often delayed.

As suggested, contingencies can be faded by gradually increasing the response requirement necessary before delivering a reinforcer. Practice Illustration 9.2 is an example of this technique. The clients in this study were expected to increasingly engage in self-feeding behavior on their own for the same amount of reinforcement. Guided practice was faded one step at a time as each trial was completed successfully and then reinforced with praise.

Practice guidelines for fading cues and reinforcers include:

1. Fade reinforcers gradually over time and evaluate target behavior after each change in the frequency or intensity of
   reinforcers.
2. Use a schedule of contingency changes to fade cues, reinforcers, and/or punishers to allow behavior to stabilize,
   fade further, and restabilize.
3. Pair cues and reinforcers developed during intervention
   with existing cues and reinforcers in the natural environment.
4. Fade punishment procedures only if negative behaviors are
   below an acceptable level.

Unplanned Generality. Occasionally, behaviors do not return to preintervention levels following the abrupt removal of
contingencies developed during intervention; this is a predictable result. Conclusive information as to why unplanned generality occurs is not available. Unplanned generality is defined as
maintenance and/or generality of behavior when generality is
not explicitly programmed into the intervention or, simply,
luck. There are several interpretations as to how this "acciden-
tal" maintenance might occur:

1. Momentum of change effort may be a stabilizing factor.
   The consequences derived from the new behavior itself
   (natural reinforcement) can maintain that behavior by producing changed expectations and satisfactions. Even the
   financial expense to the client may enhance maintenance—
   after individuals pay for service, they may feel they should
   keep what they have bought.
2. The administration of tangible reinforcers may permanently alter the behavior of the person enabling reinforcers so
   that this mediator's social response becomes a reinforcing
   consequence of the client's appropriate behavior. As an
   illustration, a teacher who praises Gayle for appropriate behavior may first notice the behavior only when she must
   give Gayle a token for each appropriate response—if this approval also has reinforcing consequences, the token economy may no longer be needed.

3. The initial use of concrete reinforcers for appropriate behavior gives the client feedback about how to get rewards.
   Operant procedures may enable clients to learn the "rules
   of the game" in a systematic way they can transfer to similar situations.
4. New pride of *status* may reinforce generality. If the individual's self-esteem is enhanced, maintenance of change is likely to be increased.

Although these all seem to be possible explanations of behavioral maintenance, generality is more likely to occur if specific programming for it is included as part of the intervention
strategy. If the worker or client observe unplanned generality,
procedures to strengthen the naturally occurring maintenance
are indicated.

Evaluating Generality

The generality of treatment effects can be evaluated by
using the methods presented in Chapter Four. In fact, evaluating generality effects proceeds almost identically to evaluating
direct intervention effects on target behaviors. In addition to
measuring a target behavior during baseline and then treatment
conditions, the practitioner includes a probe for generality. This
probe is a sampling of conditions (settings or behaviors) that are
logically predicted to be related to the target behaviors. For
example, if a worker wants to examine the setting generality of
intervention effects for reducing the disruptive classroom behaviors of a child, it is necessary to first measure the target behavior in the classroom where interventions occur (baseline). To
determine the setting generality, baseline data are collected in a
second classroom. Generality is indicated by comparing the
baseline conditions in each classroom by probes and observing
changes in the problem behavior. (See Mallon-Wenzel and others, Practice Illustration 6.1 for an illustration of generality
probe use.)

Evaluating generality does require a degree of creativity
from the evaluator. There are no fixed rules for determining

which extra-intervention settings or behaviors should be examined for generality. The practitioner and the client consider various areas of functioning to determine what behaviors and settings should be examined.

Temporal generality is evaluated by measuring the target behaviors after sessions with the worker have terminated. Data are collected for a short period at specific follow-up points.

The interval between follow-ups may begin at monthly checks and can be gradually lengthened so that data are collected more and more infrequently. For instance, two weeks after intervention has ended, Cindy's parents might be asked to collect data on both their own and Cindy's behavior, as Cindy did during the time she was meeting with the practitioner. This occurred for only one week. The family may be requested to do this again six weeks after termination, then twelve weeks, and so on. When continued behavior change is observed, the practitioner knows if the intervention effects are maintained only when data are collected. The client, however, can invoke the procedures taught during intervention and presumably can use them again if needed.

Programming for the Establishment, Maintenance, and Generality of a Self-Initiated Greeting Response Using a Token Economy

Sheila A. Lullo, Elsie M. Pinkston

Socially isolated retarded individuals show an array of demonstrated behaviors. One such category of behaviors is the lack of self-initiated greeting responses. This behavioral deficit has been observed and treated with retarded populations; two studies are most relevant for this research. Stokes, Baer, and Jackson (1974) increased the hand-wave greeting responses of four retarded children by presenting a potato chip or an M & M contingent on the occurrence of that response. Later, Stokes and Baer (1977) incorporated generality as a goal of their program by training sufficient exemplars to increase the response. As an alternative to training the response under all possible stimulus conditions, their approach involved training the clients to greet several staff, to increase the probability that they would learn to greet other individuals. The results show the importance of planning the transfer of learning when designing the intervention.

Social work practitioners should plan programs to transfer intervention effects to other settings, people, or behaviors than those for which they were originally trained. Many practitioners have not dealt with programming for transfer of learning and instead have proceeded with their intervention, assuming that transfer would occur.

This study focused on three areas: (1) the effectiveness of contingent tokens with backup reinforcers paired with naturally occurring social consequences in increasing a self-initiated verbal greeting response in sufficiently verbal but behavior-retarded clients; (2) the simultaneous use of two experimenters in programming for the generality of the response; (3) the maintenance of the response by naturally occurring social reinforcers following the removal of the token economy.

Method

Clients. Three students from a school for behavior disordered and functionally retarded children were chosen for this project: (1) Andrea, a fifteen-year-old female; (2) Becky, a sixteen-year-old female; and (3) Carl, a twelve-year-old male. These students were chosen because of the following similarities: All were sufficiently verbal to enable them to emit the desired response, none emitted the desired response, all were between twelve and sixteen years old, and a developmental goal for all was to increase their appropriate interactions with peers and adults.

Responses. The focused responses in this study were self-initiated verbal greeting responses. A self-initiated verbal greeting response was described as a response made without prompting to a person, within ten seconds after that person was present within five feet of the student, and included a minimum verbalization of "Hi," "Hello," or "Good Morning."

Setting. The response training and generality measures were recorded in the student's homeroom and the other classroom for students on the same level. The two teachers in these two classrooms were the trainers who provided consequences for the greeting responses. The two aides in the classrooms functioned as observers and were the individuals used for generality measures.

Behavioral Consequences. Two types of consequences were used to establish the self-initiated greeting response. A token system was developed so that tokens were earned by the students for emitting the response to the trainers and were cashed in weekly for material backup reinforcers. Naturally occurring potential reinforcers also were received as a result of emitting the appropriate response; these potential reinforcers were acknowledgment of the response and a greeting in reply.

Generality. For each student, checks for generality were

made by two aides, the aide in his homeroom classroom and the other classroom aide, who recorded daily whether the self-initiated greeting response was emitted by the student toward each aide. If the student emitted the self-initiated verbal greeting response to one of the aides checking for generality, it was followed by a greeting reply, but no tokens were awarded to the student. The aides did not use any prompts with the students to obtain the response.

Reliability. The teacher and aide for each client recorded the student's responses daily. As a reliability check, one of the counselors in the school observed in the two classrooms of each student at least once during every phase and recorded the student's responses to the two staff members. These data were compared with the staff members' data, and if the recordings agreed, reliability was scored at 100 percent; if they did not agree, reliability was scored as 0 percent. To determine reliability of the bus aide's data, one of the counselors observed on the bus at least twice in each phase. The data were compared and reliability determined for each student's data in each phase.

Experimental Phases

Phase 1—Baseline. During the baseline phase, no intervention for the response and no reinforcement for the response occurred. If a student emitted an appropriate response, the teachers and aides responded with an appropriate greeting and acknowledgment but made no effort to continue the interactions. Also during this phase, the teachers and aides did not greet the student unless the student initiated the greeting.

Phase 2—Reinforcement. On the day prior to the first day of intervention, the worker informed each student of the token system. They were told that if they greeted the homeroom teacher or teacher in the other classrooms, they would receive five tokens from each teacher for an appropriate greeting (a possible ten tokens). An appropriate greeting was modeled for the student. Beginning the following day, when the students emitted a self-initiated greeting to their teachers participating in the study, they received five tokens, acknowledgment, and a greeting reply. Tokens were exchanged for material rewards at the end of the morning.

Phase 3—Maintenance. During this phase, the token system was faded according to an increasing variable ratio schedule until the desired behavior was maintained by naturally occurring contingencies.

Phase 4—Monitoring. Once the self-initiated greeting was under the control of naturally occurring contingencies, the staff members decreased their data recording to two days per week. These data were recorded to monitor the durability of the rate of responding.

Research Design. A multiple-baseline-across-clients design was used (see Chapter Four) for this project. Baselines began for all three students on the same day. When the baselines were stable, treatment began with Andrea. When intervention with Andrea had progressed to the end of phase 3, treatment began with Becky, while the baseline continued with Carl. When Becky reached the end of phase 2, intervention began with Carl. During the time Becky and Carl were in the treatment phase, data continued to be recorded on Andrea as she moved through the maintenance and durability phases. Behavioral change following the change offers experimental evidence that the intervention causes the change. Hence, three changes offer three replications of the intervention effect.

Results

Phase 1 reliability scores ranged from 85 to 100 percent, and the three remaining phases showed average scores of 100 percent for all three subjects. The reliability of the data recorded for this project is very high, as demonstrated in the reliability scores achieved.

Figure 1 summarizes the results of this project. All clients showed an increase in self-initiated greetings during phase 2, the reinforcement phase, over the rate obtained in phase 1, the baseline phase. Andrea showed an average increase with the trainers from 10 to 56 percent, Becky's rate increased from 3 to 41 percent, and Carl's rate increased from 15 to 76 percent.

Figure 1. Percentage of Self-Initiated Verbal Responses.

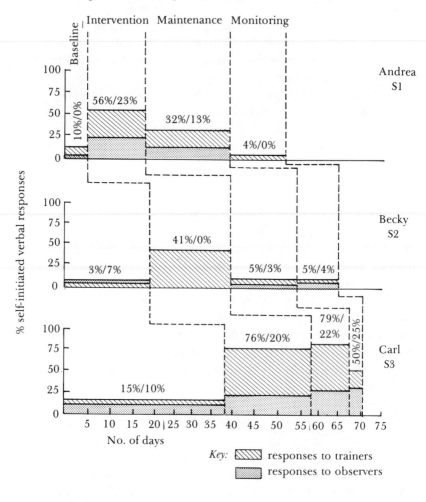

Key: responses to trainers
     responses to observers

Generality was measured by the change in the student's rate of initiations to the observers. Andrea showed increases in greetings to the observers during the treatment phase, although the increases were not as great as those obtained with the trainers. This student's rate of responding to observers increased from 0 percent in phase 1 to an average of 23 percent in phase 2. Becky did not show an increase in average greeting in phase 2 over the baseline rate with observers but showed a decrease in average response rate from 7 to 0 percent. Carl demonstrated an increase in average response rate with observers in phase 2 from 10 to 20 percent; however, as with Andrea, these increases were not as great as with the trainers.

Degree of response maintenance is evidenced by the data collected in phases 3 and 4. The rate of responding established with Andrea in phase 2 dropped 24 percent with trainers and 10 percent with observers in phase 3 when the token economy was faded and another 28 percent with trainers and 13 percent with observers in phase 4 when the token economy was completely absent. Becky's response rate with trainers dropped 36 percent in phase 3 and remained stable in phase 4; however, Becky's greeting rate with observers increased 3 percent in phase 3 and another 1 percent in phase 4. Carl demonstrated an increase of 3 percent with trainers and 2 percent with observers in phase 3. His response rate with observers increased another 3 percent in phase 4; however, it dropped 29 percent in phase 4 with trainers.

Generally, all clients demonstrated an increase in response rate in phase 2 over the rate obtained in phase 1. For all three students, this increase was greater with the trainers than with observers. Andrea's and Becky's greeting rate with trainers decreased in phase 3, while Carl showed an increase. In phase 4, Andrea continued to demonstrate a decrease in response rate, Becky's percent of self-initiated greetings remained very close to her response rate in phase 3, and Carl showed a decrease; however, the rate remained higher than baseline rate.

Discussion

This research was designed to address three areas: (1) the effectiveness of a token paired with backup reinforcers and naturally occurring social consequences in establishing a self-initiated verbal greeting response in a sufficiently verbal, behavior-disordered population; (2) the simultaneous use of two teachers for programming the generality of the response; and (3) the maintenance of the response following the removal of the token economy, leaving the naturally occurring social reinforcers to maintain the level of response achieved. This section considers each area in light of the final results obtained in the project.

Phase 2 dealt with establishing the self-initiated verbal greeting response through the use of a token economy paired with naturally occurring reinforcers issued by two trainers. All subjects demonstrated an important increase in response rate over the baseline rate with both trainers. Because the research design was a multiple baseline and all subjects seemed to demonstrate independent increases in rates during this phase, it can be reasonably assumed that the increase in response rates for each subject can be attributed to the effectiveness of the token system and social consequences.

Increases in the greeting response were greatest during phase 2 for Carl. Because Carl's trainers were different from those used with Andrea and Becky and the reinforcement menus for the token economy were individualized for the clients, it is difficult to determine what accounts for the greater increase in Carl's response rate. Possibly the items on his reinforcement menu were more valuable and more reinforcing than the items on the other two students' menus. It is also possible that Carl's relationship with the teachers affected the success of the token economy.

Each client's individual characteristics also cannot be discounted when considering the students' varying degrees of responsiveness to the token economy. One characteristic possibly related to the rates of greeting achieved during the reinforcement phase is the students' intellectual capabilities. When the success of the reinforcers in establishing the desired response was considered, this project demonstrated that the token economy paired with naturally occurring reinforcers was initially effective. A problem arises in determining whether the token economy was effective, whether the social reinforcers were effective, or whether the combination of the two led to the increase in self-initiated greetings for the three students. Because the two types of reinforcers were used simultaneously and not individually, it is impossible to discuss the effectiveness of either separately.

Phase 2 was designed to assess the degree of generality of the established response to people in the student's environment other than those with whom the response was trained. This project used the notion of training sufficient exemplars and attempted to establish the response with two teachers simultaneously. If this procedure resulted in generality, it would save the time required to train the response to generalize. Andrea demonstrated the greatest increase in response rate to observers from phase 1 to phase 2. Carl's response rate to observers decreased from 7 to 0 percent in phase 2. Considering the data on all students combined, generality did not occur to a significant degree. The degree of generality Andrea obtained in phase 2 lasted only for that phase and eventually dropped to 0 percent in phase 4. Becky demonstrated a decrease in generality from phase 1 to phase 2 and in phases 3 and 4 showed a minimal increase. Carl showed an increase from phase 1 to phase 2, and this increase continued, to a lesser degree, in phases 3 and 4. It can be speculated that the increases in generality for Becky and Carl in phases 3 and 4, when the token economy was gradually removed, indicate the increasing strength of the naturally occurring social reinforcers. If the naturally occurring reinforcers were maintaining the response, one would expect the response rate to be similar with the trainers and the observers. The facts that the students were receiving social contingencies from both the trainers and observers and no tokens from the trainers and that the degree of generality to aides increased, coming closer to the response rate demonstrated with the trainers, might suggest that the social reinforcers were maintaining the response at a level which might have been achieved for the trainers and the observers had the project continued. This idea requires additional research to be substantiated.

Some researchers have suggested that noncontingent transfer of learning represents poor discrimination by the subject. This theory may be somewhat substantiated in this study. Andrea had the lowest level of intellectual functioning and demonstrated the greatest degree of generality in phase 2. Perhaps this student was least able to discriminate between those individuals who would provide reinforcers and those who would not.

An additional factor possibly accounting for variations in generality may be each student's personal likes and dislikes for the observers. The greeting response may have transferred to the observers with whom the clients were most comfortable. It is interesting to note the very different responses of each student in relation to the observers. The variations suggest that the amount of transfer may be attributed to factors other than the use of two trainers.

Phases 3 and 4 were concerned with maintaining the greeting response and removing the token economy. In phase 3, the tokens were gradually faded, so that in phase 4 the naturally occurring consequences were left to maintain the response. Theoretically, if the naturally occurring reinforcers are potent enough, the tokens could be faded and the response rate still maintained over time. The overall results of this study indicate that this maintenance did not occur. In phase 3, when the tokens were gradually faded, Andrea and Becky demonstrated a decrease in the rate of self-initiated greetings. The rate of responding in phase 3 did remain higher than the rate during the baseline phase. This finding might indicate that some degree of maintenance occurred; however, the results seem to show that in phase 4 the rate of responding for Andrea and Becky was near baseline level.

Several reasons could account for the decline in the rate of responding. For these two students, social consequences alone may not have been potent enough to maintain the response. It is also possible that the response was not sufficiently trained before the tokens were faded. Finally, one must consider that the token may have been faded too abruptly.

Carl's self-initiated greetings increased in phase 3. His response rate was not only maintained but increased while the tokens were faded. During the monitoring phase, however, his response rate decreased but remained higher than it was in the baseline phase. Perhaps the social consequences were potent enough for response maintenance. Note that phase 4 for Carl was very short. It is possible that if this phase had been longer, the response rate might have decreased significantly.

One source of valuable information was the anecdotal information obtained from staff members not aware of the project. Staff members mentioned that Andrea seemed brighter and cheerful and greeted them in the hallways frequently. Because no data had been collected on this behavior, it cannot be reported in the results; however, it is interesting information about the positive effects of the project.

Many school staff members who were aware of the project but not involved in data collection mentioned to the experimenter that they were being greeted by the students. Had these people been gathering data, the results obtained regarding generality might have been more successful. As mentioned earlier, the students seemed to be selective as to whom they were willing to respond to. It might be most beneficial to have as many people as possible in the client's environment gather data and serve as behavioral mediators.

In summary, the results of this project indicate the following: (1) The pairing of the token economy with naturally occurring social reinforcers effectively increased the self-initiated verbal greeting response rate of these clients. (2) The reinforcement system used in this project to train the response with two trainers simultaneously did not result in a significant amount of generalization to others in the clients' environments. (3) The levels of responding achieved when token reinforcement was used was not maintained when the token system was removed.

A Training-Maintenance Program for Reestablishing Appropriate Utensil Use Among the Impaired Elderly

Donald K. Blackman, Elsie M. Pinkston

The behavior analysis perspective has at least two advantages for working with the impaired elderly. First is the assumption that behavior is changeable, unless there is empirical demonstration to the contrary (Rebok and Hoyer, 1977). This perspective is particularly useful when working with a group that has been characterized as apathetic, withdrawn, unresponsive, uninterested, and dependent. Second, it is assumed that behavior is a function of the environment; for example, behavior, even of the mentally impaired, is at least partially determined by the characteristics of their environment (Skinner, 1953; Watson and Tharp, 1972).

Operant techniques have been effective for teaching and maintaining utensil use among other institutionalized populations. Zeiler and Jersey (1968) reported a case study in which a developmentally disabled adolescent was taught to spoon-feed herself; the training procedure consisted of guided trials and chaining desired behaviors. Barton and others (1970) reported that behaviors which included eating with hands rather than utensils could be modified by temporarily denying access to food when trainees responded incorrectly. O'Brien and Azrin (1972) demonstrated that a program combining verbal instruction, imitation, and manual guidance was effective for teaching proper mealtime behaviors and that verbal praise for proper behavior and verbal correction and time-out for improper behavior were effective maintenance procedures. O'Brien, Bugle, and Azrin (1972), in a controlled case study with a severely developmentally disabled girl who ate exclusively with her hands, reported that a manual guidance procedure, in which assistance was gradually withdrawn, was effective for training proper utensil use. A posttraining interruption-extinction procedure, in which the child was stopped when she attempted to eat with her hands, was necessary, however, to maintain appropriate utensil use.

Baltes and Zerbe (1976) extended these procedures to work with the institutionalized elderly. In their study, two elderly clients with low baseline rates of self-feeding behavior exhibited substantially higher rates of independent eating when food and attention from staff were made contingent on self-feeding. These results strongly suggested that the rate of the clients' independent eating depended on the environmental change introduced by the innovative care-taking procedure.

In the present study, guided-trial and interruption procedures were adapted to reestablish utensil use at meals for a group of institutionalized elderly women who ate almost entirely with their hands. Their low rate of appropriate eating resulted in negative staff responses and deprived them of their opportunity to function at their optimum level. The training procedure was implemented during the luncheon meal. An important aspect of this study was to evaluate the usefulness of a maintenance procedure to: (1) maintain the changes established with the guided-trial training procedure during lunch and (2) establish behavioral changes at dinner, during which no guided training was used.

Evaluation Method

Setting. The program was conducted on one floor of a 200-bed home for the aged. Most residents were assigned to the unit because they needed close staff supervision and nursing care. The majority of the floor's residents spent twenty-four hours per day on the unit and were allowed to leave only with supervision. Part 1 of the study was conducted during lunch; at lunch all residents were served trays that contained food items, hot and cold beverages, and utensils. Part 2 of the study was conducted during dinner; at dinner residents sat at tables that were set with utensils, bread and butter, dessert, and cold beverages. Dinner was served in two courses: first soup and then a plate with the main course and a variety of side dishes. Trays were prepared in the same manner at both meals and in all experimental conditions.

Clients. Three potential clients were selected for treatment using the following criteria: (1) each woman used her hands almost exclusively at meals to feed herself, and (2) each woman was able to raise and lower at least one arm between her waist and nose. It was assumed that each client had a history of appropriate utensil use prior to institutionalization. Each client was described in her record as showing marked dementia, confusion, and disorientation.

Mrs. A., Mrs. B., and Mrs. C. were eighty-five, eighty-seven, and ninety-five years old, respectively, and had resided in the home from two to three years. Mrs. A. was confined to a wheelchair; Mrs. B. and Mrs. C. were ambulatory. All the women received partial assistance with all elements of self-care. Each client demonstrated some form of sensory impairment. Mrs. A. and Mrs. B. were diagnosed as hearing impaired, and Mrs. B. and Mrs. C. had cataracts. Mrs. B. and Mrs. C. were responsive to verbal stimuli, could communicate, and were able to follow directions. Mrs. A. was generally uncommunicative and was responsive only to simple requests and directions.

Study Design. This program was conducted in two parts. Part 1 was conducted during the luncheon meal from day 1 to day 100. Part 2, conducted during dinner, was run concurrently with part 1 from day 51 to day 75. A multiple-baseline-across-subjects design was used for each part. With this design, current rates of the target behaviors are recorded for all subjects prior to the beginning of intervention, and intervention is introduced on different days for each client. The effectiveness of the intervention is supported when behavioral changes occur concurrently with the introduction of the procedure.

Observation and Reliability. Independent observers recorded data in five-second intervals. Data were recorded for each client for three continuous intervals (fifteen seconds) of each minute. No observations were made during the final fifteen seconds of each minute. The order in which clients were observed changed daily.

Client behaviors were recorded using a three-category behavioral code:

1. *Appropriate self-feeding.* Holding an eating utensil by the handle; moving food in a utensil held by the handle; using hands to eat food items normally eaten with hands, such as bread or cookies.
2. *Inappropriate self-feeding.* Holding wrong end of utensil; attempting to eat with the wrong end of the utensil; eating food items normally eaten with a fork or spoon with hands only, or otherwise without the use of appropriate utensils; having hands in contact with food normally eaten with a utensil. Exclusions: using fingers as a "prop" against which food was pushed to load utensil; using hands to return food to plate.
3. *Other mealtime behaviors.* This category was recorded during any interval during which neither appropriate nor inappropriate mealtime behavior occurred. Examples were drinking, using napkin, and chewing food.

In all cases when appropriate and inappropriate self-feeding behaviors were observed as occurring at the same time (for example, when a client was holding a utensil properly in one hand but attempting to deliver food to her mouth with the other), the behavior was recorded as inappropriate.

The mealtime interventions of staff members, visitors, trainers, and other nonresidents were monitored using a three-category code:

1. *Intervention other than interruptions.* Prompt or request to perform any step of the eating process; complete feeding of client; providing physical assistance for performance of any step of the eating process. Exclusions: cutting, mixing, or arranging food; arranging plates or containers; pouring liquids. Examples: Saying "Why don't you eat some of this?"; handing subject a utensil; feeding subject.
2. *Interruption.* Use of the complete interruption procedure as described below. Although the interruption procedure included some of the behaviors described above, the first category was not recorded when interruption was recorded.

3. *No staff intervention.* This category was used for any interval in which neither category of staff intervention occurred.

Interrater reliability was assessed for all behavioral categories at least once during each study condition. Occurrence reliability was calculated separately for each category (see Chapter
Four for formula). Average occurrence reliabilities were appropriate self-feeding, 91 percent; inappropriate self-feeding, 88
percent; interruption procedure, 84 percent; and other staff interventions, 82 percent.

Part 1—Training and Maintenance During Lunch

Baseline 1. During baseline 1, all categories of data were
recorded but no systematic treatment was instituted. In this
condition, and in all others, a worker prepared each resident's
tray before each meal so that the resident would not have to
open tight containers or use a knife. Food preparation included
cutting long vegetables and other items that could not be easily
handled with a fork or spoon; buttering and slicing bread; and
opening milk cartons, juice containers, and ice cream containers.

Training 1. The training procedure was an adaptation of
the guided-trial training procedure. The process of appropriate
self-feeding was broken into seven steps: grasping a utensil by
the handle, moving the utensil to plate or dish, loading food on
the utensil, moving the utensil approximately halfway to the
mouth (throat level), moving the utensil to the mouth, opening
the mouth, and inserting the utensil into the mouth. An occurrence of independent appropriate self-feeding was defined as the
unassisted completion of all seven steps.

On the first day of training, the worker placed a spoon in
the resident's hand and then instructed her to use her spoon.
The worker then manually guided the resident through the
seven-step process and praised her upon successful completion.
If, within ten seconds of the successful trial, the client began
eating appropriately, the worker let her complete the trial independently and praised her. However, if a client did not begin a
new trial independently within ten seconds, the worker began a
new guided trial. Furthermore, when the resident engaged in in-

appropriate self-feeding, the worker interrupted and began a guided trial. The interruption procedure consisted of taking the client's hand, returning the food to the plate, cleaning the client's hands, handing her a utensil, and instructing her to use a utensil. After three successful guided trials, regardless of the number of intervening unassisted trials or inappropriate self-feeding responses, the worker guided the client through one step less than the previous trial, instructed her to complete the trial, and praised her for successful completion. This was the first step in the fading of guided trials. Fading was completed when the client was able to take the utensil in hand from the worker and use it for independent eating.

Maintenance 1. When training was completed, the worker and staff continued to use the final step of the training procedure (instructing the client to use a utensil) and interruption as the maintenance procedure. During this condition, food items were prepared and the meal was presented as during the training procedure. Then, the client was handed a utensil and instructed to use the utensil to eat. The client was praised after the first appropriate eating response. If the client attempted to use her hands to eat, however, the staff used the interruption procedure, and the client received approval only after the first successful occurrence of appropriate self-feeding. The interruption was used throughout the meal whenever a client attempted to use her hands for eating. After maintenance 1 was established on day 43, guided trials were no longer used for any clients.

Baseline 2. Workers and staff continued the maintenance 1 condition until day 75. Then, use of the maintenance condition and data collection were discontinued for two weeks. After two weeks, baseline data were again collected for each client. Workers offered assistance during baseline 2 in the same manner as during baseline 1.

Maintenance 2. Following the collection of baseline 2 data, the maintenance condition for each client was reinstated.

Part 2—Maintenance During Dinner

Baseline. On day 51, observers began collecting baseline data for each client during dinner. Although the maintenance procedure was being continued during lunch, no systematic intervention was introduced at dinner during baseline.

Maintenance. Following the collection of baseline data, the maintenance procedure was introduced at the evening meal.

Results

Each client decreased the incidence of inappropriate self-feeding during part 1 almost immediately following the introduction of training. These data further suggest that the maintenance procedure was effective for sustaining behavior change. Data are summarized in Figure 1. During baseline 1, Mrs. A.,

Figure 1. Average Daily Rates of Appropriate Eating as a Percentage of Total Intervals of Eating Recorded During Part 1.

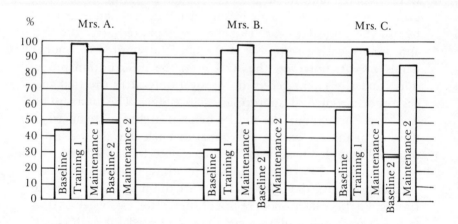

Mrs. B., and Mrs. C. exhibited appropriate self-feeding behavior during the times they were observed eating only 42 percent, 30 percent, and 58 percent of the time, respectively. When training was instituted, however, their rates of appropriate eating rose to approximately 97 percent for each client. When training was completed and the maintenance 1 condition was implemented, rates of appropriate self-feeding remained at high rates: 96 percent, 98 percent, and 91 percent, respectively.

After the maintenance procedure has been discontinued, the average rates of appropriate eating during baseline 2 fell to rates similar to those of baseline 1. When workers and staff reinstated the maintenance procedure, average rates of appropriate self-feeding again rose substantially over baseline rates.

Data from part 2 are summarized in Figure 2. Clients ex-

Figure 2. Average Daily Rates of Appropriate Eating Recorded During Part 2.

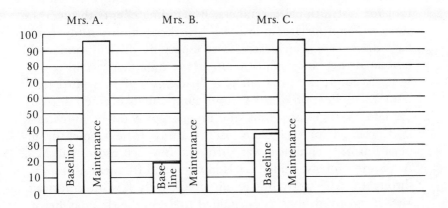

hibited low rates of appropriate self-feeding during baseline, even though high rates were being maintained during the same period at lunch. These results suggest that no transfer of training occurred between lunch and dinner. However, when the maintenance intervention was used, average rates of appropriate self-feeding rose to over 90 percent for all clients.

Discussion

Results of this evaluation supported the conclusion that operant procedures were effective for reestablishing and maintaining high rates of appropriate use among three elderly impaired clients. More specifically, these results suggest that: (1) Specially designed training procedures can be effective for reestablishing personal care behaviors which once were, but are no longer, part of the client's usual pattern of behavior; and (2) that maintenance procedures which are designed to become part of the usual institutional care-taking routine may be necessary to sustain desired behaviors for long periods. It is encouraging to see that maintenance procedures may also be effective for extending the transfer of training to other situations in which the behavior is desired.

Training-maintenance programs have at least three particular advantages for work with the institutionalized elderly. First, the training procedure is a relatively simple assessment tool for institutional caretakers. By guiding clients through the steps of appropriate utensil use, workers in this study could have discovered which steps were especially difficult and could have made necessary adjustments in the training procedure.

Second, the program is a "package" of individual techniques. Application of the various components is determined by the client's responses; thus, the program provides an individualized program for each client. In this study, for example, the application of techniques was different for each individual. Mrs. A. required many guided trials initially and frequent prompting throughout the study but required relatively few interruptions. Mrs. B. received only a few guided trials on the first day before her rate of appropriate self-feeding could be maintained with only occasional prompting and infrequent interruption. Mrs. C. also needed few guided trials and only occasional prompts; however, frequent interruptions were necessary to maintain her high rate of utensil use.

Third, the techniques and method of this study form an intervention model that may be particularly useful in institutional settings. A relatively complicated training procedure was initially used to establish high rates of desired behavior. With this model, initial training takes place under the supervision of a worker with the time and skills to provide intensive, complex training. These procedures, however, are designed to maintain high rates of behaviors with less complicated and demanding procedures. Once the desired behaviors are brought under the control of less complicated procedures that fit into the existing pattern of staff activity, other caretakers can be trained to use these maintenance procedures to sustain desired behavioral changes.

One of the most important goals of social work in institutions for the elderly is to assist residents in using institutional and personal resources to maintain an optimum level of functioning (Brody, 1979; Linsk, Howe, and Pinkston, 1975). Maintaining optimum functioning includes not only restoration but forestalling of deterioration. Sperbeck and Whitbourne (1981) suggested that behavioral deficits among the institutionalized elderly may be partially caused by inaccurate assessment (often based on pessimistic assumptions) of the ability of impaired older people to perform self-care behaviors. For example, most people use utensils appropriately at meals without special prompts or external monitoring. When impaired older people no longer use utensils appropriately under "normal" conditions (that is, without special cueing), it is often assumed that they are no longer able to perform the behavior. This study and others indicate that assumptions such as these should be questioned.

Institutions for the impaired elderly should become "prosthetic environments" that are designed to support and maintain the abilities of the residents (Butler and Lewis, 1977; Lindsley, 1964; McClannahan and Risley, 1974). In the prosthetic environment, assessment procedures will be used to determine *under what conditions* behavior can be reestablished, rather than simply *whether* behavior can be reestablished. It is likely that a well-constructed prosthetic environment will extensively use maintenance procedures.

A Single-Parent Intervention
to Increase Parenting Skills over Time

Matsujiro Shibano, Wendell H. Cox,
Tina L. Rzepnicki, Elsie M. Pinkston

The Single Parent Project (SPP) was launched to investigate and develop a short-term educational program for the amelioration of interaction problems of single parents and their children by teaching the parents child management skills. The intervention procedures were deduced from social work intervention models, concepts developed for parent-child problems (Keith, 1978; Larson and Gilbertson, 1977; Simon, 1976), and the parent training models presented and tested in the field of applied behavior analysis (Bernal, 1969, 1971; Berkowitz and Graziano, 1972; O'Dell, 1974; Patterson and others, 1975; Pinkston, Friedman, and Polster, 1981).

The program, presented here, is a part of the SPP project and adds a new dimension through the development of procedures to facilitate maintenance (or temporal generality) of acquired child management skills after the program is terminated. The total efficacy of an intervention program cannot be truly evaluated without assessing durability of intervention gains beyond the termination of the intervention (Forehand and Atkenson, 1977; Johnson and Katz, 1973; Keeley, Shemberg, and Carbonell, 1976; Stokes and Baer, 1977). It has also been recognized, implicitly and explicitly, that maintenance or temporal generality does not always occur naturally and that it is likely to occur more frequently if planned. Thus, developing and evaluating a specific training package directed toward the maintenance of parents' child management skills are important. The basic research questions in this evaluation are: (1) Does the program presented here contribute to helping single parents acquire effective child management procedures and maintain the acquired procedures beyond the termination of the program? (2) Does the program give practitioners detailed guidelines to follow?

It has been demonstrated that self-management is powerful when it is combined with other procedures, such as self-monitoring, self-evaluation, external feedback, and external reinforcement (Kanfer, 1975; Sasaki and Fukushima, 1979). In this program, therefore, generality procedures are introduced after self-monitoring, self-evaluation, and external control (worker control) have been established.

This program includes four discrete phases; each phase includes one to five guided steps. The phases are linearly arranged so that the research control can be attained optimally. Each step within phases contains some options for the worker to choose, allowing the worker to respond sensitively to the individual client's behavior change to secure the maximum program effects. Each step has a specific guideline in the form of the checklist for worker activities, including options, which may permit the worker to go back to the earlier steps, if necessary. This allows flexibility so that when the course of the training necessitates modifying intervention plans after the behavioral training phase (phase 2) has started, the worker and the parent may change intervention techniques insofar as the target behaviors remain the same. The program and its options are best presented in flowchart form (Figure 1). The duration of the program, excluding follow-up observations, is approximately eight to eleven weeks.

Through these three phases, the parent training and maintenance program concentrates on: (1) teaching parents effective child management procedures, (2) ameliorating disturbing parent-child interactions by the use of the procedures, and (3) facilitating maintenance of the acquired procedures after the program terminates.

The first two phases of the program are based on parent training procedures established by Pinkston and her colleagues in the Single Parent Project (SPP) of the University of Chicago, School of Social Service Administration.

Three additional phases are designed to facilitate and

424

Figure 1. Flowchart for Parent Training Program.

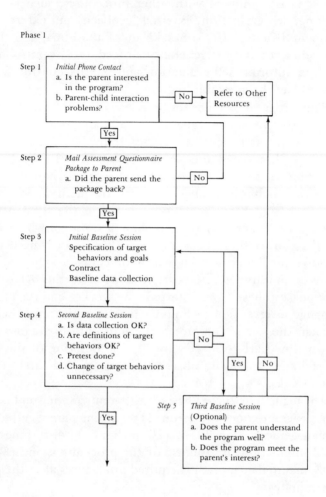

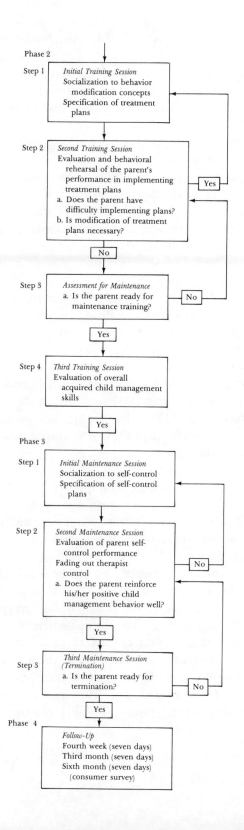

Phase 2

Step 1 | *Initial Training Session*
Socialization to behavior
   modification concepts
Specification of treatment
   plans

Step 2 | *Second Training Session*
Evaluation and behavioral
   rehearsal of the parent's
   performance in implementing
   treatment plans
a. Does the parent have
   difficulty implementing plans?
b. Is modification of treatment
   plans necessary?

Yes

No

Step 3 | *Assessment for Maintenance*
a. Is the parent ready for
   maintenance training?

No

Yes

Step 4 | *Third Training Session*
Evaluation of overall
   acquired child management
   skills

Yes

Phase 3

Step 1 | *Initial Maintenance Session*
Socialization to self-control
Specification of self-control
   plans

Step 2 | *Second Maintenance Session*
Evaluation of parent self-
   control performance
Fading out therapist
   control
a. Does the parent reinforce
   his/her positive child
   management behavior well?

No

Yes

Step 3 | *Third Maintenance Session*
(Termination)
a. Is the parent ready for
   termination?

No

Yes

Phase 4

Follow-Up
Fourth week (seven days)
Third month (seven days)
Sixth month (seven days)
   (consumer survey)

evaluate maintenance of the parent's acquired child management knowledge and skills beyond the termination of the program. In the course of these three phases, the worker's influence
is faded as the parent self-control increases.

Although specific child management procedures taught in
this program vary from family to family, depending upon the
problems they are facing, they include the following three procedures that have been deduced from the operant paradigm
(Skinner, 1938 and 1957) and applied to parent-child interaction problems: (1) differential attention (combination of positive reinforcement and extinction procedures), (2) mild punishment (time-out and response-cost procedures), and (3) contingency contracting and point systems.

Theoretical concepts behind the procedures are explained
didactically to the parents to facilitate their verbal understanding of the application of the procedures. Instructional materials,
deduced from relevant research studies, are used to supplement
the therapist in-session instructions. Parents also learn the application of the procedures by working on their child's problems
under the worker's supervision. The worker's activities involved
in this supervision are (1) feedback regarding procedure implementation, (2) modeling, (3) behavior rehearsal, and (4) positive
reinforcement (praise).

A Case Example

Clients. Mrs. H. was a thirty-four-year-old woman who
had been divorced for two years. She had difficulty managing
her eight-year-old son's, Sam's, home behavior. Her major concern was that Sam and his younger brother, Mark, six years old,
did not get along with each other. They tended to argue over
toys, TV, and so forth, which culminated in physical fighting
that disrupted the ongoing relationships of the family. Mrs. H's
other concern was that Sam tended to either forget his home
chores or came up with excuses to avoid them. She wanted to
have control over his compliance with household chores.

Setting and Worker Roles. The training program took
place within the clients' house. Throughout the training and

maintenance preparation phases, the worker's role was twofold: First, it was a consultant/educator role (Fischer, 1978) in that she did not engage directly in changing the identified behaviors of the child. The mother was the mediator in this case and actually implemented behavior change procedures. Second, the worker's role was also as a clinical/behavior change agent in that she directly engaged in altering the mother's child management behavior. In the parent training program, the mother's behavior can often be considered the target of the intervention.

Responses and Goals. Based on the assessment questionnaires and the initial interview, the mother and the worker agreed to work on Sam's problems as follows: (1) reduce the frequency of fighting, (2) increase cooperative play, (3) increase the number of chores completed, and (4) develop the mother's acquisition of appropriate child management skills (techniques) to attain the changes in her child's behaviors.

Three specific techniques appropriate for altering the child's targeted behaviors were selected: (1) differential attention to decrease fighting and to increase cooperative play, (2) time-out to decrease fighting, and (3) contingency contracting combined with a point system to increase completion of chores.

The defined behaviors include both the child's and the mother's behaviors.

1. *Mother behavior*

   Positive attention: Positive attention includes verbal praise and physical affection for your child's targeted positive behavior (cooperative play and completion of chores), for example, "Good job!" after child does household tasks. "I like the way you play together." All occasions when you use the words "super," "terrific," "cool," "great," "nice," "interesting," "fascinating" or other superlatives to describe your child's behavior are types of positive verbal attention. Hugs, kisses, pats on the head, and tickles are examples of positive physical attention.

   Negative attention: Negative attention includes verbal and physical behavior directed toward your child to stop the child's targeted negative behavior (fights, including threats):

"Stop that right now!"; "Cut it out!"; "Better stop that, or I'll spank you"; slapping, hitting, spanking, kicking, pinching, and using belt, paddle, or other object to punish child are examples of negative attention.

2. *Child behavior*

Cooperative play: Child plays nicely with his brother, which includes playing together and watching TV, and talking together without negative verbal exchange such as teasing and physical fight.

Fighting with brother: includes teasing, name-calling, yelling, and physical contact such as punching, kicking, and taking brother's property.

Chores: take out garbage, brush teeth two times per day, feed pets, take dog out, comb hair, and pick up clothes around house.

The reliability of the mother's observations was examined at least once during each experimental condition by comparing the records of a trained observer and the mother and calculating their agreement. Reliability was formulated by using occurrence agreement (see Chapter Four for formula and procedures). The average occurrence reliability for the following behaviors was cooperative play, 98 percent; fighting, 100 percent; parental positive attention, 96 percent, parental negative attention, 100 percent. These percentages were based on eight observations, and no percentage was below 80 percent.

Throughout the phases of the program, the parent was instructed in the specific skills to modify the defined behaviors and general knowledge of behavioral techniques relevant to child management. This acquisition was evaluated by a set of multiple-choice questions administered by the worker before and after the program.

Results

Child Behavior. During the baseline period, the daily frequency of Sam's fighting was 3; his fighting occurred three times a day on the average in the baseline. It went down to 1.5 times in the training phase. It was further reduced to .5 times in the maintenance preparation phase, as noted in Figure 2. The reduction was large enough for the worker and the parent to agree that the first goal of the program had been attained.

On the other hand, the frequency of the child's cooperative play was somewhat puzzling. Although it went up to 3.9 times a day in the training period from 2.9 times of the baseline, it went down to 1.7 times a day on the average in the maintenance preparation period (Figure 2). Interestingly, the total frequency of fighting and cooperative play went down quite a bit in the maintenance preparation period (2.2) compared with those of the previous phases (5.8 and 5.4). When the ratio of fighting to cooperative play was calculated, a clear reduction was detected. For example, it went down from 1.07 in the baseline to .38 in the training period and .29 in the maintenance preparation period (Figure 2).

In chore completion, there was a dramatic change from the baseline to the first and second phases of the program (Figure 2). During the baseline, the child completed 2.2 chores a day on the average. In the training and maintenance preparation periods, he completed more than 5 chores a day. The third goal of the program was attained.

Parent Behavior. The daily frequencies of parental positive and negative attentions to the child's behaviors changed in the expected direction through the training and maintenance preparation periods. The frequency of the mother's negative attention to fighting decreased from 1.7 times in the baseline to .2 in the training period. In the maintenance preparation period, the mother completely ignored the child's negative behavior. Her positive attention to cooperative play jumped up to 2.2 times a day in the training period, from .97 times a day in the baseline. The frequency of the positive attention in the maintenance preparation period was slightly lower than that in the training period. The ratio of the positive attention to the positive child behavior jumped up to 88 percent in the maintenance preparation period. Although the mother paid positive attention to the child's cooperative play only 25 percent of the time in the baseline, she paid positive attention to 56 percent and 88 percent of the positive behavior during the later phases.

As for time-out, the parent used it for 26 percent of the

Figure 2. Mean Parent and Child Behaviors.

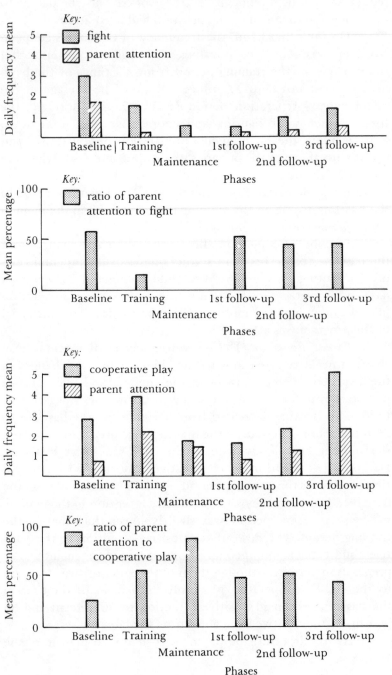

negative behavior in the training period. In the maintenance preparation period, 60 percent of the negative behavior was followed by time-out. The parent attained the fourth goal of the program.

Follow-Up for Child and Parent. Although the first follow-up was conducted on schedule, the second and third follow-ups were delayed because the child was away during the scheduled periods. The second follow-up took place five months after the program had been completed. The third follow-up was completed almost a year after the termination of the program. The numbers of observation days for the first, second, and third follow-ups were five, nine, and five, respectively.

The child's frequency of fighting remained low through all three follow-up periods (Figure 2). Although there seemed to be a tendency to increase, its frequency in the third follow-up (1.4) was about the same as in the training period (1.5.). Again, the cooperative play looks somewhat puzzling. During the first and second follow-up periods, its frequency stayed low (1.6 and 2.4, respectively), but it jumped up to 5.2 times a day in the last follow-up. In the third period, the total frequency of the negative and positive behaviors increased to a great degree. The ratio of the negative behavior to the positive behavior, however, stayed about the same throughout three follow-up phases.

The numbers of completed chores remained the same in the first, second, and third follow-up periods. They were 5.0, 4.6, and 5.2, respectively, and were well above that in the baseline period.

The frequency of the mother's negative attention to the child's fighting gradually increased in the follow-up phase. The ratio of the parent's negative attention to fighting returned close to the baseline level. She paid negative attention to 56 percent of the child's negative behavior in the baseline. In the first, second, and third follow-up periods, the ratios were 50 percent, 44 percent and 43 percent, respectively. The calculation of the ratio of the negative attention to the positive attention, however, shows that the percentage of the negative attention remained very low in all three follow-up periods. Although 71 percent of the mother's attention was negative in the base-

line, only about 20 percent of her attention was negative in the
follow-up phase (Figure 2).

The ratio of the parent's positive attention to cooperative
play maintained the level of the training period (50 percent)
throughout the follow-up phase. It never attained the high level
of the maintenance preparation period. Time-out, in the first
follow-up period, was not used. It may be that very few negative behaviors occurred during this period (.4 times a day). In
the second and third follow-up periods, the record showed that
the mother continued to use time-out only occasionally.

Discussion

Through the training phase (phase 2) and the maintenance preparation phase (phase 3), the change in the parent's
and the child's targeted behaviors took place in an expected direction, except for the frequency of cooperative play. Sam's
fighting, which occurred three times a day, occurred only once
every other day in the maintenance preparation phase. The
mother either ignored or used time-out with his fighting. No
negative attention given to the fighting was observed in the
maintenance preparation period. Five to six out of six chores
were completed regularly during the training and maintenance
preparation phases. During phase 1 (baseline) the average number of completed chores was about two.

Although the frequency of Sam's cooperative play increased in phase 2, it dropped quite a bit in phase 3 despite the
fact that the ratio of the parent's positive attention to the cooperative play increased dramatically. As mentioned earlier, the
total frequency of fighting and cooperative play also dropped
largely in this phase. Because the frequency might be somewhat
misleading due to a reduction in the total behavior, the ratios
of fighting to cooperative play and cooperative play to fighting
were calculated; the latter increased to a large extent in the
training and maintenance preparation phases as the former decreased. Why the total frequency decreased in phase 3, however, is not clear. It might be that their opportunity to be together at home may have decreased because summer had started.

Interestingly, there seems to be considerable change in the parent's behaviors from the training period to the maintenance preparation period. In the maintenance preparation phase, she paid positive attention to the cooperative play more consistently than in the previous phase. During this phase, she successfully managed to refrain from paying any negative attention. She also used time-out with fighting more often in this phase than in the training period. Although it is not feasible to isolate the effect of the maintenance preparation phase because of the nature of the design (ABC), this may suggest that phase 3, where self-control techniques were transmitted to the parent, may have further facilitated the parent's acquisition of child management skills more consistently. As for the general knowledge on behavioral techniques relevant to child management, her score in the multiple-choice test increased by 27 percent from the baseline to the postprogram evaluation.

In the follow-up phase, the frequencies of the child's fighting and daily chores remained about the same as in the training phase (phase 2). Although the child's positive behavior (cooperative play) stayed low regarding daily frequency in the first and second follow-up periods, its ratio to fighting remained above the level of the training phase.

The parent's behavioral ratio also maintained the level of the training phase, with the exception of her negative attention. In the follow-up phase, the ratio of the mother's positive attention to cooperative play remained about the same as in the training phase, although it showed a slight sign of decrease, which may not be quite surprising because it is understandable and desirable that the reinforcement schedule becomes more sparse in the maintenance period. The parent continued to use time-out with fighting 33 percent and 14 percent of the time in the second and third follow-up periods, respectively, although she did not use the procedure in the first follow-up period. As for her negative attention to fighting, the ratio returned to near baseline levels. Because the focus in parent training studies is often on changes in child behavior in training and follow-up, observational data of changes in parent behavior, especially during follow-up, have been rarely reported. However, Cox (1982) found that in the follow-up phase, the parental negative attention tended to go back to the baseline level in several cases. The ratio of parent negative attention to total negative and positive attention stayed fairly low in the follow-up phase compared with that in the baseline period, resulting in less negative attention in the follow-up periods.

In summary, this program resulted in many expected positive changes in both the child's targeted behaviors and the parent's responses, and they were maintained through the follow-up phase. The daily frequencies of the child's positive behavior (cooperative play) and parent's negative attention to fighting were exceptions. Although there were no positive changes in those behaviors as to frequency, they improved relative to the total negative and positive behavior, as the ratio data show. In other words, the interactions between the mother and child became much less negative in the training and maintenance preparation phases, and they were maintained in the follow-up phase.

The results from this case study alone cannot answer all the research questions presented earlier in this evaluation. Analysis of the results from the systematic replication of the program should answer those questions.

A Creativity Enhancement Program for Preschool Children in an Inner City Child-Parent Center

Theodore W. Lane, Miriam Z. Lane, Benjamin S. Friedman, Elizabeth M. Goetz, Elsie M. Pinkston

There has been an increasing interest in the training of creativity as an operant response. Researchers have trained preschool children in a university laboratory setting to be diverse in their blockbuilding, easel painting, Lego building, felt-pen drawing, improvisation, and dancing (Elliot and Goetz, 1971; Fallon and Goetz, 1975; Figgs, Dunn, and Herbert, 1971; Goetz and Baer, 1971, 1973; Goetz, Jones, and Weamer, 1973; Goetz and Salmonson, 1972; Goetz, 1977; Holman, Goetz, and Baer, 1976; Parsonson and Baer, 1978; Reese and LeBlanc, 1970). These studies, using single-case designs, investigated the effects of various training procedures (for example, verbal reinforcement and instructions) on creativity while the children were participating in specific activities.

In general, evidence indicates that reinforcement training produces reliable increases in response *diversity,* when applied directly, in each of the above activities. *New responses* also appear at higher rates during the reinforcement of response diversity. However, generality of novel responses to previously untrained tasks is limited and variable. Maintenance of experimental effects over time has been assessed in only two studies (Fallon and Goetz, 1975; Holman, Goetz, and Baer, 1976).

The primary purpose of this research was to assess whether the results of these studies could be used to increase new creative responses and diversity of those responses in an inner city public school consisting exclusively of black students from low-income families. The social worker had noted a low level of diversity of forms when children were drawing in the classroom and suggested a reinforcement program to increase the children's creative repertoire.

Generality of creative behavior across settings, which has not been investigated before, was measured in both a trained activity (felt-pen drawing) and in an untrained activity (collage construction). In addition, the performance of students trained by one investigator were compared with students trained by two investigators in an attempt to assess whether the added researcher would enhance generality effects into the classroom and across tasks. Finally, a larger number of subjects participated in the present study than in previous studies. The research was evaluated by using a combination of group comparison and multiple-baseline designs.

Method

Students. Eighteen subjects were selected from the four classrooms of three- and four-year-old students at an urban child-parent center. These students were black male (eleven) and female (seven) children from low-income families living in a public housing project. Fifty-three students were pretested on the felt-pen drawing activity. The eighteen students with the lowest form-diversity scores were paired based on the scores and randomly assigned to either the experimental or practice control group. Mean pretest form-diversity scores were 4.0 for the experimental group and 4.1 for the practice control group; the average age of subjects in each group was 4.4 years and 4.3 years, respectively.

Setting. The study was conducted within a child-parent center, a public school facility for low-income children and their parents. In contrast to the low student-teacher ratios of previous studies, staff for classrooms of fifteen to twenty students consisted of one teacher and an aide. Students attended the center for two and a half hours per day, five days a week, while parents attended the center for a minimum of two hours per week.

On Monday and Wednesday mornings, children in the experimental group were invited individually to a room within the child-parent center for experimental sessions lasting approximately ten minutes each. During these sessions, the children participated in the felt-pen drawing activity. Each session terminated after ten minutes of drawing, unless the child indicated that the task was completed before the time had elapsed. Children in the practice control group also engaged in felt-pen drawing on Monday and Wednesday mornings for an identical period of time. However, control children worked on the task within their respective classrooms. On Tuesday mornings, all eighteen children engaged in felt-pen drawing within their classrooms and, on Thursday mornings, all children engaged in collage construction.

Materials. Materials for the felt-pen activity included a sheet of white paper (twenty-nine by thirty-five centimeters) and three watercolor felt-tipped markers in red, blue, and green.

Collage materials included a sheet of white paper (twenty-nine by thirty-five centimeters), an envelope of red, blue, and green forms, and a cup of paste or glue. Each envelope contained six different shapes, including squares (2½ centimeters), right triangles (4½ centimeters), rectangles (2½ by 7½ centimeters), parallelograms (2½ by 10 centimeters), circles (4½ centimeters), and semicircles. For each collage session, the students received two of each shape per color, for a total of thirty-six pieces.

Behavior Definitions and Recording

Dependent Variables. A major outcome of the study was measured by changes in the form content of the children's felt-pen drawings and collage constructions. The form content of these activities was scored according to a set of defined forms appropriate to each activity. The definitions of forms for felt-pen drawings were modified from those developed previously by Holman, Goetz, and Baer (1976). The collage code was developed from the blockbuilding code established by Goetz and Baer (1973). (Copies of the codes can be obtained from E. M.

Pinkston, The University of Chicago, 969 E. 60th, Chicago IL 60637.)

Form-diversity scores, defined as the number of the twenty-five or twenty-two forms appearing at least once in any drawing or construction session, were the primary measure of change (Goetz and Baer, 1973). In addition, a new-forms score was defined as the number of these forms appearing in a drawing or construction session that had not appeared in any prior drawing or construction by a child. The number of forms appearing in the pretest was taken as the child's baseline of forms for felt-pen drawing. The new-forms measure was not scored for the child's first collage construction because all forms appearing in that session would have to be considered new. Thus, the number of forms appearing in the first collage construction was taken as the child's baseline of forms for that activity. New collage forms included all new forms appearing during and after the first baseline session (Goetz and Baer, 1973).

Independent Variables. Reinforcement training was a combination of token reinforcement and descriptive social reinforcement contingent on form diversity per product. During both experimental and baseline sessions, four experimenter behavioral categories—general praise, praise of form diversity, form-diversity prompts, and other adult attention—were recorded by an independent observer (silently watching from a few feet away) for each ten-second observation interval. In addition, the experimenter and observer each recorded the names of the specific forms reinforced during the reinforcement of form-diversity condition.

Experimenter Behavior

General praise. A word or statement that expresses general approval or admiration of the student, student's work, or the material (no reference to forms).

Praise of form diversity. A combination of praise and a simple verbal description of the form contingent on the first appearance of that form within that session (for example, "Oh, that's nice, that curved line is different!").

Form-diversity prompt. Any experimenter response that instructs the subject to draw a different form (for example, "Can you draw something different?").

Other adult attention. Any verbal response emitted by the experimenter that is directed toward the subject but not included in the previous definitions (for example, "Are you finished?").

Reliability. Throughout the duration of the study, a judge naive to experimental designs and conditions scored all the permanent product drawings and constructions, counting the number of forms appearing at least once in each session's drawing or collage. New-forms scores were also derived from these counts, comparing the identities of the forms found in a given drawing or collage to those found in all previous drawings or collages. On days unknown to the primary judge, an independent observer also scored the drawings and constructions.

Occurrence reliability was recorded for dependent and independent variables at least once for each subject in each experimental condition. Reliability was calculated by dividing the number of agreements by the number of agreements plus disagreements and multiplying by 100 percent. Mean occurrence reliability for felt-pen drawings was 76 percent, ranging by session from 66 to 84 percent. For collage construction, mean occurrence reliability was 87 percent, ranging by session from 83 to 93 percent.

To record reliability for experimenter behavior, experimental sessions were tape-recorded and scored by an independent observer for comparison to the vivo observer's data. Occurrence reliability was recorded for the first three behaviors and for total intervals of experimenter attention. Mean occurrence reliability was 82 percent for general praise, 95 percent for form-diversity praise, 87 percent for form-diversity prompts, and 87 percent for total experimenter attention.

Reliability was also recorded for forms reinforced during experimental sessions by comparing the observer's records with the experimenter's. Mean occurrence reliability was 99 percent, ranging by session from 94 to 100 percent. In addition, forms praised by the experimenter during experimental sessions were compared to those scored from the permanent products. Mean occurrence reliability was 70 percent, ranging by session from 60 to 78 percent.

Design. A combination of control group and multiple-baseline designs was used to establish experimental control. The eighteen students scoring lowest on the pretest were matched in pairs based on form-diversity scores and randomly assigned to either the experimental or practice control group. Each group participated in approximately the same number of activities during the study, but only the experimental group received reinforcement training. In the analyses of group differences, *t* tests for paired data were computed.

Besides between-group comparisons, the students in the experimental group were matched in triads based on their pretest scores and randomly assigned to one of three experimental subgroups. Two experimental subgroups (A and B) received reinforcement training by a single (different) experimenter; the third experimental subgroup (C) received reinforcement training by both experimenters in alternating sessions. A multiple-baseline-across-subjects design was used within each experimental subgroup. When comparing experimental subgroups A and B to group C, it was possible to assess whether the added experimenter enhanced generality effects.

Procedures

Pretest. All the students were pretested within the classroom on felt-pen drawing. The classroom teachers distributed the materials and gave the children simple verbal instructions to draw whatever they wanted and to use three colors. As in all subsequent classroom sessions, students participated in the activity as a group, sitting at a small table(s) until they were finished or until ten minutes had elapsed.

Baseline. During this condition, students in the experimental group participated in two experimental sessions per week. Experimenter behavior consisted mainly of general praise, with no occurrences of form-diversity praise or prompts. The experimenter sat at the table beside the child and attempted to praise the child's work twice a minute. Table 1 presents mean

Table 1. Mean Percent Ten-Second Intervals of Experimenter Behavior.

	Subjects								
	Baseline								
Behavior	*1*	*2*	*3*	*4*	*5*	*6*	*7*	*8*	*9*
General praise	31	27	31	34	34	34	34	39	31
Total attention[a]	34	34	31	36	38	39	34	47	32
Behavior	*Reinforcement Training*								
General praise	10	11	9	12	15	12	14	11	10
Form-diversity praise[b]	19	17	22	22	16	19	14	16	20
Total praise	29	28	31	34	30	31	28	27	30
Form-diversity prompts	2	1	2	1	2	6	3	3	3
Total attention[c]	32	35	37	44	35	48	34	38	38

Note: Maximum number of ten-second intervals per session = 60.

[a]Total attention consists of general praise and other adult attention.

[b]A token was presented along with each occurrence of form-diversity praise.

[c]Total attention consists of general praise, form-diversity praise, form-diversity prompts, and other adult attention.

percent 10-second intervals of experimenter behavior. Following each session, children received a preselected snack.

Also, beginning with baseline and continuing throughout the remainder of the study, students in the experimental group participated in two generality sessions per week. On Tuesdays, these children engaged in felt-pen drawing within the classroom, and on Thursday they engaged in collage construction in the classroom. Generality sessions were administered by the teachers (experimenters were not present).

Children in the practice control group participated in three felt-pen sessions and one collage session per week, the same number of activities as the experimental children. These classroom sessions were also administered by the teachers.

Reinforcement of Form Diversity. After each child's form diversity had stabilized, training was begun in a multiple-baseline fashion for each experimental subgroup. In experimental sessions, children received a combination of descriptive social praise and tokens contingent on the first appearance of any form within the current session, but not for subsequent appearances of the same form within the session. Descriptive social praise was defined as a combination of praise and a simple verbal description of the form. In addition to descriptive social praise, each subject was required to earn a predetermined number of tokens to receive the preselected snack. The daily criterion was derived from each child's current form-diversity score (Holman, Goetz, and Baer, 1976). Thus, for the initial session, the mean of the baseline form-diversity score was used. Subsequently, the criterion was raised daily by adding one new form to the previous day's form-diversity score until the baseline was doubled. The doubled baseline-criterion score was raised by one new form only after a child had achieved it on two successive days. The daily criterion was never set below the subject's mean baseline score.

During training sessions, a token card was placed on the table beside the child and a cup of tokens was placed in front of the experimenter. The token card included an adjustable arrow to indicate the daily criterion level. The following instructions were given to each child:

> Today, Mary, we're going to try something new. First I want you to pick the snack that you would like to earn. Fine! Now, to earn your snack, you have to earn this many tokens (experimenter points to arrow). The way you earn a token is by drawing different things. Each time you draw something different, I will give you a token." The experimenter demonstrated with his/her finger, describing the form made, and supplying a token, for example, "See, if you drew a straight line up and down (demonstrated with finger) that would be

something *different* (token given); and if you drew
a curvy line (demonstrated), that would be another
different thing. Now to earn your snack, you have
to work hard and earn this many tokens (experimenter points to arrow). Remember, you earn a
token each time you draw something different.
You can start when you are ready.

Experimenter behavior during this condition consisted mainly
of general praise, form-diversity praise, and form-diversity
prompts. The experimenters attempted to keep total praise and
total experimenter attention equal to baseline levels (see Table
1).

Results

Form Diversity. Figure 1 shows felt-pen diversity scores
for each child in the experimental and control groups, respectively. It appears that training resulted in enhanced form-diversity scores for experimental children. Mean form-diversity scores
during baseline and reinforcement training, respectively, were
5.7 and 8.7 for the experimental group and 6.5 and 6.1 for the
control group. Mean form-diversity scores for each child, by
condition, are in Table 2.

The t test for paired data indicated no significant differences between the two groups during baseline, t (6) = 1.3626,
$p < .30$. As predicted, however, experimental children showed
significantly greater improvement in form-diversity scores following reinforcement training than did control children, t (6) =
3.2804, $p < .01$. Because two control group children withdrew
from the center before the study was completed, two child pairs
were not included in the statistical analysis. An additional
analysis revealed that experimental children obtained significantly greater form-diversity scores during training than during
baseline, t (8) = 5.5769, $p < .001$. The analysis of variance indicated no significant differences between experimental groups A,
B, and C.

New Forms. Cumulative felt-pen new-forms scores for each

Figure 1. Felt-Pen Form-Diversity Scores of Experimental and Control
Subjects, by Condition, for Each Experimental and Generalization Session.
(Training consisted of descriptive social reinforcement and token
reinforcement for form diversity. Groups A and B received training by
single experimenters; group C received training by both experimenters.)

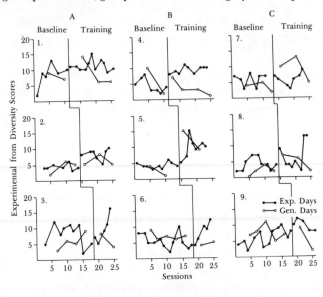

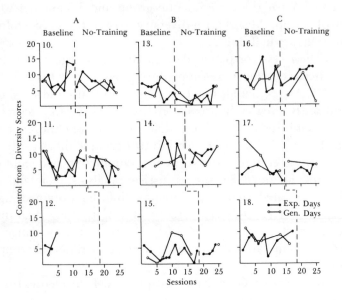

Table 2. Mean Form-Diversity Scores: Felt-Pen Drawing.

	Experimental Group				Control Group		
Subject	Pretest[a]	Baseline	Training	Subject	Pretest[a]	Baseline	No Training
A[b]:				A:			
1.	5	8.5 (8.0)	11.2 (8.7)	10.	5	9.0 (7.7)	7.4 (6.3)
2.	5	4.3 (4.3)	8.1 (6.0)	11.	5	6.1 (7.8)	5.2 (7.3)
3.	2	8.1 (5.8)	9.6 (6.0)	12.	3	—	—
B[b]				B:			
4.	1	4.6 (6.0)	9.3 (3.5)	13.	1	4.7 (5.3)	2.1 (3.7)
5.	6	4.2 (2.5)	9.7 (12.0)	14.	6	9.7 (7.3)	9.6 (9.7)
6.	5	5.4 (7.0)	8.2 (4.5)	15.	5	3.3 (4.3)	4.0 (6.0)
C[c]				C:			
7.	5	5.9 (3.7)	6.0 (9.3)	16.	5	8.4 (8.4)	9.7 (4.7)
8.	4	4.1 (2.0)	6.6 (5.0)	17.	3	3.7 (7.5)	4.4 (6.5)
9.	4	6.1 (7.6)	9.8 (5.5)	18.	4	6.9 (8.0)	—

Note: Numbers in parentheses indicate mean scores for generalization sessions. Maximum score = 25.
[a]Pretest condition consisted of only one session per subject.
[b]Reinforcement training administered by single experimenter.
[c]Reinforcement training administered by two experimenters.

child in the experimental and control groups are shown in parts 3 and 4 of Figure 2. The pretest felt-pen form-diversity scores were the baseline of new forms for each child. Each subsequent data point represents the cumulative number of new forms displayed by each child. The difference between points indicates the number of new forms displayed in that session. Because most children in each group emitted a greater number of new forms during baseline than during reinforcement training, the emergence of new forms was not restricted to periods in which different forms were being reinforced, as in previous studies. Of the nine experimental children, only one, child 5, displayed a pattern similar to previous findings, for example, a stable baseline followed by a sharp increase at the onset of intervention. Finally, the mean total number of new forms displayed by the experimental group (fourteen) was lower than the mean total number of new forms displayed by the control group (fifteen).

Generality. Generality-day felt-pen form-diversity scores for each child in the experimental and control groups, respectively, are shown in Figures 1 and 2. Generality of form diversity from experimental sessions to the classroom was clearly apparent only in child 5. Mean form-diversity scores during baseline and training, respectively, were 5.2 and 6.7 for the experimental group and 7.0 and 6.3 for the control group (see Table 2). The t test for paired data indicated no significant differences between the two groups during baseline, t (6) = 1.7399, $p < .20$. Additionally, no significant differences were found between the two groups regarding change in form-diversity scores following reinforcement training, t (6) = 1.6185, $p < .10$. No significant differences were found between experimental groups.

Cumulative new-forms scores from classroom sessions for each subject in the experimental and control groups, respectively, are shown in Figure 2. Increases in the emergence of new forms following baseline is apparent in children 1, 5, 7, and 9. However, the rate or number of new forms appearing per session was higher during baseline than during reinforcement of form diversity in the majority of children in each group (thirteen out of sixteen children). In comparison, the mean total number of new forms appearing in the experimental group (eleven) was

Figure 2. Felt-Pen Cumulative New-Forms Scores of Experimental and
Control Subject, by Condition, for Each Experimental and
Generalization Session. (Training consisted of descriptive social
reinforcement and token reinforcement for form diversity. Thus, any
changes noted in the emergence of new forms are collateral effects.
Groups A and B received training by single experimenters; group C
received training by both experimenters.)

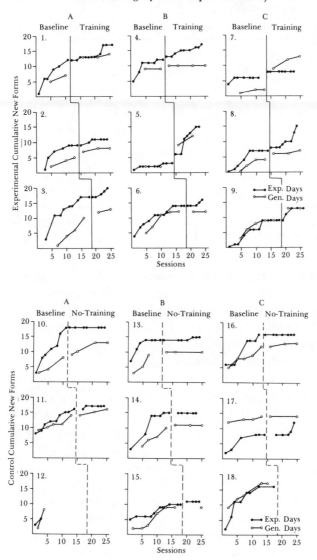

lower than the mean total number of new forms displayed by the control group (twelve).

Table 3 presents mean collage form-diversity scores for

Table 3. Mean Form-Diversity Scores: Collage Construction

| | Experimental Group | | | Control Group | |
Subject	Baseline	Training	Subject	Baseline	No Training
A:			A:		
1	1.0	0.5	10	1.5	2.8
2	2.5	1.3	11	3.0	2.7
3	3.5	1.5	12	—	—
B:			B:		
4	0.3	0.0	13	0.0	0.0
5	1.8	2.0	14	4.0	2.7
6	3.3	2.5	15	0.0	0.0
C:			C:		
7	3.0	3.0	16	3.0	3.0
8	1.0	0.0	17	0.0	0.0
9	0.4	0.0	18	2.3	—

Note: Reinforcement training was not given to either group in this activity. Maximum score = 22.

each child in the experimental and practice control groups. Although form-diversity scores were low during baseline, generality to this activity was clearly lacking.

Experimental Session Durations. Mean session duration for experimental children during baseline was 5.5 minutes (range = 1 minute to 10 minutes); mean session duration training was 8.2 minutes (range = 6 minutes to 10 minutes). Compared to baseline, mean session duration during training increased for five children (1, 2, 5, 6, and 8), decreased for one child (7), and remained the same for three children (3, 4, and 9).

Discussion

The increase in form-diversity scores by the preschoolers in this study suggests that it is possible to use the technology developed by Goetz, Baer, and their associates with university preschoolers (Goetz and Baer, 1973) to increase creativity with an inner city low-income population. Similar to previous findings, experimental children show increasing form diversity in their drawings subsequent to reinforcement training, including specific praise and tokens contingent upon diverse responding, whereas control children do not display similar increases. Thus, it appears that the analysis of creative behavior may have some practical applications within the general educational system.

Of particular interest, however, is the difference in the emergence of new forms with both the experimental and control population because emergence of new forms is not restricted to reinforcement periods. Baseline rates are higher than reinforcement rates in both groups. In addition, control children's rate of producing new forms during baseline is higher than experimental children's. One variable of possible importance in this regard is the novelty of the activity for these children and special attention paid to both groups for participation in the project by teachers, peers, and families. Also, it appears that the group sessions of the control children may play a part in their higher rate of producing new forms. Each child's drawings could serve as a model for the remaining children.

Generality across settings (experimental room and classroom) was investigated in the trained activity. This measure of generalization has not been evaluated in previous creativity studies. Generality was observed, to some extent, in four of nine experimental subjects regarding form-diversity scores. No differences, however, were noted between experimental and control children on these days. Control children had greater mean scores than experimental children in four out of seven cases. Thus, generality across settings in the trained activity was not evident in most cases.

When assessing generality to a different activity, a more stringent analysis was used than in previous studies. In this case, generality to the different activity was measured in a different setting, with the researchers absent. Neither the experimental setting nor the experimenters, then, could have served as discriminative stimuli for creative behaviors. Although previous studies have found limited generality across tasks (Holman,

Goetz, and Baer, 1976), the present study found none. This appears to support the hypothesis that previous findings have been largely the result of stimulus control (Goetz, 1977). Lack of generality of the trained activity across settings would further support this hypothesis.

Finally, in an attempt to program generality, two researchers were used to administer reinforcement training in one of the experimental groups (C). This group could then be compared to the other experimental groups that received training by single experimenters. Previous research indicated that this procedure tends to enhance generality (Corte, Wolf, and Lock, 1971; Stokes, Baer, and Jackson, 1974; Stokes and Baer, 1977), but no apparent differences between experimental groups were found in this regard.

When scoring children's finished products, reliability was substantially lower than that reported in previous studies (Goetz, 1977). A few variables in the present study appear to be related to this difference. First, the children were allowed to draw for up to ten minutes. Given the size of the paper, this tended to cause extensive overlapping of forms, making scoring less precise. Also, it was observed during experimental sessions that sometimes forms were completely covered over by subsequent drawing. This largely accounted for the low reliability found between the primary judge and the within-session observer. In addition, scoring during the session appeared to be influenced by the verbal performance of the experimenter and may have enhanced reliability. Furthermore, the previous studies were performed with the same population from whose drawings the codes were developed and also may have been influenced by the verbal performance of the experimenter.

Differences between the present and previous studies may be partly attributed to the differences in subject population. The children participating in the present study were not accustomed to token reinforcement systems. Possibly, they had not had much experience with preschool art, as is probably common for children attending a university laboratory setting. Therefore, their baseline "new-forms" behavior in art had not yet stabilized and their responses may have been reinforced by a novel experience. One informal observation was that the children were largely deficient in verbal ability. Although this was not measured, the child with the most obvious advanced verbal skills had results most similar to past findings. Thus, for child 5, direct training effects were substantial and transferred to the classroom. Also, the emergence of new forms with this student was restricted to periods of reinforcement in both experimental and generalization sessions. In future research, it would be interesting to examine verbal ability as a possible precondition for using these procedures most successfully.

Thus, the present study builds upon the existing body of creativity research in substantiating the utility of these procedures. It seems clear that the practical application of the technology and procedures developed in previous research (Goetz, 1977) can be valuable in additional settings with different populations. In future research, however, an important goal should be to develop effective generality procedures. In this regard, the sum of the research to date indicates that an effective program might include *group training within the classroom,* with reinforcement training administered by the teacher, or perhaps in the home administered by a parent or older sibling.

Children's failure to achieve and develop their maximum potential remains a serious problem in poor urban populations. Priority should be given to remediation efforts for this problem.

Summary:
Using Behavioral
Methods Effectively

◆•◆◆•◆◆•◆◆•◆◆•◆◆•◆◆•◆◆•◆◆•◆◆•◆◆•◆◆•◆◆•◆◆•◆◆•◆

The effective use of behavioral methods has relevance for a variety of populations with differing demographic characteristics and for many fields of practice. Although there are still questions about the delivery systems needed to provide behavioral and environmental interventions to people of different ages and developmental stages, of different social classes and educational levels, and with different kinds of problems, there are no specific limitations on using scientific methods to solve human problems. The practitioner-researcher model presented in this book is an experiment; its success depends on the ability of practitioners and researchers to develop practice and evaluation methods that work with a wide range of clients.

452

Most behavioral procedures have been effective in solving problems occurring in settings in which one is able to provide consequences and cues for behavior. In cases where controls are not possible, such as with involuntary clients, workers must convince clients that society has reinforcers for them if they comply with certain societal rules and standards. Obtaining adequate positive consequences for clients, or teaching clients how to obtain them, is a prerequisite for any intervention model.

We have paid special attention to linking individuals, families, and staff members of agencies. Further linkage to the community of individuals and families has also been considered as a potential source of support and reinforcement. Although we have not dealt with large-scale social systems, they are not beyond the scope of direct practice or the concepts and methods presented in this book.

A systematic, self-evaluating, and discovery-oriented approach to social work rests on a data base. Data are important to the worker but even more so to the client. The data allow clients and others in their lives to evaluate the effectiveness of the intervention, as well as to evaluate their own performance. The collection and use of such data often seem strange to both client and other social workers, who may be unaccustomed to thinking of such data as a part of the helping process. Workers who plan to use observation and data collection must sometimes educate clients and colleagues to the key role of such data in planning interventions and evaluating effects.

Once a data base is obtained, the next part of behavioral intervention is the functional analysis. The functional analysis is the worker's way of helping clients understand how they interact with their environment to achieve specific consequences and how their environment rewards or punishes them for their behavior. It is the intellectual base of behavioral practice in that it provides clients with rationales for their behavior and directs them toward an intervention; as such, functional analysis empowers clients to have some control over the contingency systems in which they live. It is also the means by which workers develop intervention plans that alter the circumstances surrounding problems and hence the conditions of clients' lives. In short, the functional analysis is the means by which workers can form working relationships with clients and help them understand their own roles in perpetuating or solving problems.

Building a Behavioral Support System

To effectively use behavioral and scientific intervention methods in social work, workers themselves need support systems. The first task in a professional environment is to look for ways to increase the amount of professional reinforcers provided to workers. Often, the most important reinforcer is the satisfaction of having worked effectively with clients; another is the encouragement and understanding offered by colleagues and supervisors.

Workers who do not receive positive support from clients and colleagues may find self-evaluation a useful way to maintain high performance standards. Since self-evaluation is controlled by the individual, it may be effective even when others are not providing reinforcement. For example, a job description may be translated into a list of specific performance requirements, which the worker can use as a yardstick of his or her effectiveness. A weekly, or even daily, list of tasks planned for clients or other activities can be periodically checked off and can help bolster one's feelings of accomplishment; such lists can also be used to set priorities and efficiently manage the ongoing workload.

Positive collegial relationships are often enhanced by educational experiences, whether organized within the agency, in cooperation with other agencies, or privately with other professionals. Inviting an outside person, perhaps a consultant or an expert in a particular area of interest, to speak to staff members or other professionals can be the stimulus for exploring significant issues and sharing common concerns. Further, many colleges and universities offer courses and workshops relevant to practice issues; they serve not only to increase workers' knowledge but also offer the opportunity to establish a support network of other professionals.

The practitioner-researcher may find additional support by attending professional association meetings; presenting papers, participating on panels, or discussing concerns and problems with others are all rewarding experiences. Organizing local interest groups and encouraging presentations on topics relevant to behavioral methods in social work practice can also be a source of reinforcement. Writing up clinical evaluations and thereby compiling data for a potential proposal or presentation helps one evaluate and put into perspective both setbacks and accomplishments. Writing for publication may not be immediately successful, but even early attempts can result in support (and not only criticism) from colleagues.

Future Practice

Scientific practice is expanding into new fields at a rapid pace. Increasingly, family therapy includes some aspects of defining and measuring the behaviors of parents and children. Other family interventions—such as child abuse treatment, sexual dysfunction interventions, and foster parent training—are developing. Behavioral medicine is becoming part of social work in health care, as are behavioral applications of scientific methods to solving problems of the elderly. Only now are these areas being evaluated. In addition, integrating scientific methods with relatively unresearched practice methods in many other areas offers opportunities for the practitioner-researcher to contribute to the knowledge base of social work and social welfare.

Within the context of social work, many professionals have not been taught to use behavioral and scientific methods to plan and evaluate their practice. Workers should thus be encouraged to participate in continuing education programs that emphasize such methods. Those who already have a solid background should present training sessions for the benefit of other staff members. Caretakers with direct client contact should be trained to record data to provide ongoing assessment of the behavioral target and to note consequences for client behaviors.

As more and more emphasis is placed on prevention, it will be necessary to teach individuals the skills to avoid difficulties before they arise. Courses might include child management classes for new parents, life-planning courses for persons of all ages, and retirement-planning courses for those in middle age. Preventive behavioral and environmental planning is a relatively unevaluated intervention technology.

Future research for clinical social workers lies in the directions of practice methods, assessment tools, extension of intervention effects, and technical development. These directions will require using current research findings and carefully defining and measuring baseline and intervention effects. In many areas, evaluation of practice methods with the clinical populations of social work practice is virtually untapped. With adequate research and practice training, social workers can uncover ways to most effectively intervene in difficult practice situations. It is therefore important to encourage this research-practice perspective in order to develop a sound data base and hence an empirical methodology for social work practice.

References

Allen, E. K., and Harris, F. R. "Elimination of a Child's Excessive Scratching by Training the Mother in Reinforcement Procedures." *Behavior Research and Therapy,* 1966, *4,* 79-84.

Allen, E. K., and others. "Effects of Social Reinforcement on Isolated Behavior of a Nursery School Child." *Child Development,* 1964, *35,* 511-518.

Anderson, K. A., and King, H. E. "Time-Out Reconsidered." *Instructional Psychology,* 1974, *1,* 11-17.

Andrasik, F., and McNamara, J. R. "Optimizing Staff Performance in an Institutional Behavior Change System." *Behavior Modification,* 1977, *1,* 235-248.

Aragona, J., Cassady, J., and Drabman, R. S. "Treating Overweight Children Through Parental Training and Contingency Contracting." *Journal of Applied Behavior Analysis,* 1975, *8,* 269-278.

Ayllon, T., and Azrin, N. H. "Reinforcement and Instructions." *Journal of the Experimental Analysis of Behavior,* 1964, *7,* 327-331.

Ayllon, T., and Azrin, N. H. *The Token Economy: A Motiva-tional System for Therapy and Rehabilitation.* New York: Appleton-Century-Crofts, 1968.

Azrin, N. H., and Foxx, R. M. *Toilet Training in Less Than a Day.* New York: Simon & Schuster, 1974.

Azrin, N. H., and Holz, W. C. "Punishment." In W. K. Honig (Ed.), *Operant Behavior: Areas of Research and Application.* New York: Appleton-Century-Crofts, 1966.

Azrin, N. H., Naster, B. J., and Jones, R. "Reciprocity Counsel-ing: A Rapid Learning-Based Procedure for Marital Counsel-ing." *Behavior Research and Therapy,* 1973, *11,* 365-382.

Azrin, N. H., and Nunn, R. G. "A Rapid Method of Eliminating Stuttering by a Regulated Breathing Approach." *Behaviour Research and Therapy,* 1974, *12,* 279-286.

Baer, D. M. "A Case for the Selective Reinforcement of Punish-ment." In C. Neuringer and J. L. Michael (Eds.), *Behavior Modification in Clinical Psychology.* New York: Appleton-Century-Crofts, 1970.

Baer, D. M. "The Analysis of Behavior and the Analysis of Prob-lems." Paper presented at the Fourth Annual Conference on Behavior Analysis in Education, Lawrence, Kans., May 1973.

Baer, D. M., and Guess, R. "Receptive Training of Adjective In-flections in Mental Retardates." *Journal of Applied Behavior Analysis,* 1971, *4,* 129-140.

Baer, D. M., and Wolf, M. M. "The Entry into Natural Commu-nities of Reinforcement." In R. Ulrich, T. Stachnik, and J. Mabry (Eds.), *Control of Human Behavior.* Vol. 2. Glenview, Ill.: Scott, Foresman, 1970.

Baer, D. M., Wolf, M. M., and Risley, T. "Some Current Dimen-sions of Applied Behavior Analysis." *Journal of Applied Be-havior Analysis,* 1968, *1,* 91-97.

Bailey, J. S., and others. "Modification of Articulation Errors of Pre-Delinquents by Their Peers." *Journal of Applied Behavior Analysis,* 1971, *4,* 265-282.

Baltes, M. M., and Zerbe, M. B. "Independence Training in Nursing Home Residents." *The Gerontologist,* 1976, *16,* 428-432.

Bandura, A. *Principles of Behavior Modification.* New York: Holt, Rinehart and Winston, 1969.

Barber, V. "Studies in the Psychology of Stuttering XVI. Rhythm

As a Distraction in Stuttering." *Journal of Speech and Hearing Disorders,* 1940, *5,* 29-42.

Barton, E. S., and others. "Improvement of Retardates' Mealtime Behavior by Time-Out Procedures Using Multiple Baseline Techniques." *Journal of Applied Behavior Analysis,* 1970, *3,* 77-84.

Beard, C., Cox, W. H., and Pinkston, E. M. "A Proposal to Implement the Parent Education Project at the Elizabeth Ludeman Development Center." Unpublished manuscript, School of Social Service Administration, University of Chicago, 1977.

Becker, W. C. *Parents Are Teachers.* Champaign, Ill.: Research Press, 1971.

Becker, W. C., and others. "The Contingent Use of Teacher Attention and Praise in Reducing Classroom Behavior Problems." *Journal of Special Education,* 1967, *1,* 287-307.

Beech, H. R., and Fransella, R. *Research and Experiment in Stuttering.* Oxford, England: Pergamon Press, 1968.

Bellack, A. S., and Hersen, M. M. *Research and Practice in Social Skills Training.* New York: Plenum, in press.

Bellack, A. S., and Schwartz, J. S. "Assessment for Self-Control Programs." In M. Hersen and A. S. Bellack (Eds.), *Behavioral Assessment: A Practical Handbook.* Elmsford, N.Y.: Pergamon Press, 1976.

Berger, R. M., and Rose, S. D. "Interpersonal Skill Training with Institutionalized Elderly Patients." *Journal of Gerontology,* 1977, *32,* 346-353.

Berkowitz, B. P., and Graziano, A. M. "Training Parents as Behavior Therapists: A Review." *Behavior Research and Therapy,* 1972, *10,* 297-317.

Bernal, M. E. "Behavior Feedback in the Modification of Brat Behaviors." *Journal of Nervous and Mental Disease,* 1969, *148,* 375-385.

Bernal, M. E. "Training Parents in Child Management." In R. H. Bradfield (Ed.), *Behavior Modification in Learning Disabilities.* San Rafael, Calif.: Academic Therapy Publications, 1971.

Bernal, M. E., and North, J. A. "A Survey of Parent Training Manuals." *Journal of Applied Behavior Analysis,* 1978, *11,* 533-544.

Bernal, M. E., and others. "Behavior Modification and the Brat

Syndrome." *Journal of Consulting Clinical Psychology,* 1968, *32,* 447-455.

Bijou, S. W., and Baer, D. M. *Child Development I: A Systematic and Experimental Theory.* New York: Appleton-Century-Crofts, 1961.

Bijou, S. W., and Baer, D. M. *Child Development II: The Universal Stage of Infancy.* New York: Appleton-Century-Crofts, 1965.

Bijou, S. W., and Baer, D. M. *Child Development: Readings in Experimental Analysis.* New York: Appleton-Century-Crofts, 1967.

Bijou, S. W., Peterson, R. F., and Ault, M. H. "A Method to Integrate Descriptive and Experimental Field Studies at the Level of Data and Empirical Concepts." *Journal of Applied Behavior Analysis,* 1968, *1,* 175-191.

Birnbrauer, J. S., and others. "Programmed Instruction in the Classroom." In L. P. Ullman and L. Krasner (Eds.), *Case Studies in Behavior Modification.* New York: Holt, Rinehart and Winston, 1965.

Blackman, D. K., Howe, M. W., and Pinkston, E. M. "Increasing Participation in Social Interaction of the Institutionalized Elderly." *The Gerontologist,* 1976, *17,* 69-76.

Blechman, E. A. "The Family Contract Game: A Tool to Teach Interpersonal Problem Solving." *Family Coordinator,* 1974, *23,* 269-281.

Blechman, E. A. "Directions in Behavior Modification Research with Women." In A. Brodsky and R. Hare-Mustin (Eds.), *Research on Psychotherapy with Women.* New York: Guilford Press, 1980.

Bostow, D. E., and Bailey, J. B. "Modification of Severe Disruptive and Aggressive Behavior Using Brief Time-Out and Reinforcement Procedures." *Journal of Applied Behavior Analysis,* 1969, *2,* 31-37.

Boudin, H. M. "Contingency Contracting as a Therapeutic Tool in the Deceleration of Amphetamine Use." *Behavior Therapy,* 1972, *3,* 604-608.

Braukmann, C. J., Kerigan, K. A., and Wolf, M. M. "Achievement Place: The Researcher's Perspectives." *Bureau of Child Research.* Lawrence: University of Kansas Press, 1976.

Briar, S. "Effective Social Work Intervention in Direct Practice:

Implications for Education." In S. Briar and others (Eds.), *Facing the Challenge*. New York: Council on Social Work Education, 1973.

Briar, S. "Incorporating Research into Education for Clinical Practice in Social Work: Towards a Clinical Science in Social Work." In A. Rubin and A. Rosenblatt (Eds.), *Sourcebook on Research Utilization*. New York: Council on Social Work Education, 1977.

Brody, E. *A Social Work Guide to Long-Term Care Facilities*. Rockville, Md.: National Institute of Mental Health, 1974.

Buchard, J. D. "Systematic Socialization: A Programmed Environment for the Rehabilitation of Antisocial Retardates." *Psychological Record*, 1967, *17*, 461-476.

Buchard, J. D., and Barrera, C. "An Analysis of Time-Out and Response Cost in a Programmed Environment." *Journal of Applied Behavior Analysis*, 1972, *5*, 271-282.

Bucher, B., and Lovaas, O. I. "Use of Aversive Stimulation in Behavior Modification." In M. R. Jones (Ed.), *Miami Symposium on the Prediction of Behaviors, 1967*. Coral Gables, Fla.: University of Miami Press, 1968.

Budd, K. S., and Baer, D. M. "Behavior Modification and the Law: Implications of Recent Judicial Decisions." *Journal of Psychiatric Law*, Summer 1976, 171-244.

Budd, K. S., Pinkston, E. M., and Green, D. R. "An Analysis of Two Parent Training Packages for Remediation of Child Aggression in Laboratory and Home Settings." Paper presented at 81st annual convention of the American Psychological Association, Montreal, September 1973.

Burnside, I. M. *Working with the Elderly: Group Processes and Techniques*. Belmont, Calif.: Duxbury Press, 1978.

Butler, R. N., and Lewis, M. I. *Aging and Mental Health*. St. Louis, Mo.: Mosby, 1977.

Christophersen, E. R., and others. "The Home Point System: Token Reinforcement Procedures for Application by Parents of Children with Behavior Problems." *Journal of Applied Behavior Analysis*, 1972, *5*, 485-499.

Clark, H. E., and others. "Time-Out as a Punishing Stimulus in Continuous and Intermittent Schedules." *Journal of Applied Behavior Analysis*, 1973, *6*, 443-455.

Cohen, S., and others. "The Support of School Behaviors by

Home-Based Reinforcement Via Parent-Child Contingency Contracts." In E. Ramp and B. Hopkins (Eds.), *A New Direction for Education: Behavior Analysis.* Lawrence: University of Kansas Press, 1971.

Compton, B. R., and Galaway, B. *Social Work Processes.* Homewood, Ill.: Dorsey Press, 1979.

Cook, T. D., and Campbell, D. T. *Quasi-Experimentation: Design and Analysis Issues for Field Settings.* Chicago: Rand McNally, 1979.

Corson, J. A. "Families as Mutual Control Systems: Optimization by Systematization of Reinforcement." In E. J. Mash, L. A. Hamerlynck, and L. C. Handy (Eds.), *Behavior Modification and Families.* New York: Brunner/Mazel, 1976.

Corte, H. E., Wolf, M. M., and Locke, B. J. "A Comparison of Procedures of Eliminating Self-Injurious Behavior of Retarded Adolescents." *Journal of Applied Behavior Analysis,* 1971, *4,* 201-213.

Cox, W. H. "Group Training of Single Parents." Unpublished dissertation, School of Social Service Administration, University of Chicago, 1982.

Cox, W. H., and others. "A Cross Validation Study of Short-Form Scales in the Evaluation of Behavioral Parent Training." Paper presented at the Association for Behavior Analysis Conference, Dearborn, May 1979.

Dahl, G. "Behaviour Modification and the Team Approach." *The Social Worker,* 1973, *41,* 144-153.

Dangel, R., and Polster, R. A. "Parents as Partners in Program Development." Paper presented at the Association for Behavior Analysis Conference, Milwaukee, May 1981.

Deitz, S. M., and Repp, A. C. "Decreasing Classroom Misbehavior Through the Use of DRL Schedules of Reinforcement." *Journal of Applied Behavior Analysis,* 1973, *6,* 457-463.

Doke, L. A., and Risley, T. R. "The Organization of Day-Care Environments: Required Versus Optional Activities." *Journal of Applied Behavior Analysis,* 1972, *5,* 405-420.

Doty, D. W., McInnis, T., and Paul, G. L. "Remediation of Negative Side Effects of an Ongoing Response-Cost System with Chronic Mental Patients." *Journal of Applied Behavior Analysis,* 1974, *7,* 191-198.

Drabman, R. S., Spitalnik, R., and O'Leary, K. D. "Teaching Self-Control to Disruptive Children." *Journal of Abnormal Psychology,* 1973, *82,* 10-16.

Ebner, M. A. "An Investigation of the Role of the Social Environment in the Generalization and Persistence of the Effects of a Behavior Modification Program." Unpublished doctoral dissertation, University of Oregon, 1967.

Eisler, R. M., Miller, P. M., and Hersen, M. "Components of Assertive Behavior." *Journal of Clinical Psychology,* 1973, *29,* 295-299.

Eisler, R. M., and others. "Situational Determinants of Assertive Behaviors." *Journal of Consulting and Clinical Psychology,* 1975, *43,* 330-340.

Ekman, P., and Friedman, W. V. "Nonverbal Behavior in Psychopathology." In R. J. Friedman and M. M. Katz (Eds.), *The Psychology of Depression: Contemporary Theory and Research.* New York: Wiley, 1974.

Elliott, C. H., and Goetz, E. M. "Creative Blockbuilding as a Function of Social Reinforcement Using an Unrestricted Creativity Code." Unpublished manuscript, University of Kansas, 1971.

Fallon, M. P., and Goetz, E. M. "The Creative Teacher: The Effects of Descriptive Social Reinforcement upon the Drawing Behavior of Three Preschool Children." *School Applications of Learning Theory,* 1975, 7 (2), 27-45.

Felixbrod, J. J., and O'Leary, K. D. "Self-Determination of Academic Standards by Children: Toward Freedom from External Control." *Journal of Educational Psychology,* 1974, *66,* 845-850.

Ferster, C. B. "Classification of Behavioral Pathology." In L. Krasner and L. P. Ullmann (Eds.), *Research in Behavior Modification.* New York: Holt, Rinehart and Winston, 1965.

Ferster, C. B. "A Functional Analysis of Depression." *American Psychologist,* 1973, *28,* 857-870.

Ferster, C. B., and Skinner, B. F. *Schedules of Reinforcement.* New York: Appleton-Century-Crofts, 1957.

Ferster, C. B., Culbertson, S., and Boren, M. C. P. *Behavior Principles.* (2nd ed.) Englewood Cliffs, N.J.: Prentice-Hall, 1975.

Figgs, S., Dunn, J., and Herbert, E. "The Effects of Primes on

Creativity in Blockbuilding." Unpublished manuscript, University of Kansas, 1971.

Fischer, J. *The Effectiveness of Social Casework.* Springfield, Ill.: Thomas, 1976.

Fischer, J. *Effective Casework Practice: An Eclectic Approach.* New York: McGraw-Hill, 1978.

Fischer, J., and Gochros, H. L. *Planned Behavior Change: Behavior Modification in Social Casework.* New York: Free Press, 1975.

Forehand, R., and Atkenson, B. M. "Generality of Treatment Effects with Parents as Therapists: A Review of Assessment and Implementation Procedures." *Behavior Therapy,* 1977, *8,* 575-593.

Foxx, R. M., and Azrin, N. H. "Reinstitution: A Method of Eliminating Aggressive-Disruptive Behavior of Retarded and Brain-Damaged Patients." *Behavior Research and Therapy,* 1972, *10,* 15-27.

Foxx, R. M., and Azrin, N. H. "The Elimination of Autistic Self-Stimulatory Behavior by Overcorrection." *Journal of Applied Behavior Analysis,* 1973, *6,* 1-14.

Frankel, A. L., and Glasser, P. H. "Behavioral Approaches to Group Work." *Social Work,* 1974, *19,* 163-176.

Fransella, F. "Rhythm as a Distraction on the Modification of Stuttering." *Behavior Research and Therapy,* 1967, *5,* 253-255.

Frederiksen, L. W., and Frederiksen, C. B. "Teacher-Determined and Self-Determined Token Reinforcement in a Special Education Classroom." *Behavior Therapy,* 1975, *6,* 310-314.

Fremouw, W. J., and Harnatz, M. G. "A Helper Model for Behavioral Treatment of Speech Anxiety." *Journal of Consulting and Clinical Psychology,* 1975, *43,* 652-660.

Friedman, B. S. "Analysis of Participation in a Training Program for Single Parents." Unpublished dissertation, School of Social Service Administration, University of Chicago, 1979.

Galloway, C., and Galloway, K. C. "Parent Groups with a Focus on Precise Behavior Management." *IMRID Papers and Reports,* 1970, *7,* 1-36.

Gambrill, E. D. *Behavior Modification: Handbook of Assess-*

ment, Intervention, and Evaluation. San Francisco: Jossey-Bass, 1977.

Gambrill, E. D. "A Behavioral Perspective of Families." In E. R. Tolson and W. J. Reid (Eds.), *Models of Family Treatment.* New York: Columbia University Press, 1981.

Gambrill, E. D., and Richey, C. A. "An Assertion Inventory for Use in Assessment and Research." *Behavior Therapy,* 1975, *6,* 547-549.

Garcia, E., Baer, D. M., and Firestone, L. "The Development of Generalized Imitation Within Topographically Determined Boundaries." *Journal of Applied Behavior Analysis,* 1971, *4,* 101-112.

Gardner, J. M. "Teaching Behavior Modification to Nonprofessionals." *Journal of Applied Behavior Analysis,* 1972, *5,* 517-521.

Glass, G. V., Willson, V. L., and Gottman, J. M. *Design and Analysis of Time-Series Experiments.* Boulder: Colorado Associated University Press, 1975.

Goetz, E. M. "A Review of the Training of Creativity as an Operant." Paper presented at the Midwestern Association of Behavior Analysis, Chicago, May 1977.

Goetz, E. M., and Baer, D. M. "Descriptive Reinforcement of 'Creative' Blockbuilding by Young Children." In A. E. Ramp and B. L. Hopkins (Eds.), *A New Direction for Education: Behavior Analysis.* Lawrence: University of Kansas Press, 1971, pp. 72-79.

Goetz, E. M., and Baer, D. M. "Social Control of Form Diversity and the Emergence of New Forms." *Journal of Applied Behavior Analysis,* 1973, *6,* 209-217.

Goetz, E. M., Holmberg, M. C., and LeBlanc, J. "DRO and Noncontingent Reinforcement as Control Procedures During the Modification of a Preschooler's Compliance." *Journal of Applied Behavior Analysis,* 1975, *8,* 77-82.

Goetz, E. M., Jones, K., and Weamer, K. "The Generalization of Creativity 'Training' in Easel Painting to Blockbuilding." Paper presented at The American Psychological Association, Montreal, September 1973.

Goetz, E. M., and Salmonson, M. M. "The Effect of General and

Descriptive Reinforcement on 'Creativity' in Easel Painting."
In G. B. Semb (Ed.), *Behavior Analysis in Education.* Lawrence: University of Kansas Press, 1972, pp. 53-61.

Goffman, E. *Asylums: Essays on the Social Situations of Mental Patients.* New York: Doubleday, 1961.

Goldiamond, I. "Stuttering and Fluency as Manipulatable Operant Response Classes." In L. Krasner and L. P. Ullman (Eds.), *Research in Behavior Modification.* New York: Holt, Rinehart and Winston, 1965.

Goldiamond, I. "Toward a Constructional Approach to Special Problems: Ethical and Constitutional Issues Raised by Applied Behavior Analysis." *Behavioralism,* 1974, *2,* 1-84.

Goldiamond, I. "Singling Out Behavior Modification for Legal Regulation on Patient Care, Psychotherapy, and Research in General." *Arizona Law Review,* 1975, *17,* 105-126.

Goldstein, A. P., Heller, K., and Sechrest, L. B. *Psychotherapy and the Psychology of Behavior Change.* New York: Wiley, 1966.

Goldstein, A. P., Sprafkin, R. M., and Gershaw, N. J. *Skill Training for Community Living: Applying Structured Learning Therapy.* Elmsford, N.Y.: Pergamon Press, 1976.

Gottman, J., and others. *A Couple's Guide to Communication.* Champaign, Ill.: Research Press, 1978.

Graziano, A. M. "Parents as Behavior Therapists." In M. Hersen, R. M. Eisler, and P. M. Miller (Eds.), *Progress in Behavior Modification.* New York: Academic Press, 1977.

Green, G. R., and Wright, J. E. "The Retrospective Approach to Collecting Baseline Data." *Social Work Research and Abstracts,* 1979, *15,* 25-30.

Greene, B. F., and others. "Measuring Client Gains for Staff-Implemented Programs." *Journal of Applied Behavior Analysis,* 1978, *11,* 395-412.

Guess, R., Sailor, W., and Baer, D. M. *Functional Speech and Language Training for the Severely Handicapped.* Pts. 1 and 2. Lawrence, Kan.: H & H Enterprises, 1977.

Hall, R. V. *Managing Behavior.* Pt. 1: *Behavior Modification: The Measurement of Behavior.* Lawrence, Kan.: H & H Enterprises, 1971a.

Hall, R. V. *Managing Behavior.* Pt. 2: *Behavior Modification: Basic Principles.* Lawrence, Kan.: H & H Enterprises, 1971b.

Hall, R. V. *Managing Behavior.* Pt. 3: *Behavior Modification: Applications in School and Home.* Lawrence, Kan.: H & H Enterprises, 1971c.

Hall, R. V., and others. "Teachers and Parents as Researchers Using Multiple Baseline Designs." *Journal of Applied Behavior Analysis,* 1970, *3,* 247-255.

Hall, R. V., and others. "The Teacher as Observer and Experimenter in the Modification of Disrupting and Talking Out Behaviors." *Journal of Applied Behavior Analysis,* 1971, *4,* 141-149.

Hall, R. V., and others. "The Effective Use of Punishment to Modify Behavior in the Classroom." In K. D. O'Leary and S. O'Leary (Eds.), *Classroom Management: The Successful Use of Behavior Modification.* Elmsford, N.Y.: Pergamon Press, 1972.

Hamilton, G. *Theory and Practice of Social Casework.* (2nd ed.) New York: Columbia University Press, 1951.

Hanf, C. "Modifying Problems in Mother-Child Interaction: Standardized Laboratory Situations." Paper presented at meeting of the Association of Behavior Therapy, Olympia, Washington, November 1968.

Hawkins, R. P., and others. "Behavior Therapy in the Home: Amelioration of Problem Parent-Child Relations with the Parent as a Therapeutic Role." *Journal of Experimental Child Psychology,* 1966, *4,* 99-107.

Henderson, R. W., and Garcia, A. B. "The Effects of Parent Training Program on the Question-Asking Behavior of Mexican-American Children." *American Educational Research Journal,* 1973, *10,* 193-201.

Herbert, E. M., and Baer, D. M. "Training Parents as Behavior Modifiers: Self-Recording Contingent Attention." *Journal of Applied Behavior Analysis,* 1973, *6,* 15-30.

Herbert, E. M., and others. "Adverse Effects of Differential Parental Attention." *Journal of Applied Behavior Analysis,* 1973, *6,* 15-30.

Hersen, M., and Barlow, D. H. *Single-Case Experimental Designs: Strategies for Studying Behavior Change.* Elmsford, N.Y.: Pergamon Press, 1976.

Hersen, M., and Bellack, A. S. "Assessment of Social Skills." In A. R. Cimimero, K. S. Calhourn, and H. E. Adams (Eds.), *Handbook for Behavioral Assessment.* New York: Wiley, 1977.

Hersen, M., and Bellack, A. S. *Behavior Therapy in the Psychiatric Setting.* Baltimore: Williams & Wilkins, 1978a.

Hersen, M., and Bellack, A. S. "Social Skills Training for Chronic Psychiatric Patients: Rationale, Research Findings, and Future Directions." *Comprehensive Psychiatry,* 1978b, *17,* 559-580.

Hersen, M., Bellack, A. S., and Turner, S. M. "Assessment of Assertiveness in Female Psychiatric Patients: Motor and Autonomic Measures." *Journal of Behavior Therapy and Experimental Psychiatry,* 1978, *9,* 11-16.

Hersen, M., Eisler, R. M., and Miller, P. M. "An Experimental Analysis of Generalization in Assertive Training." *Behavior Research and Therapy,* 1974, *12,* 295-310.

Hersen, M., and others. "Effects of Phenothazines and Social Skill Training in a Withdrawn Schizophrenic." *Journal of Clinical Psychology,* 1975, *34,* 588-594.

Hollis, F. "The Psychosocial Approach to the Practice of Casework." In R. Roberts and R. Nee (Eds.), *Theories of Social Casework.* Chicago: University of Chicago Press, 1970.

Hollis, F. *Casework: A Psychosocial Therapy.* (2nd ed.) New York: Columbia University Press, 1974.

Holman, J., Goetz, E. M., and Baer, D. M. "The Training of Creativity as an Operant and an Examination of its Generalization Characteristics." In B. C. Etzel, J. LeBlanc, and D. M. Baer (Eds.), *New Developments in Behavior Research: Theory, Methods, and Applications. In Honor of Sidney W. Bijou.* Hillsdale, N.J.: Erlbaum, 1976.

Homme, L. E., and others. *How to Use Contingency Contracting.* Champaign, Ill.: Research Press, 1969.

Howard, C. F. "Teaching a Class of Parents as Reinforcement Therapists to Treat Their Own Children." Paper presented at the Southeastern Psychological Association Annual Meeting, Louisville, April 1970.

Howe, M. W. "Casework Self-Evaluation: A Single-Subject Approach." *Social Service Review,* 1974, *48,* 1-23.

Howe, M. W. "Behavior Management of Urinary Incontinence in the Elderly." Unpublished doctoral dissertation, School of Social Service Administration, University of Chicago, 1975.

Hoyer, W. J. "Application of Operant Techniques to the Modification of Elderly Behavior." *The Gerontologist,* 1973, *13,* 18-22.

Hoyer, W. J., and others. "A Reinstatement of Verbal Behavior in Elderly Mental Patients Using Operant Procedures." *The Gerontologist,* 1974, *14,* 149-152.

Hudson, W. W. "A Measurement Package for Clinical Social Workers." Paper presented at 23rd annual program meeting of the Council of Social Work Education, Phoenix, Ariz., February 1977.

Hudson, W. W. "Development and Use of Indexes and Scales." In R. M. Grinnell (Ed.), *Social Work Research and Evaluation.* Itasca, Ill.: Peacock Publishers, 1981.

Huntsville-Madison County Mental Health Center Programs and Evaluation. Huntsville, Ala.: Huntsville County Mental Health Center, 1978.

Ingham, R. J., and Andrews, G. "Behavior Therapy and Stuttering." *Journal of Speech and Hearing Disorders,* 1973, *38,* 405-441.

Iwata, B. A., and Bailey, J. S. "Reward Versus Cost Token Systems: An Analysis of the Effects on Students and Teachers." *Journal of Applied Behavior Analysis,* 1974, *7,* 567-576.

Jackson, D. A., and Wallace, R. F. "The Modification and Generalization of Voice Loudness in a Fifteen-Year-Old Retarded Girl." *Journal of Applied Behavior Analysis,* 1974, *7,* 461-472.

Jacobson, N. S. "Problem-Solving and Contingency Contracting in the Treatment of Marital Discord." *Journal of Consulting and Clinical Psychology,* 1977, *45,* 92-100.

Jayaratne, S., and Levy, R. *Empirical Clinical Practice.* New York: Columbia University Press, 1979.

Jeffords, K., Danzig, L., and Fitzgibbons, K. "Group Training of Parents as Behavior Modifiers of their Mentally Retarded Children." Mimeographed, University of Wisconsin, 1971.

Johnson, C. A., and Katz, R. A. "Using Parents as Change Agents for Their Children: A Review." *Journal of Child Psychology and Psychiatry and Allied Disciplines,* 1973, *14,* 181-200.

Johnston, J. M. "Punishment of Human Behavior." *American Psychologist*, 1972, *27*, 1033-1057.

Jones, F. H., Fremouw, W. J., and Carples, S. "Pyramid Training of Elementary School Teachers to Use a Classroom Management 'Skill Package.'" *Journal of Applied Behavior Analysis*, 1977, *10*, 239-253.

Jones, R. J., and Azrin, N. H. "Behavioral Engineering: Stuttering as a Function of Stimulus Duration During Speech Synchronization." *Journal of Applied Behavior Analysis*, 1969, *2*, 223-229.

Jones, R. R., Reid, J. B., and Patterson, G. R. "Naturalistic Observation in Clinical Assessment." In P. McReynolds (Ed.), *Advances in Psychological Assessment*. Vol. 3. San Francisco: Jossey-Bass, 1975.

Kanfer, F. H. "Self-Management Methods." In F. H. Kanfer and A. P. Goldstein (Eds.), *Helping People Change*. Elmsford, N.Y.: Pergamon Press, 1975.

Kanfer, F. H., and Goldstein, A. P. *Helping People Change*. Elmsford, N.Y.: Pergamon Press, 1975.

Kanfer, F. H., and Saslow, G. "Behavioral Diagnosis." In C. M. Franks (Ed.), *Behavior Therapy Appraisal and Status*. New York: McGraw-Hill, 1969.

Katz, G. C., Johnson, C. A., and Gelfand, S. "Modifying the Dispensing of Reinforcers: Some Implications for Behavior Modification with Hospitalized Patients." *Behavior Therapy*, 1972, *3*, 579-588.

Kaufman, A. "Social Policy and Long-Term Care of the Aged." *Social Work*, 1980, *25*, 133-138.

Kaufman, A., and Baron, A. "Suppression of Behavior by Time-Out Punishment when Suppression Results in Loss of Positive Reinforcement." *Journal of the Experimental Analysis of Behavior*, 1968, *11*, 595-607.

Kaufman, K. F., and O'Leary, K. D. "Reward, Cost, and Self-Evaluation Procedures for Disruptive Adolescents in a Psychiatric Hospital School." *Journal of Applied Behavior Analysis*, 1972, *3*, 84-90.

Kazdin, A. E. "Response Cost: The Removal of Conditioned Reinforcers for Therapeutic Change." *Behavior Therapy*, 1972, *3*, 533-546.

Kazdin, A. E. *The Token Economy: A Review and Evaluation.* New York: Plenum, 1977.

Kazdin, A. E., and Polster, R. "Intermittent Token Reinforcement and Response Maintenance and Extinction." *Behavior Therapy,* 1973, *4,* 386-391.

Keeley, K. M., and Henderson, J. D. "A Community-Based Operant Learning Environment II: Systems and Procedures." In R. D. Rubin, and others (Eds.), *Advances in Behavior Therapy.* New York: Academic Press, 1971.

Keeley, S. M., Shemberg, K. M., and Carbonell, J. "Operant Clinical Intervention: Behavior Management or Beyond? Where is the Data?" *Behavior Therapy,* 1976, *7,* 292-305.

Keith, P. M. "Perceptions of Participants in a Family Life Education Program." *Social Casework,* 1978, *59,* 116-119.

Kifer, R. E., and others. "Training Predelinquent Youths and their Parents to Negotiate Conflict Situations." *Journal of Applied Behavior Analysis,* 1974, *7,* 357-364.

Koegel, R. L., and Rincover, A. "Treatment of Psychotic Children in a Classroom Environment: Learning in a Large Group." *Journal of Applied Behavior Analysis,* 1974, *7,* 45-59.

Kramer, T. J., and Rilling, M. "Differential Reinforcement of Low Rates: A Selective Critique." *Psychological Bulletin,* 1970, *74,* 225-254.

Kratochwill, T. R. (Ed.). *Single-Subject Research: Strategies for Evaluation of Change.* New York: Academic Press, 1978.

Kreitner, R., Reif, W. E., and Morris, M. "Measuring the Impact of Feedback on the Performance of Mental Health Technicians." *Journal of Organizational Behavior Management,* 1977, *1,* 105-109.

Kuypers, D. S., Becker, W. C., and O'Leary, K. D. "How to Make a Token System Fail." *Exceptional Children,* 1968, *35,* 101-109.

Larson, C. C., and Gilbertson, D. L. "Reducing Family Resistance to Therapy Through a Child Management Approach." *Social Casework,* 1977, *58,* 620-623.

Lawrence, H., and Sundel, M. "Behavior Modification in Adult Groups." *Social Work,* 1972, *17,* 34-43.

Lazarus, A. A. "Learning Theory and the Treatment of Depression." *Behavior Research and Therapy,* 1968, *6,* 83-89.

Leitenberg, H. "Is Time-Out from Positive Reinforcement an Aversive Event?" *Psychological Bulletin,* 1965, *64,* 428-441.

Leitenberg, H. *Handbook of Behavior Modification and Behavior Therapy.* Englewood Cliffs, N.J.: Prentice-Hall, 1976.

Levenstein, P., Kochman, A., and Roth, H. "From Laboratory to Real World: Service Delivery of the Mother-Child Home Program." *American Journal of Orthopsychiatry,* 1973, *43,* 72-78.

Levitt, J. L. "A Component Analysis of Parental Data Collection and Reporting Tasks in a Parent Education Program." Unpublished dissertation, School of Social Service Administration, University of Chicago, 1981.

Levitt, J. L., and Pinkston, E. M. "Examination of a Brief Time-Out Procedure for Bizarre and Irrelevant Verbalizations Employing Speech Teachers as Therapists." Paper presented at 5th annual Applied Behavior Analysis Conference, Dearborn, Mich., June 1979.

Levitt, J. L., and Reid, W. J. "Rapid Assessment Instruments for Social Work Practice." *Social Work Research and Abstracts,* 1981, *17,* 13-19.

Levitt, J. L., and others. "Analysis of Consumer Evaluation Across Single-Parent Studies." Paper presented at 6th annual Applied Behavior Analysis Conference, Dearborn, Mich., May 1980.

Lewinsohn, P. M. "A Behavioral Approach to Depressions." In R. J. Freidman and M. M. Katz (Eds.), *The Psychology of Depression: Contemporary Theory and Research.* New York: Wiley, 1974.

Lewinsohn, P. M., Biglan, A., and Zeiss, A. M. "Behavioral Treatment of Depression." In P. Davidson (Ed.), *The Behavioral Management of Anxiety, Depression, and Pain.* New York: Brunner/Mazel, 1976.

Lewinsohn, P. M., Weinstein, M., and Alper, T. "A Behavioral Approach to Group Treatment of Depressed Patients: A Methodological Contribution." *Journal of Clinical Psychology,* 1970, *26,* 525-532.

Liberman, R. P., King, L. W., and DeRisi, W. J. "Behavior Analysis and Therapy in Community Mental Health." In H. Leitenberg (Ed.), *Handbook of Behavior Modification and Behavior Therapy*. Englewood Cliffs, N.J.: Prentice-Hall, 1976.

Libet, J., and Lewinsohn, P. M. "Concept of Social Skill with Reference to the Behavior of Depressed Persons." *Journal of Consulting and Clinical Psychology*, 1973, *40*, 304-312.

Lindsley, O. R. "Geriatric Behavioral Prosthetics." In R. Kastenbaum (Ed.), *New Thoughts on Old Age*. New York: Springer, 1964.

Linsk, N. L., Green, G. R., and Pinkston, E. M. "Evaluation of a Home-Based Behavioral Program for Enhancing Social Supports for the Impaired Elderly." Paper presented at 34th annual scientific meeting of the Gerontological Society of America and 10th annual scientific and educational meeting of the Canadian Association on Gerontology, Toronto, November 1981.

Linsk, N. L., Howe, M. W., and Pinkston, E. M. "Behavioral Group Work in a Home for the Aged." *Social Work*, 1975, *20*, 454-463.

Lovaas, O. I., and Bucher, B. D. (Eds.). *Perspectives in Behavior Modification with Deviant Children*. Englewood Cliffs, N.J.: Prentice-Hall, 1974.

Lovaas, O. I., and others. "Some Generalization and Follow-Up Measures on Autistic Children in Behavior Therapy." *Journal of Applied Behavior Analysis*, 1973, *6*, 131-166.

Lowy, L. *Social Work with the Aging: The Challenge and Promise of the Later Years*. New York: Harper & Row, 1979.

Lutzker, J. R., and Martin, J. A. *Behavior Change*. Monterey, Calif.: Brooks/Cole, 1981.

McAllister, L. W., and others. "The Application of Operant Conditioning Techniques in a Secondary School Classroom." *Journal of Applied Behavior Analysis*, 1969, *2*, 263-277.

McClannahan, L. E., and Risley, T. "Design of Living Environments for Nursing Home Residents: Increasing Attendance at Activities." *The Gerontologist*, 1974, *14*, 236-240.

MacDonough, T. S., and Forehand, R. "Response-Contingent Time-Out: Important Parameters in Behavior Modification with Children." *Journal of Behavior Therapy and Experimental Psychiatry*, 1973, *4*, 231-236.

Madsen, C. H., Becker, W. C., and Thomas, D. R. "Rules, Praise, and Ignoring: Elements of Elementary Classroom Control." *Journal of Applied Behavior Analysis*, 1968, *1*, 139-150.

Madsen, C. H., and others. "An Analysis of the Reinforcing Function of 'Sit Down' Commands." In R. H. Parker (Ed.), *Readings in Educational Psychology*. Boston: Allyn & Bacon, 1967.

Margholin, D. I., Siegel, L. J., and Phillips, D. "Treatment and Transfer: A Search for Empirical Procedures." In M. Hersen, R. M. Eisler, and P. M. Miller (Eds.), *Progress in Behavior Modification*. Vol. 3. New York: Academic Press, 1976.

Milby, J. B. "Modification of Extreme Social Isolation by Contingent Social Reinforcement." *Journal of Applied Behavior Analysis*, 1970, *1*, 149-152.

Miller, W. H. *Systematic Parent Training: Procedures, Cases, and Issues*. Champaign, Ill.: Research Press, 1975.

Mindel, C. H. "Instrument Design and Construction." In R. M. Grinnell (Ed.), *Social Work Research and Evaluation*. Itasca, Ill.: Peacock Publishers, 1981.

Minkin, N., and others. "The Social Validation and Training of Conversational Skills." *Journal of Applied Behavior Analysis*, 1976, *9*, 127-139.

Monteger, C. A., and others. "Increasing Institutional Staff to Resident Interactions Through Inservice Training and Supervisor Approval." *Behavior Therapy*, 1977, *8*, 533-540.

Morris, R. *Alternatives to Nursing Home Care: A Proposal*. Washington, D.C.: U.S. Government Printing Office, 1971.

Mueller, D. J., and Altas, L. "Resocialization of Regressed Elderly Patients: A Behavior Management Approach." *Journal of Gerontology*, 1972, *27*, 390-392.

Mullen, E. J., and Dumpson, J. R. (Eds.). *Evaluation of Social Intervention*. San Francisco: Jossey-Bass, 1972.

Nay, W. R. "A Systematic Comparison of Instructional Techniques for Parents." *Behavior Therapy*, 1975, *6*, 14-21.

Nay, W. R. "Parents as Real Life Reinforcers: The Enhancement of Parent Training Effects Across Conditions Other than Training." In A. P. Goldstein and F. H. Kanfer (Eds.), *Maximizing Treatment Gains: Transfer Enhancement in Psychotherapy*. New York: Academic Press, 1979.

Nordquist, V. M., and Wahler, R. G. "Naturalistic Treatment of the Autistic Child." *Journal of Applied Behavior Analysis,* 1973, *6,* 79-87.

O'Brien, F., and Azrin, N. H. "Developing Proper Mealtime Behaviors of the Institutionalized Retarded." *Journal of Applied Behavior Analysis,* 1972, *5,* 389-399.

O'Brien, F., Bugle, C., and Azrin, N. H. "Training and Maintaining a Retarded Child's Proper Eating." *Journal of Applied Behavior,* 1972, *5,* 67-72.

O'Dell, S. L. "Training Parents in Behavior Modification." *Psychological Bulletin,* 1974, *81,* 418-433.

O'Dell, S. L., and others. "Predicting the Acquisition of Parenting Skills Via Four Training Methods." Unpublished paper, Department of Psychology, University of Mississippi, 1981.

O'Leary, K. D., and Becker, W. C. "Behavior Modification of an Adjustment Class: A Token Reinforcement Program." *Exceptional Children,* 1967, *33,* 637-642.

O'Leary, K. D., and Wilson, G. T. *Behavior Therapy: Application and Outcome.* Englewood Cliffs, N.J.: Prentice-Hall, 1975.

O'Leary, K. D., O'Leary, S. G., and Becker, W. C. "Modification of Deviant Sibling Interaction Patterns in the Home." *Behavior Research and Therapy,* 1967, *5,* 113-120.

Panyan, M., Boozer, H., and Morris, N. "Feedback to Attendents as a Reinforcer for Applying Operant Techniques." *Journal of Applied Behavior Analysis,* 1970, *3,* 1-4.

Parsonson, B. S., and Baer, D. M. "The Analysis and Presentation of Graphic Data." In T. R. Kratochwill (Ed.), *Single Subject Research: Strategies for Evaluating Change.* New York: Academic Press, 1978.

Patterson, G. R. *Families.* Champaign, Ill.: Research Press, 1971.

Patterson, G. R. "Intervention for Boys with Conduct Problems: Multiple Settings, Treatments, and Criteria." *Journal of Consulting and Clinical Psychology,* 1974, *42,* 471-481.

Patterson, G. R., and Brodsky, G. "A Behavior Modification Program for a Boy with Multiple Problems." *Journal of Child Psychology and Psychiatry,* 1966, *7,* 277-295.

Patterson, G. R., Cobb, J. A., and Ray, R. S. "A Social Engineering Technology for Retraining the Family of Aggressive Boys." In H. E. Adams and I. P. Unikel (Eds.), *Issues and*

Trends in Behavior Therapy. Springfield, Ill.: Thomas, 1973.

Patterson, E. T., Griffen, J. C., and Panyan, M. "Incentive Maintenance of Self-Help Skill Training Programs for Nonprofessional Personnel." *Journal of Behavior Therapy and Experimental Psychiatry,* 1976, *7,* 249-253.

Patterson, G. R., and Gullion, M. E. *Living with Children: New Methods for Parents and Teachers.* Champaign, Ill.: Research Press, 1971.

Patterson, G. R., and others. *A Social Learning Approach to Family Intervention.* Vol. 1: *Families with Aggressive Children.* Eugene, Ore.: Castalia, 1975.

Patterson, G. R., and Reid, J. B. "Intervention for Families of Aggressive Boys: A Replication Study." *Behavior Research and Therapy,* 1973, *11,* 383-394.

Pavlov, I. P. *Conditioned Reflexes.* (G. V. Anrep, Ed. and Trans.) Oxford, England: Oxford University Press, 1927.

Pavlov, I. P. *Lectures on Conditioned Reflexes.* (W. H. Gantt, Trans.) New York: International Publishers, 1928.

Perlman, H. H. *Social Casework: A Problem-Solving Process.* Chicago: University of Chicago Press, 1957.

Perlman, H. H. "The Problem-Solving Model in Social Casework." In R. W. Roberts and R. H. Nee (Eds.), *Theories of Social Casework.* Chicago: University of Chicago Press, 1970.

Peterson, R. F., and Peterson, L. R. "The Use of Positive Reinforcement in the Control of Self-Destructive Behavior in a Retarded Boy." *Journal of Experimental Child Psychology,* 1968, *6,* 351-360.

Phillips, E. L. "Achievement Place: Token Reinforcement Procedures in a Home-Style Rehabilitation Setting for 'Predelinquent' Boys." *Journal of Applied Behavior Analysis,* 1968, *1,* 213-233.

Phillips, E. L., and others. "Achievement Place: Modification of the Behaviors of Predelinquent Boys Within a Token Economy." *Journal of Applied Behavior Analysis,* 1971, *4,* 45-59.

Pincus, A. "Reminiscence in Aging and Its Implications for Social Work Practice." *Social Work,* 1972, *15,* 47-53.

Pincus, A., and Minahan, A. *Social Work Practice: Model and Method.* Itasca, Ill.: Peacock Publishers, 1973.

Pinkston, E. M., Budd, K. S., and Baer, D. M. "Modeling as a Parent Education Technique." In press.

Pinkston, E. M., Friedman, B. S., and Polster, R. P. "Parents as Agents of Behavior Change." In S. P. Schinke (Ed.), *Behavioral Methods in Social Welfare.* Hawthorne, N.Y.: Aldine, 1981.

Pinkston, E. M., and Herbert-Jackson, E. W. "Modification of Irrelevant and Bizarre Verbal Behavior Using Mother as Therapist." *Social Service Review,* 1975, *49,* 46-63.

Pinkston, E. M., and others. "Independent Control of a Preschool Child's Aggression and Peer Interaction by Contingent Teacher Attention." *Journal of Applied Behavior Analysis,* 1973, *6,* 115-124.

Polster, R. P., and Lynch, M. A. "Single-Subject Designs." In R. M. Grinnell (Ed.), *Social Work Research and Evaluation.* Itasca, Ill.: Peacock Publishers, 1981.

Polster, R. P., and Pinkston, E. M. "A Delivery System for the Treatment of Underachievement." *Social Service Review,* 1979, *53,* 35-55.

Pomerleau, O. F., Bobrove, P. H., and Smith, R. H. "Rewarding Psychiatric Aides for the Behavioral Improvement of Assigned Patients." *Journal of Applied Behavior Analysis,* 1973, *6,* 383-390.

Pommer, D. A., and Streedback, D. "Motivating Staff Performances in an Operant Learning Program for Children." *Journal of Applied Behavior Analysis,* 1974, *7,* 217-221.

Premack, D. "Toward Empirical Behavioral Laws: Positive Reinforcement." *Psychological Review,* 1959, *66,* 219-233.

Premack, D. "Reinforcement Theory." In D. Levine (Ed.), *Nebraska Symposium on Motivation.* Lincoln: University of Nebraska Press, 1965.

Quilitch, H. R. "A Comparison of Three Staff-Management Procedures." *Journal of Applied Behavior Analysis,* 1975, *8,* 59-66.

Rebok, G. W., and Hoyer, W. J. "The Functional Context of Elderly Behavior." *The Gerontologist,* 1977, *17,* 27-34.

Redd, W. H., Porterfield, A. L., and Anderson, B. L. *Behavior Modification: Behavioral Approaches to Human Problems.* New York: Random House, 1979.

Reese, E. P., Howard, J., and Reese, T. W. *Human Operant Behavior: Analysis and Application.* (2nd ed.) Dubuqe, Iowa: Brown, 1978.

Reese, N. M., and LeBlanc, J. M. "Creative Dance: A Pilot Study." Unpublished manuscript, University of Kansas, 1970.

Reid, W. J. *The Task-Centered System.* New York: Columbia University Press, 1978.

Reid, W. J., and Epstein, L. *Task-Centered Casework.* New York: Columbia University Press, 1972.

Reid, W. J., and Epstein, L. (Eds.). *Task-Centered Practice.* New York: Columbia University Press, 1977.

Rekers, G. A., Lovaas, O. I., and Low, B. "The Behavioral Treatment of a 'Transexual' Preadolescent Boy." *Journal of Abnormal Child Psychology,* 1974, *2,* 99-116.

Repp, A. C., and Deitz, S. M. "Reducing Aggressive and Self-Injurious Behavior of Institutionalized Retarded Children Through Reinforcement of Other Behaviors." In C. M. Franks and G. T. Wilson (Eds.), *Annual Review of Behavior Therapy, Theory, and Practice.* Vol. 3. New York: Brunner/Mazel, 1975.

Richmond, M. *Social Diagnosis.* New York: Free Press, 1965. (Originally published 1917, 1944.)

Richmond, M. *What Is Social Case Work?* New York: Russell Sage Foundation, 1922.

Risley, T. R., and Hart, B. M. "Developing Correspondence Between the Nonverbal and Verbal Behavior of Preschool Children." *Journal of Applied Behavior Analysis,* 1968, *1,* 267-281.

Risley, T. R., and Wolf, M. M. "Strategies for Analyzing Behavioral Change over Time." In J. Nesselroade and H. Reese (Eds.), *Life-Span Developmental Psychology.* New York: Academic Press, 1972.

Roberts, R. W., and Nee, R. H. *Theories of Social Casework.* Chicago: University of Chicago Press, 1970.

Rose, S. D. "Training Parents in Groups as Behavior Modifiers of Their Mentally Retarded Children." *Journal of Behavior Therapy and Experimental Psychiatry,* 1974, *5,* 135-140.

Rose, S. D. *Group Therapy: A Behavioral Approach.* San Francisco: Jossey-Bass, 1977.

Rose, S. D., and others. "Group Training of Parents as Behavior Modifiers of Their Own Mentally Retarded Children." Mimeographed, School of Social Work, University of Wisconsin, 1972.

Russo, S. "Adaptation in Behavior Therapy with Children." *Journal of Behavior Research and Therapy,* 1964, *2,* 43-47.

Rutman, L. *Evaluation Research Methods: A Basic Guide.* Beverly Hills, Calif.: Sage, 1977.

Sajwaj, T., Twardosz, S., and Burke, M. "Side Effects of Extinction Procedures in a Remedial Preschool." *Journal of Applied Behavior Analysis,* 1972, *5,* 163-175.

Saleebey, D. "A Proposal to Merge Humanist and Behavioral Perspectives." *Social Casework,* 1975, *56,* 468-479.

Salzberg, B. H., and others. "The Effect of Intermittent Feedback and Intermittent Contingent Access to Play and Printing of Kindergarten Children." *Journal of Applied Behavior Analysis,* 1971, *4,* 163-172.

Sasaki, M., and Fukushima, O. "The Formation of a Standard and the Increase in the Number of Correct Responses Reduced by Self-Reinforcement Procedure." *Japanese Journal of Psychology,* 1979, *50,* 136-144.

Schinke, S. P., and Wong, S. E. "Teaching Child Care Workers: A Behavioral Approach." *Child Care Quarterly,* 1978, *1,* 45-61.

Schumaker, J., and Sherman, J. A. "Training Generative Verb Usage by Imitation and Reinforcement Procedures." *Journal of Applied Behavior Analysis,* 1970, *3,* 273-292.

Schwartz, A., and Goldiamond, I. *Social Casework: A Behavioral Approach.* New York: Columbia University Press, 1975.

Schwartz, M. L., and Hawkins, R. P. "Application of Delayed Reinforcement Procedures to the Behavior of an Elementary School Child." *Journal of Applied Behavior Analysis,* 1970, *3,* 85-96.

Simon, D. M. "A Systematic Approach to Family Life Education." *Social Casework,* 1976, *57,* 511-517.

Skinner, B. F. "Two Types of Conditioned Reflex and a Pseudo Type." *Journal of General Psychology,* 1935, *12,* 66-77.

Skinner, B. F. *The Behavior of Organisms.* New York: Appleton-Century-Crofts, 1938.

Skinner, B. F. *Science and Human Behavior.* New York: Macmillan, 1953.

Skinner, B. F. *Beyond Freedom and Dignity.* New York: Knopf, 1971.

Skinner, B. F. *Cumulative Record: A Selection of Papers.* 3rd ed. New York: Appleton-Century-Crofts, 1972.

Smith, M., and Glass, G. "Meta-Analysis of Psychotherapy Outcome Studies." *American Psychologist,* 1977, *32,* 752-760.

Solnick, J. V., Rincover, A., and Peterson, C. R. "Some Determinants of the Reinforcing and Punishing Effects of Time-Out." *Journal of Applied Behavior Analysis,* 1977, *10,* 415-424.

Sperbeck, D. J., and Whitbourne, S. K. "Dependency in the Institutional Settings: A Behavioral Training Program for Geriatric Staff." *The Gerontologist,* 1981, *21,* 268-275.

Spivack, G., Platt, J. J., and Shure, M. D. *The Problem-Solving Approach to Adjustment.* San Francisco: Jossey-Bass, 1976.

Steeves, J. M., Martin, G. L., and Pear, J. J. "Self-Imposed Time-Out by Autistic Children During an Operant Training Program." *Behavior Therapy,* 1970, *1,* 371-381.

Stein, T. J. "Some Ethical Considerations of Short-Term Workshops in the Principles and Methods of Behavior Modification." *Journal of Applied Behavior Analysis,* 1975, *8,* 113-115.

Stein, T. J. *Social Work Practice in Child Welfare.* Englewood Cliffs, N.J.: Prentice-Hall, 1981.

Stein, T. J., and Gambrill, E. D. *Decision Making in Foster Care: A Training Manual.* Berkeley: University Extension Publications, University of California, 1976.

Stokes, T. F., and Baer, D. M. "An Implicit Technology of Generalization." *Journal of Applied Behavior Analysis,* 1977, *10,* 349-367.

Stokes, T. F., Baer, D. M., and Jackson, R. L. "Programming the Generalization of a Greeting Response in Four Retarded Children." *Journal of Applied Behavior Analysis,* 1974, *7,* 559-610.

Stuart, R. B. "Operant-Interpersonal Treatment of Marital Discord." *Journal of Consulting and Clinical Psychology,* 1969, *33,* 675-682.

Stuart, R. B. "Behavioral Contracting with the Families of Delinquents." *Journal of Behavior Therapy and Experimental Psychiatry,* 1971, *2,* 1-11.

Stuart, R. B. *Helping Couples Change: A Social Learning Approach to Marital Therapy.* New York: Guilford Press, 1980.

Stuart, R. B., and Lott, L. A. "Behavioral Contracting with Delinquents: A Cautionary Note." *Journal of Behavior Therapy and Experimental Psychiatry,* 1972, *3,* 161-169.

Sulzer, B., and Mayer, G. R. *Behavior Modification Procedures for School Personnel.* Hinsdale, Ill.: Dryden Press, 1972.

Sundel, M., and Sundel, S. S. *Behavior Modification in Human Services: A Systematic Introduction to Concepts and Applications.* (2nd ed.) Englewood Cliffs, N.J.: Prentice-Hall, 1982.

Tallon, R. J. "Frequency of Reinforcement as a Determinant of Time-Out Effectiveness." Unpublished thesis, Department of Psychology, Drake University, 1976.

Teigiser, K. "A Profile of Social Treatment Graduates." Unpublished manuscript, School of Social Service Administration, University of Chicago, 1980.

Tharp, R. G., and Wetzel, R. J. *Behavior Modification in the Natural Environment.* New York: Academic Press, 1969.

Thomas, D. R., Becker, W. C., and Armstrong, M. "Production and Elimination of Disruptive Behavior by Systematically Varying Teacher's Attention." *Journal of Applied Behavior Analysis,* 1968, *1,* 35-45.

Thomas, E. J. "Behavior Modification and Casework." In R. Roberts and R. Nee (Eds.), *Theories of Social Casework.* Chicago: University of Chicago Press, 1970.

Thomas, E. J. "Use of Behavioral Methods in Interpersonal Practice." In N. A. Polansky (Ed.), *Social Work Research: Methods for the Helping Professions.* (rev. ed.) Chicago: University of Chicago Press, 1975.

Thomas, E. J. "Research and Service in Single-Case Experimentation: Conflicts and Choices." *Social Work Research and Abstracts,* 1978, *14,* 20-31.

Thorndike, E. L. *Animal Intelligence: An Experimental Study of the Association Processes in Animals.* Psychological Review Monograph supplement 2, 1898.

Thorndike, E. L., and Woodworth, R. S. "The Influence of Improvement in One Mental Function Upon the Efficiency of Other Functions." *Psychological Review,* 1901, *8,* 18-25.

Tobin, S. S. "Old People." In H. Mass (Ed.), *Review of Research in Social Services.* New York: National Association of Social Workers, 1977.

Tobin, S. S., and Lieberman, M. A. *Last Home for the Aged: Critical Implications of Institutionalization.* San Francisco: Jossey-Bass, 1976.

Towle, C. *The Learner in Education for the Professions as Seen in Education for Social Work.* Chicago: University of Chicago Press, 1954.

Towle, C. *Common Human Needs.* New York: National Association of Social Workers 1965.

Traux, C. B., and Carkhuff, R. R. *Toward Effective Counseling and Psychotherapy.* Hawthorne, N.Y.: Aldine, 1967.

Turkewitz, H., O'Leary, K. D., and Ironsmith, M. "Generalization and Maintenance of Appropriate Behavior Through Self-Control." *Journal of Consulting and Clinical Psychology,* 1975, *43,* 577-583.

Wachtel, P. L. *Psychoanalysis and Behavior Therapy: Towards an Integration.* New York: Basic Books, 1977.

Wahler, R. G. "Oppositional Children: A Quest for Parental Reinforcement Control." *Journal of Applied Behavior Analysis,* 1969a, *2,* 159-170.

Wahler, R. G. "Setting Generality: Some Specific and General Effects of Child Behavior Therapy." *Journal of Applied Behavior Analysis,* 1969b, *2,* 239-246.

Wahler, R. G., and others. "Mothers as Behavior Therapists for Their Children." *Behavior Research and Therapy,* 1965, *3,* 113-124.

Walker, H. M., and Buckley, N. K. *Token Reinforcement Techniques.* Eugene, Ore.: Engelmann-Becker Press, 1974.

Watson, D., and Tharp, R. *Self-Directed Behavior: Self-Modification for Personal Adjustment.* Monterey, Calif.: Brooks/Cole, 1972.

Watson, J. B., and Rayner, R. "Conditioned Emotional Reactions." *Journal of Experimental Psychology,* 1920, *3,* 1-14.

Weiss, C. H. *Evaluation Research: Methods of Assessing Program Effectiveness.* Englewood Cliffs, N.J.: Prentice-Hall, 1972.

Weiss, R. L., Hops, H., and Patterson, G. R. "A Framework for Conceptualizing Marital Conflict: A Technology for Altering It, Some Data for Evaluating It." In L. A. Hamerlynck, L. C. Hancy, and E. J. Mash (Eds.), *Behavior Change: Methodology, Concepts, and Practice.* Champaign, Ill.: Research Press, 1973.

Weissman, A. L. "Industrial Social Services: Linkage Technology." *Social Casework,* 1975, *55,* 50-54.

Welsch, L. C., Radicker, J., and Krapfl, J. E. "Effects of Feedback on Daily Completion of Behavior Modification Projects." *Mental Retardation,* 1973, *11,* 24-27.

Wetzel, R. J., and others. "Outpatient Treatment of Autistic Behavior." *Behavior Research and Therapy,* 1966, *4,* 169-177.

Whalen, C. K., and Henker, B. A. "Pyramid Theory in a Hospital for the Retarded." *American Journal of Mental Deficiency,* 1971, *75,* 414-434.

White, G. D., Nielson, G., and Johnson, S. M. "Time-Out Duration and the Suppression of Deviant Behavior in Children." *Journal of Applied Behavior Analysis,* 1972, *5,* 111-120.

Whittaker, J. K. *Social Treatment: An Approach to Interpersonal Helping.* Hawthorne, N.Y.: Aldine, 1974.

Wilson, G. T., and Evans, I. M. "The Therapist-Client Relationship in Behavior Therapy." In A. S. Gunman and A. M. Razin (Eds.), *Effective Psychotherapy: A Handbook of Research.* Elmsford, N.Y.: Pergamon Press, 1977.

Winkler, R. C. "Management of Chronic Psychiatric Patients by a Token Reinforcement System." *Journal of Applied Behavior Analysis,* 1970, *3,* 47-55.

Wodarski, J. S., and Bagarazzi, D. I. *Behavioral Social Work.* New York: Human Sciences Press, 1979.

Wolf, M. M. "Social Validity: The Case for the Subjective Measurement or How Applied Behavior Analysis Is Finding Its Heart." *Journal of Applied Behavior Analysis,* 1978, *11,* 203-214.

Wolf, M. M., Risley, T. R., and Mees, H. "Application of Operant Conditioning Procedures to the Behavior Problems of an Autistic Child." *Behavior Research and Therapy,* 1964, *1,* 305-312.

Wyatt vs. Stickney. In B. J. Ennis and P. P. Friedman (Eds.), *Legal Rights of the Mentally Retarded.* Vol. 1. New York: Practicing Law Institute, 1974.

Zeilberger, J., Sampen, S., and Sloane, H. N. "Modification of a Child's Problem Behaviors in the Home with the Mother as Therapist." *Journal of Applied Behavior Analysis,* 1968, *1,* 47-53.

Zeiler, M. D. "Other Behavior: Consequences of Reinforcing Not Responding." *Journal of Psychology,* 1970, *74,* 149-155.

Zeiler, M. D., and Jersey, S. S. "Development of Behavior: Self-Feeding." *Journal of Consulting and Clinical Psychology,* 1968, *32,* 164-168.

Name Index

A

Allen, E. K., 172, 261, 457
Alper, T., 364, 472
Altas, L., 342, 474
Anderson, B. L., 16, 20, 52, 105, 193, 477
Anderson, K. A., 320, 322, 457
Andrasik, F., 302, 457
Andrews, G., 233, 469
Aragona, J., 214, 457
Armstrong, M., 172, 481
Atkenson, B. M., 422, 464
Ault, M. H., 65, 67, 283, 460
Ayllon, T., 24, 172, 182, 288, 457-458
Azrin, N. H., 24, 31, 71, 159, 172, 173, 182, 209, 213, 233, 251, 288, 292, 412, 457-458, 464, 470, 475

B

Baer, D. M., 2, 5, 17, 45, 47, 65, 76, 78, 175, 192, 209, 217, 247, 329, 376, 382, 389, 390, 395, 402, 422, 435, 437, 438, 442, 448, 449-450, 458, 460, 461, 465, 466, 467, 468, 475, 477, 480-481
Bagarazzi, D. I., 105, 483
Bailey, J. B., 31, 173, 251, 320, 460
Bailey, J. S., 24, 25-26, 78, 307, 458, 469
Baltes, M. M., 413, 458
Bandura, A., 32, 100, 184, 207, 458
Banzett, L. K., 52, 281, 304, 306, 353-363
Barber, V., 233, 459
Barlow, D. H., 48, 65, 74, 78, 136, 161
Baron, A., 321, 470
Barrera, C., 30-31, 213, 318, 320-321, 322, 338, 339, 340, 461
Barton, E. S., 78, 412, 459
Beard, C., 298, 459
Becker, W. C., 172, 182, 215, 247, 248, 249, 250, 253, 262, 264,

485

265, 289, 296, 394, 459, 471, 474, 475, 481
Beech, H. R., 233, 459
Bellack, A. S., 82-83, 112, 140, 142, 157, 278, 459, 467-468
Berger, R. M., 342, 459
Berkowitz, B. P., 183, 209, 247, 261, 422, 459
Bernal, M. E., 99, 247, 249, 261, 422, 459-460
Bijou, S. W., 17, 65, 67, 283, 460
Birnbrauer, J. S., 320, 460
Blackman, D. K., 26, 44, 217, 294, 305, 382, 390, 392, 412-421, 460
Blechman, E. A., 197, 393, 460
Bobrove, P. H., 302, 303, 477
Boozer, H., 80, 302, 475
Boren, M. C. P., 21, 463
Bostow, D. E., 31, 173, 251, 320, 460
Boudin, H. M., 214, 460
Braukmann, C. J., 70, 460
Briar, S., 2, 6, 13, 74, 461
Brodsky, G., 247, 475
Brody, E., 220, 421, 461
Buchard, J. D., 30-31, 213, 318, 320-321, 322, 338, 339, 340, 461
Bucher, B. D., 30, 213, 461, 473
Buckley, N. K., 322, 482
Budd, K. S., 192, 247, 461, 477
Bugle, C., 412, 475
Burke, M., 78, 479
Butler, R. N., 421, 461

C

Campbell, D. T., 341, 462
Carbonell, J., 422, 471
Carkhuff, R. R., 35, 482
Carples, S., 298, 470
Cassady, J., 214, 457
Christophersen, E. R., 247, 461
Clark, H. E., 31, 251, 461
Cobb, J. A., 158, 249, 475-476
Cohen, S., 214, 461-462
Compton, B. R., 272, 462
Cook, T. D., 341, 462
Corte, H. E., 80, 173, 450, 462
Cox, W. H., 46, 72, 123, 233-246, 284, 298, 422-434, 459, 462

Culbertson, S., 21, 463

D

Dahl, G., 272, 462
Dangel, R., 13, 70, 100, 183, 462
Danzig, L., 261, 469
Deitz, S. M., 173, 182, 353-354, 462, 478
DeRisi, W. J., 75, 472-473
Doke, L. A., 287, 462
Doty, D. W., 25, 462
Dougherty, R., 47, 51, 281, 282, 284, 288, 293, 305, 320-341
Drabman, R. S., 214, 386, 457, 463
Dumpson, J. R., 3, 381, 474
Dunn, J., 435, 463-464

E

Ebner, M. A., 247, 463
Eisler, R. M., 141, 156, 463, 468
Ekman, P., 139-140, 463
Elliott, C. H., 435, 463
Epstein, L., 9, 15, 38, 60, 89, 478
Evans, I. M., 34, 483

F

Fallon, M. P., 435, 463
Felixbrod, J. J., 386, 463
Ferster, C. B., 21, 139, 288, 353, 463
Figgs, S., 435, 463-464
Firestone, L., 78, 465
Fischer, J., 2, 3, 8, 13, 35, 38, 52, 74, 105, 185, 273, 381, 427, 464
Fitzgibbons, K., 261, 469
Fixsen, D. L., 135
Forehand, R., 320, 422, 464, 473
Foxx, R. M., 31, 173, 209, 213, 251, 458, 464
Frankel, A. L., 342, 464
Fransella, F., 233, 459, 464
Frederiksen, C. B., 386, 464
Frederiksen, L. W., 386, 464
Fremouw, W. J., 298, 464, 470
Friedman, B. S., 10, 46, 47, 51, 57, 73, 102, 185, 207, 209, 247-260, 261, 281, 282, 284, 288,

293, 305, 320-341, 422, 435-451, 464, 477
Friedman, W. V., 139-140, 463
Fukushima, O., 423, 479

G

Galaway, B., 272, 462
Galloway, C., 261, 464
Galloway, K. C., 261, 464
Gambrill, E. D., 8, 13, 27, 52, 71, 74, 105, 140, 175, 183, 209, 214, 215, 464-465, 480
Garcia, A. B., 247, 467
Garcia, E., 78, 465
Gardner, J. M., 297, 465
Gelfand, S., 303, 470
Gershaw, N. J., 140, 466
Gilbertson, D. L., 422, 471
Glass, G. V., 74, 89, 465, 480
Glasser, P. H., 342, 464
Gochros, H. L., 2, 105, 185, 273, 464
Goertz, E. M., 173, 182, 435-451, 463, 465-466, 468
Goffman, E., 280, 466
Goldiamond, I., 37, 44, 63, 106, 191, 193, 210, 233, 250, 466, 479
Goldstein, A. P., 34, 140, 379, 466, 470
Gottman, J., 158, 466
Gottman, J. M., 74, 465
Graziano, A. M., 98, 183, 209, 247, 261, 422, 459, 466
Green, D. R., 274, 461
Green, G. R., 45, 52, 64, 72, 120, 191, 192, 201, 203, 219, 220-232, 281-282, 288, 291, 293, 304, 307-319, 390, 466, 473
Greene, B. F., 302, 466
Griffen, J. C., 302, 476
Guess, R., 78, 209, 458, 466
Gullion, M. E., 249, 262, 476

H

Hall, R. V., 30, 78, 138, 225, 298, 307, 466-467
Hamilton, G., 190, 467

Hanf, C., 247, 249, 467
Harnatz, M. G., 298, 464
Harris, F. R., 261, 457
Hart, B. M., 78, 478
Hawkins, R. P., 78, 247, 467, 479
Heller, K., 379, 466
Henderson, P. D., 261-271
Henderson, R. W., 247, 467
Henker, B. A., 298, 483
Herbert, E. M., 23, 47, 99, 208, 247, 249, 250, 435, 463-464, 467
Herbert-Jackson, E. W., 44, 99, 209, 213, 247, 477
Hersen, M., 48, 65, 74, 78, 82-83, 136, 140, 141, 142, 156, 157, 161, 278, 459, 463, 467-468
Hollis, F., 38, 190, 378, 468
Holman, J., 435, 437, 442, 449-450, 468
Holmberg, M. C., 173, 182, 465
Holz, W. C., 24, 213, 292, 458
Homme, L. E., 27, 129, 214, 251, 265, 468
Hops, H., 393, 483
Howard, C. F., 261, 468
Howard, J., 298, 307, 478
Howe, M. W., 4, 26, 44, 175, 193, 217, 272, 344, 421, 460, 468, 473
Hoyer, W. J., 220, 342, 412, 469, 477
Hudson, W. W., 71, 72, 79, 123, 144, 157, 160, 167, 170, 284, 469

I

Ingham, R. J., 233, 469
Ironsmith, M., 386, 482
Iwata, B. A., 24, 25-26, 307, 469

J

Jackson, D. A., 381, 469
Jackson, R. L., 389, 402, 450, 480-481
Jacobson, N. S., 214, 469
Jayaratne, S., 2, 13, 74, 136, 469
Jeffords, K., 261, 469
Jersey, S. S., 412, 484

Johnson, C. A., 183, 247, 303, 422, 469, 470
Johnson, S. M., 322, 340, 483
Johnston, J. M., 292, 470
Jones, F. H., 298, 470
Jones, K., 435, 465
Jones, R. J., 71, 159, 233, 458, 470
Jones, R. R., 47, 73, 470

K

Kanfer, F. H., 20-21, 34, 423, 470
Katz, G. C., 303, 470
Katz, R. A., 183, 247, 422, 469
Kaufman, A., 220, 321, 470
Kaufman, K. F., 24, 25, 213, 307, 318, 470
Kazdin, A. E., 13, 23, 24, 126, 210, 287, 288, 310, 320, 321, 381, 386, 390, 391-392, 470-471
Keeley, S. M., 422, 471
Keith, P. M., 422, 471
Kerigan, K. A., 70, 460
Kifer, R. E., 159, 163, 471
King, H. E., 320, 322, 457
King, L. W., 75, 472-473
Kochman, A., 247, 472
Koegel, R. L., 381, 471
Kramer, T. J., 353, 471
Krapfl, J. E., 299, 483
Kratochwill, T. R., 137, 471
Kreitner, R., 302, 471
Kuypers, D. S., 172, 289, 296, 471

L

Lane, M. Z., 435-451
Lane, T. W., 110, 435-451
Larson, C. C., 422, 471
Lawrence, H., 342, 471
Lazarus, A. A., 364, 471
LeBlanc, J., 173, 182, 465
LeBlanc, J. M., 435, 478
Leitenberg, H., 52, 105, 320, 321, 472
Levenstein, P., 247, 472
Levitt, J. L., 46, 123, 204, 305, 472
Levy, R., 2, 13, 74, 136, 469

Lewinsohn, P. M., 139, 364, 472, 473
Lewis, M. I., 421, 461
Liberman, R. P., 75, 472-473
Libet, J., 139, 364, 473
Lieberman, M. A., 220, 482
Lindsley, O. R., 194, 342, 421, 473
Linsk, N. L., 26, 50, 64, 72, 77, 191, 192, 201, 204, 219, 220-232, 272, 281, 282, 284, 292, 304, 306, 342-352, 390, 421, 473
Locke, B. J., 80, 173, 450, 462
Lott, L. A., 214, 215, 481
Lovaas, O. I., 30, 209, 213, 461, 473, 478
Love, B. T., 261-271
Low, B., 209, 478
Lowy, L., 220, 473
Lullo, S. A., 26, 81, 382, 390, 392, 396, 402-411
Lutzker, J. R., 70, 100, 473
Lynch, M. A., 74, 247-260, 477

M

McAllister, L. W., 78, 473
McCabe, M. M., 45, 52, 65, 78, 101, 118, 137, 139-170, 392
McClannahan, L. E., 276, 342, 421, 473
MacDonough, T. S., 320, 473
McInnis, T., 25, 462
McNamara, J. R., 302, 457
Madsen, C. H., 172, 474
Mallon-Wenzel, C. M., 52, 118, 120, 130, 137, 139-170, 400
Margholin, D. I., 395, 474
Martin, G. L., 321, 339, 480
Martin, J. A., 70, 100, 473
Mayer, G. R., 298, 481
Mees, H., 31, 251, 484
Milby, J. B., 78, 474
Miller, P. M., 141, 156, 463, 468
Miller, W. H., 248, 474
Minahan, A., 38, 89, 476
Mindel, C. H., 71, 474
Minkin, N., 13, 70, 474
Molick, R., 18, 49, 53, 72, 196,

204, 207-208, 219, 261-271, 284, 294, 304, 364-375
Monteger, C. A., 302, 303, 474
Morris, M., 302, 471
Morris, N., 80, 302, 475
Morris, R., 220, 474
Moses, C. A., 29, 100, 118, 130, 171-182
Mueller, D. J., 342, 474
Mullen, E. J., 3, 381, 474

N

Naster, B. J., 71, 159, 458
Nay, W. R., 32, 98, 99, 100, 474
Nee, R. H., 105, 276, 478
Nielson, G., 322, 340, 483
Nordquist, V. M., 209, 475
North, J. A., 99, 249, 459
Nunn, R. G., 233, 458

O

O'Brien, F., 412, 475
O'Dell, S. L., 72, 98, 100, 183, 209, 230, 247, 261, 394, 422, 475
O'Leary, K. D., 21, 24, 25, 105, 172, 213, 247, 289, 296, 307, 318, 386, 396, 463, 470, 471, 475, 482
O'Leary, S. G., 247, 475

P

Panyan, M., 80, 302, 475, 476
Parsonson, B. S., 435, 475
Patterson, G. R., 24, 47, 71, 73, 158, 190, 209, 213, 214, 247, 248, 249, 262, 302, 309, 393, 422, 470, 475-476, 483
Paul, G. L., 25, 462
Pavlov, I. P., 17, 476
Pear, J. J., 321, 339, 480
Perlman, H. H., 6, 10, 15, 38, 378, 393, 476
Peterson, C. R., 339, 480
Peterson, L. R., 172-173, 476
Peterson, R. F., 65, 67, 172-173, 283, 460, 476

Phillips, D., 395, 474
Phillips, E. L., 24, 70, 135, 172, 476
Pincus, A., 38, 89, 275, 476
Pinkston, E. M., 18, 26, 29, 30, 43, 44, 47, 49, 50, 51, 52, 64, 66, 67, 70-71, 72, 77, 81, 88, 99, 102, 139-182, 185, 191, 192, 195, 201, 204, 207, 209, 213, 217, 219, 220-271, 272, 281-282, 284, 288, 291, 292, 293, 294, 298, 304, 305, 306, 307-352, 364-375, 382, 386, 389, 390, 392, 396, 402-421, 422-451, 459, 460, 461, 472, 473, 477
Platt, J. J., 393, 480
Polster, R. A., 13, 70, 100, 183, 462
Polster, R. P., 44, 47, 67, 74, 102, 185, 195, 207, 209, 247-260, 261, 272, 386, 391, 422, 471, 477
Pomerleau, O. F., 302, 303, 477
Pommer, D. A., 302, 303, 477
Porterfield, A. L., 16, 20, 52, 105, 193, 477
Premack, D., 292, 477

Q

Quilitch, H. R., 302, 477

R

Radicker, J., 299, 483
Ray, R. S., 158, 249, 475-476
Rayner, R., 17, 483
Rebok, G. W., 220, 412, 477
Redd, W. H., 16, 20, 52, 105, 193, 477
Reese, E. P., 298, 307, 478
Reese, N. M., 435, 478
Reese, T. W., 298, 307, 478
Reid, J. B., 47, 73, 190, 470, 476
Reid, W. J., 9, 15, 38, 60, 74, 89, 123, 139-170, 472, 478
Reif, W. E., 302, 471
Rekers, G. A., 209, 478

Repp, A. C., 173, 182, 353-354, 462, 478
Richey, C. A., 71, 465
Richmond, M., 5, 15, 190, 276, 478
Rilling, M., 353, 471
Rincover, A., 339, 381, 471, 480
Risley, T. R., 2, 5, 17, 31, 45, 65, 76, 78, 175, 251, 276, 287, 329, 376, 421, 458, 462, 473, 478, 484
Roberts, R. W., 105, 276, 478
Rose, S. D., 99, 101, 249, 261, 342, 459, 478-479
Roth, H., 247, 472
Russo, S., 247, 249, 479
Rutman, L., 275, 479
Rzepnicki, T. L., 192, 196, 203, 210, 219, 233-246, 390, 422-434

S

Sailor, W., 209, 466
Sajwaj, T., 78, 479
Saleebey, D., 297, 479
Salmonson, M. M., 435, 465-466
Salzberg, B. H., 78, 479
Sampen, S., 172, 247, 261, 484
Sasaki, M., 423, 479
Saslow, G., 20-21, 470
Schinke, S. P., 303, 479
Schumaker, J., 78, 479
Schwartz, A., 37, 63, 193, 479
Schwartz, J. S., 112, 459
Schwartz, M. L., 78, 479
Sechrest, L. B., 379, 466
Shemberg, K. M., 422, 471
Sherman, J. A., 78, 479
Shibano, M., 45, 233-246, 383, 385, 390, 392, 422-434
Shure, M. B., 393, 480
Siegel, L. J., 395, 474
Simon, D. M., 422, 479
Skinner, B. F., 3, 17, 34, 43, 158, 288, 353, 412, 426, 463, 479-480
Sloane, H. N., 172, 247, 261, 484
Smith, M., 89, 480
Smith, R. H., 302, 303, 477
Solnick, J. V., 339, 480
Sperbeck, D. J., 421, 480

Spitalnik, R., 386, 463
Spivack, G., 393, 480
Sprafkin, R. M., 140, 466
Steeves, J. M., 321, 339, 480
Stein, T. J., 27, 191, 297, 480
Stokes, T. F., 376, 381, 389, 390, 395, 402, 422, 450, 480-481
Streedback, D., 302, 303, 477
Stuart, R. B., 71, 159, 214, 215, 218, 481
Sulzer, B., 298, 481
Sundel, M., 105, 342, 471, 481
Sundel, S. S., 105, 481

T

Tallon, R. J., 321, 339, 481
Teigiser, K., 6, 481
Tharp, R. G., 108, 127, 171, 288, 295, 394, 412, 481, 483
Thomas, D. R., 172, 474, 481
Thomas, E. J., 2, 3, 74, 75, 184, 185, 216, 481-482
Thorndike, E. L., 17, 378, 482
Tobin, S. S., 220, 482
Towle, C., 3, 15, 482
Truax, C. B., 35, 482
Turkewitz, H., 386, 482
Turner, S. M., 140, 468
Twardosz, S., 78, 479

W

Wachtel, P. L., 297, 482
Wahler, R. G., 78, 171, 208, 209, 213, 247, 381, 475, 482
Walker, H. M., 322, 482
Wallace, R. F., 381, 469
Watson, D., 108, 127, 412, 483
Watson, J. B., 17, 483
Weamer, K., 435, 465
Weinstein, M., 364, 472
Weiss, C. H., 341, 483
Weiss, R. L., 393, 483
Weissman, A. L., 211, 483
Welsch, L. C., 299, 483
Wetzel, R. J., 171, 247, 288, 295, 394, 481, 483
Whalen, C. K., 298, 483

Whitbourne, S. K., 421, 480
White, G. D., 322, 340, 483
Whittaker, J. K., 108, 483
Willson, V. L., 74, 465
Wilson, G. T., 21, 34, 105, 475, 483
Winkler, R. C., 24, 483
Wodarski, J. S., 105, 483
Wolf, M. M., 2, 5, 17, 31, 45, 65,
    70, 76, 78, 80, 135, 173, 175,
    251, 329, 376, 382, 450, 458,
    460, 462, 478, 484

Wong, S. E., 303, 479
Woodworth, R. S., 378, 482
Wright, J. E., 45, 120, 203, 466

Z

Zeilberger, J., 172, 247, 261, 484
Zeiler, M. D., 173, 181, 182, 412,
    484
Zerbe, M. B., 413, 458

Subject Index

A

AB design, for self-management evaluation, 137

ABAB reversal design, in experimental research, 76-78

Access to problem, and change agent selection, 109-110

Achievement Place Group Home: fading at, 398; and social validation, 70; and teaching interactions, 134, 135

Aftercare program, multiple-replication design for, 86-87

Agency, as change setting: for creativity enhancement, 436-437; for elderly, 343; for families, 200-201; for negotiation, 159-160; for prosocial behavior, 171, 182; role requirements of, 108-109; selection of, 117-118; for social-skills training, 141. *See also* Institutions

Agent. *See* Change agent

Aggressive behavior: clinical multiple-baseline design for, 88; intervention-reversal design for, 85

Anecdotal observation: for data base, 62-63; in group social work, 344

Applied behavior analysis. *See* Behavior analysis

Assessment: and baseline data, 47-49; and data recording, 46-47; and desirable outcomes, 40-41, 196, 275-276; for elderly, 223; of family intervention, 190-205; and generality, 382-388; for individual intervention, 113-117; initial, 38-40; in institutions, 274-276; in intervention model, 38-49; measurement techniques for, 45-46; preliminary analysis in, 113-114; and resources available, 41-42; of target behaviors, 42-45. *See also* Data assessment

Attention, from parent, and stuttering, 233-246. *See also* Differential attention

Attitude changes, as indirect measure, 72-73

Aversive event, as punishment, 29-30;

B

Baseline data: and assessment, 47-49; for creativity enhancement, 441-442; for elderly, 223-224, 416; and follow-up, 59; and graphing, 48-49; for greeting response, 404; for negotiation, 162-163; in parent training, 253; and problem behaviors, 48; for prosocial behavior, 176; in social-skills training, 142-143, 145-146; stability of, 75; for stuttering, 235-236, 237; validity of, 48

Baseline/intervention design, for clinical evaluation, 84

Behavior analysis: analytical component of, 7-8; assumptions in, 412; and behavioral and environmental variables, 6-7; conceptually systematic component of, 9-10; designing interventions, training, and evaluation in, 49-55; educational component of, 10-11; effective use of, 452-456; and effectiveness, 11; elements in, 2, 5-13; follow-up for, 58-60; and generality, 12, 380-382; intervention model for, 38-60; practice and research integrated by, 14; rationale for, 13-15; as research area, 17; and scientific method commitment, 5-6; and social relevance, 12-13; technological component of, 8-9; training in, and generality, 393-394

Behavior change: in behavior analysis, 6-7; contingency contracting for, 27-28; environmental relationships to, 7; extinction procedures for, 28-29; and functional and contingency analysis, 20-22; generality of, 10; interventions

for, 20-32; maintenance of, 55, 57-58; modeling procedures for, 31-32; principles of, 16-32; punishment procedures for, 29-31; reinforcement procedures for, 22-27

Behavioral Assertive Test, 141

Behavioral Assertiveness Test, Revised, 141

Behavioral data, and reinforcement opportunities, 287

Behavioral principles: for institutional change agents, 296-298; in parent training, 253-254

Behavioral Principles Knowledge Inventory, 230

Behavioral training, for implementation, 53

Behavioral trap, concept of, 382-383

Behaviors: aggressive, 85, 88; frequency, duration, and intensity of, 64-65; incompatible, 211; and law of effect, 17; multiple baselines across, 78-80, 145, 150, 156-157, 239; operant, 18; out-of-session, and generality, 392-393; problem, defining, 115-116; rate of, assessment of, 193-194; specification of, 230; theory of, 17-20. *See also* Prosocial behavior intervention; Target behaviors

C

Change, concept of, 378. *See also* Behavior change

Change agent: abilities of, 186; access of, 186; administrative support for, 278; agreement by, 94; analysis of, 92-104; assessing, 93-96; benefit to, 95; client as, 97-98; and client behavior, 95; client relationship with, 94-95; concept of, 93; cues for training of, 99-100; educational level of, 95-96; feedback for training of, 101-102; health of, 96; and initial assessment, 40; instruction for, 98-99; for intervention, 53; maintenance of, 103-104; modeling for, 100-101; motivation of, 187; rehearsal for, 101; reinforcement for, 102-104; resources of, 277; responsibilities of, 199; selecting, 93-98; selecting, for family intervention, 197-200; selecting, for individual interventions, 109-113; selecting, in institution, 276-278; self-evaluation of, 104; skill level of, 96; social worker as, 97, 184, 273-274, 427; time needed by, 95; training of, 98-102, 296-304

Change setting. See Setting

Checklists: for systematic practice, 89; in training, 301-302

Chicago, University of: Behavior Analysis Research Laboratory at, 233; School of Social Service Administration at, 4, 423; social treatment graduates of, 6

Child Attitude Toward Mother, 123

Child's Attitude Toward Father, 160, 169

Client: for behavioral social work, 221-222; characteristics of, and change agent selection, 112; for creativity enhancement, 436; for differential reinforcement, 354-355; education of, 132-135; for greeting response, 403; for group social work, 343; multiple baseline across, 80-82; for negotiation, 159-160; for parenting skills, 426; for prosocial behavior, 174, 365; for response cost, 308; for retarded adults program, 262; role and setting requirements of, 107-108; for social-skills training, 140-141; for stuttering intervention, 234-235; for time-out, 322; for utensil use, 414; voluntary or nonvoluntary, 112

Clinical evaluation: analysis of, 84-88; clinical multiple-baseline design for, 87-88; intervention-reversal design in, 84-85; multiple-replication design for, 85-87

Clinical multiple-baseline design, for clinical evaluation, 87-88

Coding: for negotiation, 161-162; for stuttering, 236-237

Coercive interactions, intervention in, 247-260

Commands, verbal, and prosocial behavior, 175, 177, 179, 181

Communication: complete, in negotiation, 161, 163; modification of, 158-170

Community: as change setting, for family, 201-203; resources of, 42, 186, 195-196, 211-212

Consultative triad, concept of, 171

Consumer satisfaction, as indirect measure, 73

Contingencies: group, 294; modifying, and generality, 397-398

Contingency analysis: and behavior change, 20-22; concept of, 21-22

Contingency contracting: for behavior change, 27-28; concept of, 27, 214; for elderly, 224, 226-230; in family intervention, 214-216; for individual intervention, 129; in institutions, 293-294; and maintenance, 215-216; and negotiation, 27-28, 215; parental training in, 251, 254-255; in parenting skills, 426, 427; with retarded adults, 262-271

Contingency control: and change agent selection, 110-111; in family interventions, 198-199

Contingency exchanges, for prosocial behavior, 370-372

Contracts. See Contingency contracting

Creativity enhancement: discussion of, 448-451; method for, 436-437; procedures for, 440-443; program for, analysis of, 435-451; reinforcement in, 438-440, 442-443, 450; results of, 443-448; target behaviors in, 437-438; theoretical background for, 435-436

Criterion-changing design, for self-management evaluation, 138

Cues: for change agent training, 99-100; for elderly, 342; environmental, 195; for fluency, 238, 244; in individual intervention, 127; for prosocial behavior, 371; and reinforcement, 26-27; removing, and generality, 386-387

D

Data: independent observers for, 122-123; observational, 120-123; retrospective, 119-120; and self-recording methods, 122

Data assessment: and baseline data, 124; in family intervention, 205; for group social work, 351; for individual intervention, 123-125; in institutions, 284

Data base: building, 61-73; direct observation for, 62-63, 65-67; indirect measures for, 69-73; and permanent product data, 67

Data collection: for elderly, 225; for group social work, 344-345; for individual intervention, 119-123; for negotiation, 160

Data recording: and assessment, 46-47; for differential reinforcement, 356-357; for elderly, 223-224, 230; in family intervention, 188, 203-205; in institutions, 280-284; in parent training, 253; for prosocial behavior, 366-367; and reliability, 283; skills for, 47; for stuttering, 235-236; for time-out, 326-327, 338; training in, 298-300

Depression: concept of, 364; and prosocial behavior, 364-375; and social-skills training, 139-157

Design, research: for creativity enhancement, 440; for elderly, 224-225; for negotiation, 160-161; for response cost, 311-312; for retarded adults, 265-266; for stuttering, 239-242. See also AB; Baseline/intervention; Clinical multiple-baseline; Criterion-changing; Intervention-reversal;

Multiple-baseline-across-behavior; Multiple-baseline-across-settings; Multiple-replication; Reversal; Single-case; and Withdrawal design

Diary, structured, for data base, 63

Differential attention: cueing for, 99-100; as extinction procedure, 28-29; in family intervention, 208; in individual intervention, 126; by parent, 426, 427-428, 429, 431-432, 433; parent training in, 250-251; as reinforcement, 23

Differential reinforcement of a low rate of behavior (DRL): advantage of, 363; analysis of, 353-363; concept of, 353; discussion of, 362-363; method for, 354-357; procedures for, 357-359; results of, 359-361; theoretical background of, 353-354

Differential reinforcement of other behavior (DRO), and prosocial behavior, 172-173, 176-177, 181-182

Direct influence: concept of, 106; evaluation in, 136; observational data for, 120-121; punishment in, 127-128; reinforcement for, 126-127; self-management compared with, 121; worker role in, 106-107

Direct observation: for data base, 62-63, 65-67; for group social work, 344-345; in institutions, 282; measurement by, 45-46; reliability of, 67-69

Discontinuance, issue of, 10

E

Education, as behavior analysis component, 10-11. See also Instruction; Training

Effect, law of, and behavior, 17

Effectiveness: and behavior analysis, 11; defined, 3; evaluation of, 61-91; of family techniques, 217-218; of token system, 307-319

Elderly: advantages of training-maintenance programs for, 420-421; behavioral social work with, 220-232; discussion of intervention for, 230-232, 419-421; in institutions, 342-352, 412-421; medical consultation for, 231; method for, 221-222, 413-416; procedures for, 222-225; prosthetic environments for, 421; results for, 225-230, 418-419; theoretical background for, 221-222, 412-413; training-maintenance program for, 412-421

Elderly Support Project (ESP), 221

Environment: altering, 3-4, 50, 192; assessment of, 194-195; as behavior analysis variable, 6-7; behavior change related to, 7; natural, as change setting, 118-119; natural, and generality, 382-384; prosthetic, concept of, 421; and target behavior, 44

Evaluation: axioms for, 71; clinical, 84-88; data base for, 61-73, 135-136; direct observation for, 65-67; and experimental research, 74-83; for follow-up, 58-59; of generality, 400-401; in individual intervention, 135-138; in institutions, 304-305; of intervention, 54, 61-91; by systematic practice, 88-91

Experimental control, concept of, 7

Experimental research: ABAB reversal design in, 76-78; analysis of, 74-83; multiple-baseline designs in, 78-83

Extinction: for behavior change, 28-29; in combination with reinforcement, 28; concept of, 19-20; and prosocial behavior, 172

Eye contact, and social-skills training, 143, 147, 151

F

Fading: of contingencies, 398; for elderly, 417; and greeting response, 410

Family: assessment for intervention with, 190-205; coercion of, 191-192; coercive interactions in, 247-260; concept of, 183; of elderly, 220-232; and evaluation, 216-219; findings on, 217-219; intervention with, 183-271; issues in intervention with, 206-207; negotiation in, 158-170; with retarded adults, 261-271; and roles for workers and family members, 184-190; strategy choice for, 206-209; and stuttering treatment, 233-246; techniques for, 209-216

Family members: responsibilities of, 188-190; roles of, 184-185; training of, 216

Feedback: for change agent training, 101-102; and modeling, 32; in parent training, 255

Fine conditions, and time-out, 325-341

Fluency, structured program for, 233-246

Follow-up: and baseline data, 59; for behavior analysis, 58-60; in parent training, 256; in social-skills training, 149; and termination, 59-60

Functional analysis: and alterations needed, 50; analytical dimensions of, 20-21; and behavior change, 20-22; concept of, 7-8, 20; and intervention, 49-50; role of, 453-454; topographical analysis compared with, 124; and whose behavior, 50

G

Generality: across activities, 449-450; analysis of, 376-451; and assessment, 382-388; and behavior analysis, 12, 380-382, 393-394; of behavior change, 10; concept of, 12; and contingency modification, 397-398; of creativity enhancement program, 435-451; and cue removal, 386-387;

of differential reinforcement, 358-359, 362-363; evaluation of, 400-401; failure to achieve, 379-380; of greeting response, 402-411; guidelines for, 384, 385, 386, 387, 388, 391, 392-393, 394, 395-397, 399; in individual intervention, 130-132; in institutions, 305-306; and instruction, 395-396; and intermittent reinforcement, 391-392; and intervention, 388-394; and out-of-session behavior, 392-393; of parenting skills, 422-434; and program substitution, 396-397; and reinforcement schedule, 384-385; and research, 380-382; and self-management, 385-386; across settings, 449; and significant others, 387-388; in social-skills training, 148-149, 152, 155-156; and stimulus conditions, 389-391; and termination, 394-400; types of, 377; unplanned, 399-400; of utensil use by elderly, 412-421. *See also* Maintenance

Generalized Contentment Scale (GCS), 123; and social-skills training, 144, 152-154, 155

Graphing: and data assessment, 124-125; in family intervention, 205; for stuttering, 239-243

Greeting response: discussion of, 407-411; experimental phases for, 404-405; generality of, 402-411; method for, 403-404; results of, 405-407; and social reinforcers, 408-410; across subjects, 81; theoretical background of, 402-403

Group social work: conclusions on, 350-352; in institutions, 342-352; methods for, 343-346; results of, 346-350; theoretical background for, 342. *See also* Social work

H

Home as change setting: for elderly,

220-232; for families, 200; for negotiation, 165; for parenting skills, 426-427; for retarded adults, 262-263; for stuttering, 235

I

Ignore-protect-reinforce, as extinction procedure, 28-29

Ignore-redirect-reinforce, as extinction procedure, 28-29

Incompatible behavior, concept of, 211

Index of Marital Satisfaction, 123

Index of Parental Attitudes, 160, 169

Index of Self-Concept, 123

Index of Self-Esteem (ISE), 144, 152-154, 155

Index of Sexual Satisfaction, 123

Individuals: assessment for, 113-117; change agent selection for, 109-113; change setting selection for, 117-119; data assessment for, 123-125; data collection for, 119-123; evaluation of interventions for, 135-138; implementing intervention for, 132-135; interventions with, 105-182; negotiation training for, 158-170; prosocial behavior for, 171-182; role and setting requirements for, 106-109; selecting intervention procedures for, 125-132; social-skills training for, 139-157

Influence. *See* Direct influence

Information sources, in family intervention, 203-205

Initial assessment: and change agent, 40; and client motivation, 39; and relevant problems, 38-39; and what behavior, 39-40; and whose behavior for change, 39

Initiations, reinforcement for, 368-370

Institutions: assessment in, 274-276; change agent training in, 296-304; as change setting for elderly, 413-414; as change setting for family, 201, 222, 279-280; as change setting for retarded children, 403; data assessment in, 284; data recording in, 280-284; differential reinforcement in, 353-363; evaluation in, 304-305; generality and maintenance in, 305-306; group social work with elderly in, 342-352; group training in, 297-298; interventions in, analysis of, 272-375; prosocial behavior for depressed girl in, 364-375; punishment in, 292-294; reinforcement in, 285-292; resources available in, 276-278; response cost in, 307-319; response requirements and contingencies in, 280; role and setting considerations in, 273-274; staff feedback and reinforcement in, 302-304; structures for implementation in, 274; techniques in, 285-296; time-out and response cost in, 320-341; token systems in, 287-292. *See also* Agency, as change setting

Instruction: in change agent training, 98-99; and generality, 395-396; for group parent training, 263-264; in parent training, 248-249. *See also* Training

Instrumentation, for data collection, 123

Intensity, measurement of, 65

Interval samples, for direct observation, 67

Intervention: assessment in, 38-49; as behavior analysis model, 38-60; for behavior change, 20-32; and behavior maintenance, 52; change agent for, 53; choosing, in institutions, 294-295; contingency analysis for, 131-132; contingency contracting as, 27-28; designing, 49-55; developing and implementing, 33-60; evaluation of, 54, 61-91; extending effects of, 376-451; extinction procedures as, 28-29; with families, 183-271; and functional analysis of data, 49-50; and functional and contingency analysis, 20-22; and generality, 388-394; implementing, 53-54; and inappropriate behavior, 51; for individuals, 105-182; for institutions, 272-375; interviews for, 34-38; learning as result of, 377-379; modeling as, 31-32; package of, for individuals, 130, 134; package of, negotiation in, 160; package of, for prosocial behavior, 176-177, 181-182; for positive behaviors, 50-51; punishment as, 29-31; reinforcement as, 22-27; revising, 55, 56; selecting, for individuals, 125-132; social relevance of, 295-296; strategy for, 50-53

Intervention-reversal design, for clinical evaluation, 84-85

Interviews: characteristics of, 35-38; in family intervention, 203; and functional aspects of client behavior, 36-38; goals for, 34; intake, 263; for interventions, 34-38; mutual shaping in, 36; as nonpunishing, 35-36; for observational data, 120; reinforcement in, 36

Issue identification, in negotiation, 161, 163, 166

L

Learning: as result of intervention, 377-379; transfer of, 378-379, 420

M

Maintenance: of behavior change, 55, 57-58; consequences for, 57-58; and contracts, 215-216; and differential attention, 251; for elderly, 225, 226, 231, 416-418; in family intervention, 187; in institutions, 305-306; and intervention, 52; of negotiation, 170;

and scheduling, 57. *See also* Generality

Manuals, in parent training, 249-250

Materials, for group parent training, 263

Measurement: for assessment, 45-46; by direct observation, 45-46

Measures: indirect, for data base, 69-73; of parent training, 265-266; for prosocial behavior, 174-175; for social-skills training, 141-144

Modeling: for behavior change, 31-32; for change agent training, 100-101; in combinations, 32; in family intervention, 207; and feedback, 32; for greeting response, 404; in individual intervention, 129-130; in institutions, 294; for negotiation, 163; in parent training, 249, 255; and rehearsal, 32

Multiple baseline, for self-management evaluation, 137-138

Multiple-baseline-across-behavior design: in experimental research, 78-80; in social-skills training, 145, 150, 156-157; for stuttering, 239

Multiple-baseline-across-clients, for greeting response, 405

Multiple-baseline-across-settings design, in experimental research, 82-83

Multiple-baseline-across-subjects: for elderly, 414; in experimental research, 80-82

Multiple-replication design, for clinical evaluation, 85-87

N

Negative reinforcement, concept of, 18-19. *See also* Reinforcement

Negotiation: analysis of training in, 158-170; and contracts, 27-28, 215; discussion of, 168-170; intervention for, 162-165; method in, 159-162; reinforcement for, 370-372; results of, 166-168; with retarded adults, 261-271; theoretical background for, 158-159

O

Observations: anecdotal, 62-63, 344; for data recording training, 299-300; direct, 45-46, 62-63, 65-69, 282, 344-345; for elderly, 414-416; in family intervention, 204-205; of family members, 46; of frequency, duration, and latency, 66; informal, 281; in institutions, 281-283; for negotiation, 162-163, 165; for prosocial behavior, 174, 180-181, 366-367; recording periods for, 282-283; for reinforcement opportunities, 286; repeated over time, 66; for response cost, 308, 310; for target behavior definition, 281-282; for time-out, 326-327

Operant behaviors, concept of, 18

Option suggestion, in negotiation, 161, 163, 166-167

Outcomes, desirable: and assessment, 40-41, 196, 275-276; behaviorally defined, 114-115

Overcorrection: parent training in, 251; as punishment, 31

P

Parent: attention from, and stuttering, 233-246; as backup reinforcer, 271; as change agent, 234-246; and contracts, 251, 254-255, 426, 427; differential attention by, 426, 427-428, 429, 431-432, 433; positive consequences needed for, 246; responsibilities of, in training, 252-253; time-out by, 426, 429, 431, 432, 433

Parent Education Program, 248-260

Parent training: analysis of, 247-260; assessment and evaluation in, 256-257; case example of, 257-259; data sources in, 257;

discussion of, 259-260; in groups, 261-271; home assignments for, 264-265; home visits for, 265; implementation of, 251-256; initial contact for, 251-252; orientation to, 252-253; procedures in, 248-251; theoretical background for, 247-248

Parent Training Program, 263-271

Parental Attitude Scale, 123

Parenting skills: case example of, 426-428; discussion of, 432-434; follow-up for, 431-432; maintenance of, over time, 422-434; results of, 428-432; theoretical background for, 422-426

Participation, and group social work, 345-346, 348-351

Play, and prosocial behavior, 175, 177, 178, 180, 181

Point system. *See* Token system

Positive punishment: concept of, 128; in family intervention, 213. *See also* Punishment

Positive reinforcement, concept of, 18. *See also* Reinforcement

Practice evaluation. *See* Clinical evaluation

Practice model, concept of, 33

Pre- and posttest design: for group parent training, 265-267; as indirect measures, 72

Preschool children, creativity enhancement for, 435-451

Problem-severity scales, as indirect measure, 70-71

Problems: assessment of, 192-193; as observable events, 63-64; reconceptualized, 90

Procedures: concept of, 50-51; specificity of, 8-9

Prompt and praise, for elderly, 225-226

Prosocial behavior intervention: analysis of, 171-182; for depressed girl, 364-375; discussion of, 181-182, 374-375; methods for, 173-175, 365-367; and positive staff feedback, 371, 373-374; procedures for, 176-177;

reinforcement for, 365-375; results of, 177-181; across settings, 83; theoretical background of, 171-173, 364-365

Punishment: for behavior change, 29-31; in combination, 29; concept of, 19; in family intervention, 208, 212-214; guidelines for, 127; for individual interventions, 127-129; in institutions, 292-294; positive, 128, 213; uses of, 29

Q

Question technique: in group social work, 343, 345-346, 347-348, 350; as reversal design, 77-78

Questionnaires: for data recording, 283-284; as indirect measure, 72

R

Rapid Assessment Instruments, 123

Recruitment, for group parent training, 262-263

Referral sources: assessment of, 191-192; for elderly, 222-223

Rehearsal: for change agent training, 101; and modeling, 32; in parent training, 249, 255

Reinforcement: advantages of, 292; backup, 310; for behavior change, 22-27; for change agent, 102-104; in creativity enhancement, 438-440, 442-443, 450; cueing and, 26-27; in family intervention, 207-208, 209-210; and generality, 384-385, 391-392; for greeting response, 404-405; immediate and backup, 254; for individual intervention, 125-127; in institutions, 285-292; intermittent, and generality, 391-392; interval schedule for, 22; for prosocial behavior, 365-375; ratio schedule of, 21-22; schedules of, 21-22, 384-385

Reinforcement opportunity: concept of, 26; in family intervention, 186, 189, 208, 210-212; and greeting response, 411; in home, 230-232; in individual intervention, 108, 126-127; in institutions, 285-287

Reinforcers: concept of, 22; primary and social, 22; for token system, 288

Relaxation of upper body, and social-skills training, 143-144, 147, 151-152

Relevance, social: and behavior analysis, 12-13; as intervention criteria, 295-296; and target behavior, and generality, 380

Reliability: acceptable level of, 68; concept of, 48; in creativity enhancement, 439-440, 450; and data recording, 283; for differential reinforcement, 357; of direct observation, 67-69; formulas for calculating, 68-69; for greeting response, 404; occurrence and nonoccurrence, 68; and time-out, 328-329; total, 68-69

Reminder status, and time-out, 324

Resources: assessment of, 41-42, 116-117, 197; client behaviors as, 42; community, 42; community, in family intervention, 186, 195-196, 211-212; in institutions, 276-278; supportive relationships as, 41-42

Response. See Greeting response

Response-cost: analysis of, 307-319; combined with reinforcers, 30; concept of, 307; different values of, 340; discussion of, 316-319; experimental design for, 311-312; in family intervention, 212-213; in individual intervention, 128; in institutions, 293; method for, 308-310; procedure for, 310-311; as punishment, 30-31; results of, 312-316; side effects of, 30-31; and specific contingencies, 310-311; theoretical background of, 307-

308; time-out compared with, 320-341

Responses, reinforcement for, 367-368

Retarded adults: discussion of program for, 270-271; methods for, 262-266; parent training for, 261-271; results with, 266-270; theoretical background on, 261-262

Reversal design: ABAB type of, 76-78; for group social work, 345-346; for prosocial behavior, 175, 366-367; for retarded adults, 266; and time-out, 329

Role play: for change agent training, 101; for group parent training, 265; for social-skills training, 141-144

Role requirements: for individual intervention, 106-109; in institutions, 273-274

S

Scientific methods: analysis of, 1-15; and behavior analysis, 5-6; defining practice with, 3-13; journals on, 2; need for, 1-2

Self-management: agency as change setting in, 118; client role in, 108; concept of, 106; and contingency contracts, 129; data collection for, 121-122; direct influence compared with, 121; evaluation in, 136-137; and generality, 385-386; modeling in, 130; in parenting skills, 423, 433; and punishment, 128-129; reinforcement for, 127; training in, 132-135; worker role in, 107

Self-report measures, and social-skills training, 144-145, 155, 157

Setting: agency as, 108-109, 117-118, 141, 159-160, 171, 182, 343, 436-437; for creativity enhancement, 436-437; for differential reinforcement, 355; for elderly, 222, 413-414; for family

interventions, 200-203; for greeting response, 403; home as, 165,
200, 220-232, 235, 262-263,
426-427; for individual intervention, 106-109, 117-119; institutions as, 201, 222, 273-274, 279-
280, 403, 413-414; multiple
baselines across, 82-83; for negotiation, 159-160; for parenting
skills, 426-427; for prosocial behavior, 173-174, 365-366; for response cost, 308; for social-skills
training, 141; for time-out, 322-
323
Shaping: in family intervention,
207; mutual, in interviews, 36;
as reinforcement technique, 22-
23
Sharing, and prosocial behavior,
175, 177, 179, 181
Shore Training Center (Skokie, Illinois), 262
Side effects: of positive punishment,
213; potency related to, 318; of
punishment, 292; of response
cost, 30-31; of token system,
24-26, 307-319
Simulation, for negotiation, 163-
165
Single-case designs: as analytical
component, 8; in experimental
research, 74-76; in self-management, 137-138
Single Parent Project, 234, 422-434
Social attention, and prosocial behavior, 176, 180
Social relevance. See Relevance, social
Social skill, concept of, 139
Social-skills training: analysis of,
139-157; across behaviors, 78-
80; discussion of, 154-157; method for, 140-149; procedure for,
145; results of, 149-154; theoretical background for, 139-140
Social validation, as indirect measure, 70
Social work: data base for, 453; future practice in, 455-456; scien-

tific methods in, 1-15. See also
Group social work; Worker
Special education class, time-out
and response-cost procedures in,
320-341
Speech loudness, and social skills
training, 143, 147, 151
Stability, concept of, 48
Staff, for elderly, 222
Statements, positive, negative, or
neutral, in negotiation, 161-162,
167, 168
Stimulus conditions: and generality, 389-391; for greeting response, 409
Stuttering: discussion of, 244-246;
intervention in, analysis of, 233-
246; method for, 234-237; procedures for, 237-243; results for,
243-244; theoretical background
for, 233-234
Subjects. See Client
Systematic practice: analysis of, 88-
91; and observable terms, 89-90

T

Tantrums: contingency analysis for,
21-22; parent training for, 257-
259
Target behaviors: assessment of, 42-
45; characteristics of, and change
agent selection, 111-112; circumstances for, 43-44; in creativity
enhancement, 437-438; for differential reinforcement, 356; for
elderly, 223, 415, 416; and environment, 44; and generality, 382-
384; for greeting response, 403;
for group social work, 343-344;
observable, 43, 44; observation
for, 281-282; in parent training,
253, 255; for parenting skills,
427-431; for prosocial behavior,
367; for response cost, 309; social relevance of, and generality,
380; for social-skills training,
143-144; specification of, 236-
237; and time-out, 325, 328;

time period for, 44-45; and token systems, 288. *See also* Behaviors
Teachers, as change agents, 171-172
Techniques, concept of, 51
Technology, as behavior analysis
component, 8-9
Termination: concept of, 394-395;
and follow-up, 59-60; and generality, 394-400; of group social
work, 346; in parent training,
256
Time-out: concept of, 320-321; discussion of, 337-341; in family
intervention, 213-214; in individual intervention, 128; in institutions, 293; methods for, 322-
329; by parent, 426, 429, 431,
432, 433; parent training in, 251;
procedures for, 323-325; as punishment, 31; as reinforcer, 339-
340; and response bursts, 338-
339; response cost compared
with, 320-341; results of, 330-
337; and teacher praise and negative attention, 328, 332, 335;
theoretical background of, 320-
322; training for, 325-326
Time sample. *See* Interval samples
Token system: client training for,
289-290; components of, 24;
contingency development for,
288; effectiveness and side effects of, 307-319; evaluation of,
290-291; fading of, 291; in family intervention, 210; for greeting response, 402-411; implementing, 289; individual, 291; in
individual intervention, 126; in
institutions, 287-292; negative
side effects of, 24-26; in parent
training, 255; and people of
equal status, 24; for prosocial
behavior, 172, 176, 177, 182; rehearsal for, 290; as reinforcement
technique, 23-26; and reinforcer
potentiation, 290; reinforcers
for, assessment of, 288; response-

cost type of, 30-31; settings for,
24-25; staff training for, 289;
and target behaviors, 288; and
time-out procedures, 321-341
Topographical analysis, concept of,
124
Training: for change agent, 98-102;
in data recording, 298-300; for
elderly, 416-418; feedback and
reinforcement in, 302-304; for
fluency, 237-239; guided-trial,
416-417; in intervention application, 300-302; in intervention
formulation, 300; pyramid model
of, 298; sessions of, for social
skills, 146-148; for time-out,
325-326; transfer of, 420; within-session, for negotiation, 163-
165. *See also* Instruction; Parent
training; Social-skills training

U

Utensil use, training-maintenance
program for, 412-421

V

Validity, concept of, 48

W

Withdrawal design, for differential
reinforcement, 355-356
Worker: as behavioral analyst, 273;
as change agent, 97, 184, 273-
274, 427; characteristics of, and
change agent selection, 112-113;
family intervention roles of, 184-
188; as reinforcer, 103; responsibilities of, in family intervention,
185-188; responsibilities of, in
parent training, 252; role and
setting requirements of, 106-107;
roles of, for parenting skills, 426-
427; self-evaluation by, 454;
support system for, 454-455
Wyatt vs. Stickney, 320, 484

DATE DUE